Gendered Passages

PETER LANG
New York • Washington, D.C./Baltimore • Bern
Frankfurt am Main • Berlin • Brussels • Vienna • Oxford

YUKARI TAKAI

Gendered Passages

French-Canadian Migration
to Lowell, Massachusetts,
1900–1920

PETER LANG
New York • Washington, D.C./Baltimore • Bern
Frankfurt am Main • Berlin • Brussels • Vienna • Oxford

Library of Congress Cataloging-in-Publication Data
Takai, Yukari.
Gendered passages: French-Canadian migration to Lowell,
Massachusetts, 1900-1920 / Yukari Takai.
p. cm.
Includes bibliographical references and index.
1. French-Canadians—Massachusetts—Lowell—Social conditions—
20th century. 2. Immigrants—Massachusetts—Lowell—History—20th century.
3. Sex role—Massachusetts—Lowell—History—20th century. 4. Textile workers—Massachusetts—
Lowell—History—20th century. 5. French-Canadians—Employment—Massachusetts—Lowell—
History—20th century. 6. Lowell (Mass.)—Social conditions—20th century. 7. Lowell (Mass.)—
Economic conditions—20th century. 8. Lowell (Mass.)—Ethnic relations—History—20th century.
9. Lowell (Mass.)—Emigration and immigration—History—20th century. 10. Québec
(Province)—Emigration and immigration—History—20th century. I. Title.
F74.L9T35   974.4'4004114—dc22   2006022526
ISBN 978-0-8204-8672-7 (hardcover)
ISBN 978-1-4331-0496-1 (paperback)

Bibliographic information published by **Die Deutsche Bibliothek**.
Die Deutsche Bibliothek lists this publication in the "Deutsche
Nationalbibliografie"; detailed bibliographic data is available
on the Internet at http://dnb.ddb.de/.

Cover art: a roving tender piecing-up a broken end of cotton roving
in the Pacific Mills of Lawrence, Massachusetts, ca. 1915. Many women and men
in Lowell at the time worked in similar conditions in the city's textile factories.
(Courtesy of the American Textile History Museum, Lowell, MA)

The paper in this book meets the guidelines for permanence and durability
of the Committee on Production Guidelines for Book Longevity
of the Council of Library Resources.

© 2008 Peter Lang Publishing, Inc., New York
29 Broadway, 18th floor, New York, NY 10006
www.peterlang.com

All rights reserved.
Reprint or reproduction, even partially, in all forms such as microfilm,
xerography, microfiche, microcard, and offset strictly prohibited.

Printed in the United States of America

TO MY PARENTS,
Takai Setsuko and Takai Tadashige

Contents

List of Tables ix

List of Illustrations xi

Acknowledgments xiii

Note on Language and Terminology xvii

Introduction 1

CHAPTER ONE
To the Wrong Side of the Border 10

CHAPTER TWO
Lowell after Paternalism 32

CHAPTER THREE
The Transnational Mobility and Family Networks of French Canadians 62

CHAPTER FOUR
American or Ethnic Workers? : Work, Family and Masculinity
 of French-Canadian Men 87

CHAPTER FIVE
"You Gotta Keep Going" : Paid Work Performed
 by French-Canadian Women 130

CHAPTER SIX
More Than a Defence of the Traditional Family : The Unpaid Work
 of French-Canadian Women 161

Epilogue 180

APPENDIX A
Longitudinal Data and the Nominal Record-Linkage Method 185

APPENDIX B
The Classification of Work 187

Notes 189

Selected Bibliography 227

Index 245

Tables

1. Population of Lowell by Country of Birth, 1826-1920 35
2. French-Canadian Population in Selected New England Cities, 1860-1920 38
3. Manufacturing Sectors in Lowell, 1899-1920 43
4. Distribution of Foreign-Born Persons in Lowell, Each Specified by Number of Years in the U.S., by Birthplace of Individuals, 1908-1909 .. 45
5. Distribution of Lowell-bound French Canadians by Place of Birth, 1904-1920 69
6. Distribution of Lowell-bound French Canadians by Place of Last Permanent Residence, 1904-1920 70
7. Locations of Previous Sojourns in the United States of Lowell-bound French Canadians 80
8. Relation of Contact Persons to Lowell-bound French Canadians 83
9. Age Distribution by Ethnic Group in Lowell, 1910 and 1920 92
10. Age Distribution of the French-Canadian Immigrant Population by Gender, Lowell, 1910 and 1920 93
11. Relationship of Immigrants to Household Head, Lowell, 1910 and 1920 94
12. Age Distribution of the French-Canadian Working Population by Gender, Lowell, 1910 and 1920 95
13. Occupational Distribution of Male Workers in Five Ethnic Groups, Lowell, 1910 97
14. Occupational Distribution of Male Workers in Five Ethnic Groups, Lowell, 1920 97
15. Number of Sampled French-Canadian Men Working as Labourers in Lowell, 1910 and 1920 98

16. Leading Occupations of French-Canadian and Irish Men in the Manual Labour Sector, Lowell, 1910 and 1920 99
17. Household Budgets of Selected French-Canadian Families in Lowell 113
18. Occupational Distribution of Female Workers in Five Ethnic Groups, Lowell, 1910 (Number of Individuals per 100 Workers) 134
19. Occupational Distribution of Female Workers in Five Ethnic Groups, Lowell, 1920 (Number of Individuals per 100 Workers) 135
20. Marital Statuses of French-Canadian Female Workers in Lowell, 1910 and 1920 (Number of Individuals per 100 Workers) 136
21. Age Distribution of French-Canadian Female Workers in Lowell by Marital Status, 1910 and 1920 (Number of Individuals per 100 Workers) 137
22. Distribution of Household Relationships of French-Canadian Wage-Earning Women by Marital Status, Lowell, 1910 and 1920 141
23. Paid Labour Participation Rates of French-Canadian Married Women by Life Cycle, 1910 and 1920 149
24. Distribution of French-Canadian Married Female Workers According to the Patterns of Wage-earning in Their Household, Lowell, 1910 and 1920 151

Illustrations

Maps

1. Québec, New Brunswick, and New England, ca. 1900......................... xviii
2. Southern and Eastern Québec, ca. 1900 xix
3. Lowell, Massachusetts, ca. 1900..xx

Figures

1. Merrimack Manufacturing Employees, ca. 1900 40
2. Austin Block in Little Canada, ca. 1900 53
3. Trolley Lines on Central Street, ca. 1900.. 54
4. Central Street Construction Work, ca. 1910... 90
5. Barber Shop, ca. 1910.. 106
6. J.G. Roche (Portuguese) Grocery Store, 1907.. 107
7. Saloon Owner and Employees, ca. 1900.. 108
8. Male Workers in one of the Spinning Rooms at the Merrimack
   Manufacturing, ca. 1900 120
9. B.F. Keith's Theatre, 1913. 123
10. A Portuguese Worker's Family on the Beach, ca. 1910......................... 129
11. Female Knitters in the Shaw Stocking Company, ca. 1915.................... 133
12. Portuguese Female Spinners, 1907... 146
13. Mill Employees, ca. 1917 148
14. Children in Front of Clothes Lines, ca. 1910 166

Acknowledgments

This book is a product of the past several years of my life. It began as a modest research paper for a graduate seminar at the Université de Montréal, turned into a doctoral thesis, and finally, grew to stand as a book, in which, I sincerely hope, attentive readers will find something interesting and useful. It also evolved with my personal experience. As a foreign student, a migrant woman, a returnee, and, then a remigrant, I have moved from one city to another in Canada, the United States, and Japan since I first tackled the issue of French-Canadian migration. At each passage, I lived and worked among women and men who taught me the arts of crossing and, at times, bending many boundaries. My own experience and ingenuity and the persistence of the hardworking people I met in the course of my research into the past sustained and enriched this book.

I am delighted to have the chance to express my thanks to the many people who have helped along the way. I am indebted, first, to friends in Lowell, Massachusetts and Nashua, New Hampshire and their numerous "cousins" in Québec, who helped me to understand human histories of the transnational region across the Canada-U.S. border. I have accumulated weighty academic debts to my teachers as well. I thank my professors at the Université de Montréal. Bruno Ramirez, my thesis advisor, suggested that I might write a thesis on French-Canadian migration. Denyse Baillargeon, Jacques Rouillard, Thomas Ingersoll, Claude Morin, Bettina Bradbury at the Département d'histoire, then or now, Deirdre Meintel at the Département d'anthropologie, and the Groupe de recherches sur l'ethnicité et société (GRÈS)—all taught me to read and write history, migration, and gender. Yves Frenette at Glendon College, York University, exterior member of my dissertation committee, read portions of the manuscript and offered me sound advice and good cheer. The late Ninomiya Hiroyuki ushered me into the world of social history at Tokyo University of Foreign Studies. The late Konami Takashi at Gaigo, Kobayashi Junko, then at Seisen Women's College, and Yui Daizaburo, then at Hitotsubashi University, also played special roles as long-distance and long-time supporters of this project.

I have relied on the good offices of several archivists and librarians. I would like to thank in particular Martha Mayo and Janine Whitcomb at the Center for Lowell History at the University of Massachusetts in Lowell, Daniel Olivier at the Salle Gagnon at the Bibliothèque Municipale de Montréal, and Bernard Robert at the Salle de Documentation at the Département d'histoire at the Université de Montréal, without whose goodwill and resourcefulness, this book would have been of much poorer quality.

A number of friends, fellow colleagues, and students deserve my heartfelt thank-yous for their support and bursts of inspiration. Yves Otis and Nelson Ouellet gave me advice, suggestions, and much needed encouragement for collecting and analysing data for this study. David Palmer and Jean Lamarre read part of my manuscripts when I desperately needed feedback. Special acknowledgments also go to Brian Bergstrom for editing and Joyce Wong and Julia Buckingham who scrupulously proofread the entire manuscript. My thanks also go to my students at Glendon College, York University, for their reading and feedback. Taniguchi Hiromi, Isabelle Mimeault, Josiane Legall, Peter Cook, and Nicolas Rivain undoubtedly heard a lot more about the challenge of writing this book than they wanted to. Warm thanks to all of them for accompanying me on some of my research trips to Lowell, help with going over tens of thousands of lines of data collected from the federal manuscript censuses, or reading early versions of the manuscript more than once. Michèle Bessette, Patricia Bittar, Livia and Jean-Pierre Monnet, Akémi and Michel Mallette, the late Attilio, Jacqueline, and Eliza Janniello, Nicola Zavaglia, Jean Dorion and Tsunezuka Hiromi, Shelagh and Drew Webster, and the late Josephine Fowler animated my spirits with a good sense of humour, tentative ears, wonderful dishes, and much more. Sato Nobuyuki and Alain Mallette pitched in at the last stage of production and assisted with preparation of the tables and formatting the text. Carolyn King created the maps. Julia Buckingham compiled the index with help of Jane Lanktree. Carla Ayukawa at Evolution Professional Design Consultants Ltd. offered me well-timed suggestions and precious help for cover production. Publication of this book suffered lengthy delay after the contract was arranged by Phyllis Korper, Senior Acquisitions Editor at Peter Lang Publishing, part of the reason being that the four consecutive editors passed my manuscript from one to another. Jackie Pavlovic, the Production Supervisor, graciously wrapped up the task of completing the production process.

I have benefited from fellowships and grants. The Rotary International Graduate Overseas Fellowship; the International Council for Canadian Studies Canada Award; the Faculté des études supérieures of the Université de Montréal Bourse d'excellence; the Japanese Society for the Promotion of

Sciences Graduate Fellowship and Junior Faculty Grant; the Japan-United States Educational Commission (Fulbright) Research Grant; and the Aichi Prefectural University Chancellor's Special Research Grant brought with them precious time to research and write.

For permission to reproduce photographs used in the illustrations of this book, I would like to acknowledge the Center for Lowell History at the University of Massachusetts in Lowell and the American Textile History Museum in Lowell.

Parts of this book have been published in different forms in the following journals: Chapter 3 was published in an abridged form as "The Family Networks and Geographic Mobility of French-Canadian Immigrants in Early-Twentieth-Century Lowell, Massachusetts" in *Journal of Family History* 26, 3 (July 2001). Ideas developed in Chapters 4, 5, and 6 appeared in "Shared Earnings, Unequal Responsibilities: Paid Work of Single French-Canadian Immigrant Women in Lowell, Massachusetts," *Labour/Le Travail* 47 (Spring 2001); "Sexe et expérience de travail comme critères migratoires: le cas des immigrantes canadiennes-françaises à Lowell, Massachusetts au début du vingtième siècle," *Francophone d'Amérique*, 11 (2001); and "An 'Adapting' Mechanism in the Process of Immigration: An Age and Gender Profile of French-Canadian Immigrants in an Early-Twentieth-Century Textile City," (*Imin katei ni miru tekiou no mekanizumu*), *The Annual Review of Canadian Studies* (*Kanada Kenkyu Nenpô*), 20 (2000).

Finally, only two persons saw me from the beginning to the end of this project: Takai Setsuko and Takai Tadashige, my dear parents. Their confidence, patience, and love have always been boundless for the daughter "adrift." To them, I dedicate this book.

Yukari Takai
Toronto, June 2008

Note on Language and Terminology

Some readers may object to my use of the term "French Canadian" as it refers to, in a narrow sense of the term, men and women who were born in French Canada, immigrated to the U.S. and remained Canadian without being naturalized. The expression then suggests exclusion of naturalized Americans of Canadian descent and more importantly, of a growing number of American-born sons and daughters of immigrant parentage. The latter brought an important change to a sense of their own and their community throughout New England in the late nineteenth century as a growing number came to identify themselves as Franco-Americans rather than *Canadiens* living in the United States.[1] The intention of this study is, however, to depict experience of both Canadian-born and American-born men and women of French-Canadian background. In line with a usage common in U.S. government documents of the early twentieth century, I employ the term "French Canadians" to refer to immigrants and their descendants of French-Canadian background.

The terms "immigrant" and "immigration" connote a sense of permanency when a foreign-born person leaves her or his country of origin to move to a destination in another country for permanent settlement with or without the intention of becoming a naturalized citizen. As a number of scholars in im/migration history point out, however, not all migrants are immigrants. In this study, I prefer to use the terms "migrant" and "migration" to refer to the people on the move and those who lived and worked in Lowell, Massachusetts and elsewhere, unless the phrases become too repetitive. My choice arises from the awareness that these terms better reflect the concept of migration as a process, rather than a more traditional view of immigration as a one-way, one-time movement.

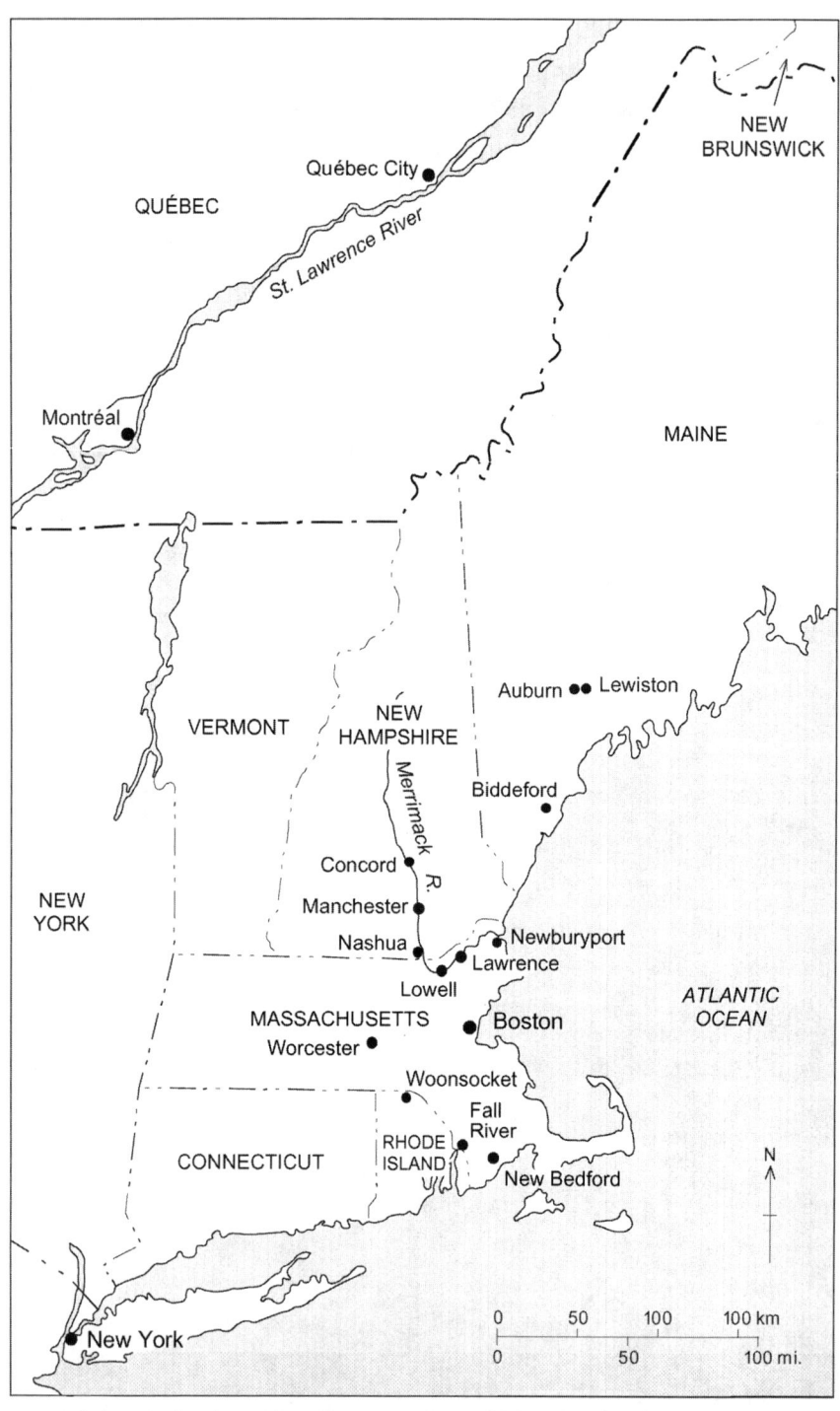

Map 1. Québec, New Brunswick, and New England, ca. 1900

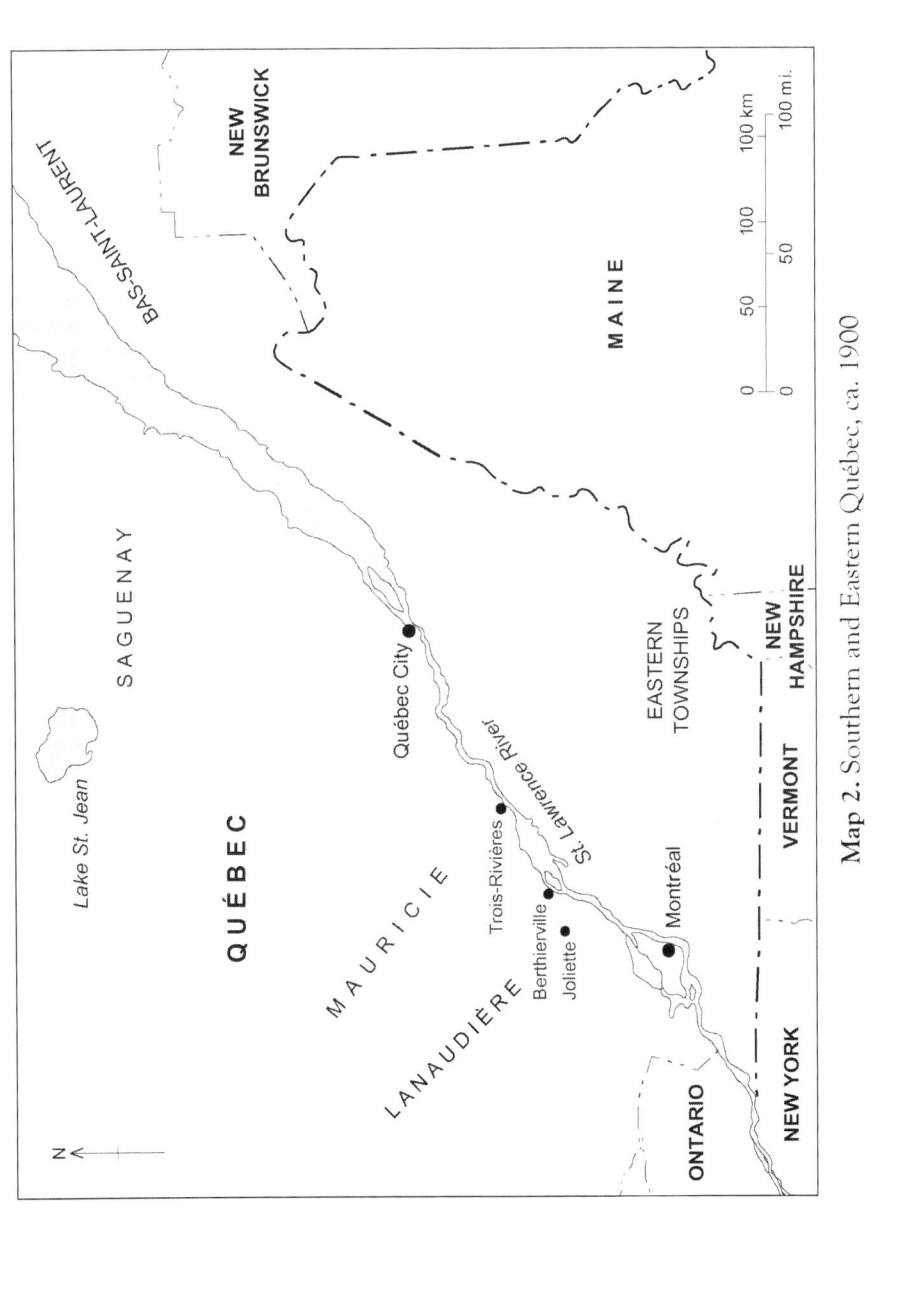

Map 2. Southern and Eastern Québec, ca. 1900

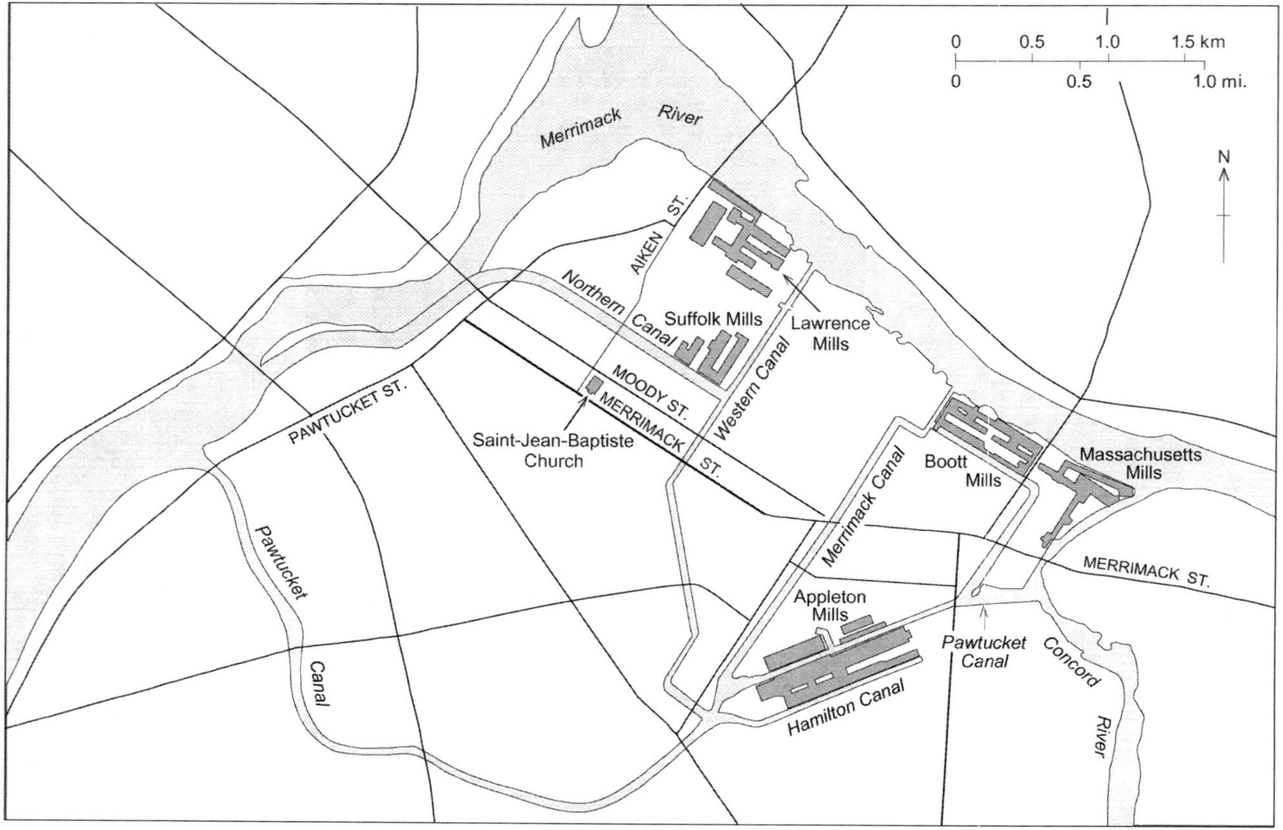

Map 3. Lowell, Massachusetts, ca. 1900

Introduction

This book is about French-Canadian women, men, and children who left their homes in search of a better life in early-twentieth-century Lowell, Massachusetts. The questions posed in this study are simple ones. What was the role of a family in the course of migration, and how did women and men respond to the challenges of moving to, and settling in, Lowell? To answer these questions I argue that it is necessary to consider this migration as a phenomenon consisting of a series of processes and not as a linear progression toward inevitable assimilation or Americanization. I also emphasize the importance of introducing a gendered perspective in order to recognize the diversity of strategies employed by migrating women and men, whose respective interests were alternately in harmony and conflict as they went through the migration and settlement processes.

French Canadians formed by far the largest group among the foreign-born population in early-twentieth-century Lowell. They constituted about one quarter of the city's population. Despite this important presence of French-Canadian immigrants and their descendants in that U.S. city in particular and the northeastern and mid-western U.S. more generally, and despite scholarly efforts among American and Canadian scholars to analyze this continental migration across the U.S.,[1] French Canadians in the U.S. have not received the attention they deserve in the larger field of migration history. The relative marginality of *Canadiens* in the U.S. becomes even more glaring when one considers the number, the duration, and distinctive—yet changing—patterns of movement that characterized this group of migrants as they moved south of the border. According to demographer Yolande Lavoie, the number of migrating French Canadians reached about 1,000,000, representing one in ten *Canadiens*, and continued over the span of one hundred years from about 1830 to 1930.[2] The majority moved in family units with a large number of children, as was the case for Jan-Anna and Charles Bédard, Annie and Delphis Brière's family, and Mary-Louise Clermont and her family, as well as many others like them who headed for Lowell in the early twentieth century and were following the well-known paths explored by their predecessors in the last century. Their stories as they are narrated in this book highlight issues such as the porous nature of the U.S.-Canadian border; the transnational mobility and circular migration; the central role of family and kin networks; paid and unpaid work performed by French-Canadian men and women; and gendered dimensions of migrant family lives including the ideology of family wage, working-class masculinities, and the division of labour. An analysis of these themes reveals how fundamental gender and family were for French-Canadians on the move; it also shows how essential the French-Canadian presence was in shaping the social history not only of Lowell, but also that of the transborder region of Québec and eastern New England.

The migration of French-Canadian women and men is unique in many ways. The geographical proximity and railroad links—only a day's ride—to places like Lowell set their migration distinct from their European and Asian contemporaries, whose travel to North America inevitably included trans-oceanic voyages. In this regard, French-Canadian migration to New England has a common, although a hitherto rarely acknowledged, link with the Great Migration of African Americans from the South to the Northern and Western cities, as well as Mexican migration to California before and after the Mexican Revolution in 1910. The difference, however, is that African Americans and Mexicans (before 1910) were leaving an oppressive socio-political climate, which was not the case with French Canadians, at least not to the same extent. The essential factor for French Canadians was economic, much like that of another important, yet even more neglected, cross-border movement of Anglo Canadians.[3]

Although comparison *per se* is beyond the scope of this book, one of the contributions this book seeks to make derives from a desire to raise awareness of the commonality and divergence which underpin human movement of divergent groups from regional and continental perspectives. From the vantage point of the border being crossed, French-Canadian migration emerges as a distinct yet not atypical, population movement. Their migration calls for placement in a broader, continental perspective, rather than the one limited to a single "community study."[4] To this end, my approach privileges the entire process of migration, rather than singling out the "adjustment" period that took place only after migrants' settlement in Lowell. What comes into focus through this new perspective are the journeys of French-Canadian men, women, and children from rural parishes in the Lanaudière, or an economic centre of a region, such as Shawinigan Falls, to the province's, and also Canada's, commercial and political centre, Montréal, then to Lowell, with a possible return to Canada. As this book will show, such processes of movement or migration criss-crossed the northeastern part of the continent and the U.S.-Canadian border, and far from constituting a mono-directional, one-time displacement, it linked several localities on both sides of the border. The complexity and multiplicity of such movements challenge explanations (such as dichotomous views of migration that rely on push-pull factors, oppositions made between pre-industrial versus industrial societies, or the "immigration paradigm" intricately linked to assumptions deriving from U.S. exceptionalism) embedded in earlier studies as too simplistic. My work seeks to recreate, albeit partly, the socially expansive space that French-Canadian men and women constructed over a period of a lifetime, or even generations, connecting many localities in Québec and New England in their processes of movement to, and settlement in, the city of Lowell.[5]

The issue of gender in French-Canadian migrant families provides another important focus for this book. The paradigm shift in migration history from *the uprooted* to *the transplanted*[6] encouraged the depiction of immigrant families as a source of cultural resilience and cohesion for the ethnic communities. As historian Donna Gabaccia has pointed out, however, it is ironic that until recently few migration studies have treated the lives of women seriously, given the emphasis placed on the role of the family as a whole.[7] Many blithely addressed such questions in terms of the family's decision to emigrate, its work ethic, and their collective values, while tending to neglect how men, women, and children negotiated their shares of these responsibilities and decisions. Others emphasized the solidarity of migrant families in facing the difficulties produced by an urban industrial milieu without considering the question of gender and power relations within families. As a result, most writing has highlighted the experiences of men, while marginalizing those of women. As Franca Iacovetta has cogently summed up, this tendency has buttressed a view of the family as a monolithic, co-operative, and non-gendered collective that "acted in a self-interested manner."[8]

Thomas Dublin, on his part, has pointed out that despite the increasing attention being paid to the functions of the family as a survival unit and to the economic roles of women in the changing economy, studies exploring migrants' family economy tend to view families, rather than individuals, as historical actors.[9] The very title of Tamara Hareven's seminal work, *Family Time and Industrial Time*, on French-Canadian and other migrant families in Manchester, New Hampshire, in the late nineteenth and early twentieth centuries is indicative of this propensity to consider the family as an active historical subject, rather than as an arena in which individuals struggle through co-operation and conflict.[10] Likewise, a number of important works on the family economy, labour participation, sociocultural transformations, and persistence of French-Canadian culture in a dozen other New England communities notwithstanding, little consideration has been given to the distinctive roles played by French-Canadian women within or outside the home.[11] Such a gap in knowledge is further strengthened by some of the practices that highlighted the importance of the family to the cross-border movements of this group. Those practices included French-Canadian migration centred around family units with a large number of children; the employment of young children, often in their early teens, who contributed their entire earnings to the family budgets; and family networks that placed many sons and daughters in the same workplace with their parents.[12] In accordance with the emphasis placed on the centrality of family in broader migration literature, these and other features have helped to propagate the image of co-operative and monolithic French-Canadian families.

In this book, I seek to redress the dearth of gendered perspectives found in the earlier depiction of French-Canadian migrant families. To this end, I graciously draw on advances in women's and gender history, which have provided new ways to view American, Canadian, and, to a lesser extent, migrant families.[13] Family decisions were not necessarily made in the best interest of all members. Migrant and working-class families emerged as arenas of multiple relations wherein loci of support and tension were mediated among members—husbands, wives, sons, and daughters—who wielded unequal power. Families thus provided a contested terrain rather than a monolithic block and held the potential to be a site of both support and oppression, and possibly resistance, especially for women.[14] Such a perspective compels me to draw a more comprehensive portrait of the lives of French-Canadian women and men, whose perspectives, expectations, and responsibilities often set them apart from one another.[15]

In the story that follows, I seek to understand how French Canadians responded to the respective dynamics of both the society of departure and the society of destination. To do so, I raise a series of questions. Who were these migrants? What was the economic and social context they left behind? How did they organize their journey to Lowell? In what ways did these men, women, and children construct their new lives in Lowell? How did women's and men's experiences of migration and settlement differ from, or converge with, one another as they confronted difficulties and savoured moments of pleasure in the urban, industrial milieu of Lowell? An analysis of these questions leads me to explore the dynamic and complex ways in which migration, work, family, and gender shaped the lives of French-Canadian women and men and their descendants bound for, or living in, Lowell as that industrial city underwent a series of radical transformations in the early twentieth century.

In many ways, Lowell is an attractive setting in which to explore these questions as they revolve around the dynamics of migration, family, work, and gender. The city of Lowell, located about forty kilometres northwest of Boston, was one of the leading centres of the textile industry in the United States. Since its inception as a city, textile production, particularly of cottons but also of woolens and hosiery, had been Lowell's principal industry. The city's textile factories recruited workers first from the surrounding rural communities in the 1830s and 1840s, then from Ireland and, increasingly, from Canada throughout the late nineteenth century, until "new immigrants" from Eastern and Southern European countries arrived in the city *en masse* starting at the turn of the century and continuing well into the early twentieth century. French Canadians, however, represented the largest immigrant group in the city since the last third of the nineteenth century.[16]

Lowell was situated in a volatile environment between the closing decade of the nineteenth century and the outbreak of World War I. As Progressivism reached its height, the city's textile factories had to comply with the pressure to curtail child labour. Increased wartime production and the draft after 1917, coupled with a halt on trans-Atlantic migration, created an acute labour shortage that the region's economy, and indeed the nation's economy, had never known. The intense demand for labour temporarily offset the curb on young child workers. It also benefited protest movements and labour radicalism momentarily, although labour's gains remained marginal in Lowell.[17] This is largely because of the greater proportion of unskilled workers and the ethnic composition of the city's textile employees, which made it more difficult for these workers and their families to benefit from the successful industrial reorganization that workers in the neighbouring city of Lawrence seemed to enjoy,[18] although both cities were under a particular pattern of corporate ownership (non-residents forming a unified group with commonly shared directorates), in which the board members shared pertinent information including blacklisted workers.

The labour shortage boosted workers' wages several times. However, with wartime inflation propelling food prices to an exorbitant level, wages—if one adjusts them in keeping with these variables—barely kept pace. For example, potatoes more than doubled in price during one month in 1916, whereas in the same year and the following, wages rose twice each year in the Boott Manufacturing factories, one of the city's largest textile corporations, recording a just below 50-percent rise in two years.[19] Thus, French-Canadian and other working families found their lives severely burdened even during the short-lived boom years, and the situation was worse during the long years of industrial decline and recession.

While the political, economic, and social changes mentioned above were profoundly re-shaping the lives of French Canadians already in the city, they also had an impact on the prospective migrants on the other side of the border.

During the first two decades of the twentieth century, French-Canadian migration to the U.S. declined to nearly half the level recorded in the peak years of migration. The number of Quebecers crossing the border to the United States fell to 80,000 in 1910-20, down from 150,000 in 1880-90. A brief moment of prosperity that boosted the Canadian and Québec economies added to the factors leading to declines in the population migrating out of the province.[20] By the turn of the century, the proportion of French Canadians within Lowell's foreign-born and foreign-parented population remained constant at over one quarter (or about 24,000).[21] By 1920, the majority of French Canadians in Lowell were those born in the United States, a clear sign that the immigrant influx from Canada had passed its peak and the population growth of this group in Lowell had become more and more dependent on natural, internal growth.[22]

A variety of qualitative sources, such as newspaper articles, oral histories, and governmental research conducted at the time, have proven essential in exploring the questions posed in this study, especially when these sources were combined with data drawn from selected quantitative sources. The latter includes the U.S. federal decennial manuscript census schedules and the *Soundex Index to Canadian Border Entries through the St. Albans, Vermont, District, 1895-1924*, Records of Immigration and Naturalization Service, Record Group 85, Washington, D.C. (hereafter referred to as the *Border Entry*).[23] Unlike manuscript census schedules, which have become a traditional tool of investigation for social historians, the Border Entry have begun to be explored only recently. The wealth of information contained in the *Border Entry* pertains to all the individuals, regardless of their nationalities, who entered the U.S. from Canada. People crossing the U.S.'s northern border in the early twentieth century provided information on their birthplace, last permanent residence, whether or not they had been to the U.S. prior to the recorded entry, and if so, where and how long; their occupation, name, age and relationship of accompanying persons, and persons they expected to meet upon arrival at a U.S. destination. A historian can thus reconstruct, albeit partly, migration itineraries from the longitudinal records of migrants and their families derived from the *Border Entry*—at birth, before crossing the border, and upon entry. Longitudinal data, as opposed to cross-sectional data, derived from the *Border Entry* afford one with a crucial methodological advantage in order to offset some of the problems inherent in the census manuscripts. The most conspicuous of such problems relate to information on the families that functions like a series of snapshot-like pictures. One is thus left with life histories of these migrating people at one moment in the evolution of their life cycles.

Another advantage the historian can draw from the *Border Entry* also relates to the longitudinal analysis this source enables one to conduct. While the traditional oral histories contain retrospective information about a migrant's past, the *Border Entry* provide longitudinal data recorded at different moments of a migrant's life. This does not invalidate the use of oral history accounts. But the longitudinal data collected from the *Border Entry*, as used in this study in combination with the records drawn from the decennial U.S. Federal census schedules with a method of direct nominal record linkage, shed new light on aspects of the French-Canadian migration at micro levels, i.e., individual and municipal levels, in systematic ways that few other sources have enabled researchers to do.[24]

It is easier to raise simple questions than to answer them. My efforts to introduce a gendered perspective into my narrative are at times constrained and frustrated by the sources (or lack thereof) created in the past. Among such sources, this study has drawn upon municipal records of the assistance given to the destitute, the *Case History Records for the Overseers of the Poor*. Because only a part of these files was available for consultation at the time of my research, the migration itineraries reconstructed from this source pertain to only a small segment of the migrant population. In addition, my endeavour to reconstruct the past from the available sources, such as the *Border Entry* and the decennial censuses discussed above, has been challenged by some limitations inherent in the very nature of such records. They tell little about matters such as the authority of the male household head, conflicts between parents and children, and tensions among siblings—some of the central issues in the investigation of gender relations within the family. Oral history accounts are helpful in providing details that fill in these gaps of knowledge left by the quantitative sources. The story that follows is thus a partial attempt to tackle the questions of gender and family in the lives of French-Canadian migrants.

In chapters 1 and 2, I outline the economic and social contexts of life and work in late-nineteenth- and early-twentieth-century Québec and Lowell. The societies of departure and destination formed by French-Canadian migrants underwent profound changes during this period. In Québec, the processes of urbanization and industrialization radically transformed the rural, and mostly agricultural, landscape of the province although at an uneven pace. Transition also occurred in agricultural production itself, which changed from a subsistence to a commercialized farming practice that involved a concomitant shift toward specialization. The combined effects of these changes sharpened the class divide between those who did and did not own land, while creating a great number of wage earners. French Canadians, especially those belonging to the latter two groups—landless farmers and wage-workers—had to make difficult choices for their survival, since a good proportion of both worked as *journaliers*, or day labourers. More than a few chose to leave their homeland, and many ended up in Lowell, Massachusetts.

At about the same time across the border, industrialists in Lowell were faced with mounting difficulties. These stemmed from fierce competition from the Southern textile industry, the intensification of the labour process, and, most importantly, a series of laws adopted throughout the New England states that raised the legal age of working children and instituted compulsory schooling. The need to reduce production costs incited the mill management to abandon paternalistic policies, which provided amenity and control through company-run boardinghouses, church services, and reading and music facilities. New managerial priorities replaced these benefits with increasingly cost-efficient policies. French Canadians, on their part, also adjusted their migration patterns to the new dynamics of the local labour markets. The number of Canadians arriving in Lowell declined, the number of young children among migrants also decreased, and the population growth of this group in the city became increasingly dependent on natural increase.

In chapter 3, I offer a longitudinal analysis of the migration of French Canadians. Their geographic movements were often multidirectional. Lowell was not necessarily their ultimate place of settlement, although the city continued to stand as a destination for many. In comparison to their nineteenth-century predecessors,[25] a greater number of Lowell's French Canadians in the twentieth century had been to places in the U.S., mostly Lowell, before their recorded journey. The complexity and diversity of French Canadians' itineraries were deeply rooted in the family and kin networks involved. At the same time, emerging patterns of women and men moving "alone," whose migration did not lead to family reunification, at least in the short term, points to important changes in the role of the family in the process of migration.

Chapters 4, 5, and 6 turn to the "settlement" period—the time after the migrants' arrival in Lowell. To what extent did the socioeconomic profiles of French-Canadian men change or remain the same? What implication does this have for the formation of their senses of themselves, or their masculinities as workers, fathers, and/or husbands? The degree of their occupational progress, however limited this may have been, suggests the centrality of family and ethnic ties that continued to define Lowell's segmented labour markets. It also points to the centrality of gender ideologies that informed their skills, wages, and responsibilities as male workers, on the one hand, and their power, privilege, and senses of entitlement and pressure as husbands and fathers, on the other.

Finally, chapters 5 and 6 assess the paid and unpaid work of French-Canadian women. They explore demographic factors such as age and marital status, on the one hand, and another important, yet subtler set of factors including living arrangements and household organization, on the other, that defined French-Canadian women's financial and non-financial responsibilities. Defying the conventional view that assumes that a woman's age and marital status were decisive in setting patterns of their labour market participation, Lowell's French-Canadian women of the same age group and marital status undertook different shares of economic responsibility. Indeed, they commonly shouldered the heaviest share of non-monetary responsibilities at home regardless of their employment status. The responsibilities and expectations of these women, distinct from those of their husbands, fathers, and male siblings, reflected complex interpersonal dynamics where different and, at times, conflicting interests had to be negotiated in not necessarily equal terms, but in accordance with each member's power and authority within the family and the larger society.

CHAPTER ONE

To the Wrong Side of the Border

In February of 1909, a daily newspaper in Lowell quoted a Québec deputy in the Canadian Commons who lamented that despite increasing Canadian prosperity, the development of Québec's agriculture in recent years, and efforts by the government to promote colonization, "the deplorable exodus of [his] people from the province to the States had not yet ceased." This Member of Parliament argued that Canada should put all her strength into repatriating the 2,000,000 "Canadians" who were "on the wrong side of the border." In the opinion of the Honourable Member, a renewed injection of subsidies into efforts to colonize the province's hinterland was in order. The Lowell daily, however, seriously questioned the efficiency of the remedy proposed to staunch the flow of French Canadians leaving the province:

> It is hard to see [...] where the government got its money's worth out of the colonizing agents it paid fatly to deliver glowing lectures in French-American centres on the advantages of Lake St. John or other bucolic regions. Their efforts in this town [Lowell], for instance, were notoriously futile, and it wasn't in any case their oratory which drew back to Canada the few families which did leave ... for the old home.[1]

The complex issue of French-Canadian emigration and the efforts of political and religious leaders to repatriate, and, if possible, halt the population drain out of the province were at stake. According to this Lowell newspaper, the French-Canadian exodus to New England textile centres was so strong that repatriation projects would not have any significant effect in changing the flow of population. Farmers, labourers, and industrial workers leaving rural villages and towns as well as cities led this southward migration to Lowell. Under what circumstances did they leave the province? How did women and men respond to the changes moulding their daily lives? What motivated them to move across the border? What were their alternatives? These are the questions addressed in this chapter.

Before turning to my analysis, a few words need to be said about the shift in paradigm in the study of migration. With the emergence of new immigration history over three and a half decades ago, proponents of new yet diverse approaches in an historical inquiry of migration have challenged the hitherto prevalent model of one-way and one-time trans-Atlantic migration.[2] Instead, they underline the continuity of geographical mobility as the multi-directional phenomenon within and outside national boundaries.[3] French-Canadian migration is no exception to such diversity and continuity of geographical mobility. Yet, the existing literature has tended to ignore the important link that connected intra- and inter-provincial migration, on the one hand, and the cross-border movement of French Canadians, on the other.[4] With important exceptions such as studies by Bruno Ramirez and Yves Frenette,[5] such neglect was partly because of the methodological difficulty and partly because of the conceptual bias that demarcates internal from transnational migration inherent in the study of migration history in general. This chapter is an attempt to tackle this lacuna by exploring forces of change in turn-of-the-century Québec and the nature and significance of *colonization* upon the prospective migrants to the U.S.

The Rise of Cities

The French-Canadian exodus was largely a response to structural changes that had radically transformed Québec's rural economy. In the late nineteenth century, rapid population increases in rural regions resulted in a shortage of land. The shift toward commercialized farming precipitated a rise in the number of rural wage earners already made vulnerable to fluctuations in prices and yields. In the early twentieth century, French Canadians departed from a province undergoing profound changes that rendered it quite different from the place their predecessors had known in the 1870s and 1880s. A key driving force behind this radical transformation lay in the urbanization and industrialization of the province—two factors that accompanied the increasing thrust of capitalism into ever more remote regions of the province. Indeed, the proportion of urban dwellers versus rural counterparts in Québec reversed during the first three decades of the twentieth century. In 1901, one in three Quebecers lived in cities; two decades later, one in two did, and by 1931, the proportions of urban and rural dwellers had switched places completely, the former reaching nearly 60 percent. As industrialization progressively commanded greater numbers of wage earners, as factory-made commodities increasingly replaced hand-made goods, and as the commercialization of agriculture deepened the divide between those who owned land and those who did not, few Quebecers were left untouched by the growing forces of change.[6]

The process of urbanization proceeded at an uneven pace, varying by region and parish. As early as the end of the nineteenth century, two metropolitan areas—Montréal and, to a lesser extent, Québec City—dominated the province's urban networks. The population of the Montréal metropolitan region doubled its size every twenty years, from 171,000 in 1881 to 346,000 in 1901, and then to 714,000 in 1921. The population of Québec City increased as well, although in a less spectacular manner, swelling from 62,000 in 1881 to 69,000 in 1901, and to 101,000 in 1921. A half-dozen small to middle-sized cities scattered across the Montreal Plain and the Eastern Townships—including Saint-Jérôme, Sainte-Thérèse, Sherbrooke, St.-Hyacinthe, Sorel, and Granby—also expanded at various rates, though they by no means challenged the supremacy of the province's "prime cities."[7]

Joliette, in the Lanaudière region, is a case in point. Although its population increased slowly from 3,000 to 4,000 during the last third of the nineteenth century, the city began to grow rapidly after the turn of the century. Its population increased by 1.5 times per decade, from 4,220 in 1901 to 6,346 in 1911, and then to 9,116 in 1921.[8] Together with the smaller, yet also important, regional centre Berthierville and the rural areas surrounding it—such as Saint-Jean-de-Matha, Sainte-Émilie-de-l'Énergie and Sainte-Mélanie—Joliette became home to a substantial number of those who emigrated from the Lanaudière region to Lowell, Massachusetts.

In addition to the growth of the existing urban networks within the province's primary metropolitan areas, as well as its small-to-mid-sized cities, the opening decades of the new century also saw the birth of urban centres in peripheral regions. In the Mauricie, Saguenay-Lac-Saint-Jean, and Abitibi regions, urbanization was closely linked to the development of natural resources. In the Mauricie, for example, the opening of a hydroelectric plant at turn-of-the-century Shawinigan Falls, located about thirty kilometres north of Trois-Rivières, boosted rapid economic growth in the Upper Mauricie region. Exploitation of other natural resources and the large-scale production of products such as paper and pulp, aluminium, and carborundum further sustained this regional development.[9] The expansion of Shawinigan Falls best symbolizes this regional evolution. Its population increased from a little over 2,700 in 1901, the time of its inception as a village, to 4,300 a decade later, and then to 11,000 another decade later. Paradoxical as it may seem, it was this newly born city that ended up sending a leading number of provincial inhabitants from the Mauricie region to Lowell.[10]

The accelerated paces of urbanization, industrialization, and the modernization of commercial activities in Québec in the early twentieth century did not, however, mean that the province's agricultural sector was vanishing. Rather, new urban development was largely limited to a sprinkling of new and older commercial and industrial centres that co-existed with agricultural activities throughout much of the province. Nevertheless, the expansion of existing cities and the creation of new ones bore major consequences on the province's agriculture. One of the most remarkable of these was the heightened demand for agricultural products from Québec. It is true that as early as 1854, the Reciprocity Treaty with the U.S. and the subsequent American Civil War had both served to stimulate the province's agricultural production. After a brief period of reciprocal trade in 1865-66, the American market closed, but by then Québec had found a new opening in Great Britain for its agricultural products, such as butter and cheese. However, it was not until after the turn of the century, largely due to the urban expansion within the province detailed above and in the Prairies, that more and more Québec farmers reoriented their production toward commercialization, focusing their activities on specialization in producing goods such as vegetables, meat, and dairy products.[11]

The Commercialization and Specialization of Agriculture

The transition from subsistence to commercialized farming accelerated profound social changes and was undeniably one of the factors behind the large-scale migration out of the province. Dairy production came to dominate the province's agricultural output. It reflected more distinctly than any other agricultural sector the shift in agricultural production that had been occurring since the last third of the nineteenth century. Figures for Québec alone are not available, but cheese exports from Québec and Ontario combined amounted to less than $100,000 before 1865, but reached $1.1 million by 1871.[12] The increase in butter production was less dramatic. Before 1856, the yearly value of butter exports from Québec and Ontario never exceeded $200,000, but by 1859 it surpassed $500,000 and, with the opening of the British market, it rose to $1.3 million by 1865 and to $2.9 million by 1871.[13] After this marked rise, butter production doubled during the period from 1871 to 1921, going from 24,289 pounds to 48,630 pounds per year.[14]

In the province of Québec, the production of cheese and, to a lesser extent, butter, which until then had been a backbreaking task usually assigned to women, was gradually taken over by factories.[15] Whereas butter production in the rest of the country largely remained in the hands of women, with only a third of the output produced in factories, in Québec, the production of butter in factories had already exceeded home production by 1916.[16] Ontario was undergoing the same shift from home- to factory-produced butter, but the process there was not as rapid as it was in Québec. However, this transformation in dairy production did not proceed uniformly throughout the province, and in regions with limited access to outside markets, subsistence farming still persisted.[17]

The years from 1890 to 1910 marked a high point for Québec's agricultural industry. The number of dairy cows increased by more than 200,000 in the 1890s, and the number of factories producing cheese and, later, butter also increased quickly: from a combined total of 162 in 1886 to 728 in 1891, and then to 1,992 in 1900, although it decreased slightly to 1,867 two decades later. The increase in cheese production grew by more than seven times, from a yearly average of 585,000 pounds for the period from 1860 to 1880 to 4,261,000 pounds in 1890. The volume of butter production was less spectacular but rose by 90 percent from 1860 to 1890. The total value of manufactured products also increased: during the three decades between 1891 and 1919, it rose from $2,919,000 to $15,305,488 for cheese, and from $268,000 to $1,369,384 for butter.[18]

The rapid increase in pork and poultry production is another indicator of the progress of commercial agriculture.[19] Farmers fed pigs with by-products (*petit lait*) from dairy production. This practice contributed to making pork the second largest animal product in Québec, while poultry doubled its numbers between 1890 and 1910. This process of commercialization proceeded concurrently with that of specialization. For instance, farmers in the Bellechasse and the Montmagny regions bred horses for export to the American market. The increase in dairy farming and horse breeding, in turn, resulted in the production of hay nearly doubling during the decades between 1870 and 1910. There was also animal husbandry practiced in the Eastern Townships, the cultivation of vegetables and fruits occurring in the rural belts surrounding Montréal and Québec City, and the cultivation of tobacco taking place in the Joliette region.[20] The shift toward market-oriented production did not, however, end subsistence farming. Even farmers growing crops such as grains and potatoes for the purposes of commercial markets still devoted most of their energy to farming for their own consumption. Thus, Québec's agriculture was, on the whole, a distinctive mix of production of *grandes cultures* (grains and potatoes), livestock breeding, and the cultivation of fruits and garden vegetables.

Commercialized agriculture, with its concomitant trend toward specialization, meant that not only were farmers vulnerable to the fluctuating needs of the market, but they also became more dependent on the market for products which they had hitherto produced themselves. Moreover, in order to maximize their profits, a proportion of farmers expanded their operations and invested in expensive machinery. Doing so, they accumulated huge debts, which, according to Yves Roby, forced a significant number of them to borrow money from notaries and general store owners.[21] Under the combined effects of successive devastating crop failures in 1888, 1889, and 1890, acute international competition in the marketplace, and restrictions on market access imposed by protectionist measures such as the McKinley Tariff in the United States, some farmers had to turn to usurers in an attempt to repay creditors. Others sought to escape this vicious cycle of mounting debt by temporarily leaving the countryside in search of employment in the industrial centres within and outside the province, and in the U.S.[22]

Bruno Ramirez has developed a different take on the direct causal relationship between indebtedness and emigration that Roby delineates in his work. According to Ramirez, the transition from subsistence farming to commercial farming widened the gap that already divided the minority of commercial farmers from the small farmholders and landless farmers who made up the majority. As early as the 1870s, the first category of prosperous farmers had acquired a growing amount of farm land and practised considerable agricultural specialization. These commercial farmers, such as Prosper Allard in Berthier County,[23] likely provided seasonal employment for the second category of small farmholders and landless farmers. Most of the emigrating French Canadians in the 1870s and 1880s came from the expanding latter category—including *journaliers* and small landholders, though a substantial number were both.[24]

In the early twentieth century, the ongoing transformation of agriculture profoundly touched the lives of a greater number of Québec farmers. For example, the concentration of land in the hands of a relatively small number of prosperous commercial farmers accelerated unabatedly. The other, apparently new, phenomenon was the gradual decrease in the number of small landholders and landless farmers; from 1891 to 1931, the number of landless farmers decreased from 175,000 to 136,000. The transformation can also be observed in the changes in the average acreage of farms that occurred during this period. The average size of a farm rose steadily, from 103 acres (of which 53 acres were arable land) in 1901, to 127 acres (of which 66 acres were arable land) in 1921.[25] Certainly, an increase in the average acreage held does not translate directly into growth in productivity or production. Likewise, the decreasing number of small farm-holders does not mean that they acquired a larger proportion of arable land. Rather, these figures include a significant portion of landholding settlers, whose newly acquired lands contained tracts of forests yet to be cultivated. This was especially the case in the peripheral regions. To the great disappointment of many, the land they came to possess often failed to yield crops sufficient to keep their families above the survival line. Consequently, a great number of farmers would accept any available opportunity to sell their labour for wages in order to make up for their eroding means of survival. Some worked as farm labourers as had been done in the late nineteenth century; but by the new century, an increasing number worked as general day labourers.

The work of *journaliers* included haying and harvesting during the cultivation period and hauling during the off-season on family-owned farms; construction work at railroads and later, road sites; and, increasingly after the turn of the century, maintenance and various other industrial jobs in nearby towns and cities, as well as in the countryside. This type of employment was irregular by nature, and in most cases, wages were insufficient to compensate for the loss of subsistence farming. In addition to the lack of any form of job security, other chronic problems persisted, including increased difficulties of accessing land, population pressure, and natural disasters. Not surprisingly, such a combination of factors made day labourers the best candidates to migrate, temporarily or permanently, out of their rural villages and towns in search of jobs for a quick and hopefully steady income.

Women in a Society of Transition

The socioeconomic reality of early-twentieth-century Québec provided another incentive, especially for women, to move with their families to the urban industrial centres of New England. As has been discussed earlier, as commercial farming became the dominant form of agriculture in Québec, the site of dairy production shifted, for the most part, from farms to factories. The relocation of cheese-making, in particular, exemplified the way in which what had previously been a domestic chore for women was transformed into a large-scale industrial enterprise. Such transformation, however, did not necessarily reduce the workload for women. Farm women no longer had to do the tedious job of churning butter, but since they had a number of other extremely time-consuming tasks, they continued to labour as much as ever. Such tasks ranged from poultry raising, to gardening, to the making of honey and maple sugar for family use or to trade or sell, all of which remained for a long time the work of women.[26]

The profound impact of this shift of production sites on women's lives in Québec's countryside notwithstanding, women were not immediately removed from the process of dairying; rather, their displacement was gradual. Moreover, such a process of simultaneous change and continuity in the content of women's tasks was not unique to Québec, and many of their counterparts in the neighbouring province of Ontario also experienced a similar shift. In both provinces, women had initially made up a significant proportion of the labour force in cheese factories, and in 1871, they constituted one third of these workers. Even as cheese-producing factories increased in number, however, the proportion of women workers declined. By the turn of the century, not a single woman was recorded as working in a cheese factory in Canada.[27] The manufacture of butter, in contrast, remained for a longer time in the hands of women.[28] This was principally because butter was more expensive to produce in factories than cheese. To put it another way, the fact that butter production required less space and equipment and demanded fewer specialized skills than cheese meant that it could continue to be made more readily at home most likely by women.

Regardless of the change in the content of their work, most rural women at home and in manufacturing saw themselves being marginalized and felt excluded from the decision-making processes involved in the management of farming activities. This was the case for dairy production as it became central, lucrative, and based on the exchange of cash. In the mid-nineteenth century, women had "helped out," as women themselves stated, regularly or occasionally. They had been responsible for certain tasks in the field, especially those related to haying, picking, laying in swath, weeding, and bedding, and by doing so, they continued to help out in the early years of mechanization.[29] It is important to note that the variety of their work and the sphere of their responsibilities were often restricted to sites of non-cereal production (outside the *grande culture*). Examples include: henhouses, cowsheds, vegetable gardens and, most importantly, kitchens, where daily meals were prepared, canning was done, and dairy products were made.[30] In the early twentieth century, as Martine Tremblay has observed, the place traditionally assigned to women narrowed even further, and the decision-making power and responsibilities of men increased. This was largely a result of the further progression of market-oriented farming, which at times modified, and at other times intensified, the existing division of labour along gender lines on the farm. In apparent contradiction to this, however, the process of mechanization that accompanied the commercialization of agricultural production also pressed women to increase their contribution to the tasks in the field. This was especially true when the scarcity of financial means made it impossible for the family to employ an *engagé*, or paid worker—a situation commonly faced by farming families in Québec—or when children were too young to take part in the work on the fields.[31] As a result, the working conditions of women in the field merged with those of farm labourers, thus intensifying the lack of recognition of women's contributions in the field, on the part of the male heads of the families. This meant that the progression of the commercialization of farming and the mechanization that went with it heightened the degree to which women were marginalized on the farm. It is not difficult to imagine then that when women sought to resist the marginalization underway, and when they found out about the wide range of opportunities for wage-earning across the border, few must have hesitated to leave their parishes behind either temporarily or permanently, often bringing their families along with them.

While changes in the processes and sites of production stemming from the commercialization and specialization of agriculture redefined the existing division of labour between women and men on the farm, the further industrialization of the countryside and peripheral regions also modified women's work within the household. As factory-made commodities became more readily available and accessible, women's domestic tasks shifted from producing goods for consumption within the family to obtaining and consuming manufactured products. This change occurred gradually and unevenly as rural French-Canadian women continued to produce some of the daily necessities, such as soap, candles, canned foods, and bread, on their farms, yet also began to replace these goods with commercial products with increasing frequency. Moreover, during the last quarter of the nineteenth century, a growing number of families living in remote corners of the province also began to enjoy the new luxury of mail-order shopping, or *l'achat en ville*, as they called it, since they were able in this way to experience the thrill of "shopping in town" without actually having to go into town. In the course of industrialization and commercialization, whereby "country cloth and fabrics were increasingly replaced by cotton, printed cotton, tweed, and commercial sheets,"[32] this slow and uneven process of redefining women's work did not decrease their overall responsibilities. Farm women were no longer burdened with spinning and weaving cloth themselves but instead became dependent on cash to buy machine-made fabrics. Now women had to make sure that their households had sufficient money to buy necessities made increasingly available through advertisements and mail order, rather than producing them as they had done earlier.

While women's and their families' need for cash income intensified, women, particularly in rural areas, ran into difficulties earning money. When social services were negligible and household technology primitive, it must have been extremely difficult, if not impossible, for married women to combine wage work with household work. Another disincentive to seeking employment outside the household stemmed from the fact that the type and amount of work available to French-Canadian women in rural Québec were limited and the wages were quite low. Furthermore, religious and sociocultural norms at the time dictated that a woman's place was in the home. As *reines du foyer*, or "queens of the household," women were to cook, clean, mend, and take care of everyone at home, as we have discussed earlier, and often had a multitude of other chores to attend to outside the house as well.

The children of farming families, much like their urban counterparts, were expected to contribute from an early age to the collective welfare of the household. Their participation in household work was characteristic of both subsistence-oriented and market-oriented patterns of production. Moreover, children, especially daughters, had to help their mothers with heavy domestic chores. Denise Lemieux and Lucie Mercier assert that in almost all families, there was an unmarried daughter who was charged with "taking care of an infirm mother or young orphan nephews, and it was considered a duty."[33] An example of this kind of dutiful young woman is provided in Agusutine Linteau's description of her sister:

> My sister Hélène has to leave the school to become the right hand of my Mom who is sick. The children called her T'Len and everyone loved her for her natural gaiety and her great generosity for receiving everyone who lived far away from the family's residence. During the vacation, Mom takes boarders: young girls of the office.[34]

Hélène's devotion to her family illustrates one of the most important roles played by older daughters. Their household duties continued until the death of their parents, which left single women like Hélène at a loss, for then they had to adapt, at a fairly late stage of their life, to earning wages.[35]

Colonisation and Repatriation as a Less Viable Alternative

Although a number of marginalized rural Quebecers left for the U.S. in response to economic and social transformations, emigration was not their only option. Another possibility would have been to move to regions designated for colonization, an option that provincial government officials and the Catholic clergy strongly encouraged during a series of "*colonisation*" campaigns conducted in order to direct its surplus population toward the hinterlands of the St. Lawrence Valley.

The colonization policy had three clear objectives: to promote agriculture in the hinterlands, to populate these areas, and to transform them into sites of repatriation or alternative migration for Quebecers. The third objective did not constitute the initial aim of settlement but as growing numbers of French Canadians left their parishes for the U.S., this objective became a central goal of the colonization policy. Underlying the rhetoric of peopling the hinterlands were the political and religious elites' motives for promoting colonization, motives that defined the nature of this social and national project.[36]

Colonization was therefore more than just a settlement policy; it was a social project by which French-Canadian leaders attempted to incite rural Quebecers to fulfill the duty of the "French-Canadian race," as they referred to themselves. The political elite and the Catholic clergy believed that taming Québec's forests would preserve their civilization against the threats of Protestantism, secularization, marginalization, and anglicization. French-Canadian frontier settlement was, as Bruno Ramirez has argued, "Turner's frontier thesis in reverse."[37] Whereas the American frontier, according to Frederick Jackson Turner, would produce "new, freer, proto-democratic men," settling the French-Canadian frontier would preserve cherished elements of traditional society: Catholicism, the French language, and the family.[38] The regions north of Montréal, Mauricie, Saguenay-Lac-Saint-Jean, the inland region of the Bas-Saint-Laurent, the Eastern Townships, and later, the Témiscamingue region—all came under the plough of colonization.[39]

From early on, nationalist leaders believed that colonization would become the principal means of slowing and, if possible, halting the population flowing toward the "wrong side of the border." As the departure of Quebecers to manufacturing centres in New England reached its peak in the 1870s and 1880s, supporters of the colonization policy emphasized the need to keep the French-Canadian population in the province. Premier Honoré Mercier and Father François-Xavier-Antoine Labelle from Saint-Jérôme-de-Terrebonne claimed that migration toward the cities, especially the urban centres of the United States, would result in the moral corruption of rural Quebecers, who would be unable to withstand the pressure to assimilate and secularize. Expatriates in the U.S., they argued, must be rescued from cultural extermination; thus, repatriation of the population already residing outside of the province became an integral part of colonization policy.

In the 1890s, T. Saint-Pierre, the French secretary of the Workers Congress of Canada also decried the migration of his people into the "manufacturing states," or *États de manufacture,* that lay to the south. Saint-Pierre lamented that French Canadians who went to the U.S. in search of fortune and did not find it faced ruin.[40] If that was true, however, why did these emigrants often write letters to their families and friends in Québec boasting of their positions in the U.S.? Why could they spend so much money when they returned to their homeland? St.-Pierre's replies were that French Canadians are naturally light-hearted and proud; back in Québec, they simply wanted to impress their acquaintances that they had money. St.-Pierre continued, "This is a common effect of human vanity."[41] Thus, he concluded by stating that it was best to set aside prejudice and vanity and to never leave the native land in the first place. In this way, his discourse joined that of clerical and political efforts, all of which maintained that the best way for potential migrants to make a living in Québec was to go to the virgin land, the *régions de colonisation,* extending across Saguenay-Lac-Saint-Jean, Bas-du-Fleuve, Mauricie, Lanaudière, and Outaouais.

The zeal of the nationalist leaders did not simply remain as words, but was translated into various concrete actions. They set up colonization societies, sent repatriation agents throughout New England towns and cities, and published brochures, maps, and advertisements in Québécois and Franco-American newspapers. Supporters of colonization and repatriation loaded their discourse with dichotomous rhetoric, turning the site of colonization into a sort of demarcation line between the birthplace of civilization and the state of savagery. For instance, a local newspaper in Joliette, *l'Étoile du Nord,* frequently published articles calling for visitors to take part in organized excursions to future sites of colonization. On September 8, 1904, the paper announced a visit to the valley of the Mattawin and Lake Saint-Ignace in a northern colonization region. The trip would offer a great opportunity, emphasized the anonymous author, for the future settlers to observe, firsthand, the wealth of resources available in the region; to examine the construction work of railroads; and to attend the birth of a settlement where the processes of *défrichements,* or "clearing," and settlement had recently displaced the former state of savagery. In addition, read the announcement, the excursion would be accompanied by "distinguished persons," including government officials and representatives of the Catholic Church. The announcement concluded by reminding the readers to seriously consider the "question of colonization" and the obligations of a "true patriot."[42] The consideration of these matters, the writer hoped, would inevitably urge a great number of potential settlers to join this organized voyage.

Despite the concerted efforts to campaign for the colonization, the results of such endeavours were mixed at best. As Paul-André Linteau observes, colonization provided the short-term benefit of alleviating the pressure of overpopulation in the province's seigneurial parishes, and it also had the long-term advantage of establishing new regions in the province's hinterlands. Nevertheless, as a means of stemming the tide of emigration to the United States, *colonisation* failed.[43] For instance, although the population grew from 17,000 to 37,000 between 1871 and 1901 in the Saguenay, one of the most important colonization regions,[44] this rate was only marginally higher than the French-Canadian population increase in a New England textile city such as Lowell or Fall River.[45] The population increase in the Mauricie region, which swelled from 98,294 to 124,328 during the same period, was more significant than that of the Saguenay-Lac-Saint-Jean region; yet this increase largely reflected the development of regional commercial/industrial centres such as Trois-Rivières and Grand'Mère.[46]

For many, colonization provided only a temporary solution to enduring problems as a significant number of people drifted out of the colonization regions in the second half of the nineteenth century. In the Bas-Saint-Laurent, for example, outward migration began to exceed inward migration as early as the 1860s. In the 1880s, this migration out of the area had reached a peak of 16,924 in a population of 59,128.[47] The phenomenon of de-population was not unique to the Bas-Saint-Laurent but was also found in other major colonization regions.[48]

By the early twentieth century, the population flow out of the *régions de la colonisation* accelerated in some areas. In other places, the colonization movement entered its last phase. The earliest regions subjected to colonization, such as the Lac-Saint-Jean region, were running out of uncleared land for settlers, while new regions for exploitation were located in extremely remote areas, such as Témiscamingue in the Northeast, the Outaouais valley in the west, and the valley of the Mattawin, which lay northwest of the already settled counties of Berthier and Joliette in the Lanaudière region. Not all the efforts to promote colonization and repatriation met with disappointing results, however. The *Société de colonisation de Montréal* praised the successful work that reportedly brought over 1,700 "Canadians in the United States" to settle in the province between 1898 and 1907.[49] But among those who returned to Canada, a significant number left again for the United States. T. A. Brisson of the *Société générale de colonisation et rapatriement* conceded that, as far as the Saguenay region was concerned, repatriation efforts had failed. A large number of those who returned from the U.S. and settled in colonization regions decided to leave the province once again. Some even convinced friends and family members to join them as they went back to the United States. In his annual report of 1905, Dr. Brisson, referring to the 1902-1903 recession and its effects on New England textile centres, wrote:

> When the crisis came in the United States three years ago, a larger number than one would believe of our emigrated compatriots returned to Canada. In spite of attempts to retain them, a larger number of those who had come back to us returned, or are now returning to foreign parts ... as the opportunity occurs for them to take advantage of the reopening of the American manufactures ... The greater part of those who are leaving now are those who had already been away and it is feared that no efforts can wholly prevent this.[50]

Indeed, a significant number of French Canadians crossed the border several times during their lifetime. Many also moved from one factory town to another within New England. It was unlikely that they had monopoly over such practices but because of the extent of their frequent displacement among the factories within New England and across the border, according to Pierre Anctil, they deserved the nickname: "*coureurs de facterie,*"[51] or those who moved from one factory to another, a play on words with the expression *coureurs des bois* for the fur trade in New France.

The failure to colonize and repatriate can be largely explained by the relative attraction of emigration. The harsh conditions of extreme cold and backbreaking work in the colonization areas, coupled with the instability stemming from the volatile agro-forestry economy, could arguably be endured by young rural Quebecers, whether single men or members of small families, but not by older individuals or larger families. Typically, young rural Quebecers left for a colonization region and stayed there for a while, living on a combination of subsistence farming and seasonal forestry employment. Once their families became too large to be sustained with available resources, they left the area and were replaced by younger settlers.[52]

In addition, the high turnover in the population of the colonization regions resulted from the region's inability to effectively absorb the incoming settlers. After the developmental boom created by railroad and road construction ended, the colonization regions simply could not sustain previous levels of employment, or a sufficient variety of work, to support all of the settlers who had ventured to the area. In the regions of Rivière-du-Loup and Témiscouata, for example, the forestry and railroad industries, which linked the region to the metropolitan market and to sources of investment, initially provided the driving force for the region's development. The advent of railroads brought in workers, not only from other regions in Québec, but also from as far away as Europe.[53] Moreover, it provided regional farmers with access to outside markets and stimulated the development of the forestry industry and that of agricultural settlement.[54] But once the construction work was completed, the boom came to an abrupt end. Antonio Lechasseur estimates that in 1877, just a year after the completion of the railroad, the first contingent of emigrants had already left the Bas-Saint-Laurent region *en masse*. By the 1880s, migration out of the Rimouski region, the hardest-hit area in the Bas-Saint-Laurent, reached its peak with a 36 percent drop in population over ten years.[55] The ultimate destination of these people is not known; some, no doubt, left for Montréal and other urban centres within the province, some might have migrated to western Canada, while a large proportion must have left for the urban industrial centres of New England.

Perhaps the most immediate obstacle for colonization was the physical and psychological isolation imposed on the settlers and their families as they attempted to live in these remote locations. This isolation seemed even more unbearable when viewed against the "pull" of American cities. Emigration to

New England textile centres presented the promise of immediate and tangible economic rewards at the end of the day, week, or month. Becoming a wage earner in the U.S. also meant making higher salaries in comparison to those in Québec. Furthermore, textile factories in New England welcomed the employment of not only adults, but also their children, at least until the turn of the century when strict anti-child labour laws were implemented.[56] In contrast, working on one's own plot of land in Québec's hinterlands might have provided one with the pride of ownership, yet it also meant waiting for one entire agricultural season before income could be obtained from crop yields. Moreover, such economic advantages could be had after a day trip by train to the south. And above all, the American option offered potential migrants crucial sociocultural assets, including the chance to become part of one of the most "institutionally complete," to use Raymond Breton's term, Francophone communities in the region, with French-Canadian churches, parish schools, and a variety of shops. In the beginning of the twentieth century, Fall River, Massachusetts, for example, held the largest French-speaking population after Montréal in North America.[57] Such advantages offered by the manufacturing centres in Massachusetts and other New England states must have easily outweighed the disadvantages,[58] demonstrating the hollowness of the rhetoric used by the promoters of colonization, who often praised the "tender and pleasant life led by happy residents in our Canadian countryside," as opposed to the "harsh life of those who lived in the underground of the mines or prisons of American manufacturing."[59]

One may conclude, therefore, that the failure of political efforts to stem the tide of migration to the United States did not simply reflect the inability of the concerned provincial elite to impose its will upon the migrating population. During the twentieth century, the provincial government pursued the construction and maintenance of railroads and increasingly, of roads, conceiving them as an infrastructure of utmost importance, and therefore spending the largest proportion of the colonization budgets on these transportation links. Yet such efforts fell far short of either breaking the barriers of isolation or creating sufficient work to keep settlers within the recently opened regions of colonization.[60] As Ramirez has argued, for the late-nineteenth-century French Canadians, rather than any abstract nationalist argument about the preservation of Catholic French-Canadian culture, it may have been the settlers' perception of family needs and capacities, and most importantly, their knowledge of particular local labour markets that shaped the decision of Quebecers in the early twentieth century to either become or remain settlers in an isolated region of the province or to work in the industrial centres of the United States.[61] The choice was not necessarily an easy one. Life in the city meant hard work and at least a temporary stay in a foreign land. On the other hand, life in the colonization regions meant even harder work, offset perhaps by the promise of securing land; yet this land often provided too poor a yield to ensure the survival of one's family. For many in the late nineteenth century, decision-making was a complex process involving years of experimentation, reconsideration, accidents, and failures. But in the new century, a growing proportion had already acquired experience living and working in Lowell and other industrial cities in the U.S. for a period of time. Thus, when they decided to move across the border, many of them must have done so with the certainty of finding what they were looking for, i.e., jobs and the wages necessary to better their lots.

The Homeland of Lowell-Bound Migrants: Lanaudière and Mauricie

In the twentieth century, a leading proportion of Lowell-bound French Canadians originated from regions of either older or relatively recent settlement. Lanaudière was one such region, and another was Mauricie. A close analysis of Lowell-bound migrants from the Lanaudière and the Mauricie sheds light on important aspects of the complex mechanisms by which human movement took place amidst ongoing industrialization and urbanization. The majority of the emigrants from these regions were, indeed, from rural areas, but not all were farmers. A significant minority had lived and worked in urban, industrial milieux prior to their recorded travel across the border.[62]

For a leading proportion of Lanaudière migrants bound for Lowell, two cities, Joliette and Berthierville, together with their surrounding rural parishes, formed a part of an important constellation of departure points within the web of migratory networks. Situated at the immediate backwater of the St. Lawrence, a land that contained rich soil suitable for agriculture, Joliette had become the veritable commercial, industrial, and service centre of the Lanaudière region after the mid-nineteenth century when neighbouring territories came under the purview of colonization.[63] Berthierville, much smaller in population, was located on the North Shore, at the strategic crossroad along the *Chemin du Roi* linking Montréal to Québec City, and was within a ferry ride's distance of Sorel, another key commercial centre on the Southern Shore of the Saint Lawrence River. Berthierville thus bridged the path for travelers from the North Shore as they moved to the Eastern Townships and the U.S.[64]

When migrants from Lanaudière passed through these cities on their way to Lowell, their journeys were much more than mere adventures into a strange land. Many were tracing a familiar path they themselves had taken some time earlier. The majority, comprising two out of three emigrants from the region, had lived and worked in Lowell, and thus left their parishes knowing what they would find at their destination. Moreover, a good proportion already possessed the skills necessary to find work in the textile city. This was in sharp contrast to their predecessors in the 1870s and 1880s, most of whom were rural families with little or no work experience in the textile industry. A substantial proportion of emigrants from the Lanaudière region in the new century were not, strictly speaking, rural farmers. Instead, before their recorded move to Lowell, they had become urban dwellers—some in their home province and others, increasingly, in the U.S.[65]

Hermine Adam and his family, for instance, illustrate the multiple moves conducted by a considerable proportion of the residents of Lanaudière. After residing in Lowell for fifteen years, this thirty-eight-year-old weaver and his family went back to their native town of Joliette. Was their voyage back to Canada motivated by an unexpected loss of employment experienced by one or more of their family members? Or was it a long-awaited return home, after having earned and saved the desired amount of money in the textile city? We do not know. What we do know is that in February 1909, the Adams crossed the border again, this time southward, heading for the New England city they had previously known so well. Their migration unit consisted of seven children including Alphonsa and Philomena, ages sixteen and seventeen, respectively, who were identified as cotton mill operatives, and their five younger siblings ranging in age from three to thirteen. Some or all of the four elder members of the family, i.e., Hermine, Alexandria, Alphonsa and Philomena, might have begun their careers as textile mill operators in Lowell during their former stay in that city.[66] Another example is the case of forty-three-year-old Herménégilde Adam. In April 1913, Herménégilde left his native parish of Ste.-Béatrice, Québec, for Lowell. He traveled with his wife, Leah, who was forty-six years old, and five children ranging in age from three to fourteen. Like Hermine Adam and his family, Herménégilde's family had lived in Lowell as long as six years before their recorded trip in 1913.[67] Yet another example is Céline Archambault, a thirty-five-year-old single domestic who headed for Lowell seven years after Herménégilde Adam's voyage. In January 1920, Céline departed St.-Jean-de-Matha with her parents, Hercule and Marion. Like the Adams, Céline and her parents had once lived in the U.S. Responding to an American border official who questioned them about their former stay in the U.S., the family reported that they had resided in various localities in the southern Republic between 1914 and 1919.[68]

The marked flow of migrants between villages and urban centres in Québec and Lowell was not a phenomenon unique to Lanaudière, but rather was a part of a broader process that shaped, to varying degrees, several regions of the province. Mauricie, just northeast of Lanaudière, was another region that saw the departure of a significant number of its residents to the United States. In the last quarter of the nineteenth century, Trois-Rivières, the regional capital of Mauricie and the third largest city of the province, underwent a period of stagnation. After a period of rapid growth resulting in an increase of 2,572 people from 6,098 in 1861 to 8,670 in 1881, the population of the fluvial city actually decreased to 8,334 during the following decade. In 1901, the city's population rose to just below 10,000, but its pace of expansion did not regain the level recorded three decades earlier.[69] This slowdown in the city's population growth in large part resulted from a serious setback that hit the region's lumber industry.

The lumber companies relied heavily on the seasonal workforce drawn from both nearby parishes and the remote colonization regions. The rural families in these regions, especially those living in the colonization settlements, drew from seasonal work in the forestry industry, in combination with and supplementing their agricultural activities, a common strategy for survival. Agricultural settlers sent young male members of their families out to the lumber camps during the winter, usually from October to April. As they did so, they made sure that there would be sufficient labour power left behind to take care of the family farm, which in any event was relatively inactive during that season.[70] Extra income procured in this manner made a significant difference in their household economy. Also, partaking in forestry work bore an important cultural meaning for settlers' and farmers' sons. To leave for the forest for the first time in one's life was a rite of passage and marked an important step into manhood. It tested their endurance, both physical and mental, amidst the harsh working conditions of the camp, far away from their mothers, sisters, and younger siblings. It could also mean initiation to smoking and drinking in the company of adult men. And above all, it proved a young man's capacity to earn wages, however limited they might be, and to contribute directly to the household economy. In these ways, the forestry activities and the income thus generated by these male workers enabled their families to sustain, reinforce, and even extend traditional practices proper to their local economy, while simultaneously serving the modern and developed industries and services. As Gérard Bouchard has asserted, insofar as the latter relied on the former in a similar manner, these systems operated in relative "structural harmony."[71]

Yet, at the same time, the involvement of those men in forestry work transformed the domestic roles traditionally assumed by men and women. In the parish of Saint-Justin, for instance, married women, who spent a large proportion of the year alone, had to assume greater responsibility for the maintenance of the household. They had to make decisions regarding the education of their children and were in charge of the animals as well as the cultivation of the fields.[72]

Exact figures are not available for determining what portion of the household budget was derived from a forestry worker's earnings. However, the importance of this source of income became clear when the market price of lumber declined, and families were pushed to a status of bare subsistence. When things became unbearable, as they did in Mauricie during the closing decades of the nineteenth century, families engaged in agro-forestry activities left the region for elsewhere. It would be a mistake, however, to suggest that families who derived income from forestry were always in financial distress. During the period between 1869 and 1875 and again between the beginning of World War I and the outbreak of the Great Depression, with the years 1921-22 being a notable exception, forestry workers received acceptable wages for their hard labour. During the war, wages in the forestry industry rose to an all-time high due to the greater demand for forestry. In 1921, however, wages dropped by twenty-two percent.[73]

The working day for forestry workers lasted *d'une noirceur à l'autre*, or from dawn to dusk. Workers would labour as long as eleven to fourteen hours a day in extremely cold temperatures. At times, the density of the forest and the depth of the snow forced these men to work without horses (*travailler à la "bunch"*), and so they had to transport logs weighing as much as three hundred pounds by hand back to the accessible trail, covering distances of 200 to 300 feet. Moreover, the workers had to deduct from their earnings the cost of necessities such as blankets, tools, and underwear, which they were forced to purchase at exorbitant prices from the company. In addition to this exploitation, the men had to endure three- to six-month-long work assignments in isolated forests far away from their families.[74]

The lumber companies exploited these agro-forestry workers by keeping them barely above the subsistence level. And yet, the meagre cash income procured through this seasonal work in the forests made an important difference in the lives of many rural families. In some cases, it allowed landless farmers and small landholders to buy land for their children, or to settle on new land. But for a greater number, it was simply a way to get by, to put enough food on the table, and to keep themselves warm with the minimum of necessary clothing. Thus, when cutbacks in the forestry industry made it impossible for those families to fall back on this crucial means of supplementing their subsistence, their lives were put at risk.

The opening of the new century swept away the sluggishness of the previous decades. The establishment of resource industries in Upper Mauricie reinvigorated the existing urban centres and created new ones, boosting the regional economy. Smaller and mid-size cities, such as Shawinigan Falls, Grand'Mère, La Tuque, and, later, Cap-de-la-Madeleine, grew quickly, while the oldest regional centre, Trois-Rivières, renewed the pace of its expansion.[75] Of these expanding cities, Shawinigan Falls stood out as a site from which a leading proportion of the emigrants I studied departed for Lowell.

This produces an apparent contradiction—that the urban expansion of certain quarters of Mauricie, especially Shawinigan Falls, coincided with a draining of its population. One may explain this by noting how the departing migrants, allegedly originating from urban centres such as Shawinigan Falls, had in fact been residents of neighbouring rural parishes such as Saint-Tite. Even so, this would not have raised the number of residents from Shawinigan Falls so disproportionately above that of Lowell-bound emigrants from other parts of Mauricie, since such an effect would have been observable in other localities as well. A more plausible hypothesis would be that this newborn industrial centre failed to offer sufficient employment to support workers who had moved to the city in search of new job opportunities and by extension, support for their families. The production of hydro-electricity, aluminium, and pulp and paper called for the establishment of large-scale enterprises financed heavily, if not entirely, by foreign capital and required a great number of workers. In 1898, for instance, American money and technology initiated the construction of a huge dam in Shawinigan, the first of its scale in the province.[76] The project also attracted a number of day labourers from the surrounding rural areas and beyond. Once construction was completed, however, the capital-intensive industry did not provide alternative employment for its workers. The "surplus population" left the region, hoping to find other means of survival elsewhere.

Furthermore, the expansion of railroad networks facilitated migration out of once isolated, peripheral regions. A glance at a local Joliette newspaper finds a number of advertisements that were regularly placed by a railroad company, the Grand Nord. The company announced daily service connecting Shawinigan Falls, Grand'Mère, and Québec City to and from Joliette. Upon arrival in Joliette, a traveler could then change to another line, the Boston & Maine, which ran daily between Joliette and destinations in New England such as Manchester in New Hampshire and Nashua, Worcester, and Lowell in Massachusetts.[77] An emigrant who took a train departing Shawinigan Falls at six o'clock in the morning would arrive in Lowell at six o'clock in the evening of the same day without paying an exorbitant fare for his or her ticket. These railroad networks were the very vehicles by which the political and religious leaders of the province had sought to achieve their goals of promoting colonization and repatriation and thereby halt the southward flow of French Canadians across the border. Considering that, one cannot but note with irony how these lines served, essentially, to facilitate the undermining of the national project they were established to promote.

Thanks to the excellent railway system, emigrants from Mauricie, much like their contemporaries from Lanaudière, gained first-hand experience of living and working in the U.S. relatively easily. Such was the case with Isidore Auger. Born in the rural parish of Saint-Ursule in Mauricie, Isidore had resided in Lowell for over ten years. In 1910, when he was twenty-eight years old, he moved back to his home country. No one knows whether he was tired of his trials in the textile city or simply wanted to change his life, but in any case, after moving back to Québec, he worked as a farmer in the Shawinigan Falls region. Given the precarious conditions under which many farming families lived and worked in Québec at the time, it is most likely that Isidore would also have worked temporarily at a forestry camp. In late September of 1915, Isidore, by then thirty-three, decided to leave for Lowell again. The experience he gained working and living in Lowell, coupled with the skills, knowledge, and, most importantly, the connections he had built up from his earlier residence in that city, must have proved to be decisive factors motivating him to move south. Isidore crossed the border again, accompanied by his wife, Ursulle, who was thirty years old, and their six young children, who ranged in age from eleven months to eight years.[78]

The itineraries of Isidore and many others like him point to a qualitative difference between his generation of migrants and the French Canadians who migrated in the last century, a population characterized, according to Bruno Ramirez, by "a generalized lack of industrial skills."[79] In the early twentieth century, a substantial proportion of migrants leaving Mauricie and Lanaudière, and possibly other regions as well, was comprised of a more select group of workers, who already possessed the skills and experience required to work in the textile factories.

*****

This chapter has explored the homeland of French-Canadian migrants who left for Lowell and other New England localities in the early twentieth century. Going to the *États* had provided an important means of economic improvement for French-Canadian families in the late nineteenth century. In the twentieth century, it continued to do so, but at the same time, growing forces of change engraved distinct contours into the socioeconomic profiles of departing French-Canadian men and women. Although labourers and farmers continued to constitute the majority of emigrants, a growing number had previously accrued industrial experience in Canada. Moreover, for many, going to Lowell was not an adventure into an unknown land: many had stayed in Lowell prior to their recorded travel to that city and were leaving for that same city again. Finally, emigration was not the only possibility of survival for French-Canadian families, but the fact remains that many indeed opted for this choice. Some did so after they had attempted the alternative of settling in the *colonisation* regions. Increasingly, others left the province repeatedly, building on previous experiences of having lived and worked in textile centres in the U.S.

Viewed in this light, the departure of a number of French Canadians to New England textile centres in the early twentieth century emerges as something much more complex than a straightforward flight from poverty or overpopulation. Nor were French Canadians like moths attracted by the dazzling lights of American industrial cities. Well before their departure to the United States, their homeland had been touched by rapid yet uneven processes of urbanization, industrialization, commercialization, and proletarianization. The consequences of industrial capitalism in Québec, as manifested in the spread of commercial agriculture, manufactured goods, and wage-earning activities, were the major causes of French-Canadian emigration. As the next chapter shows, however, even more compelling forces for directing and shaping French-Canadian migration to a destination such as Lowell were human networks of family, kin, and acquaintance. Forced to choose from limited possibilities, French-Canadian women, men, boys, and girls who moved across the border now had to face another reality in their adopted home, which was being shaped by some of the same forces that were transforming the homeland they had left behind.

CHAPTER TWO

Lowell after Paternalism

While numbers of rural French Canadians chose emigration as one possible option in response to the adverse effects of industrial capitalism, they also had to adjust to the forces of change and the new socioeconomic conditions that were shaping New England in the early twentieth century. Increasingly fierce competition from the Southern textile industry incited Lowell's industrialists to abandon their paternalistic policies and instead to aggressively seek more cost-efficient policies. The intensification of the labour process coupled with a series of laws adopted throughout New England states served to remove, to some extent, children from the workforce by curbing the number of teenagers eligible to work and making enrollment in schools compulsory. The young workers, who had formerly provided the region's textile industry with cheap and diligent labour, did not disappear all together but were gradually replaced by an influx of "new immigrants" from southern and eastern Europe.

Such changes produced an immediate impact on the dynamics of the local labour market and on the French-Canadian migration to New England. From 1900 to 1920, the number of French Canadians moving to the U.S. declined to nearly half of what it had been during the highest recorded period, three decades earlier.[1] In Lowell, the influx of migrants from French Canada also declined, and their population growth within the city slowed to a rate commensurate with natural growth. Moreover, the number of French-Canadian residents decreased from 24,000 in 1900 to 23,208 in 1910 with a slight increase of up to 23,699 in 1920. The number of first generation migrants for the same period also fell from 14,674 to 12,296, and then to 10,180.[2]

How did the downward trend in French-Canadian migration to Lowell relate to the radical transformation occurring in the political economy of the textile city? In order to address this question, this chapter first looks at Lowell's evolution as the nation's leading textile centre. This chapter will then consider the ways in which French-Canadian workers and residents of that city, with the largest concentration in textile manufacturing, accommodated challenges stemming from such transformations in the factory, on the street, and at home. As French Canadians came to form a permanent feature of the city, they extended the geographical parameters of their living quarters in the city. French Canadians also diversified their class status with a growing number of small businesses populating the streets of the *Petit Canada*. While many French-Canadian families continued to live in tenement buildings, or "blocks," and work in mills where life-threatening accidents were common, their community thrived with a number of small businesses and the dynamic everyday sociability both within their own group and without.

From Yankee Town to Immigrant City

Lowell owes its modern origins to a decision, made by a party of Boston merchants in 1821, to build an industrial city of an unprecedented order and scale devoted to the production of textiles. Nathan Appleton and Patrick Tracy Jackson were among the first entrepreneurial industrialists who visited what was then called East Chelmsford, "a sleepy little farming village,"[3] in order to investigate the grounds. These prosperous merchants-turned-industrialists immediately liked the place. It was only forty kilometres away from Boston, at the junction of the Merrimack and Concord Rivers, just below the Pawtucket Falls. It was located on both the Pawtucket Canal, which could easily be enlarged for waterpower purposes, and on the Merrimack Canal, which offered daily freight and passage service to Boston.[4] In sum, the place was ideal for the production of cotton cloth.

Though not present at the visit with Messieurs Appleton and Jackson, Francis Cabot Lowell was responsible for the successful realization of the nation's first textile centre in Waltham seven years earlier. The namesake of the new city had died before his colleagues planned a second centre for integrated textile production. Lowell was a representative member of the wealthy merchant shipping class, later known as the Boston Associates, of Newburyport and Boston. The Cabots, Lowells, Jacksons, Duttons, and Wendells—just to name a few—married among themselves and formed a clique of power and prestige.[5]

Within a few months of their first visit to the town, the Boston Associates purchased the land and waterpower rights in East Chelmsford. They then incorporated the Merrimack Manufacturing Company and structured it based on the pattern of the first integrated manufacturing factory at Waltham, which had been built during the War of 1812. Its first labour agent, Kirk Boott, brought more than five hundred common Irish labourers to the site. Housing them in tent camps, he put them to work enlarging the Middlesex Canal as well as building the first factories and boardinghouses there. By September of 1823,

Merrimack Manufacturing turned its first wheel and in November, produced its first cloth.[6]

The immediate success of the Merrimack Manufacturing Company led to the establishment of several new firms.[7] By 1850, these factories were producing over one million yards of cloth per week and employed more than 10,000 workers.[8] Lowell became—and, until the Civil War, remained—the largest centre of textile production in the United States. During the early years of its rapid industrial expansion, the population of Lowell grew significantly. It rose from 200 in 1820 to 6,000 in 1830, to 18,000 in 1836, and then to more than 33,000 in 1850, until it became the second largest city in Massachusetts. (See Table 1.) Moreover, Lowell's success inspired the development of other "mill towns" throughout New England, based on the Waltham-Lowell-style operation, i.e., integrated manufacturing.[9]

The textile corporations had a determining influence on the expansion of Lowell. They controlled development by virtue of their ownership of almost three quarters of the city's land. As the principal taxpayers in the community, the corporations had a significant influence on the local government.[10] Moreover, these Lowell corporations were a somewhat unified group. By means of the concentration of stock ownership and commonly shared directorates, they centralized the power in the hands of a relatively small number of investors. These owners, the Boston Associates, did their best to minimize competition among the companies they controlled.[11] Lastly, the fact that Lowell's investors were non-residents, unlike the manufacturing owners in other industrial cities such as Troy in New York State,[12] added a special feature. This absence of human engagement would become much more visible when difficulty hit the city.

The successful functioning of the "Lowell system" attracted a large number of workers to the city. Those who fuelled the burgeoning industry's first years of growth were mostly young, unmarried women coming from the surrounding countryside. These "Yankee girls" were attracted to textile manufacturing by the unprecedented opportunity to earn wages. The arrival of a large number of young women from the American countryside in the textile city also reflected the efficiency of the textile corporations' recruitment strategy, which, among other things, emphasized the high moral standards enforced by management. At the outset, the corporate managers were trying to dissociate themselves from the image of "dark satanic mills" attributed to English textile factories by strictly regulating the behaviour of female workers in the factories and boardinghouses. Under the banner of corporate paternalism, the managers successfully achieved this objective. Their success impressed at least one English visitor to Lowell in

Table 1. Population of Lowell by Country of Birth, 1826-1920

	Total Population of the City	Canada, French	Canada, English	Ireland	Greece	Portugal#	Turkey	Armenia	Russia	Poland
1826	2,500									
1830	6,474									
1840	20,796									
1850	33,383									
1860	36,827									
1870	40,928									
1880	59,475	*7,758		10,670	3	26	-	-	5	6
1885	-	6,438	1,380	11,681	2	43	-	-	7	-
1890	77,696	**15,742	-	12,671	2	107	-	-	107	5
1895	-	12,843	1,565	12,550	213	310	107	-	252	113
1900	94,969	***14,674	***4,485	12,147	1,203	482	84	-	291	441
1905	94,869	11,603	2,779	11,020	2,020	924	190	135	708	463
1910	106,294	12,291	4,049	9,983	3,782	1,449	637	-	1,840	-
1920	112,759	10,180	3,682	7,453	3,733	1,666	-	357	916	2,298

Sources: Immigration Commission, *Immigrants in Industry*, vol. 10, 232; *Thirteenth U.S. Federal Census*, 1910, vol. 2, Population, 868; *Fourteenth U.S. Federal Census*, 1920, vol. 1, Population, 229, vol. 2, 854-55.

Notes: 1. *Including Canada (English); **including Canada (English) and Newfoundland; ***Including Newfoundland; #Including the Azores Islands.
2. Figures for the population by birthplace are not available for the period before 1880.

1840. Charles Dickens wrote admiringly of the female operatives in his *American Notes*:

> These girls, as I have said were all well dressed; and that phrase necessarily includes extreme cleanliness. They had serviceable bonnets, good warm cloaks, and shawls; and were not above clogs and pattens. [...] They were healthy in appearance, many of them remarkably so, and had the manners and deportment of young women; not of degraded brutes of burden.[13]

The system was a far cry from perfection, for these women sporadically organized strikes in the 1830s to protest wage cuts. Nevertheless, in general, paternalism was very profitable for investors in the early years.[14] The owners of the Lowell factories explicitly targeted female workers instead of male ones, since the latter had higher expectations with respect to wages. Women workers were not only classified as less skilled, and therefore less expensive, but also considered to be less prone to importing subversive ideas about workers' rights.[15] These women did not have prior experience in industrial work. More importantly, in keeping with the personnel policy of these corporations, these female operatives worked for only a few years before marriage and thus lacked long-term career goals. Inexpensive and unlikely to organize themselves against management, the Yankee women represented an ideal workforce for the industrialists.

Within less than thirty years after the establishment of the first textile factories in Lowell, the city's workforce and the paternalistic policies that characterized the early years of its textile corporations began to change. As early as the 1830s, the New England textile manufacturers had become concerned with high production costs compared to their Southern competitors. In order to reduce costs, they gradually closed the boardinghouses and other "amenities" for workers that had once constituted one of the central features of the Lowell system. They also introduced the practices of the "speed-up" and the "stretch-out," which in combination increased the operating speed of the machinery while making workers responsible for additional looms and spinning frames.[16] As workloads increased and wages fell, working conditions rapidly deteriorated. The imperatives for the textile firms to increase productivity also led to the introduction of spinning mules in the late 1840s. Consequently, the mule spinners were burdened with an average workload that was two-and-a-half times greater than the normal workload for throstle spinners.[17]

The changes mentioned thus far—wage cuts, speed-ups, and stretch-outs, together with technological innovation—had a profound impact on the Lowell factories after 1836, and especially after the Civil War. These developments, as Thomas Dublin notes, steadily brought about the re-composition of the textile industry's workforce, a transformation that eliminated the high degree of homogeneity of the earlier period. The decline in the number of Yankee women in the textile workforce, on the one hand, and the increase in the numbers of migrants in the city, on the other, beginning with the massive arrival of the Irish after 1845,[18] propelled the most dramatic change in Lowell's textile labour force: the rapid and significant increase in the proportion of immigrant workers.

From the middle of the century, the population of the city underwent an important transformation. Lowell's population decreased from 36,000 in 1860 to 31,000 in 1865. This was largely due to the temporary shut-down of the factories during the Civil War, which had greatly reduced supplies of southern cotton. The cut in textile production left some 10,000 workers out of work, many of whom subsequently moved out of the city. However, the reopening of cotton factory operations after the Civil War brought in a new flood of immigrants. As a large number of new workers arrived, first from Ireland, and then from French Canada, its population increased to 41,000 in 1870, and then to slightly less than 50,000 by 1875 (see Table 1).[19]

French Canadians made up the largest number of arrivals to take advantage of the city's post-war boom. The reopening of the Lowell mills and their subsequent expansion coincided with recurrent agricultural difficulties that ravaged Québec's rural areas. Moreover, newly completed railways facilitated the transportation of a significant number of French-Canadian families to New England cities. As a result, Lowell's mere 100 French Canadians in 1865 increased to 1,200 by 1868, and to 2,000, representing 5 percent of the city's total population, in 1870. In 1885, the state census listed 6,438 French-Canadian and 1,380 English-Canadian residents in Lowell (see Table 2).[20] By 1900, the number of workers of Canadian origin living in Lowell (including both those born in French Canada and those born in the U.S.) rose to 24,000. Among them, French Canadians numbered more than 14,000, forming the largest group of foreign-borns in the city (16 percent).[21] The arrival of French Canadians in large numbers supplied a cheap and diligent labour force, which was much needed by the textile industry. More importantly, the majority of these *Canadiens* came to the city in family units containing large numbers of young children. This was a supplementary advantage for a textile industry wanting a great number of unskilled workers during a time when no laws prohibited the employment of children. From 1870 to 1900, the number of French Canadians entering the New England textile cities reached its highest level, with 510,000 migrants crossing the border southward. This meant that, at the time, one in every ten Quebecers was moving across the border.[22] As a result of this and other human movements, what was once a predominantly

Table 2. French-Canadian Population in Selected New England Cities, 1860-1920

Year	Lowell	Fall River	Woonsocket	Holyoke	Fitchburg	Biddeford	Worcester	Lawrence
1860*	266	-	794	165	-	-	386	84
1880*	10,000	9,000	5,593	6,000	500	4,301	3,500	2,500
1885**	6,438	8,219	-	5,067	741	-	2,794	1,921
1890***	16,000	17,000	9,200	-	-	8,150	-	4,459
1895**	12,843	17,079	-	6,347	2,899	-	4,219	4,637
1900*	24,000	33,000	17,000	15,500	7,200	16,500	15,300	11,500
1910#	23,208	32,033	-	-	-	-	-	-
1920#	23,699	28,368	22,189	13,785	-	-	-	-

Sources: *Ralph Vicero, "French-Canadian Immigration," 173, 289, 294; **Census of Massachusetts, 1875, vol. 1, 743, Census of Massachusetts, 1885; ***Guignard, "History of Franco-American Immigration"; #Fourteenth U.S. Federal Census, 1920, vol. 2, Population, 455, 926-29, 953-55. See also Paul Raymond Dauphinais, "Structure and Strategy," 58, table 2.

Anglo-American town grew into a bustling immigrant city[23] in the post-war years.

Lowell in the Early Twentieth Century

Early-twentieth-century Lowell was a multiethnic city with at least forty different nationalities represented within its population. In 1900, three quarters of the city's population was comprised of migrants and their children; a decade later only 20 percent, of the over 100,000 city residents, were born in the U.S. to U.S.-born parents. The percentage of foreign-born residents was one of the highest in the United States—41 percent in 1910, as compared to the national average of 15 percent and the Massachusetts average of 32 percent.[24] Among the foreign-born population, French Canadians were the largest group: more than one out of four (28 percent) foreign-born whites in Lowell were French Canadians, followed by the Irish (23 percent). Smaller in number, but growing at a faster rate, were the new arrivals from southern and eastern Europe, including Greeks (9 percent), Portuguese (3 percent), Turks (2 percent), and Lithuanian Jews from Russia, Lithuania, and Poland (percent unspecified).[25]

By the twentieth century, French Canadians had clearly become a permanent feature of the culturally diverse population of Lowell. Despite the massive influxes of "new immigrants," the proportion of the French Canadians remained constant, comprising a little over one quarter of the population (or about 24,000). The majority of the Canadian-born residents had come to the city during the last century, while the population of the U.S.-born Lowellites increased.[26] By 1910, slightly less than half (48 percent) of the French Canadians in Lowell were second-generation citizens. A decade later, the latter formed the majority (57 percent) of the city's French-Canadian population. The growth and settlement of the second generation further solidified French-Canadian social and cultural institutions in the city, which included their own Catholic church, the *Église Saint-Jean-Baptiste*, French-speaking parish schools, French-language newspapers, and a growing number of small shops in and around the *Petit Canada* district.

As the French-Canadian community grew, the city transformed into a mature industrial centre with a diversified economy. Textile manufacturing, particularly in the cotton sector, continued to dominate the city's economic activity (see Table 3). The total number of those engaged in the cotton industry did not change significantly during the first decade of the twentieth century. In 1910, the largest proportion of the labour force worked in cotton manufacturing, totaling around 14,000 men, women, and children out of

40 • GENDERED PASSAGES •

Figure 1. Merrimack Manufacturing employees, ca. 1900. (Courtesy of Lowell Historical Society, Lowell Museum Collection.)

100,000 Lowell residents. During the same decade, over 10,000 workers were toiling in other textile and textile-related industries, including woolen, worsted and felt goods, and wool hats; specialty thread products; and dyeing and the finishing of textiles outside the textile factories. This meant that slightly over half of the city's industrial workers were employed in the textile industry. By 1920, this figure decreased to 47 percent.[27]

While the textile industry dominated the economic development of Lowell, other industries also grew in the city. The number of non-textile industry products accounted for eleven million dollars, over one sixth the value of the city's textile industry products. Among non-textile industries, the most important was the textile machinery industry, established to meet the growing demand of local companies. By 1920, twelve firms manufacturing machine parts and factory tools employed over 2,000 workers. The value of their production alone was over seven million dollars. The Lowell Machine Shop did not limit its production to textile machinery. It also manufactured a number of steam locomotives for the expanding railroad networks throughout New England. In addition to such traditional industries as shoe manufacturing, the city's economic base was further enlarged by supplying a growing national market for patent medicines. The Hood and Ayer companies, as well as Father John's Medicine, were prominent in this field. Further diversification came with the development of boiler works, scale-makers, and breweries. During World War I, munitions firms like the U.S. Cartridge Company also thrived.[28] These transformations had a profound impact on the ethnic composition of the work force—an aspect that will be later explored in further detail in a later chapter.

The period from 1900 to 1924 was one of relative expansion for the U.S. textile industry. The rates of development were, however, uneven throughout the country. In New England, the number of spindles grew from 15.1 to 20.3 million, an increase of 32 percent, while the Southern textile industry saw an increase from 4.4 to 16.3 million spindles, an expansion of 270 percent. The strength of the South as a competitor became obvious when Southern firms, which had been built largely with Northern capital, paid off their debts in the 1920s.[29]

The impact of nation-wide competition and market restructuring was not the first blow. Greater competition added more difficulties to Lowell's textile industry, which had begun its decline in economic standing as early as the late nineteenth century. In 1890, despite its relative expansion, the neighbouring city of Fall River had surpassed Lowell in the number of textile employees and had become the nation's largest producer of textiles. This was because geographic factors and technological advancement both worked against

Lowell's textile manufacturing industry. As steam power came into general use towards the end of the nineteenth century, the inland location of Lowell on the falls—a crucial advantage in the early Industrial Revolution, when the factories relied on the waterpower from the Merrimack to turn their wheels—blocked its development.

As steam power came into general use in the last third of the nineteenth century, Lowell's location on the falls for water power meant that the crucial advantage in the early industrial Revolution blocked the city's opportunities for continued success. Lowell did not have access to the transportation benefits of shoreline shipping and sea-borne coal, whereas the coastal towns of Fall River and New Bedford did.[30]

In the early twentieth century, economic difficulties in Lowell slowed down or even stopped the growth of the French-Canadian population. For instance, a textile strike in the spring of 1903 culminated in the closing of factories and precipitated the emigration of a cluster of French Canadians out of Lowell: between 1900 and 1905, the French-Canadian population decreased by some three thousand residents. The industrial depression of 1907 and 1908 again changed the composition of the migrant population, driving out even more French-Canadian workers and their families, as well as other immigrants.[31] Among those who left the city, some returned to Canada, while others sought work elsewhere in the United States. Consequently, the total French-Canadian population of the city (including both those born in Canada and those born in the U.S.) fell again, from 23,000 (24 percent of the city's population) in 1905 to 21,000 (21 percent of the population) in 1909. In 1910, the number of French Canadians rose again to over 23,000, representing one quarter of the city's population.

World War I created a temporary boom in the U.S. economy. Europeans needed more food, clothes, and weapons than they could produce. When the U.S. entered the war in April 1917, the war-time mobilization further stimulated the demand for American manufacturing and farming products, especially uniforms, armaments, and food provisions. The increased demand proved profitable for U.S. businesses, pulling the nation's economy out of the recession that had plagued the country since 1913. By 1917, the gross national product of the U.S. surged to 20 percent above the level that had been recorded three years earlier. Between August 1914 and March 1917, the United States shipped arms to the Allies worth about 2.2 billion dollars, an amount comparable to the value of all American exports in 1913 totaled together. It also sold iron, steel, copper, and oil to the Allies, all of which were paid for by loans from U.S. banks.[32]

Just when workers were in more demand than ever in U.S. factories, fields, and mines, the Great War also disrupted trans-Atlantic travel, resulting in a sharp drop in the migration flow from Europe. In 1914, more than one million Europeans had traveled to the U.S. The following year, the number fell to less than 200,000. In 1918, it further dropped to merely 31,000. That same year, the unemployment rate dropped to the record-low of just 2.4 percent, down from over 15 percent just three years earlier.[33]

Table 3. Manufacturing Sectors in Lowell, 1899-1920

Cotton goods, including cotton small wares	1920	13	12,927	60,831,000
	1910	11	14,003	24,744,000
	1904	11	13,173	19,384,000
	1899	8	13,847	17,039,000
Dyeing and finishing textiles done outside the textile factories	1920	5	1,063	5,369,000
	1910	-	-	-
	1904	-	-	-
	1899	-	-	-
Foundry and machine-shop products	1920	17	681	2,284,000
	1910	35	2,735	4,332,000
	1904	34	2,403	3,439,000
	1899	47	3,088	4,258,000
Lumber and timber products	1920	6	130	1,131,000
	1910	17	462	1,066,171
	1904	12	450	938,000
	1899	11	379	728,000
Patent medicines, compounds, and druggists' preparations	1920	5	198	1,562,804
	1910	7	257	1,130,000
	1904	6	369	1,471,000
	1899	7	-	1,790,000
Textile machinery and parts	1920	12	2,333	7,185,000
	1910	-	-	-
	1904	35	2,294	3,438,729
	1899	-	-	-
Woolen, worsted, and felt goods and wool hats	1920	13	2,045	9,798,000
	1910	12	3,187	6,105,000
	1904	9	2,690	4,558,000
	1899	8	2,551	4,689,000

Sources: 1910 U.S. Compiled by author from *Thirteenth U.S. Federal Census*, Manufacturing, 527; *Fourteenth U.S. Federal Census*, Manufacturing, 160-62; Census of Massachusetts, 1905, 101.

The labour shortage propelled American manufacturers' growing dependence on previously disdained groups, such as women, African Americans, Appalachian whites, and migrants from Mexico and Canada, although the latter no longer suffered from the same degree of contempt as did other groups of workers. During the three years between 1915 and 1918, Canadian migrants to the United States arrived in numbers equivalent to about one third of all those entering the United States. This was remarkable given that Canada was experiencing a comparable shortage in its labour force.[34] Textile production centres throughout New England surged again, allowing this region to recapture its spot as the most preferred destination for French-Canadian expatriates. For the first time since the late nineteenth century, Lowell's textile workers enjoyed a series of wage hikes. From 1912 to 1916, as a result of war-time orders, increased production, and a scarcity of workers, wages rose twice in the Boott factories, one of the oldest textile manufacturers in Lowell. Workers' wages increased first by 10 percent, then by 8 percent. In 1917, the wage increases reached their highest levels following two additional 10-percent raises.[35]

When the war came to an end, a sudden decrease in exports, accompanied by increases in imports of cloth, high prices for cotton, and a general depression, seriously hampered the U.S. textile industry. Each of these factors left the textile factories to fight over a smaller and more competitive market share. At first, the factory owners responded to the pressure by inciting their workers to greater productivity, but ultimately, when things became unbearable, they either temporarily or permanently closed down their operations in New England and moved parts or all of their operations to the South.[36]

Within this changing economy, a significant proportion of Lowell's French Canadians were employed in textile factories. By 1909, French-Canadian workers represented the largest ethnic group within the labour force of the city's cotton industry, making up approximately 17 percent of the workers in the industry.[37] The Immigration Commission collected data on the demographic and socioeconomic profiles of leading immigrant groups in Lowell and New England during the 1908-1909 years. In their report, *Immigrants in Industries*, the Commission revealed that in comparison to the Irish and the English, a far larger proportion (82 percent) of French-Canadian cotton textile workers in the city had been in the United States for less than twenty years (see Table 4). Moreover, in comparison to more recent migrants (Portuguese and Greeks), a greater proportion of French Canadians indicated that they had lived in the United States for less than five years: a little less than one third of the French Canadians in Lowell fell into this category. These figures reflect the fact that despite the decreasing number of French-Canadian arrivals in the city, the migratory influx from Canada had not come to a standstill. A February 1909 newspaper article published in a local daily also confirmed the presence of "a score of the pupils, fresh [sic] arrived from Canada with their families," who applied for admission at the evening schools that the French-Canadian boys and girls working in the mills had to attend in order to learn English.[38] Overall, however, by the opening decade of the twentieth century, those recently arrived from Québec were in the minority. The majority of Lowell's Canadian-born population had arrived in the city before 1900. On the whole, French Canadians, including both long-time residents and recent arrivals, had to face a labour market that differed substantially from the one their nineteenth-century forerunners had taken advantage of.

Table 4. Distribution of Foreign-Born Persons in Lowell, Each Specified by Number of Years in the U.S., by Birthplace of Individuals, 1908-1909

Birthplace	Number in Sample	Percentage Under 5 years	Under 10 years	Under 20 years
Canada (French)	336	29.8	49.4	81.5
England	34	-	8.8	32.4
Greece	921	78.1	96.5	100.0
Ireland	122	14.8	24.6	54.9
Portugal	367	26.7	62.4	92.1
Total (N)	1,781			
Average (Percentage)	-	52.5	73.9	90.5

Source: Immigration Commission, *Immigrants in Industries*, vol. 10, 236.

Anti-Child Labour Movements and the Changing Face of the Textile Labour Force

By the early twentieth century, the labour force of the textile industry in New England had radically changed in terms of the age and ethnicity, and to a lesser degree, gender of the workers. The number of children (males under sixteen and females under fifteen) in the workforce of New England's cotton factories had decreased, from 17,704 in 1880 to 10,165 in 1890, and then to 9,835 in 1905.[39] The children had begun to be replaced by adults and older adolescents drawn from the "new immigrants" of Southern and Eastern Europe, and by married women from "old immigrant" groups like Irish and French Canadians. Such restructuring was largely a result of a series of efforts made by

Progressive reformers, legislators, and labour unions, together with the effects of technological development and the intensifying labour process.[40]

In Lowell, the general decline of child labour in the first decades of the new century was momentarily reversed by the sudden rise in demand generated by the World War I boom. Industrialists were keen to take full advantage of this demand for production. The textile industry, like the cartridge industry, needed to respond to this new demand by expanding its labour force. This included the newly arrived immigrants and children younger than sixteen years old. The demand for the latter grew as the entry of migrants from Southern and Eastern European countries was temporarily halted during the war years. As a result, while the total number of wage earners over sixteen years of age hovered around 30,000 in the first two decades of the century, the number of working youth under sixteen fluctuated considerably and fell by more than half, from 1,200 in 1909 to 538 in 1914, only to rise again to 1,000 in 1919.[41]

The transformation of local labour market conditions had an enormous impact on French-Canadian migration. During the 1870s and 1880s, at the height of this human movement, children had constituted not only the largest group within its ranks but also one of the most important resources a family possessed. This was due to the fact that the wages of children were often what made the migration profitable for the family. Three decades later, French-Canadian children no longer played the same crucial role in financially contributing to their household. Working for wages became a reality for only a handful of youths and even the effects of the war-time boom did not fundamentally challenge this. In 1910, only less than 6 percent of Lowell's French-Canadian children aged between ten and fourteen were wage earners. This figure was smaller than the average for the state of Massachusetts as a whole; 9 percent for U.S.-born children of U.S.-born parents, and 14 percent for U.S.-born children of foreign-born parentage.[42] In Québec, the percentage of child workers was markedly higher for the same period: 17 percent in 1900, 6 percent in 1910, and 12 percent in 1915.[43] Even if the census figures for Lowell's French Canadians fail to include a significant number of working children whose parents and employers feared having to pay fines for violating the law, they nonetheless indicated a drastic decrease from the situation in the late nineteenth century. During this period, eight out of ten French-Canadian children could be found at work rather than school. By 1920, the percentage of working children among French Canadians further declined: only less than 3 percent of children aged between ten and fourteen were working in Lowell's industries.[44] Such figures corroborate an observation made by Yves Frenette and Sylvie Beaudreau in other New England localities: the decrease of child labour among French-Canadian migrants suggests the adaptation of their household strategy and the departure from a familiar practice in their province of origin.[45]

Among factors that led to this general decline in the number of young children working in Lowell and other textile centres in New England was a prolonged struggle that dated back to the 1870s and had culminated in national efforts to enforce a series of child labour laws. At the same time, such efforts also strove toward the enactment of labour laws aimed at protecting working women.[46] As early as 1836, Massachusetts passed the first state child labour law to prohibit the employment of children under fifteen in any factory unless they were attending school.[47] The law remained highly symbolic at the time when about 40 percent of all factory workers in New England were between the ages of seven and sixteen. Half a century later, however, social and political sentiment against child work began to spread in the state of Massachusetts and the nation as a whole. In 1890, one in five children in the U.S. was working full time.[48] In 1898, the Commonwealth banned the employment of children under the age of fourteen years in any factory, workshop or mercantile establishment. One and a half decades later, this law was extended to include children working in the home. During the Depression, however, the state changed its approach to anti-child labour. Whereas earlier laws restricted the working hours of children between the ages of fourteen and sixteen, the new law in 1933 prohibited labour for children under the age of sixteen, either at home or in an industry, during school hours.[49]

At the federal level, Congress passed its first child labour law in 1916. It prohibited the employment of children under fifteen years of age in mines and quarries and prevented children under fourteen from being employed in other types of work such as manufacturing. It also prohibited night work for children under sixteen and their working more than eight hours per day and forty-eight hours per week. Only a year later, the Supreme Court judged the law unconstitutional. Congress then tried to restrict the practice of child labour in another way. In 1919, it imposed a tax on the profits of businesses using children under fourteen years of age or employing workers between fourteen and sixteen for more than eight hours a day. This attempt, however, was again found unconstitutional three years later. While neither the state nor federal government was able to ensure observance of the laws until the 1930s, their repeated efforts were highly effective in turning child labour into a national sin, in the factory and at home.[50]

Scholars have pointed out two sharply conflicting views regarding the proper place of children in American society.[51] On one hand, for child labour reformers, including a vocal segment of middle-class American women, early childhood labour represented unjustified parental exploitation, an unacceptable practice which had to be ended immediately.[52] Another main source of opposition to child labour came from the labour movement—glassblowers, mule spinners, weavers, and coal miners unions, for example—and the politicians who represented them.[53] On the other hand, their opponents, largely composed of industrialists and some church leaders, supported children's productive work as being not only economically indispensable, but a legitimate social practice as well. In this debate, the material value of a useful wage-earning child was directly "counterposed to the moral value of an economically useless but emotionally priceless child."[54]

The child labour reform movement was by no means a polarized struggle pitting middle-class reformers and labour unions against immigrant families.[55] Middle-class reformers, most of whom were women, did not work in concert with union leaders. Instead, these ladies kept a distance from the unionists, believing that failure to do so would result in defining the anti-child labour movement as an issue of "radical" labour politics, which had grown repugnant to them after a series of labour conflicts dating back to as early as the 1890s. For the middle-class reformers, child labour was, above all, a moral issue. Accordingly, they directed their efforts at the national level and toward a series of local campaigns in order to control "neglectful" mothers and "ignorant" foreigners who kept their children out of school and sent them to the factories. In other words, female supporters of the Progressive reform viewed child labour as a reflection of the foreign values upheld by their migrant parents. They disdained working class families "who have no civilization, no decency, no anything but covetousness and who would with pleasure immolate their offspring on the shrine of the golden calf."[56] This preconception understandably made middle class reformers ill at ease with the everyday lives of the working class. Therefore, in a number of industrial cities in the U.S., these reformers sympathized with the financial hardships of the working class, yet rarely understood or approved of the strategies that these working-class families used to support their lives.[57]

By the turn of the century, the fervour displayed by the proponents of the anti-child labour movement from various milieux demanded that "the ethical norm of working-class life [be] that children should not be sent to work before they finished half a dozen years of elementary education, unless the death, desertion or disability of the father made it unavoidable."[58] But newcomers from the rural regions of the United States and abroad neither shared, nor could afford to share, such beliefs. Not surprisingly, more than a few migrant families looked for ways to get around the law. In Manchester, New Hampshire, for instance, a daughter of French-Canadian migrants, "Cora" Pellerin, recounts that when she was ten, her father obtained for her a copy of a birth certificate under the name of her deceased older sister, whose name had been Cora. Using that certificate, she would pass as a fourteen-year-old and thereby be allowed to work legally.[59]

When young children worked for wages, they tended to do so within the same industry, if not the same factory, as older members of their family. Thirteen-year-old William Leclair exemplifies one such case. This Massachusetts-born son of French-Canadian parents was the second oldest child and the only one working for wages in the Leclair household at the time when the census was taken. His thirty-seven-year-old mother, Mélanie, was working as a finisher in a textile factory, and his forty-two-year-old, Maine-born father, Louis, was a stone mason. None of his four siblings—Yvonne, fourteen years old, Théodore, eleven, Jeanette, nine, and Issne(?), six—worked for wages.[60] Yet another young French-Canadian child, fourteen-year-old Yvonne Catarette, worked as a bobbin-girl in a cotton mill. Her father, her elder brother James (twenty-one), and sister, Miralda (nineteen), all worked in the cotton factories as a sweeper, yard labourer and stitcher, respectively.[61]

Why then was it a common practice among French-Canadian parents to have their children work within physical proximity of their family members? It was perhaps simply the result of a parent's or family's access to information regarding available jobs in the mill, which meant in many cases merely talking to a foreman. As Tamara Hareven has shown, this practice was also advantageous for employers because the management could count on the family to initiate the newcomers into the routine at the factories.[62] For instance, some parents preferred having their young children sit by their side in the lint-filled spinning room, rather than leaving them at home or on the street during break periods.[63] By doing so, parents could feel a sense of security and could, albeit to a limited extent, supervise and protect these new workers.

As the twentieth century progressed further, a greater number of French-Canadian and other working-class families chose to send married women in place of children into the labour markets, indicating a modification of their survival strategies.[64] Moreover, many also showed their adaptation to the new labour market conditions even before their departure for Lowell. French-Canadian families with a large number of young children, who would have migrated to New England centres of industry in earlier decades, were now less likely to do so and instead, remained in Québec or sent one or more family members south of the border unaccompanied.[65] These new strategies for adaptation resulted in the general aging of the migrating population and in an increase in the proportion of women who had experience in textile manufacturing while living in Québec before emigration.[66]

Scholars have pointed out that equally, if not more, important than the legislative efforts to curtail the number of working children, was the intensifying labour process. This had a decisive impact on the changing composition of the textile work force.[67] The effects of anti-child labour laws in curbing the number of working children in the factories were limited and uneven. However, the Progressive reformers placed additional strains on the New England and mid-Atlantic textile industries, which were already struggling against mounting competition from their Southern counterparts. Moreover, with the expansion of the cotton sector in the final decades of the nineteenth century, technological improvements did not offset the growing demand for labour, even though the supply of child labour was dwindling. Consequently, textile manufacturers forced workers to operate a greater number of outmoded, worn-out machines more quickly under stricter supervision than in earlier periods. Child workers in their early teens hardly possessed sufficient physical strength to cope with this intensified labour process because it resulted in injuries, accidents, and even death on a daily basis in these factories. The industry found an inexpensive replacement for child labour among the newly arriving adult immigrants, whose lack of marketable skills, as well as the very fact of being new to the local labour market, prevented them from obtaining better-paid and less physically demanding jobs.[68] Together with the other transformations discussed above, these new workers from Southern and Eastern Europe brought about further change in the composition of the labour force in terms of age, gender, and ethnicity.

Houses, Streets, and Community

As changing economic conditions transformed the workplace of Lowell's French Canadians, a different set of challenges had to be met at home. Overcrowding was a common problem in the city's poorer neighbourhoods. In Little Canada, French Canadians were often blamed for this situation as a number of exaggerated accounts of some contemporary observers suggest.[69] But in reality, the state of French Canadians' housing conditions improved remarkably by the early twentieth century, indicating the betterment of their economic life in general.

In 1881, the writer of the *Annual Report of the Board of Health* observed the abominable overcrowding, which he described as comparable to that found in the Chinese community. This reference invoked a racially derogatory connotation attached to this group at the time. The reporter wrote:

One of the newest buildings in "Little Canada," a huge, three-story, flatroof caravansary, 206 by 44 feet, has a population of 396. Every tenement in this building (four rooms usually, except the end ones) has two dark rooms, lighted by small high windows into the kitchen only; and totally dark unventilated rooms are not infrequent through the entire district. The inside rooms are, many of them, perfectly dark; there being no windows of any description, nor ventilation save by the door, while the numbers of their occupants remind one of the Chinese.[70]

A physician calling on a patient in one of these "dens" was horrified to find "the family and boarders in such close quarters, that the two younger children had been put to bed in the kitchen sink." These sinks had no traps. One tenement of five rooms was occupied by a family of eight, and they claimed to be able to accommodate seven boarders.[71]

Such accusations continued well into the twentieth century. In 1920, for instance, Frederick W. Coburn, a local historian in Lowell, wrote about Little Canada as "the residential quarter of at first a majority of the Lowell French" who were "housed for the most part in flimsy structures ranging from renovated horse sheds up to a large wooden 'block' containing thirty-two tenements."[72] George F. Kenngott, a Harvard graduate and a priest, wrote that most French Canadians in Lowell lived in wooden tenement "blocks" lacking sufficient light and ventilation. Even in those buildings which had windows, many rooms were dark at three o'clock in the afternoon because the buildings stood so close to one another. The only place to hang the laundry was over the windows of another tenement, and this practice blocked what little light might have otherwise entered.[73]

The streets on which tenement buildings were built resembled a "public dump."[74] As early as the 1880s, a reporter from the *Lowell Daily Citizen* stated that the city had "the finest mills and the dirtiest streets" he had ever seen. Not only were the streets murky, but the atmosphere that pervaded them was "ladened with the vilest of odours generated by the decaying vegetable and animal matter."[75] Three decades later, the scene on the city streets had hardly changed. Muddy and dusty streets in the neighbourhoods of the textile factories, such as Tremont Street, remained "the common receptacles for rubbish and refuse and poor substitutes for suitable playgrounds for the children."[76] Backyards, in many cases, were also in a deplorable condition. "Rags, ashes, papers, potato parings, all are dumped into the yard, and often when the sink-drain is clogged, the water is thrown into the back yard until cesspools gather. Open garbage barrels in the back yards are another menace."[77]

Contemporary allegations with respect to the housing conditions of French Canadians, however, do not fully reflect the changing reality. Although Little Canada was frequently referred to as the principal living quarters of the city's French-Canadian migrants, as early as 1880, less than one in five French

Canadians lived in this section of the city. Almost 70 percent of those listed in the census were found to live in two other sections of the city: the Old and New Depots, located near the textile factories. Moreover, the population living in *Petit Canada* was far from exclusively French-Canadian: one in every two households was French-Canadian, but the rest were a mixture of English, Irish, and American homes.[78]

During the following four decades, French Canadians moved further out from the city centre to new neighbourhoods, as had earlier waves of Irish immigrants. According to reports of the state and municipal Bureaus of Health, these included Pawtucketville on the north side of the Street Bridge, and Centralville, a section farther east, which began at the north end of the Aiken Street Bridge. French Canadians shared this sector of the city with a good proportion of the Polish community, as well as with a few people from other nationalities.[79]

By the first decade of the twentieth century, while French Canadians continued to be criticized for their overcrowding, a portion of them continued to move out of the centre to various parts of the city. Their housing conditions reached a level that was, in the opinion of George Kenngott, "generally good" in comparison to the deplorable conditions of the Greeks, Portuguese, and Turks who often crammed into the old tenement buildings.[80] Although, as he recorded, some of the properties occupied by French Canadians were old and without conveniences (many of them lacked bathtubs or water-flushing privies), they were "comfortable" and "usually clean."[81]

The Immigration Commission Report further confirmed the comparatively favourable conditions of French-Canadian housing. In contrast to Greek and Portuguese households, which on average held 6.7 and 9.4 persons respectively, a French-Canadian household had 5.8 people. The figure for the English was 4.6 people, while that for residents born in the U.S. to an American father was as low as 4.3. As for rent, while French Canadians paid less ($9.59) per apartment than the Portuguese ($9.92), the amount paid per person was higher, with French Canadians paying 1.6 times more than the Portuguese.[82] These figures suggest that, contrary to popular conceptions, the housing conditions of French Canadians actually exceeded the level reached by more recent immigrants to the city. This is because the recent arrivals, no doubt forced by circumstances, had to crowd the maximum number of people into small apartments. In any event, the underlying reason for the overcrowding and poor living conditions experienced by many immigrant families was the abysmally low wages paid by employers locked in fierce competition with one another.

In contrast to the dark and filthy "corporation streets" near the textile factories, the bustling commercial streets nearby provided a stage for the more

Figure 2. Austin Block on Coolidge Street in Little Canada, ca. 1900. (Courtesy of the University of Massachusetts Lowell)

pleasurable aspects of the everyday life of working-class families. As the testimony of its inhabitants reveals, this constellation of street vendors and small businesses, together with more established institutions such as the Church and parish schools, nurtured a sense of community in the neighbourhood.[83] Yvonne Lagassé, who was born in 1906 and lived all her life in Lowell, depicts Little Canada as a small village where one found stores of all sorts: "Meat, groceries, the furniture store ... candy stores, and even the piano store of Monsieur Délisle's. I tell you, [that was] the joy of *Petit Canada*—there was everything!"[84]

Although conventionally considered a French-Canadian enclave, *le Petit Canada* was in reality less segregated than its name suggested, thus confirming Dirk Hoerder's observation regarding the mixing of different ethnic groups in other cities.[85] Its location within walking distance of the textile factories made *le Petit Canada* particularly attractive to recently arrived workers and their families, many of whom lacked the funds to afford streetcar fare. Offering a range of small stores, often run by French Canadians or other migrants, Little Canada in

Figure 3. Trolley lines extended the geographic boundaries of working-class neighbourhoods, allowing for extension into areas farther from the immediate vicinity of the textile mills in the mid-nineteenth century. Here, a view of Central Street from Merrimack Street, ca. 1900. (Courtesy of the Lowell Museum—Lowell Historical Society.)

the early twentieth century was a lively and culturally diverse neighbourhood. "Everyone spoke French, including several families with names such as O'Beirne, O'Flahavan, Moore, Murtagh, Thompson, O'Brien, Lord, Sawyer, Thurber, Sigman, Tumas, Protopapas, Brady, and Grady."[86] Ethnologist Brigitte Lane notes that as a result of ethnically mixed living conditions, there was also Francization of names among Irish or other immigrants within the French-speaking district.[87] Having a French-sounding name might have helped them to build a closer relationship with their French-Canadian neighbours, a consideration that might have been important to small business owners in the district.

Father Morrissette depicted *le Petit Canada* as it "used to be," recounting memories of the great Church fire in 1912 and of World War I, among other things. Moody Street, "once the St.-Catherine [the central commercial street in downtown Montréal]" of French Canadians in Lowell, hosted Chinese, Jewish, and Greek businesses nestled amongst those managed by French Canadians. He continued:

> There were restaurants, cafés, groceries, delis, bakeries, big and small variety stores, garages, Bellerose's bicycle shop, Rousseau's doughnuts, Philias "Garçon" Rochette's poolroom, Rochette's automobiles, mayor Beaudry's block-housing, Monsieur Rocheville's block-building, Monsieur Rocheville's monkey, Brownstein's shoes and Harvey's, the old Greek shoe-shiner, who also cleaned men's hats, the amiable cobbler April [and] the Chinese laundry.[88]

Commodity stores were not the only established businesses. Referring to later years, Father Morrissette added that there were also stores for hobbies and leisure activities such as "photographer Charlie Landry" and "Lambert Lounge [...] where one could often attend first-class shows."[89] In addition, *Petit Canada* counted a great number of cafés (*buvettes*) and candy shops (*magasins à candé*).[90] This commercial growth in Little Canada in number and range marked a qualitative change from the 1870s. According to a study by Frances Early, at this time "French Canadians were not providing many retail or professional services for their own people."[91] Such development accelerated in the Roaring Twenties. Thus, the community was becoming further integrated, cohesive, and diversified over time—a clear sign of the maturity of the French-Canadian population in Lowell.

The lives of French Canadians in Lowell were also punctuated and animated by the passage of *peddleurs*, or traveling salespeople. As Lane observed, visits by icemen, fruit and vegetable peddlers, soapmen, ragmen, kindling women, or umbrella fixers appeared to be "one of the great events of everyday life."[92] Yvonne Lagassé's account illustrates this point:

> We didn't have to go to the city to buy what we needed... Monday morning, a big fellow would pass with a horse and later, a car. And he would shout: "Soap! Soap!" We would go down quickly. He would give us a big bar of soap [in exchange] for what we had: bones, grease or spoiled, left-over meat. We would give him that—our grease! And sometimes, a kind of potash he would want to give me, he would give us for our grease. We asked for that! That washed the boards, the alleys.[93]

At a time when most houses did not have electricity or refrigerators, ice was an indispensable commodity needed to keep food from spoiling. Most families had iceboxes which had to be replenished with ice twice a day in hot weather. As working families often did their grocery shopping on Saturday afternoons, their only time off from factory work, icemen made sure to pass by during this time: "Those poor men who worked especially Saturday," remembers Lagassé.[94]

Some peddlers enjoyed a close relationship with certain clients and were invited into the house. Lagassé recalls Monsieur Jean-Baptiste Dalphond, who sold all kinds of fruits and vegetables. He would go to grandmother Lafortune's house where, instead of calling from outside, he would climb the stairs and ask Lagassé's grandmother if she needed anything that day. The grandmother would let him take a seat and serve him a cup of tea and a homemade sweet, a *beigne* or *galette*. She would then say: "Listen Baptiste, I want to have good yellow bananas, I don't want black bananas." Lagassé added: "Canadians liked those men [peddlers]."[95] As the time passed, they disappeared from the daily scene, no doubt replaced by the growing presence of small stores.

Like the small store owners in Little Canada, street vendors were not exclusively French-Canadian. Other migrant vendors, including Jewish and Syrian merchants, came to French-Canadian houses. Lagassé recalls:

> We had ragmen that we called "buyers of rags." There was one, there were many who passed, and who shouted: "Rag! Rag!" And then, there was one who had horses, who had a cart with two wheels. We would call him: "Caïf, my Jew!" Children would run after him. These were Jews who bought rags, bottles and flasks. Had one cent, two cents. Sometimes, the rags, they were two pounds for one cent ...."[96]

Lagassé also pleasantly remembers the visits of a Syrian woman peddler, who came to Yvonne Lagassé's aunt's tenement. Unable to pronounce her aunt's name Geoffroy, correctly, the merchant woman called her "Madame Afroi."[97] Lagassé recounts: "We enjoyed listening to her speak: '*Puy* good pants! Today, good laces! You will see it, it will last for a long time.'"[98] Despite the haze of nostalgia, these examples remind us that the visits of street merchants enlivened, though briefly, the daily lives of Lowell's French Canadians.

Proximity to neighbours, regular visits by peddlers, and a number of shops run by fellow French Canadians, as well as those of other backgrounds—all of these things provided opportunities for Lowell's French-Canadian migrants to knit together a neighbourhood network and share a sense of community life. This does not mean that people socialized all together. Rather, social spaces circumscribed along ethnic and linguistic lines coexisted. This is evident in the vibrant culture of the Greek coffeehouses where only Greek men, but no women or men of other ethnicities, all gathered after supper. They would sit there, drink Greek coffee, read Greek newspapers, and talk about politics in Greece.[99] Nevertheless, the glimpse of everyday life shown in the previous pages suggests that the microcosm that French-Canadian men and women created in early-twentieth-century Lowell was not hermetically segregated by ethnicity. On the contrary, it was a community in which people of different cultural backgrounds came in close and frequent contact with each other. Such a universe might have helped men and women within and beyond their own ethnic group to share experiences and articulate the common needs, difficulties and injustices that remained ever-present in the workplace.

Illness, Injury, and Death

While French Canadians improved their living standards at home and diversified their community life, their health and welfare were often jeopardized by the disastrous effects of contaminated city water, clogged drain systems, leaking privies, rubbish-strewn streets, and above all, hazardous, life-threatening workplace conditions. Despite some improvements to the general quality of life, infant mortality rates among French Canadians were painfully high, no doubt due to the combined effects of poor living standards. The high infant mortality rate was a direct result of the harmful effects of low quality of foods, especially milk, poor education, and, most importantly, the poor quality of the general sanitary conditions.[100] In 1909, 60 percent of the total number of French-Canadian deaths were found among children under six years old.[101] The city's alarmingly high rates of morbidity from tuberculosis and respiratory diseases (particularly among French Canadians)[102] were partly attributed to the housing conditions endured by most of the city's working-class families. The 1909 report by the Board of Health of the City of Lowell described some of the housing of the workers and their families as veritable "tuberculosis incubator[s]." One tenement block recorded "six deaths in five successive families."[103] In addition, interview accounts reveal that French-Canadian women tirelessly scrubbed "the warped, wide-board floors and scour[ed] the battered stairs and hallways."[104] Nonetheless, as historian Mary H. Blewett has observed, efforts to enforce high standards of domestic cleanliness were easily undermined by the crippling effects of dusty wooden tenements and garbage-strewn streets. After a workday of ten hours or more, workers came home to eat and sleep in these sunless, crowded quarters, where contagious diseases spread easily.

The day began early for the textile factory workers. An immigrant daughter describes an early-twentieth-century morning street scene in "the Acre," a once predominantly Irish neighbourhood which had, by the early twentieth century, transformed into a more culturally mixed area:

> Every morning at a quarter to six, every door in the Acre would open, and we'd all troop out, down to the Merrimack. The Prescott, the Boott, or the Tremont and Suffolk. We'd all be going down Merrimack Street in those days in the early morning. It was crowded with the mill workers going to work. No people in cars. There was no cars, and the streets were lined with people. And we'd be laughing and singing, going along. Some of us. And some of us were very upset at getting up and figuring there wasn't much to look forward to. But, so what, some of us looked at it this way. It's got to be. What else are you going to do? You can't stay home; your mother won't let you. You've got to go to work.[105]

Whether they liked it or not, for most workers above the legal minimum working age, spending the longest hours of their day at the factory was an unchangeable fact of life.

The hardest part of the workday was not getting up early; it was the working conditions waiting inside the factory gates. Although long working hours were gradually limited for women and children, many mill workers consistently risked their health and welfare amidst hazardous working conditions that resulted from neglect on the part of mill owners. Textile workers laboured in a hot, humid, dust-filled environment surrounded by the ear-splitting noise of the spinning and weaving machines. In order to prevent thread from breaking, operation rooms had to be kept humid, and while the air was sprayed regularly with water and the windows were nailed shut, "fly," or cotton dust permeated the air.[106] Before the advent of the Draper automatic looms in the 1880s, as many as 70 percent of textile workers died of respiratory diseases. At about the same time, among Massachusetts farmers, fatal respiratory illnesses only affected 4 percent.[107] One migrant child recalls the shocking sight of her mother working as a spinner in the Merrimack Mill:

> I didn't know our mother worked so hard. The cotton was all over. They [factory workers] were breathing this cotton. No masks, noisy, terrible. Terrible! They never saw the sun.[108]

She continued:

> My mother worked in the spinning room and the cotton was so thick that the nostrils would fill with cotton. They'd be throwing up, they'd come home throwing up cotton.

From their nose, from their mouth. Their hair was full of cotton. Some of them would wear little caps to cover their hair. It was terrible. They worked from six to six. They never saw the sun.[109]

A cotton spinner said in an interview that "the sanitation was not good." Given the working environment, "not good" is something of an understatement. Another worker recounted that there were no ladies' rooms, just toilets, and "oh, the less said, the better!" She recounted a story of one of the toolers in the velvet room who sharpened the velvet-cutting knives: he found a cockroach, put a string on its leg, and kept it. "That was his pet," she said. There were also rats. She continued: "We had a bench where we used to sit and change into our old shoes. We'd take them out from under [the bench], and the rats would hop out."[110]

Cockroach dung caused pulmonary disorders, while rats and other insects transmitted contagious diseases. Drinking canal water was also dangerous, as it possibly caused dysentery and tuberculosis. Concerned about this practice, the Massachusetts Mills put up a notice in five languages (English, French, Portuguese, Polish, and Greek) to warn against drinking canal water. However, because there were only a few toilets for hundreds of workers and because they were allowed only a short break for lunch, many turned to drinking canal water and fell sick.[111]

The neglect of working amenities was also conspicuous in other places. Since smoking was severely forbidden, many male workers resorted to tobacco-chewing to soothe their dry throats, which were irritated from the dusty, lint-filled air. In the absence of sufficient cuspidors, they spat the chewed tobacco on the floor. As a result of this habit, bacteria was mixed with dried floor dust and stirred up in the air. As the loomfixers had to kneel or lie down on the dirty floors in order to make necessary adjustments to even dirtier machines, they tended to breathe in floor dust.[112]

Until the introduction of the Draper loom, a new machine that sported a self-threading shuttle, operators had to manually draw the thread through the ceramic eye in the side of the old-style shuttle. The fastest way to perform this operation was with "a quick, sucking kiss."[113] If the first weaver to do this operation had a communicable disease, such as tuberculosis, the second one was almost certain to contract it. Even if an operative was fortunate enough to be spared from contracting tuberculosis while working with the "kiss-of-death" shuttle, he or she continually inhaled lint, dyestuffs, and other foreign matter.[114]

Textile factories were dangerous places to work. French-Canadian textile workers in Lowell, especially those in cotton manufacturing, toiled on outmoded, worn-out machines in aging brick buildings, from Monday to Saturday, ten to twelve hours a day. They were exempt from work on Saturday afternoons. The narrow aisles between machines and the crowded conditions in the factories made cleaning and repair difficult, and also prevented proper lighting. Workers were placed so close to open pulleys, belts, and gears, which constantly vibrated and produced ear-splitting noise, that an accident could easily happen if a worker made a wrong move by even so much as an inch. Most commonly, accidents occurred while workers cleaned the machinery, since they fed the machines by hand rather than with tools. Accidents also occurred when, in a bid to save time, workers attempted to remove foreign objects or replace a drive belt without stopping the machine. In almost every instance, "carelessness" was attributed to the employees and not to the factory.[115]

A young French-Canadian twister, Blanche Graham, almost lost her little finger in a twister machine when she was trying to remove something caught in the gears. She used to climb up a twister machine to clean the top part of the machine when there was something caught up in it. One day she was cleaning the gears and had her little finger caught in them. She pulled it out quickly and saw it was squashed. She said: "I seen [sic.] stars. I came down and showed it to the boss, and he said, Oh my God! what happened? I told him, and he said, Well, you had no business getting up there!"[116] Pressured by the factory's policy for maximizing productivity and efficiency, Blanche probably felt compelled to remove the stuck threads from the machine while it was still in operation.[117] As this and other cases illustrate, workers who were injured while attempting to comply with the productivity policy received condemnation rather than sympathy.

With little progress made in implementing safety measures, dangerous working conditions in textile factories remained unchanged even as late as the post-World War I period. One machine oiler remembers a terrible accident that occurred to a fellow worker. During overtime, when there were only two workers assigned to a room, his co-worker got his hand caught inside a cylinder. The fellow was screaming, the machine belt was squeaking, and there was no one else but the oiler in the room. He immediately shut down that machine and then stopped all of the other machines in the working room. He tried to get the strippers off the fellow's hand, but he was unable to do so. He ran into different rooms to get the fixer, and, finally, lifted the machine off the oiler's hand. He recalls: "I couldn't bear to look at his hand. It was just like a hamburger; you could see the bone." After he got the man's hand out, the fixer went to call the boss to get an ambulance. The boss turned to the oiler and said: "*Why did you shut your machines down?*" The oiler described:

> I says, what did you want me to do? Leave the machines run? With no one there, and the guy's hand caught? And have all the machines jammed up? He says, Well, you

should have called the next room and got help and keep the machines going. I says, Okay. 'Cause if you talk too much, you're fired.[118]

Life-threatening accidents frequently occurred in the factories. A woman whose long hair was caught in an uncovered belt had her scalp ripped right off.[119] Doffers and feeders usually ate lunch next to their machines while they were in operation. One doffer, who used to put his sandwich on top of the coil and then "start eating the wool and sandwich together," told his boss that he wanted to be an oiler. He wanted to "eat in peace." After the man had had the oiler's job for about six months, his loose shirt-tail got caught between the pulleys, turning him upside down and smashing his skull against a card. It "split his head right open." Within a year, he was dead, probably from a concussion. "That's how dangerous the job was," lamented a worker who had laboured alongside the deceased.[120]

******

The evolution of Lowell over the century from the nation's leading textile centre into a symbol of declining industry entailed the passing of the corporate paternalism that had characterized the early years. The combination of cost-efficient labour policies of the textile corporations on one hand and laws restricting the employment of child workers on the other, brought to the forefront radical changes in terms of the ethnicity, age, and gender of the textile worker population in the city. Amidst such transformation, French Canadians carved for themselves a distinct and permanent place within the city's economic, social, and cultural universe. This was sometimes in cooperation, and at other times in competition, with their neighbours, both old and new.

The experiences of the city's migrant workers and their families were not uniform. The diverse cultural backgrounds and work experiences of these working families, who had become residents at different times and under different circumstances, were among major factors for the inequalities in their socioeconomic statuses. Moreover, the local labour market offered very different work opportunities to the men, women, and children within any given ethnic group. Transcending these differences, however, was the centrality of family in the lives of all the migrants. The family remained one of the most important institutions in the industrial city, its primordial function being to ensure day-to-day, as well as generation-to-generation, survival. Of course, not all French-Canadian migrants and their descendants moved or lived with their families. Nonetheless, as the next chapter reveals, whether single or married, men, women, boys, and girls were all deeply embedded in a network of family and kinship.

CHAPTER THREE

The Transnational Mobility and Family Networks of French Canadians

Foreign entrants into the United States arriving by way of Canada troubled Progressive America deeply. What brought this issue home to the U.S. policymakers, immigration authorities, and labour organizers was the unsealed nature of its northern border: the U.S. Immigration failed to enforce its border to the north (and also, the border to the south) and, consequently, hundreds of thousands of foreigners from Canada, as well as from Asia and Europe, entered the United States, many without proper inspection. In 1900, Canadian-born residents living in the U.S. numbered close to 1,180,000, corresponding to over one fifth (22 percent) of Canada's population at the time. If their U.S.-born children and other descendants are added to this total, the number more than doubles, totaling over half (55 percent) of Canada's population.[1] A far more serious concern for American officials was the Asian and European migrants who arrived in the United States via Canada. Approximately 50, 000 Europeans landed in Canada in 1891, only to travel into the U.S. by what one immigration official described as "circuitous routes" within six months. Frustrating to the U.S. Immigration authority was the vast number of immigrants circumventing the U.S. immigration process. The state of quasi-open borders to the north and south and the extent of human movement beyond the control of the U.S. authority led the Commissioner-General of Immigration, Herman Stump, to write about "numerous arrivals from foreign contiguous territory," the exact number of which was "impossible" to specify. He continued, "Many of these are Canadians, some are Mexicans, but large numbers are doubtless transoceanic aliens—who, after a brief residence beyond our northern and southern boundaries, migrate to this country [the U.S.]."[2]

Despite the depth of frustration created by such human flow across the U.S.'s northern border at the time, relatively few scholars in transnational migration history have been able to systematically investigate the complex patterns of migrants' cross-border mobility. This is the flip side of the voluminous attention given to the study of the process of settlement and insertion, as opposed to the process of migration and documented in a substantial number of "community studies" within a single American locality. These works depict U.S. cities as places of settlement where newcomers were transformed into new workers and new citizens. Such a perspective has strengthened the widely held assumption, or "myth of the migration paradigm," as Donna Gabaccia has critically called it.[3] At the same time, the epistemological emphasis on the process of becoming an American (or remaining a permanent stranger) has undermined the study of the process of movement or the process of migration as secondary to such analytical focus.

Scholarship in French-Canadian migration is no exception to this general tendency. As a masterful work by Tamara K. Hareven epitomizes, the fundamental importance of a U.S. locality as a place of "settlement" has been explored in depth as far as the process of settlement is concerned. It also highlights the centrality of family and kin networks both as a unit of migration to and a source of information about an American industrial city, Manchester, New Hampshire.[4] Without neglecting a small yet important number of studies that counter this over-arching tendency,[5] research efforts in this field have also privileged the process of settlement and insertion. This was partly because of the powerful role that cities in industrial America played in attracting workers of diverse origins and cultures.

This chapter departs from the hitherto dominant study of the settlement process—with a perspective that connotes a sense of permanency and one-way and one-step movement from one place to another. Instead, it joins critics of the "American-centred view of migration," as Frank Thistlethwaite has once called it, and the more recent, burgeoning studies of scholars who bring together migration history and borderland studies.[6] Questions that need to be considered are the following. What roles did families play in the process of movements as they pertain to French Canadians headed for Lowell? What were the contours of migration paths of Lowell-bound French Canadians? What characterized their units and patterns of movement? What were their perceptions of their own move, family strategies, and the values they attached to their place of settlement, whether it turned out to be temporary or permanent? Evidence derived from an analysis of longitudinal data[7] sheds light on the diverse, yet continued process of movement, a process in which the fundamental roles of family and kin networks persisted and were modified. It also reveals that in contributing to and benefiting from family networks, men and women played different roles and lived their experience of migration differently.

A focus on the process of migration does not mean to question that many who moved to Lowell, over years or generations, experienced a degree of assimilation, integration, and Americanization. But there were also many others who returned to Québec after a variable length of residence in Lowell, while others moved on to another destination. Others still went back to Lowell after going back to Québec. The diversity and complexity of migration passages reconstructed from the process of movement pertaining to farmers, factory workers, wives, and children among Lowell's French Canadians suggest a new way to look at migration that is "less narrowly focused and ideologically loaded," as Karen Fog Olwig has critically referred to it,[8] than the migration paradigm, which was—and continues to be—closely tied to cultural and social assumptions positing the U.S. as the only and ultimate land of promise.

The Enforcement of the Border

Beginning in the 1890s, the United States strengthened its effort to tighten inspection along the Canada-U.S. border. This resulted in the expansion of the federal bureaucracy, in its administrative and legislative capacities, as a custodian of human mobility. This new role of the federal government was compatible with the spirit of the Progressive era, which also produced factory regulations, women's protective laws, and anti-child labour laws. The first step of this effort was made effective by the creation of the Office of the Superintendent of Immigration following the Immigration Act of 1891. What subsequently became the U.S. Bureau of Immigration set up a string of checkpoints along the northern border, manning them with immigration inspectors. This replaced the former customs officers who had until this point checked entrants along with the luggage they carried.[9] By 1908, as a result of the installation of inland inspection points along the northern border, Canadians had to answer all the questions posed at the border along with every other aspiring cross-border migrant. These questions included name, age, gender, birthplace, last permanent place of residence, destination, race, occupation, intention to stay in the U.S. temporarily or permanently, and, if necessary, dates and period of one's prior residence in the U.S. All of these details were considered critical to an immigration official's decision to accept or reject a migrant's entry into the U.S.

Admission of Canadians was the norm, rather than the exception, as over 90 percent reached their U.S. destinations without being barred at the border.[10] Therefore, fear of rejection remained essentially psychological, rather than real, for most Canadian travelers. When entry was indeed denied, in most cases the reasons ranged narrowly from suspicion of prostitution to ill health to lack of money—which would potentially make them "public charges."[11] This contrasted sharply with the high risk taken by Asian border-crossers, who were routinely submitted to more rigorous inspections, frequent rejections, and occasional deportation when seeking admission at immigration stations on the coastal seaports.[12] Although Canadians experienced some significant consequences of a type of border control that reduced their "freedom of circulation" across the border following 1908,[13] the extent of the exclusionary barriers Canadians came to face with was considerably lower than those against which Asians and certain Europeans had to fight for their admission.

This is not to suggest, however, that Canadians were entirely free from nativist feelings in the United States. As early as 1900s, labour organizations and governmental agencies—frequently interconnected by blood and marital relations—raised voices of criticism against French-Canadian workers. This was particularly evident when business slowed down and the textile industry consequently cut down the quantity of production, laid off workers, or shut down some of its factories in Lowell or in other parts of the region. In 1901, Terrence Vincent Powderly, president of the Knights of Labour and a brother of the Commissioner-General of Immigration declared that "[French-]Canadian labour was not necessary to keep the cotton mills running" in New England, and that Canadian labour had "depressed wages and ha[d] checked increase of native population," since young men and women "can no longer afford to marry." This resulted in not only an economic loss but also "a loss of human resources." By this, Powderly was referring exclusively to American-born men and women of American-born parentage. The "human gain" from the influx of French Canadians was not an issue for consideration.[14]

Whether such discourse was effective in shielding the American labour market from the perceived Canadian invasion is doubtful. But one thing is clear: as scholars have noted, accusations against French-Canadian workers in the early twentieth century were rarely couched in racial terms, unlike in the previous century, when they were explicitly attacked as "Chinese of the East [Coast]."[15] By then anti-Canadian discussion came to centre more heavily on labour protectionism, a discourse structured around protecting "American workers" from the intrusion of foreign workers. A similar tide of anti-Canadian workers resurfaced some two decades later when the AFL campaigned for the restriction of Canadian immigration.[16] By that time, as Catherine Collomp has observed, it became even clearer that the "labour diplomacy"[17] of the AFL leader Samuel Gompers tactfully distinguished the anti-Canadian tenor of its language and rhetoric from xenophobic declarations used against newcomers from countries such as Japan, the Philippines, Mexico, Italy, Greece, Portugal, Russia, and Poland, who headed for factories, shops, and worksites in the Eastern and Western cities in unprecedented numbers. Both English- and French-speaking

Canadians comprised a good proportion of Gompers' "international" constituency across the Canada-U.S. border. In contrast, immigrants from Asia, Latin America and southern and eastern Europe represented cheap (and therefore threatening) labour, inassimilable perpetual foreigners, or purportedly dangerous radicals. In the minds of American labour authorities, these new immigrant workers were classified as undesirable.

Migration Processes of French Canadians

If the relative leniency with which the U.S. sought to guard the northern border left it more open for French Canadians than for transoceanic migrants, family networks provided a determining factor shaping French Canadians' decisions regarding when, where, and with whom to migrate. The complex and diverse routes emerging from the examination of the process of migration pertaining to Lowell-bound French-Canadian women and men throw into relief the deep, yet changing roles of family and kin networks for men and women on the move. They also reveal the gender-specific roles husbands and wives, sons and daughters, and brothers and sisters played not only in conducting their own migration process but in helping conduct that of their family members' as well.

Of Rural Origin? : The Migration Field of French Canadians

Historians of French-Canadian migration have called into question the too simplistic depictions of this group as rural *habitants* and Québec as a pre-industrial "folk society."[18] By doing so, they have echoed a broader tendency in migration history, a shift in paradigm that contested the early emphasis placed on the rural, preindustrial backgrounds of immigrant workers. True, many French-Canadians did hail from rural villages in the late nineteenth century, as Frances Early's study of Lowell-bound immigrants in the 1870s and 1880s has shown.[19] But a degree of proletarianization was a familiar experience for many French Canadians even before heading for New England mill towns.[20] The majority of French-Canadian male migrants in Rhode Island in the 1870s, although born in rural parishes, had worked as day labourers in the urban or rural commercial/industrial centres of Québec. Similarly, a number of French Canadians in Manchester, New Hampshire, at the turn of the twentieth century had already been exposed to what Tamara Harevan has called "industrial time" in Québec through either their own employment or that of their family members.[21]

Unlike their predecessors in the last third of the nineteenth century who originated mainly from rural villages, Lowell-bound migrants in the early twentieth century whom I studied reported that their geographic backgrounds encompassed more than just rural communities back in Québec. This important change resulted largely from the industrialization and urbanization that swept the province at the turn of the century. The majority continued to leave for Lowell directly from rural localities, but growing numbers were leaving from the industrial or commercial centres of the region, and sometimes, indeed, from the province's metropolis, Montréal.

Underlying the diversity of migrants' origins was a thread of common childhood experiences: an overwhelming proportion of the Lowell-bound French Canadians I studied were born in rural villages of Québec, Ontario, and New Brunswick with populations of three thousand or less.[22] Such was the case with Samuel Bergeron, a sixty-three-year-old labourer from Saint-Croix, Québec. A minority (16 percent) of the sampled population was born either in mid-sized towns or in large cities with a population ranging between three and six thousand (See Table 5). Madame Ouellette and her family from the rural village of Sainte Elizabeth, Québec, epitomize the majority of French-Canadian migrants who moved directly to Lowell from a rural parish in Québec. The Ouellettes went to Lowell when Madame Ouellette was ten years old (*circa* 1917-20). Her new life in the textile city contrasted sharply with what she had known living on a Québec farm. She recalls:

> Oh yes, my Lord! In Canada we were on land that was so huge. A huge piece of land. My parents only had three sons. And one was nineteen years old, another, fifteen, and the youngest one was only five. So they did not have enough boys to work on the land. Myself, I worked, you know. I was only nine.[23]

A large number of the French-Canadian migrants to Lowell were born in rural parishes, but not all of them moved directly to Lowell from their birthplaces. Rather, nearly a third of the French Canadians I studied had moved to urban centres in Canada before migrating to the U.S. James Cadorette and Louis Gill are among the examples of these "step migrants." James, fifty-two years old and a labourer, was born in the small parish of Saint-Rose-de-Makinac, and moved to Trois-Rivières, the regional centre of Mauricie, and the third largest city of the province, before going to Lowell on July 7, 1916. Louis Gill, a native of Saint-Thomas, Québec, also went to Trois-Rivières, and subsequently migrated to Lowell with a Trois-Rivières-born son, Samuel, on September 5, 1923. Migrants like Cadorette, Gill, and a number of others who had resided in urban centres such as Joliette, Lévis, Montréal, Sherbrooke, Thetford Mines, Trois-Rivières, Ottawa, or Berthierville[24] just before migrating to Lowell made up about 31 percent, or double the number of sampled French Canadians born in each locality (Table 6).

Lowell-bound French Canadians further suggest that Montréal played a particularly important role as a sojourning place for a minority of French-Canadian migrants. A significant minority (17 percent) of those who had previously lived in urban centres indicated Montréal as their last permanent residence before crossing the border to the south. Among these men and women, however, only Edmont Ayotte, a twenty-three-year-old machinist, was born there. Others were born elsewhere—Berthierville, Joliette, Cornwall, St.-Raymond, and St(e).-Brigide—and went to Montréal before moving on to Lowell.[25] The majority of previous Montréal residents among the sampled French Canadians were therefore not Montrealers by birth.

As Canada's commercial and industrial metropolis, Montréal had long attracted a substantial number of rural French Canadians. In the early twentieth century, a growing number of French Canadians continued to arrive in that city, and some subsequently moved on to the U.S. An important minority of Lowell's French Canadians had taken this route, as the following examples illustrate. On September 9, 1916, Irené (sic.) Beauregard (born in La Presentation) and Maria (born in St. Paul) both listed Montréal as their last permanent residence in Canada before entering the U.S. The couple reported Lewiston, Maine, as their destination when they crossed the border. In 1920, they appeared in the census manuscript as residents of Lowell.[26] Based on the data available, we do not know whether the couple moved to Lowell after having been to Lewiston, or changed their plans and went directly to Lowell instead. Nor do we know the reasons for their move to Lowell after, or without stopping in Lewiston. What is known is that having moved from the countryside to small cities or to Montréal, French Canadians like the Beauregards frequently experienced the shift from the rhythms of rural labour to those of the urban workplace before moving to the United States.

Diversity and Continuity in Occupational Experience

Statistics derived from the Immigration Commission's report *Immigrants in Industries* further confirm my observations on the background of French-Canadian migrants. Although a majority of those who migrated to

Table 5. Distribution of Lowell-bound French Canadians by Birthplace, 1904-1920

Birthplace	Number	Percentage
Cities with population over 6,000 in 1911	23	15.0
Joliette	12	
Lévis	2	
Manchester	3	
Montréal	1	
Ottawa	1	
Sherbrooke	1	
Thetford Mines	1	
Trois-Rivières	3	
Towns with population over 3,000	2	1.3
Berthierville	2	
Villages with population of 3,000 or less	113	74.3
Bic	15	
Bury	2	
Châteauguay	3	
Matane	2	
Saint-Basile	2	
Sainte-Béatrix	8	
Saint-Clément	2	
Sainte-Élizabeth	2	
Saint-Étienne	3	
Saint-Félix	2	
Saint-Jean-de-Matha	12	
Saint-Paulin	8	
Saint-Raymond	2	
Saint-Ubald	3	
Saint-Winceslas	2	
Stanstead	2	
Stottsville	2	
Tignish	2	
Other locations in Québec	37	
Other locations in New Brunswick	1	
Other locations in Ontario	1	
Unidentified	14	
Total	152	100.0

Sources: Compiled by author from the sample of the *Soundex Index to Canadian Border Entry*.

Table 6. Distribution of Lowell-bound French Canadians by Place of Last Permanent Residence, 1904-1920

Last Permanent Residence	Number	Percentage
Cities with population over 6,000 in 1911	31	20.0
Joliette	13	
Lévis	2	
Montréal	8	
Sherbrooke	1	
Thetford Mines	1	
Trois-Rivières	3	
Lowell	3	
Towns with population over 3,000 in 1911	16	10.5
Berthier	1	
Grand'Mère	2	
Shawinigan (Bay and Falls)	13	
Villages with population of 3,000 or less	104	68.4
Acton Jct.	2	
Bic	16	
Bury	3	
Deseronto, Ontario	2	
Lacolle	2	
Matane	2	
Notre-Dame-de-Pierreville	2	
Pierreville	2	
Saint-Clément	3	
Saint-Félix	4	
Saint-Félix-de-Valois	7	
Saint-François	3	
Saint-Jean-de-Matha	10	
Saint-Tite	2	
Saint-Ubald	4	
Stanstead	2	
Sainte-Émile-de-l'Énergie	2	
Tignish	2	
Woodlands	2	
Other locations in Québec	19	
Other locations in New Brunswick	2	
Other locations in Ontario	4	
Unidentified	0	
Total	152	100.0

Sources: Compiled by author from the sample of the *Soundex Index to Canadian Border Entry*.

Lowell were born in rural and agricultural localities, their occupations before migration were not limited to agriculture. Furthermore, not only had a growing number of twentieth-century migrants from French Canada experienced wage-work before going to the United States,[27] but in addition, many had previously worked in the industrial sector, notably the textile industry. This was particularly true for women. According to *Immigrants in Industries*, while over half (54 percent) of city A's (i.e., Lowell) sampled Canadian-born male cotton textile workers had been engaged in farm labour before going to the U.S., a minority (9 percent) had worked in textile factories. Among the city's female French-Canadian cotton textile workers, one half (51 percent) had worked on a farm, while a strikingly high proportion (23 percent) had worked in textile factories.[28] Joseph Boisvert, a weaver from Grand'Mère, Eugine Côté, a warper and native of St.-Julie, and Laura Boudreau, an eighteen-year-old millhand whose place of birth was unknown—all illustrate that, for a good proportion of French Canadians, and for women in particular, working in Lowell's textile factories was not an entirely new experience.[29] Rather it was a continuation of their industrial experience from Canada. This meant an important change from the occupational profile of their predecessors: unlike nineteenth-century migrants, who had worked mostly as agricultural labourers and landless farmers before emigrating,[30] more and more Lowell-bound French-Canadian migrants in the twentieth century had been engaged in a wider range of wage-earning activities in Canada.

Such changes, it should be emphasized, were new as far as the extent of French-Canadian occupational engagement was concerned. The continuity of occupational experience before and after migration was itself not a new phenomenon. As Bruno Ramirez has observed in the last third of the nineteenth century when the *journaliers* made up the dominant occupational group among French-Canadian male out-migrants, industrial New England did not cause a kind of occupational rupture that historians had once tended to depict. This was because once in a New England town, French-Canadian male migrants, many of whom had worked as *journaliers*, or farm labourers or day labourers in Québec, "continued to sell their labour in the local unskilled labour markets," including textile factories, as general labourers.[31] In early-twentieth-century Lowell, this was no longer true for a growing majority. More and more French-Canadian workers, especially men and, to a lesser extent, women, came to join the ranks of occupational hierarchy as weavers, carders, loomfixers, and even second hands.[32] Thus, they fashioned a notable extension in upward mobility from mostly unskilled work in the last century to semi- or, indeed, skilled work in the new century.

French Canadians listed in the *Border Entry* further corroborate the observation from the Immigration Commission that the occupational profiles of French-Canadian migrants underwent a marked transformation, from the nineteenth-century farm labourer into the early-twentieth-century urban industrial worker.[33] Farm labourers like Émile and Napoléon Frenette, seventeen and eighteen years old from La Patrie, were now a definite minority. In contrast, people like thirty-year-old general labourer Arthur Mandeville, who was born in Contrecoeur and then worked in St.-Henri, and another labourer, forty-year-old David Durand, a native of Chicoutimi who then worked in Winooski, Vermont, made up a growing portion of Lowell-bound migrants, who had provided much-needed labour power to Québec's rapidly transforming rural areas before moving to Lowell. Several factors account for this change. The end of the construction boom in the province created masses of newly unemployed labourers. Many subsequently moved to other regions, others went to larger cities such as Montréal, and a proportion of them moved on to south of the border.[34] Moreover, the boom in Québec's cotton manufacturing industry at the turn of the century created industrial employment for thousands of French Canadians, particularly women workers.[35] These workers would later bring that experience south of the border in search of better wages, which contributed to further reduction of the proportion of French Canadians who migrated to Lowell from localities dependent on subsistence farming.

It is also important to note that the change in French Canadians' occupational backgrounds indicates the significant role that women came to assume in the materializing migration of their families. This may have reflected a historical change that occurred in what Ramirez has called the "selection mechanism" of migrating populations.[36] This mechanism functioned to send specific migrants whose skills best corresponded to the needs of the local labour markets within the destinations. A close analysis of my data pertaining to the sampled immigrants in Lowell reveals that changes in the selection mechanism in the early twentieth century did not affect all the prospective migrants equally but involved specific portions of the migration population, and women in particular. In the opening decades of the twentieth century, the French Canadians' southward immigration was no longer contingent on the number of working children within a household, as was the case in the 1870s and 1880s when being a French-Canadian child meant working in a textile factory.[37] By the early twentieth century, as young workers in their early teens were increasingly barred from work sites because of the implementation of a series of anti-child labour laws, New England textile industries had to fight an increasingly difficult competition with southern industry, which was free from such restrictions. "New immigrants" from Southern and Eastern Europe provided this labour force until trans-Atlantic migration came to a sudden halt during World War I. The management of Lowell's textile mills then turned more vigorously to women workers, including many married women and those belonging to both the "old" and "new" immigrant groups already in the city. These shifts in labour recruitment practices likely contributed to heightening the levels of skill and experience that French-Canadian immigrant women, and, to a lesser extent, men, had acquired in Québec's textile production factories.

Data derived from the census manuscripts corroborate the above observation that French-Canadian migration to Lowell became more and more dependent on family resources other than children, one of the most important of which was the industrial work experience of married women. By the opening two decades of the twentieth century, French-Canadian immigrant men found better-paid and possibly more regular employment in the city's labour markets. A higher percentage of French-Canadian female wage earners, including both those who were born in Canada and the United States, were employed as semi-skilled and skilled workers. Conversely, a lower percentage of French-Canadian women, when compared to their male counterparts, worked as unskilled labourers.[38] These findings suggest that although the largest portion of the French-Canadian household income was still brought home by male household heads,[39] the wage contribution made by French-Canadian women contributed crucially to the standard of living of their families. Women's wages must have been even more appreciated when the proportion of the contribution made by young children declined substantially.[40]

As a part of this trend, one such migrant labourer, Mary Louise Clermont, brought her occupational experience as a weaver in the textile industry with her as she crossed from one side of the border to the other. In late December of 1908, she moved to the U.S. with her parents, two sisters, and her brother. Her parents and sister Priscilla had worked as labourers in Québec. Annie, another sister, was not working for wages and her brother Remeus was listed as a loom sweeper. Twelve years later, the U.S. census manuscript recorded Mary Louise as an inspector in a hosiery factory. This was one of the highest occupational positions that a French-Canadian migrant woman might achieve in the textile manufacturing industry. At that time, Mary Louise's household consisted of her widowed mother, who did not possess a means of paid employment, and her two sisters, who worked as moulders in a hosiery factory. Remeus had presumably moved out. Mary Louise's industrial experience as a weaver, a skill in high demand in the early-twentieth-century Lowell factory, was undoubtedly an important asset for her labourer-headed family as they moved to Lowell.[41]

There were also cases of women who did not list any occupation in Québec but became textile workers after they moved to Lowell. Linking the data drawn from the federal census with those from the *Border Entry* provides us with examples of ostensibly new industrial workers like Annie Brière and Emma Côté. In September 1909, thirty-six-year-old Annie went to Lowell with her husband, a thirty-three-year-old labourer, and three children aged ten, seven and four. Annie answered "none" as to her occupation in Canada. A year later, the 1910 census listed her as a weaver in a cotton factory in Lowell.[42] How typical was the case of Annie's quick occupational ascent? We do not know. We do know that weaving was skilled work, which, according to an oral history account, required a relatively short period of training that lasted from a few weeks to six months.[43] It is then possible that Annie learned the trade rapidly during the time between her arrival in Lowell in September and the census enumeration in April of the following year. Alternatively, Annie's case may have reflected the general tendency among official enumerators to improperly list women's former employment in Québec. Another, more likely scenario is that Annie herself might have neglected to report her former job. In either case, it is safe to surmise that Annie had probably had some industrial experience in Québec before marriage or childbearing but was not working for wages at the time of her family's immigration. When asked at the border about her occupation, Annie answered that she was not employed.

Gender and labour historian Joy Parr has pointed out that single female migrants have not been that historically uncommon. This was particularly the case for skilled, wage-earning women, such as the Midland emigrants who moved to Paris, Ontario.[44] Likewise, one might expect that a large number of French-Canadian women with skill and experience such as Mary Louise would have traveled south of the border unaccompanied by their male family members. My findings show otherwise. An overwhelming majority (73 percent) of the French-Canadian women I studied went to Lowell with their families, while only a quarter did so without families. Without neglecting the minority who moved alone, the overall patterns confirm the continuity of a key characteristic of French-Canadian migration from the late nineteenth century, that is, of movement primarily in family units.

The above findings suggest that for the majority of French-Canadian women in the early twentieth century, for both those with and those without paid work experience in Canada, migration continued to be a family project—traveling to, and settling in, Lowell as part of a family. For example, Hermine Frenette, a twenty-year-old domestic from La Patrie, Québec, crossed the border southward with her family on April 28, 1909. Hermine was traveling with her fifty-year-old mother Emma, listed as having no paid work; her labourer brother, Napoléon, eighteen years old; another brother Émile, a seventeen-year-old farm labourer; and her two youngest siblings, Albertine, eleven, and Ovila, six, neither of whom worked for wages. Another example is Marie Chouinard, a twenty-year-old single woman listed as having had a "job" (unspecified) in Lac-Saint-Jean, Québec, before she went to Lowell with six family members on October 29, 1909. She was the oldest daughter in her family. Her father, George, forty-eight years old, was a farmer, while her mother, Mary, was a housewife. Her brother Joseph, eighteen, also had had an unspecified "job." Two younger brothers and a sister, ages eleven, nine, and five years old, were not listed as paid workers in Québec.[45]

The cases of Hermine, Marie, and many other French-Canadian women traveling with their families suggest that despite the valuable skills and/or experience a significant number of the migrant women possessed, they continued to be, to use Louise Tilly and Joan Scott's phrase, "an arm of the family economy."[46] On this subject, Thomas Dublin has asserted that as far as the process of settlement is concerned, French-Canadian female workers in Lowell's textile factories in 1900 had enjoyed far less of the economic and social independence than the Yankee mill girls in the antebellum period had done.[47] Major patterns in French-Canadian women's migration confirm the continuity of this historical process in the course of migration as well, i.e., the centrality of family, instead of individuals, defining the course of movement from Québec to Lowell.

What explains, then, the differences in migration patterns between French-Canadian women in Lowell and Midland women in Paris, Ontario? The different labour market dynamics encountered by French-Canadian migrants both at home and at their destination, compared to those met by the Midland emigrant women, militated against the construction of such migration patterns. For one thing, Québec's agro-economy at the turn of the century was based upon the parallel development of small-scale commercial agriculture and the persistence of a rural subsistence economy. While a good number of small land-holding and landless farmers worked as *journaliers*, or general labourers, on the land or in rural commercial centres, many of these men's wives and daughters cultivated vegetables and fruits, and a few even kept cows and pigs, on a small plot of land that the family owned. By doing so, these women continued to ensure the subsistence of their families, even when they earned wages. Moreover, French-Canadian women generally married early compared to their Swedish or English counterparts. Subsequently, few single French-Canadian women moved out of their parishes of origin unaccompanied by male family members. Therefore, specific types of agricultural organization and divisions of labour, which sustained a family-based subsistence economy that went along with commercial agriculture in Québec, constructed part of the structural basis restricting women's autonomy over their geographic mobility.[48]

These same structural conditions led to the predominance of migration patterns within which women rarely initiated the migration of their families. The case of Lowell's French-Canadian migrants contrasts sharply with a pattern of chain migration observed in early-twentieth-century Paris, Ontario, where men were frequently the last, rather than the first, in kin groups to go abroad, "reluctantly following the initiative of female family members."[49] Instead, a major pattern of French-Canadian migration emerging from oral history accounts was that a father and son would first move temporarily to a chosen destination in the U.S., find work, and then either return to Québec or send for the rest of the family and bring them south of the border.

Another factor that shaped the migration pattern of French-Canadian women can be found among the general economic conditions in Lowell. The New England city was, strictly speaking, no longer a mono-industrial city by the early twentieth century. As Lowell gradually diversified its economic activities, it made it easier for French-Canadian men and women to find employment in a broader range of jobs, including many outside the textile industry, such as machinery, shoe, and cartridge factories. More importantly, the city's textile industry, while consistently the largest employer within Lowell's local labour market, was facing a series of challenges that arose from increased competition from southern industry, technological innovation, and the implementation of anti-child labour laws, leading to a general downturn that continued as the century progressed, save for a brief period of upswing during the war years. Coupled with changes to the local labour market, what this meant for Lowell's French-Canadian immigrant families was that their women were "highly valued for their ability to earn immediate cash once in the new land" as historian Ardis Cameron observed among the migrant women in the neighbouring textile city of Lawrence, Massachusetts.[50] At the same time, given this socioeconomic reality in Lowell—the economic difficulties of the textile industry and the expanding employment opportunities in sectors outside the textile industry—it made more sense for those women to move from one setting to another with a family, since a composite family wage could then be relied upon.

Notwithstanding the impacts of the socioeconomic transformation both at home and at the point of arrival, the leading pattern of family migration discussed above should not gloss over cases of the significant minority who crossed the border alone. Of the sampled French-Canadian migrant women of all ages without any paid work experience listed before crossing the border, 17 percent migrated alone, as opposed to more than 80 percent who traveled accompanied. In contrast, of those who had had an occupation in Canada, a little over half traveled with their family members, while another half journeyed unaccompanied to Lowell. Claudia and Valentine Ducharme were listed as having worked as factory operatives in Québec before their journey to Lowell in 1919. Unlike Mary Louise, the Ducharme sisters traveled without other family members to Lowell. Their years of residence in Lowell suggest that the two sisters were probably on their way back to that New England city after their visit to Québec. The following year, the U.S. federal census recorded Claudia working in a cotton factory as a relatively well-paid velvet finisher and Valentine as a housemaid for a private family.[51] The example of one of the Ducharme sisters shows a continuing occupational experience of "elite" female textile workers.

Most of these "lone" female travelers with work experience went to join their sisters, who had already moved to Lowell. Their pattern of migration raises a question: What did it mean to travel *alone*? While discussion of the issue will follow in greater detail, it can be suggested, for the moment, that although having had paid work experience in Canada was not a sufficient condition for a French-Canadian woman to migrate alone, the experience nevertheless made an important difference in making her southward move possible.

Families on the Move? : Separation, Reunification, and "Lone" Migrants

Although the family-centred dimension of French-Canadian migration continued in the early twentieth century, for many who moved with their families, cross-border journeys entailed variable periods of family separation with or without entailing family reunification. Three examples taken from interviews with Yvonne Lagassé illustrate various patterns of family migration. In each case, the migration of the entire family followed the departure of some family members, "pioneer immigrants," who themselves often followed the paths blazed by other kin members. These pioneer migrants—all men in the case of Lagassé's families—first looked for jobs, checked the prospects of work for the rest of the family and then had their family join them in Lowell. Various lengths of family separation suggest that migrant families weighed available resources in their decisions, as well as various concerns, such as financial needs, maintenance of their family farm, preparation for sale or collateral, and above all, family unity, and devised ways to best address these considerations.

Yvonne Lagassé's grandmother had a nephew, Gaspard Beaudry, who had spent time in Fitchburg, Massachusetts, moved to Lowell, and then returned to Canada "pour s'promener."[52] He went to see Lagassé's grandmother, Madame Loiselle, in Saint-Jean-de-Matha in Lanaudière. Was Gaspard making a short visit home while still living in Lowell, or had he left this city to return permanently to Canada? Lagassé does not tell us. What we do know is that Beaudry encouraged Grandmother Loiselle to move her family to the city. He told the grandmother: "You'll go to Lowell. You've got lots of girls. They'll all work there."[53] The family did not leave all together at this point; neither did the daughters depart as Beaudry suggested. Instead, Grandfather Loiselle and his eldest son went down to Lowell. Before this trip, the grandfather had been to places as far away as British Columbia for two years, but he was not earning enough to support his family. Once in Lowell, he and his son found abundant work building the foundations of houses within *Petit Canada*. After a few weeks, Grandfather Loiselle went back to St.-Jean-de-Matha in Québec. Determined to move his entire family to Lowell, Grandfather Loiselle told his wife, "Take nothing but clothes."[54] They sold everything, "the house, the mill, and well, everything,"[55] and left for Lowell with their ten children. The family separation thus lasted only some weeks for Lagassé's maternal family.

Interestingly, in contrast to the Loiselles, the Lagassés, Lagassé's husband's family, took a considerably longer time to decide to move the whole family to Lowell. The two sons in the family—Lagassé's husband and his older brother—and a labourer, *un engagé*, worked on the family farm. Her father-in-law was working for the Boston & Maine Railroad Corporation, which meant that he was away from home all year long, except for two winter months when he took a leave and returned to Canada to help his family prepare the hay. Lagassé recounts:

> My father-in-law, he made money on the trains. He spent the winter on the trains here and there and after that, he spent the winter in Canada helping make hay, and other things.... And then finally, the old woman, she got tired of it ... you know! [...] There was an *engagé* (helper), for example, and he stayed there. And after that, there were two sons. My husband and the other, the oldest one—his name was Clarence. And he stayed in Canada. All the family stayed in Canada. Only her husband stayed a lot of time here [in the U.S.] because he made money on the trains.[56]

Yvonne Lagassé's accounts of her two families, the Loiselles and the Lagassés, point to the different family strategies employed by each. While one branch of the family decided to migrate shortly after the first voyage of the "pioneering" members (father and son), the other took years before moving the entire family to Lowell. It remains to be explored whether or not the different lengths of time taken by the two families to move to Lowell were at all contingent upon the availability of prospective wage workers, particularly of unmarried daughters.

Families not infrequently split across the border and created new families on each side. Roger Brunelle recounts one such family migration that began with his great-grandfather at the turn of the century. He describes it as follows:

That was a passage [from Québec to Lowell], which was made for a lot of other families between 1870 and 1920. It happened to us—the first contacts of the Brunelles with Lowell—it was—in the middle—about a century ago—in 1880. [...] So my great-grandfather stayed here in Lowell since 1899 until 1906. Then he returned to Canada and most of his daughters and sons did as well. But my grandfather stayed here [in Lowell]. He married my grandmother in 1907 and they remained here. In 1908 he bought a house on the Beaver Street and the family lives there still today.[57]

As far as family strategy is concerned, scholars have debated its definition and its relevance as an analytical notion. For instance, Cynthia Comacchio has asked whether a strategy was necessary for a family to look for supplementary income when times were tight or if some form of supplementing the primary breadwinner's wages was the only conceivable immediate response to the problems the family faced.[58] In the same vein, one may question whether the reuniting of family members on the other side of the border was based on strategy or was an intuitive response. The oral history accounts of Yvonne Lagassé and Roger Brunelle discussed above show that there were different alternatives regarding when, how, and where a migrant would bring his or her family together. The variety of such options, as limited as they might have been, allows one to argue that there was a margin of autonomy within which these French-Canadian migrants could search for the best possible way to improve the well-being of their families. Augmented as well by the privileged status accorded to them by the U.S. border control, one may argue that French Canadians exercised such autonomy to a far greater extent than those belonging to targeted groups from Asia and Southern and Eastern Europe in the same period.

If French-Canadian migration in the first two decades of the new century often entailed various periods of family separation, it also required many to travel between Canada and the U.S. more than once. As many as two thirds of the sampled French Canadians (66 percent) in Lowell had previously spent time in the United States (see Table 7). Among them, an overwhelming proportion (81 percent) had resided in Lowell. Of those who had not lived in Lowell, a good proportion had lived and worked in neighbouring cities in Massachusetts, particularly in Boston (40 kilometers, or 25 miles, southwest of Lowell) and other New England industrial centres. Only three migrants had previously resided outside of New England. These findings not only illustrate the extent of the geographic mobility of French-Canadian migrants but also point to the tendency for Lowell-bound migrants to return to a city or a region where they had once resided, regardless of the length of their former residence.

Table 7. Locations of Previous Sojourn in the United States of Lowell-bound French Canadians

Response to the question: "Had one been to the U.S. before?"	Number	Percentage
Yes	100	65.8
No	52	34.2
Total	152	100.0
Location of previous sojourn in the U.S.		
Other than Lowell	12	11.9
Massachusetts		
Boston	3	
Unspecified	2	
New Hampshire		
Manchester	1	
Nashua	1	
Maine		
Caribou	1	
Connecticut		
Willimantic	1	
New York		
New York City	1	
Washington		
Seattle	1	
Wisconsin	1	
Unidentified	7	6.9
Total	101	100.0

Sources: Compiled by author from the sample of the *Soundex Index to Canadian Border Entry*.

Note: One individual named two localities. This created the difference in the total number of the response "Yes" (100) and the total number of the listed localities (101).

The Bédards and the Brières are two of many families whose itineraries illustrated extremely high geographic mobility both before and after their arrival in the United States. Jan-Anna and Charles Bédard did not choose Lowell as their only and ultimate destination. They had been to neighbouring cities in New England before going to that city. Canadian-born Jan-Anna traveled to Fall River, Massachusetts when she was "very young." She had lived in Fall River for sixteen years before her marriage to Canadian-born Charles and the birth of their first daughter. Jan-Anna and Charles then moved to Woonsocket, Rhode

Island, and lived there for five years. In June of 1893, the couple, now with four children, left Woonsocket and moved to Lowell. After a short time, they returned to Canada, and then in 1900, went back to Lowell.

The Brière family, for their part, typifies the majority of French Canadians in the early twentieth century who moved several times between their natal village and Lowell. The birthplace of their children suggests that the couple, Annie (born in Saint-Tite) and Delphis (born in Louisville), lived most of the early years of their married life in St.-Tite in Mauricie, with the exception of the six years from 1899 to 1905, when they resided in Lowell. In addition, Delphis had been to that city earlier, in 1889, when he was thirteen years old. On 24 September 1909, the Brières crossed the border as they journeyed to Lowell, this time to stay. They traveled with their young children, Béatrice, ten years old, William, seven, and Arthur, four. In the following year, the Brières were listed as residing in Lowell. Annie was working as a weaver and Delphis as a box maker. The couple had four children, Béatrice, William, Arthur, and Joseph, a Massachusetts-born son.[59]

The high mobility that some French Canadians, like the Brières and the Bédards, experienced and the various lengths of family separation many others endured lead one to join in contesting the once predominant view of migration that assumed an abrupt one-step transplantation of previously sedentary villagers to industrial cities. Historians such as Yves Frenette and Bruno Ramirez have revealed that the migration paths of French Canadians in the nineteenth century had encompassed the "colonization regions" of the province before their cross-border journeys to the textile towns in New England, and in some cases, they also included previous stays in American towns and cities.[60] My analysis of French-Canadian migrants in early-twentieth-century Lowell has confirmed the continuity in the geographical moves prior to their recorded cross-border travel south. Although many migrated in family units and did become a "permanent element" of the city by the turn of the twentieth century, for significant numbers of families like the Brières and the Bédards, moving to Lowell was part of larger life trajectories. Their migration consisted with a series of movements of variable distances and durations. Oral history accounts further suggest that the diversity of these migration practices was ultimately linked by a common purpose, i.e., one of a family's well-being. This meant, above all, the economic survival of the family, but economic stability was not the sole determinant of the migrants' decision to move. Ultimately, perhaps, the most important considerations for these men and women on the move were when, how, and where to bring their families together, or how to make a living on one or both sides of the border.

The Extent of Migrant Networks

By the early twentieth century, French-Canadian migrants to Lowell had become less dependent on the organized efforts that characterized the migration of their predecessors. Recruiting agents sent by American textile companies, railway ticket agents, and French-Canadian Catholic priests settled in New England, all of whom made up a major part of the nineteenth-century labour system, were now replaced by more diffused personal networks of families, friends, and neighbours who had already lived and worked in Lowell. Although documenting these immigrant networks over time is an exceedingly difficult task, *Border Entry* again helps us to shed some light on this issue.[61]

For the period lasting from 1900 to 1920, data derived from *Border Entry* highlight the centrality of family in knitting these informal webs of information and support. Migrants were asked to provide the name and relation of a contact person whom they intended to meet upon their arrival in Lowell, and their answers pointed to the crucial presence of contact persons at their destination. Nearly all the identified contact persons (99 percent) of Lowell-bound French Canadians in the early twentieth century were members of family or kin. Contact persons falling outside of this category accounted only for a tiny minority (see Table 8). Among members of extended families, cousins made up the largest proportion of contact persons (17 percent), followed by brothers and sisters, uncles, and brothers-in-law.[62] The indispensable presence of a contact person at a migrant's destination confirms a key characteristic of French-Canadian migration in the early twentieth century: it was a movement built primarily on family and kinship networks—what Ramirez and Otis have termed an informal sponsored immigration.[63] As early as the 1870s and 1880s, changes in the roles played by formal and informal agents of migration had become noticeable as the presence of a contact person among family, kin, friends, and acquaintances constituted an increasingly important element in directing French-Canadian migrants. At the same time, French-Canadian migrants to Lowell had become less dependent on the organized efforts that characterized the migration of their predecessors. By the early twentieth century, this shift became decisive. Recruiting agents, who had made up a major part of the nineteenth-century labour system, were now replaced by more diffused personal networks of families, friends, and neighbours who had lived and worked in Lowell. The presence of the latter, many of whom were acting as contact persons, had come to play a more complex and articulate role. Such a change suggests the extent of "maturity" that French- Canadian migration had acquired by the early new century. The more knowledge and detailed information French Canadians gained about the job market and housing

Table 8. Relation of Contact Persons to Lowell-bound French Canadians

	Number	Percentage
Immediate family	66	53.7
Husband	4	3.3
Wife	6	4.9
Son	11	8.9
Daughter	0	0
Father	13	10.6
Mother	2	1.6
Brother	16	13.0
Sister	14	11.4
Extended family	56	45.5
Father-in-law	2	1.6
Mother-in-law	0	0
Brother-in-law	9	7.3
Sister-in-law	1	0.8
Son- or daughter-in-law	0	0
Grandfather	8	6.5
Grandmother	0	0
Uncle	10	8.1
Aunt	3	2.4
Cousin	21	17.1
Niece	0	0
Nephew	2	1.6
Institution	1	0.8
Convent	1	0.8
Total	123	100.0

Sources: Compiled by author from the sample of the *Soundex Index to Canadian Border Entry*.

conditions awaiting them at their destination, and the more institutionally complete their community grew, the less dependent migrants had to be on formal recruiting agents. Letters and visits from family members already in the U.S., and a flaunting display on the part of Franco Americans of conspicuous consumption in the form of gold chains, new hats, or, later, automobiles on occasions of their visits home must have provided prospective migrants with a wealth of information, either practical or exaggerated, regarding when, where, and with whom they should move and find work.

It is also important to note that the contact person was rarely a member of the migrant's nuclear family. This was probably the corollary of the fact that migration units of French Canadians were frequently composed of immediate family members. In the case of a separate family movement whereby the rest of the family went to join the "pioneer migrants" at a later date, the pioneers were likely to assume the role of contact persons. The relatively high percentage of sons and fathers among contact persons, in contrast to the extremely low percentage of wives and daughters, corroborates the fact that few French-Canadian women initiated their families' migration. Although the extremely low rate of husbands showing up as contact persons in my data contradicts this observation to some extent, a more extensive examination of the migration units will help us to clarify this point.

Finally, one may discern the gender-specific aspect of the contact persons waiting at the destination for those allegedly solitary migrant women discussed earlier. Although female members of the family and kin were a minority among the contact persons, sisters played a significant role in directing the small contingent of single French-Canadian women who went to Lowell unaccompanied. There were approximately the same number of sisters as there were brothers listed as contact persons for the sampled migrants. Among them, a good proportion of lone male migrants listed their male as well as female siblings as the person waiting to meet them in Lowell. In contrast, all of the unaccompanied female migrants except one in my sample recorded their sisters as contact persons. For example, Anna Aubert, native of Dubie, Canada, entered the U.S. in mid-September 1912. The twenty-four-year-old single dressmaker gave her sister's name as the contact person in Lowell. Seven years later, Béatrice Audet, 19 years old, left her native village of Stanstead, Québec, and headed for Lowell, where her married sister was waiting to meet her. Audet was a telephone operator. The examples of Anna, Béatrice, and several other women suggest that, in addition to an occupational skill, the presence of a female sibling at the destination, probably more than that of a male counterpart, was a crucial factor for a minority of unmarried women to carry out the project of crossing the border alone. Sisters at the destination must have been expected to provide emotional support, immediate help in finding a job, and, possibly, the economic foundation for setting up joint households for their unaccompanied female siblings. At a time when company-run boardinghouses disappeared along with other "amenities" that the textile corporations had previously provided for mill girls during the last century, the range of immediate and practical help that sisters at the destination offered for their newly arrived siblings must have been even more valuable. Although brothers, too, were likely trusted to assume similar roles, the difference was that they did so with respect to the larger unit of the family as a whole, while sisters were especially counted on by their female siblings. Unfortunately, detailed portraits of sisters and brothers who acted as contact persons are not to be found in the *Border Entry*. Within the limitations of available findings, however, one may conclude that neither geographical distance nor increasingly "individual" movement isolated migrants from their families. Rather migration served to remake family ties in a gender-selective manner as an integral and active part of family networks that extended to both sides of the border.

******

This chapter has shed light on some of the complex and diverse processes of French-Canadian migration to early-twentieth-century Lowell. Migration itineraries, occupational experiences, patterns of family migration or separation, and the indispensable presence of contact persons have shown that the decision to migrate was made on well-informed and pondered judgments on the part of the men and women on the move. The propensity among some of Lowell's French Canadians to move several times in their lifetime does not necessarily contradict an earlier finding that revealed the limited transience of a large proportion of French-Canadian cotton workers in New England.[64] Cross-border migration was only one, though probably the most important, result of the French Canadians' growing capacity to move to locales that stood out as being the most advantageous on their "cognitive map."[65]

Many thus struck out in new directions, but as Dirk Hoerder would say, they were only new as far as they changed their immediate living and working circumstances.[66] However, after they crossed the border, and many did so more than once, they found themselves in a world rather familiar to them. For Annie and Delphis Brière and many others like them, Lowell was a place where they had resided before moving back to a small village in Québec; now they were heading for that New England city once again. Yvonne Lagassé and her family had a cousin, Gaspard, who worked in Lowell and who, during his visit to Québec, tried to persuade the Lagassés to send their girls to Lowell where they could find plenty of jobs. The variable expressions of such transnational mobility and interactions among current, prospective, and returning migrants which sustained such "remarkable geographic mobility,"[67] to borrow the expression of Yves Roby, have highlighted the central role that family and kin networks continued to play in the early twentieth century in linking geographically separate localities and labour markets across and within the international boundary. Furthermore, family not only provided Lowell-bound migrant men and women with such indispensable connections, but for the great majority, it also functioned as a fundamental unit of movement and the very reason for displacement.

The enduring importance of family notwithstanding, French-Canadian migrants in the early twentieth century also propelled significant change in the place accorded to family. In what could be called an individualist turn, a growing minority of women and men now moved "alone" without the company of their family members, and their migration did not necessarily entail family reunification after a lengthy period of family separation. It would be erroneous to consider such movement as lone migration, however. For instance, nineteen years old and single, Béatrice Audet left her native village in Québec by herself, but she was to be met by her married sister once she arrived in Lowell. The previous pages have illustrated that even when these migrants moved alone, their migration was deeply rooted in the matrix of family and kin networks in the early twentieth century. While the emerging pattern of migration, in contrast to the previous practice of more strictly framed family movement in the nineteenth century, involved both single women and men, when women moved alone, the presence of female siblings at the destination was more crucial than that of their male counterparts. Gender thus shaped the process of movement of these French Canadians in subtle but fundamental ways.

CHAPTER FOUR

American or Ethnic Workers? : Work, Family, and Masculinity of French-Canadian Men

In January 1899, at a hearing before the U.S. Industrial Commission on Immigration, Herman Stump, former Commissioner-General of the Bureau of Immigration, expressed his view on the prominence of the French-Canadian workers in New England and the alleged disappearance of American "mill class" workers from New England localities. When asked whether he believed there were not enough "native Americans to fill the lower grades," Stump replied: "I say simply that there are more working-men in the United States than are necessary. The labour market [in the United States] is overstocked." When further asked about his thoughts on whether or not the mills of New England could run without those "Canadians [who] came in and took the places," Stump stated: "Most assuredly they could." Concurring with the point raised by the inquirer, Stump seemed to reason that it was because of the lack of what he deemed decent wages to raise a family that there was no longer any "mill class" among "American workers." "Let them [the mill owners] pay living wages," he urged, "and they can get all the help they want." He concluded, "I think that industry would flourish again if [U.S.-born] young men and women [of U.S.-parentage] could afford to marry and raise families."[1]

The ex-Commissioner-General's response is important in several regards. Stump's words were not couched in racial terms, reflecting a rhetorical strategy which was to be echoed in the restrictionist discourse of the AFL leader. Samuel Gompers deliberately emphasized the need for labour protectionism over the fear of nativist concerns as he campaigned against Canadian immigration two decades later.[2] This marked a clear difference when compared to the invectives launched against French-Canadian workers in New England textile cities some three decades earlier, when Carroll Davidson Wright, head of the Massachusetts Bureau of Statistics of Labor, derogatorily called French-Canadian workers "Chinese of the East (coast)" in his report.[3] At the same time, and perhaps most importantly, Stump's words reveal the lack of recognition on his part that French-Canadian workers, especially male workers, were moving up the occupational hierarchy in the changing political economy of early-twentieth-century New England, particularly in Lowell.

Admittedly, such progress was limited as the overwhelming majority of Lowell's French Canadians remained manual workers. Nevertheless, the distinct shift upward in socioeconomic status of Lowell's French Canadians placed them in line with what historians of migration and labour have shown over the years: that industrial cities and towns in the turn-of-the-century and early-twentieth-century U.S. were not as conducive to the socioeconomic mobility of immigrants as was previously believed. As husbands and fathers, migrant men contributed long hours of arduous work in order to provide for the well-being of the family, be it through home ownership, their children's education, or simply by keeping their families adequately fed.[4]

The emphasis on the growing importance of French-Canadian men's financial role alone, however, risks leaving the broader meanings of work, skills, and wages for them and their families unexamined. It also speaks little to the power and peril at play in these men's perception of themselves, which revolved around a sense of entitlement and responsibility as the real or symbolic male breadwinner. Recent developments in the scholarship on gendered meanings of work, its hierarchy,[5] and whiteness studies and its critics[6] have produced valuable insights to reflect on these issues. I am not in a position to discuss the diversity of the economic and cultural interactions that may have defined racial, gendered, or ethnicized categories and subjectivities of French Canadians in Lowell.[7] This chapter takes another approach, focusing on the working-class experiences of Lowell's French-Canadian men (and, to a lesser extent, women) that emerge from a combination of the data drawn from federal manuscript censuses and oral history accounts. What were the demographic profiles of French-Canadian men and women in comparison to other major American and immigrant groups in that city? To what extent did the socioeconomic profiles of French-Canadian male workers change over the time period under study? What did wage work mean for working-class French-Canadian men on the job, at home, and in the community? How did it shape a sense of themselves as fathers and husbands, and/or white American male workers? Evidence discussed in the following pages suggests that a change in the socioeconomic status of French-Canadian male workers and their U.S.-born sons did not have as much bearing on the emergence of a sense of themselves as white "American" workers. Rather, keeping up the image of the male breadwinner as dictated by the model derived from the family wage ideology likely preoccupied most French-Canadian men and their families more deeply. This is largely because of the very extent and nature of their upward mobility, I argue, which served as a basis from which French-Canadian men distilled as much a feeling of ambiguity as a sense of power and prerogative as fathers and husbands in their families.

The ideology of the family wage, or to be more precise, the living wage, as contemporaries referred to it,[8] held special importance in social and family life in the nineteenth and early twentieth century America. American views on married men, women, and wage work were dominated by the idea that held wives' and mothers' dependence on the sole wages of the breadwinner husbands as desirable, and women's employment as a misfortune. This normative ideology did not preclude women from earning money to support their families. Rather, significant variations existed according to race and class among the holders of such views, as well as changes in their perceptions over time.[9] Yet in late-nineteenth-century and the early-twentieth-century New England, the family wage ideology, using the phrases of Ardis Cameron, unified "an array of strange bedfellows"[10] ranging from radicals, to Progressive reformers, to the corporate elite, to labour organizers, and even to political leaders including the president of the U.S., Theodore Roosevelt. For them, the ideal man was a breadwinner husband whose sole wages supported his unemployed wife and children.

The hegemony of this family wage ideology, however, was constantly being undermined. In turn-of-the-century Lawrence, daily routines, unsteady economic conditions, and a skewed sex ratio in the textile factories unsettled the ground for upholding that ideology.[11] At times, men did housework and attended to young children, which was work normally performed by women. The household economies of most French-Canadian migrant families were similar to those in Lowell in the 1870s.[12] Frequent unemployment or underemployment forced men to remain idle while their wives and children worked for wages in the textile factories. In a political economy in which the wages of male workers remained constantly insufficient, therefore, the model of the family wage ideology was more of an ideal than a reality for a large proportion of working-class families.

Notwithstanding the difficulty of complying fully with the ideological norm, the family wage ideology continued to shape, in even more significant ways, the lives of most French-Canadian and other working-class families in early-twentieth-century Lowell. More and more of Lowell's French-Canadian husbands and fathers engaged in jobs that paid higher and possibly more stable wages. This in turn helped, at least partly, their households cope with another, even more important change: the significant decrease of children's wage contributions, brought about by the strict implementation of child labour laws. In 1875, the Massachusetts Bureau of Statistics of Labor reported in its annual

Figure 4. Workers rebuilding a bridge over Central Street, ca. 1910. (Courtesy of the Center for Lowell History, University of Massachusetts Lowell.)

report that among twenty-six French-Canadian households, none of the wives were listed as working, while thirty-six children (ages unspecified) earned wages. Children contributed as much as 39 percent of the total income of these families. Three decades later, the proportion of their earnings had fallen to 29 percent, although French-Canadian children still remained the most important wage earners after male heads.[13] In addition to men's improved wage-earning capacity, an increasing number of married French-Canadian women entered the paid labour market, thus providing another stream of income to make up for the loss of children's wages. The dearth of data for Lowell does not allow us to measure the exact rate of labour market participation for married women in earlier periods. However, in the early twentieth century, as many as a quarter of French-Canadian wives (26 percent in 1910 and 23 percent in 1920) worked for wages.[14]

It is in this context of radical transformation occurring in French-Canadian households that this chapter addresses the questions posed above. Before doing so, one needs to know who these French Canadians were. An analysis of three demographic profiles will help to ascertain what important demographic changes occurred within this group. These demographics relate to the age distribution of the residential, migrating, and working population of those of French-Canadian background in the city.[15]

Demographic Profiles of French Canadians in Lowell

During the decade between 1910 and 1920, French Canadians in Lowell, including both those born in Canada and in the U.S., were becoming older (Table 9). The proportion of young children, who had constituted the largest proportion of this group a few decades earlier, decreased steadily. Conversely, the percentage of adults aged forty-five and over increased. George Chouinard, James Cadorette, and Maxime Clermont exemplify typical French-Canadian male migrants of this period. George was a forty-eight-year-old farmer, a native of Lac-St.-Jean; James, fifty-two, was a labourer from St.-Rose-de-Makinac; and Maxime, another labourer, left St.-Jean-de-Matha for Lowell at the age of fifty-eight. All three migrated with their families while their children were in their late teens or older.[16]

Table 10, which excludes those born in the U.S. (second generation), provides a graphic representation of the aging of Lowell's migrant French-Canadian population. The proportion of children fourteen years old and younger declined substantially. In 1910, approximately 10 percent (one out of eight males and one out of ten females) belonged to this age group. A decade

Table 9. Age Distribution by Ethnic Group in Lowell, 1910 and 1920 (Number of Individuals per 100)

Age group	French Canadian	Irish	American	Portuguese	Greek
1910					
14 and under	33.8	22.6	26.0	43.6	6.6
15 to 24	20.8	18.0	19.4	25.5	41.2
25 to 34	16.2	17.3	16.6	16.0	29.7
35 to 44	13.0	18.0	11.8	12.8	10.4
45 and over	16.2	23.9	26.3	2.1	9.3
Total	100.0	100.0	100.0	100.0	100.0
(N)	(1,102)	(1,501)	(918)	(94)	(182)
1920					
14 and under	32.4	14.2	36.0	40.9	33.9
15 to 24	18.8	16.6	15.1	18.2	18.3
25 to 34	15.7	17.0	13.3	16.4	20.5
35 to 44	13.1	18.5	10.6	17.6	16.5
45 and over	21.7	33.7	25.0	6.9	10.9
Total	100.0	100.0	100.0	100.0	100.0
(N)	(1,152)	(1,468)	(1,201)	(159)	(322)

Sources: Compiled by author from the *Thirteenth and Fourteenth U.S. Federal Census Schedules.*

later, the proportion of this age bracket declined further, representing less than 5 percent of the migrant population. Conversely, the majority (59 percent of the men and 63 percent of the women) belonged to the most active age group, between fifteen and forty-five years of age, in 1910; the percentage remained at about the same level in 1920. One quarter of Lowell's French-Canadian arrivals in 1910 was composed of those aged forty-five and over, somewhat below the proportion of their Irish contemporaries (40 percent), but significantly higher than that of more recent arrivals, such as the Portuguese and the Greeks (only 3 percent and 10 percent respectively in the same age bracket). In 1920, the proportion of this older age group among French-Canadian men and women rose even further, representing about half of the migrating population.

Despite the decrease of the proportion of French-Canadian children in their teens, a large percentage of Lowell's French-Canadian households continued to include sons and daughters, representing the highest level among the five ethnic/migrant groups studied for this analysis besides the Portuguese in 1920 (Table 11). Many sons and daughters were likely adult children of

Table 10. Age Distribution of the French-Canadian Migrant Population by Gender, Lowell, 1910 and 1920 (Number of Individuals per 100)

Age group	Men	Women
1910		
14 and under	13.3	9.8
15 to 24	20.0	20.3
25 to 34	20.0	22.9
35 to 44	19.3	20.0
45 and over	27.4	27.0
Total	100.0	100.0
(N)	(285)	(315)
1920		
14 and under	5.3	3.9
15 to 24	9.6	7.4
25 to 34	15.3	17.9
35 to 44	22.0	25.8
45 and over	47.8	45.0
Total	100.0	100.0
(N)	(209)	(228)

Sources: Compiled by author from the *Thirteenth and Fourteenth U.S. Federal Census Schedules*.

working age who contributed wages to the household. (Not shown in the table.) In 1910 and 1920, sons and daughters accounted for about half of the French-Canadian households I studied. About 40 percent of the American, Irish, and Portuguese population consisted of sons and daughters. By contrast, children represented only slightly more than 10 percent of the Greek population.

French-Canadian households occasionally expanded to include individuals beyond members of the nuclear family, such as those directly related to the household head: brothers, sisters, brothers-in-law, sisters-in-law, parents, parents-in-law, cousins, nieces, nephews, and grandchildren. A small proportion of French Canadians, Irish, and Americans were boarders and lodgers, mostly but not exclusively unrelated to the household head, whereas this category made up by far a greater proportion of Portuguese and Greek households (35 percent and 53 percent, respectively, in 1910). The percentages of the latter two groups dropped (to 15 percent and 3 percent, respectively) over the decade, likely reflecting the growth of family formation.

Table 11. Relationship of French Canadians to Household Head, Lowell, 1910 and 1920 (Number of Individuals per 100)

	French Canadian	Irish	American	Portuguese	Greek
1910					
Head	19.1	23.2	23.4	11.7	16.5
Wife	14.5	15.7	13.9	9.6	6.0
Daughter	25.8	20.5	20.2	18.1	6.0
Son	26.4	18.7	20.4	19.1	7.7
Other family member	5.9	9.0	9.9	6.4	11.0
Lodger	5.4	9.0	8.2	35.1	52.7
Servant	0.7	1.7	-	-	-
Unidentified	2.2	2.3	4.0	-	-
Total	100.0	100.0	100.0	100.0	100.0
(N)	(1,102)	(1,501)	(918)	(94)	(182)
1920					
Head	19.9	25.1	20.1	17.6	21.4
Wife	15.5	16.8	12.4	17.0	13.4
Daughter	26.3	18.5	25.2	30.8	18.9
Son	25.7	17.6	22.9	25.2	22.0
Other family member	6.7	8.3	10	2.6	7.8
Lodger	5.5	8.4	8.2	6.3	15.2
Servant	0	0.7	0.2	-	-
Unidentified	0.3	3.5	0.7	0.6	1.2
Total	100.0	100.0	100.0	100.0	100.0
(N)	(1,155)	(1,468)	(1,201)	(159)	(322)

Sources: Compiled by author from *Thirteenth and Fourteenth U.S. Federal Census Schedules*.

Finally, corresponding to the overall aging of the city's French-Canadian population, the age distribution of the working population of this group reveals even more clearly the shifts in age distribution occurring among male and female workers (Table 12). Whereas in the 1870s, children in their early teens constituted a major pillar of wage earners contributing to French-Canadian households, in early twentieth century Lowell, a very small proportion (3 percent in 1910, and less than 2 percent in 1920) of French-Canadian children (mostly U.S.-born) aged fourteen and under was employed. Moreover, the proportion of male workers in the most active age group (from fifteen to forty-five years old) decreased from 84 percent to 67 percent, while the proportion of male workers aged forty-five years and over increased from a quarter to one third. For female workers, the change was more gradual and

Table 12. Age Distribution of the French-Canadian Working Population by Gender, Lowell, 1910 and 1920 (Number of Individuals per 100)

Age group	Men	Women
1910		
14 and under	1.8	1.6
15 to 24	29.0	49.7
25 to 34	24.3	18.0
35 to 44	20.4	18.5
45 and over	24.6	12.2
Total	100.0	100.0
(N)	(330)	(189)
1920		
14 and under	0.6	2.5
15 to 24	26.1	41.8
25 to 34	23.1	26.9
35 to 44	18.2	13.4
45 and over	31.9	15.4
Total	100.0	100.0
(N)	(328)	(201)

Sources: Compiled by author from *Thirteenth and Fourteenth U.S. Federal Census Schedules*.

diverse (from 86 percent to 82 percent and 12 percent to 15 percent, respectively).

The change occurring to the residential, migrating, and working populations of French Canadians in Lowell discussed above, the decrease in number and the increase in age, suggests in part the effects brought about by the nation-wide campaign for implementing anti-child labour laws, which was especially strong in the New England states. The Commonwealth adopted these laws that prohibited the employment of children under fourteen years of age in any factory, workshop, or mercantile establishment in 1898,[17] making it increasingly difficult for French-Canadian families to send their youngsters to work in textile factories.

The intensification of the labour processes in textile factories was another and possibly more important factor that reduced the presence of young teenage children in the factories.[18] A vocal segment of the French-Canadian elite also criticized child labour, an opposition not against but rather, in step with the efforts of American officials and reformers. A series of articles in *l'Étoile de Lowell*, a French language newspaper published in Lowell, reminded

French-Canadian working families of the consequences of sending young children to work at the mills. In 1905, an unnamed writer denounced it as "cruelty" to send children to workshops and factories "before their body and soul are sufficiently developed."[19] The writer claimed children should be placed in a school, not in the mill. "Is it not a shame for a strong and powerful nation [such as that of the French Canadians]," another article asked rhetorically, "that thousands of young children are deprived of all intellectual training"?[20]

To what extent such caveats from the ethnic elite or the entreaties of state and federal authorities reached the ears—and minds—of working-class French-Canadian families is another issue. Various measures to deceive law enforcement—such as entering the name of a relative, a neighbour or even a deceased older sister or brother on a work certificate of a younger child or simply lying about one's age—are well known.[21] Nevertheless, in light of the statistics discussed above, national and ethnic campaigns against child labour did have some important effects on reducing the number of Lowell's French-Canadian (and other) children working for wages.

Occupations Held by Lowell's French-Canadian Men[22]

If the changes occurring in Lowell's local labour markets had an immediate impact on the migration flow from French Canada, one of the direct consequences was the upward shift in the economic status of French-Canadian workers already in the city. The range of occupations listed for French-Canadian men rose from 107 in 1910 to 127 in 1920, an increase of almost 20 percent. The variety of jobs they held was small in comparison to the range of jobs held by their Irish counterparts (182 occupations in 1910 and 172 in 1920). Nevertheless, compared to those in the late-nineteenth-century cohort, a greater proportion by far of French-Canadian men found employment in semi-skilled and skilled trades.[23]

Manual Workers

Four types of manual workers—day labourers, textile workers, mechanics, and craft workers—illustrate the extent to which French-Canadian men improved their occupational profiles (see Tables 13 and 14). One of the clearest signs pointing to this distinct upward shift was the decrease in the number of day labourers. The proportion of day labourers decreased from 14 percent in 1910 to 8 percent in 1920, and the absolute number in my sample also declined from forty-six to twenty-seven, a decrease of almost 40 percent (see Table 15).

Table 13. Occupational Distribution of Male Workers in Five Ethnic Groups, Lowell, 1910 (Number of Individuals per 100)

	French Canadian	Irish	American	Portuguese	Greek
Manual Workers	77.2	71.9	54.7	92.6	88.3
Unskilled	23.9	18.3	9.1	22.2	28.9
Semi- and skilled	53.3	53.6	45.6	70.4	59.4
White Collar	10.0	18.3	28.5	-	-
Lower white collar (clerical, etc.)	6.1	11.3	19.0	-	-
Upper white collar	3.9	7.0	9.5	-	-
Professional	2.4	1.3	3.3	-	-
Independent	4.8	5.0	8.0	7.4	5.5
Other	5.5	3.7	5.1	-	5.5
Total	100.0	100.0	100.0	100.0	100.0
(N)	(330)	(459)	(274)	(27)	(128)

Source: Compiled by author from *Thirteenth U.S. Federal Census Schedules.*

Table 14. Occupational Distribution of Male Workers in Five Ethnic Groups, Lowell, 1920 (Number of Individuals per 100)

	French Canadian	Irish	American	Portuguese	Greek
Manual workers	79.7	71.6	58.4	91.3	78.7
Unskilled	16.5	22.2	11.9	39.6	24.4
Semi- and skilled	63.4	49.4	46.5	52.1	54.3
White collar	12.5	20.8	25.7	6.3	6.3
Lower white collar (clerical, etc.)	5.8	13.2	11.9	4.2	5.5
Upper white collar	6.7	7.6	13.8	2.1	0.8
Professional	0.9	0.4	4.5	-	1.6
Independent	3.4	4.7	9.0	2.1	11.8
Other (Number)	3.4	2.5	2.6	-	0.8
Total	100.0	100.0	100.0	100.0	100.0
(N)	(328)	(486)	(312)	(48)	(127)

Source: Compiled by author from *Fourteenth U.S. Federal Census Schedules.*

Table 15. Number of Sampled French-Canadian Men Working
as Labourers in Lowell, 1910 and 1920

Birthplace	1910	1920
Canada, French	38	18
(Percent of labourers among Canadian-born workers)	(16.2%)	(10.0%)
United States	8	9
(Percent of labourers among U.S.-born workers)	(8.7%)	(6.1%)
Total	46	27
(Percent of total number of French-Canadian labourers)	(13.9%)	(8.2%)
Number of French-Canadian Male Workers	330	328

Source: Compiled by author from *Fourteenth U.S. Federal Census Schedules.*

Moreover, the proportion of industrial occupations for which less expertise was required—back boys, bobbin boys, yarn boys, sweepers, and various kinds of helpers—remained small (below 10 percent). This is a significant change from 1870, when two out of three French-Canadian adult men in the city toiled as unskilled workers. Six out of ten of these unskilled workers were day labourers.[24] The proportion of male household heads among day labourers also decreased. By the new century, the proportion of these labourers among Canadian-born husbands and fathers dropped from 65 percent in 1910 to 56 percent in 1920, while the proportion of their sons remained at approximately 30 percent over the decade. Pierre Lalonde was one of the few French-Canadian day labourers listed as a household head in the 1920 census. It is difficult to imagine how the fifty-year-old day labourer could have supported his family of eight—including his thirty-eight-year-old wife, Amanda, and seven children aged from four to fourteen—with his meagre wage.[25]

By far the leading occupational category, comprising eight out of ten French-Canadian men, was manual industrial worker (Table 16). Among this group, nearly 60 percent were employed in textile manufacturing as either skilled or semi-skilled workers, such as carders, weavers, spinners, slashers, knitters, loomfixers, and operatives, or what are now referred to as machine operators. Among those in non-textile manufacturing were shoe cutters, stitchers, and bobbin makers. Michel De[s]marais was one such industrial worker. He migrated to the U.S. in 1885, and two and a half decades later, he was working as a textile machine operator. His wife Angélina, thirty-three years old, worked as a looper at a hosiery factory.[26]

The second largest group of workers among French-Canadian men worked as machinists, mechanics, and engineers. The percentage of those listed as having mechanic-related occupations almost doubled over the decade from

1910 to 1920, signaling another sign of the improvements in the occupational profile of Lowell's French-Canadian men. Arthur Lambert and his sons were part of this growing number of mechanical workers. Arthur, a thirty-five-year-old widower, worked as a machinist in a garage, while his two single brothers, Adélard, twenty-four, and Victor, twenty, worked in a machine shop.[27] Like the

Table 16. Leading Occupations of French-Canadian and Irish Men in the Manual Labour Sector, Lowell, 1910 and 1920 (Number of Individuals per 100)

French-Canadian Male Workers		1910	1920
Unskilled		23.9	16.5
	Labourers	14.2	8.3
	Others	9.7	8.2
Skilled and semi-skilled		53.3	63.4
	Operatives and other semi-skilled	34.8	36.8
	Machinists	6.8	12.6
	Carpenters and other craft workers	7.1	12.2
Total		100.0	100.0
(Number of male workers in the above jobs)		(225)	(250)
Percentage of the above workers in the total number of French-Canadian male workers		69.2	76.7
Irish Male Workers			
Unskilled		17.6	22.2
	Labourers	10.4	15.3
	Others	7.2	6.9
Skilled and semi-skilled		47.3	49.4
	Operatives and other semi-skilled	32.9	25.7
	Machinists	9.6	5.0
	Carpenters and other craft workers	4.8	11.2
Total		100.0	100.0
(Number of male workers in the above jobs)		(268)	(300)
Percentage of the above workers in the total number of Irish male workers		58.4	62.1

Sources: Compiled by author from *Thirteenth U.S. Census Schedules* and *Fourteenth U.S. Census Schedules*.

Lamberts, many French-Canadian men working as mechanics had family members—fathers, uncles, sons, and brothers, for example—who worked in the same occupation. When there was a job opening, a machinist father, uncle, or cousin might inform his boss that a son, brother, or nephew could work in the same line. An older and more experienced family member would also teach the trade to his junior. This is reminiscent of the ideal of the family labour system in the Amoskeag textile mills in turn-of-the-century Manchester, New Hampshire, where French-Canadian and other working families had family members and relatives working for the same factory, in the same section, and on the same machinery.[28] The practice of the Lambert brothers and many other French-Canadian men in mechanics suggests that the key role of family networks also became increasingly salient to families engaged in a greater range of industries other than the narrowly defined textile industry, including the machinery industry. Put another way, family-centred networks, which occasionally extended to non-family member of co-ethnics, were among the factors that spurred the growth in the numbers of mechanic-related workers among French-Canadian male—but not female—workers in the early twentieth century. In such ways, family networks sustained and re-shaped ethnically segregated and gender-segregated labour markets.

The third leading occupational group among Lowell's French-Canadian male workers was craft workers, such as carpenters, plumbers, tinsmiths, blacksmiths, and tanners. Forty-four-year-old carpenter Alfred Parent was one of them. The wages of the skilled craft worker needed supplementary wage earners such as Alfred's son Raymond, eighteen years old, who worked as an engineer assistant at a textile school.[29]

The change in occupational distribution characterized by the four groups of workers discussed above—day labourers on the decline and textile workers, mechanics, and craft workers on the rise—suggests that French-Canadian male workers were catching up and, at times, even outpacing Irish counterparts, their long-time competitors in Lowell's labour markets. In contrast to the decrease in the proportion of French-Canadian labourers, the proportion of Irish male labourers increased from 10 percent to 15 percent during the decade under study. Moreover, the growth in the numbers of French-Canadian men in the three occupational groups—skilled and semi-skilled workers in the textile factories, in machine shops, and involved in crafts (37 percent, 13 percent, and 12 percent, respectively)—were higher than those of their Irish counterparts (representing 26 percent, 5 percent and 11 percent, respectively). More importantly, French-Canadian men in the cotton textile industry earned more than their Irish counterparts. Between 1908 and 1909, their weekly wages averaged $9.77 a week, outstripping those of Irish workers ($9.70) for the first time, though only by a few cents.[30]

The shift upward among Lowell's French-Canadian male workers became clearer when compared to the occupational status occupied by more recent arrivals from Southern and Eastern Europe. Contrary to the significant decrease in the proportion of unskilled workers among French-Canadian men (from one in four in 1910 to one in six in 1920), the proportion of this category remained high among Greek (one in four in both years) and Portuguese male workers (one in five in 1910 and two in five in 1920).[31] Was this possibly because of the fact that the labour pool of early-twentieth-century Lowell, lacking any notable population of black workers, perhaps placed Greeks and Portuguese against French Canadians? Could such articulation of Lowell's socioeconomic hierarchy based on ethnicity be comparable to the experiences of Irish workers elsewhere who had defended their "wages of whiteness" against black workers in the second half of the nineteenth century?[32] In ways similar to Irish workers, one might argue, French-Canadian male workers in early-twentieth-century Lowell were making important progress up the wage scale of whiteness or Americanness, although their upward mobility was largely limited to manual sectors.

However, evidence that supports any further analogy of French Canadians with Irish workers (and "in-between people," who hailed mostly from Southern and Eastern Europe), is thin. Admittedly, Lowell's French-Canadian experience is too limited in time and geography to evaluate the diversity and complexity of the discussion of male immigrants belonging to a variety of ethnic groups, who reshaped themselves into a racially conscious component of the American working class.[33] One thing is clear: French-Canadian men's occupational advancement and their sense of self, as we shall discuss in the following pages, suggest that working-class French-Canadian men perceived their upward socioeconomic mobility not so much as a progress up the scale of a racial hierarchy or toward a greater proximity to becoming (white) American workers. Rather, their concern was more narrowly focused on a sense of themselves as fathers and husbands, or the French-Canadian version of masculinity, a large part of which hinged on men's capacity to provide for their families.

This does not preclude voices of ethnic leaders, as discussed earlier, who urged their community to shed the role of "producers of mill workers." Such admonitions indicate the deliberate efforts being made to distinguish French-Canadian people from the Greek, Portuguese, Lithuanian, and Turkish arrivals of recent date, who made up a growing proportion of the city's factory workforce. They also suggest that the writer of the French-Canadian newspaper article learned the existing social hierarchy in Lowell factories, according to which newcomers from Southern and Eastern Europe were placed at the bottom of the ethnically segmented labour markets. But that even these remarks were free of any reference to racial codification—such that French Canadians would be identified as white American workers—suggests important differences that distinguished the experience of French-Canadian men from that of Irish or "in-between people." According to scholars such as Barrett and Roediger, for these Europeans of old and new immigrant waves, the notion of "whiteness" offers adequate explanation for the benefit derived from their becoming white American workers. In contrast, Timothy J. Meagher has argued in his study of a neighbouring city of Worcester, Massachusetts that the local labour market of that city, with a tiny Chinese population and a small number of African Americans, did not offer to the same extent the advantages of whiteness and of a white identity to the city's Irish Americans as did cities such as San Francisco, St. Louis, and New York.[34] In a similar vein, one may argue that the absence of significant numbers of nonwhite "others" in Lowell, who could be imagined as veritable competitors of French Canadians, was among the factors that led to their distinct experience. It follows, then, that a "racial trap" does not appear to have caught—or perhaps, it did not even exist for—Lowell's French Canadians in the early twentieth century. For those workers, being able to earn higher wages implied little progress toward the status of American-ness or a march toward "becoming white." For the articulate elite, it represented above all a way to honour the strength of the "French-Canadian race," as they referred to themselves, rather than a way to attain the prize of being viewed as white American workers.

While the majority of working-class families continued to send their fathers, sons, nephews, and uncles to the mill regardless of the exhortations of the ethnic elite, the urge to avoid millwork came from elsewhere. A small number of men and women in French-Canadian working families refused work at the textile factories. As Henry Paradis's father said to Paradis's mother: "I'll make sure that our children do not go to work in the mill."[35] Having worked at the Suffolk Mill for forty-eight years, the elder Paradis must have known the difficulties and injustices commonly experienced while working at a textile factory. This father's opposition ended in vain, however, when with few alternatives for earning wages, Henry took a job at a mill.

In the case of Hubert LaFleur, the injury of his father had a greater impact on his decision to leave his job at the mill. The elder LaFleur was a mule spinner in the Shaw Hosiery. He tended a spinning machine about 80 centimetres, or 2.5 feet, in length with beams running on open tracks. He would watch the frame, do his work quickly and pull out. One day, he was a fraction of a second late and was caught between the mule frames. The beams stabbed into his body, leaving him covered in bruises. "There wasn't an inch of his body that wasn't black and blue. [...] We never thought that my father would live because he stopped both sides of the machine with his body," LaFleur explained. "He suffered blue murder. I'll always remember that."[36]

LaFleur's father survived the accident, however. What saved him was his own body. His father, being a big man weighing about 100 kilograms, or 220 pounds, could withstand the pressure and the beams did not completely pierce through his body. What was more, he returned to work after the injury. "That's all he ever done, you know. Because he was a mule-spinner all his life," said LaFleur.[37]

The gravity of his father's accident, along with the lack of compensation he received from the mill, added to LaFleur's dislike of the millwork. He had been working at the mill since the age of fourteen, since he did not want to go to school and his father told him: "You're going to work." He began working at a bobbin shop and then moved to the Hamilton mills for a year or so. He was a bobbin-boy and yarn boy, an "errands boy" who set in the bobbins and took them off when they were filled. At seventeen, shortly after his father's accident, LaFleur quit the mill. "There was no future; I didn't care for it. I didn't like the smell and the heat. It was awful warm," he recalled. He was lucky, however, because he had an uncle, Jack Pomerleau, who worked as an auto mechanic and taught LaFleur the trade. LaFleur respected him for that. "He was a crackerjack mechanic. [...] A very clever man." LaFleur eventually found a job in the Depot Cash Market as a mechanic and liked it. "As a mechanic," he proudly stated, "I never lost a day's work in my life."[38]

White-Collar and Supervisory Workers

Despite the working-class profile of the majority of Lowell's French-Canadian men, a significant minority were white-collar workers, small entrepreneurs, and professionals. Irené Beauregard, a thirty-two-year-old clerk at American Express, was one of them.[39] Many, like Irené, occupied lower-level, semi-skilled positions of white-collar jobs, such as salesmen, clerks, watchmen, and police officers. A small number were in the upper echelon of the white-collar world, working as foremen, second hands, inspectors, managers, or teachers, all of which required a comparatively high degree of responsibility, knowledge, and skills.[40] In 1920, the proportion of French-Canadian men in the upper echelons of white-collar jobs and professions grew significantly from the level recorded a decade earlier, signalling another sign of the occupational progress made by this group.

Phillip Cinqmars was one of the small but growing minority of Lowell's French-Canadian men working as an upper-level white-collar worker. In 1881, young Phillip had migrated with his Canadian-born parents to Lowell. Forty years later, he was working as a second hand, making up a privileged segment of the French-Canadian workforce. His oldest son, Robert, twenty-four, was also working in a cotton factory as a weaver. Neither his forty-three-year-old wife, Gertrude, nor his three other sons aged between five and eleven, listed any occupation. Phillip's father-in-law, a seventy-four-year-old widower, worked as a machinist and likely contributed additional earnings to the household.[41] The wages of three male workers at skilled and semi-supervisory levels must have assured a degree of financial stability to Phillip's household.

Finally, a very small number held the supervisory position of foreman, one of the highest positions French-Canadian men could achieve within a textile factory. Alfred Clément and Joseph Poirier were two of those fortunate few. Alfred, forty-seven years old, was employed at a shoe shop and Joseph, fifty-seven years old, at a tannery. Both were Massachusetts-born sons of Canadian parents. They must have supported their households with comparatively little worry.[42]

Independent Shopkeepers and Professionals

One of the alternatives to the harsh realities of wage work for French-Canadian men was to run a business of their own catering to the needs of their neighbours and co-ethnics. A small nucleus of independent shopkeepers and professionals made up the middle-class elite of the French-Canadian community in Lowell.[43] The ethnic *petite bourgeoisie* was mostly composed of owners of small businesses (such as fruit and vegetable stores, candy stores, butcher shops, bakeries, barbers, clothiers, and jewelers). Also included in the group were building contractors (including wood yard owners and carpenters), boardinghouse and restaurant owners, and a very small number of professionals (such as physicians and pharmacists). Although small in number, the range of services they offered placed these independent businesses and trades at the core of everyday life of the French-Canadian (and other) migrants in the city. Yvonne Lagassé vividly describes the variety of small stores in Little Canada.

> The stores, there were a lot! We didn't have to go downtown when we needed something. First, I will start with Cheever Street. [...] There was Mademoiselle Coutu who ran a beauty salon, after that, there was Monsieur Racette who had a store, who kept candy store. After that, there came a meat shop. Later, it became a Monsieur Parent who bought that. After that, yet another Racette who had a meat shop. After that came Monsieur Mayotte who had a bakery, who baked bread and, Saturday evening, cooked beans. And then, there were Mademoiselle Dubois, Mademoiselle Rita

Dubois, who is today Madame Brunelle. And after that, Albert Sawyer. [...] After that, on the other side of the street, there was a Madame Laurent who had a shop. Before her, it was Monsieur Millette [...] (we called him "Little Heart Millette") who had another small candy store. After that, we had a shoe repairer shop, a Monsieur Ouellette. After that, the pharmacy Toupin at the corner of Aiken Street and Cheever Street.[44]

Business offered Lowell's French-Canadian migrants a far more attractive option than blue-collar work. Shop owners escaped the pressures of industrial work in the textile factories and enjoyed a sense of autonomy. Therefore, a move from labourer or textile worker to small business owner represented an important step for migrants and their descendants.[45] Nonetheless, maintaining a store was demanding work. For instance, bakeries in Little Canada, which sold cooked beans as well as bread, began their preparations at four o'clock in the morning.[46] In addition to the long hours of exhausting work, storeowners constantly faced the risk of financial ruin by extending credit to hard-pressed clients. Lagassé recalls a bakery on Ward Street:

> On the other side of the street, on the left, was the good Monsieur—here comes Monsieur Langlois! He was generous, really generous. You know in those days, people were paid Saturday noon—at noon, ten to noon, a quarter to noon. People in the grocery stores did not have money on hand like today. They bought by credit. There was a book. They noted what they bought. They marked it in a book. At the end of the week, people went to pay. There were a lot of people who did not work at times. They gave, two, three dollars on their bill. Monsieur Langlois never said a word. His wife sometimes didn't like that. He said, "Oh, they will pay us!" I tell you that Monsieur Langlois, oh, he was generous![47]

Langlois' charity may well have remained within the bounds of financial prudence. Still, Langlois, like many other small business owners, had to live with the threat of failure.

Despite the constant risk of bankruptcy, these small shop owners—many of whom were of French-Canadian descent, but also including those who owned neighbouring businesses such as Jewish stores and Chinese laundries—nurtured a sense of community with their clientele. Lagassé warmly remembers some of the storeowners, such as Madame Coutu who sold hats made to order ("She was superb!"), and Monsieur Landry, the owner of a candy store, who walked with a cane because he was paralyzed in both of his legs. His daughter worked with him in his shop. They occasionally made "grab bags," little bags in which they threw three or four candies, twisted at the top, and sold for a penny.[48]

The proportion of independent shopkeepers and professionals dwindled both among French-Canadian and Irish men during the period under study (see Tables 13 and 14). In 1910, 7 percent of French-Canadian male workers in Lowell were in this category, compared to 6 percent and 10 percent, respectively,

Figure 5. Barber shops were among the numerous small businesses springing up in Little Canada during the 1910s. (Courtesy of Lowell Historical Society.)

for their Irish and American counterparts. By 1920, the proportion of French Canadians in this category declined to 4 percent, that of the Irish to 5 percent, while the proportion of Americans increased to 14 percent.

Curiously, the decrease in the number of French-Canadian small businesses occurred at about the same time as the proportion of Greek and Portuguese shopkeepers increased. In 1920, a relatively large proportion (12 percent) of Greeks worked as independent shopkeepers and businessmen, up from 6 percent a decade earlier (Tables 13 and 14). Michael Katranes was one of them. The thirty-nine-year-old migrated to the U.S. in 1907. Three years later, he was listed as running a coffeehouse, "a very inexpensive club house" for Greek men in the city. They would frequent this meeting place to play cards, smoke their narghile, or "hubble-bubble," discuss Greek politics, and exchange news from home as well as information about jobs in the city and elsewhere. In the words of Nicholas Georgoulis, "it was just a place for the guys to hang out" and he added with a laugh, "[It was] all men! Oh yes. Never saw a female in there."[49]

Figure 6. J.G. Roche Grocery Store (Portuguese), on Charles Street, 1907. (Courtesy of Lowell Historical Society.)

What explains the decline in the proportion of independent shopkeepers among French-Canadian men? Business failures must have been an important cause but this may not be the only reason. It may have reflected the lack of stability or permanence of the ethnic *bourgeoisie*, who was not exactly

108 • GENDERED PASSAGES •

Figure 7. A saloon owner and his employees provide another example of an independent business in Lowell, ca. 1900. (Courtesy of Lowell Historical Society, Lowell Museum Collection.)

representative of the "middle-class" in the contemporary sense, but, rather, was a group of people who might easily make the transition between these independent occupations and industrial or white-collar jobs by changing course in either direction. Undoubtedly, one moved from business ownership to textile work more unwillingly than one did in the opposite direction. Nevertheless, conjunctural factors—such as the World War I boom, which created a high demand for labour power and concomitantly, a series of wage increases—may have made this sort of interchangeability less overwhelming. At times these people might have run bakeries and grocery stores, while at other times, such as during economic expansion, a significant number would have gone into the factories. When the factories began to downsize or close down their operations, some might have returned to their small businesses.

Another, more likely scenario is that, forced by bankruptcy or other difficulties, a fraction of those who had been working as independent businessmen or shopkeepers abandoned their businesses and then either left the city or remained there and became clerks or salesmen in shops run by others. In turn-of-the-century Fall River, Massachusetts, prospective small business owners among French Canadians commonly worked as employees for other shop owners.[50] Many did so in order to save money and to learn the trade before they opened a business of their own. When faced with financial difficulties, former shop owners in Lowell might return to this practice, in hopes of getting by and possibly accumulating enough money to repurchase one's business when things improved.

Virginia Yans-McLaughlin has observed yet another strategy employed in early-twentieth-century New York City. In most small workshops of the Jewish garment industry, which required little capital investment, artisan bosses worked beside their employees, and, more often than not, "the boss himself had just climbed out of the ranks of wage labour and could easily slide back to his former status."[51] In contemporary Lowell, few of the self-employed would likely have accepted such changes. This is because, unlike the small-scale garment shops where a number of New York Jews worked, the large-scale production of Lowell's textile and other industries drew a social divide, by no means fixed but clearly marked nonetheless, between the ethnic *petite bourgeoisie* and the majority of working-class compatriots. Such a division would create a sense of pride amongst the privileged class of business owners and would in turn limit their occupational interchangeability within the non-manual, white-collar sectors.

The Lowest Paid Workers

Despite overall improvements in occupational standing, the majority of Lowell's French-Canadian men were unable to earn enough to support their families. An examination of the weekly wages, annual incomes, and costs of living during this period reveals the harsh reality faced by working-class families in Lowell. Furthermore, with chronic unemployment and dangerous working conditions, these workers and their families constantly faced the threat of suddenly losing what meagre wages they received.

Cotton textile workers were among the lowest paid workers despite their long working hours. According to Shirley Zebroski, in 1900, a textile operative brought home $0.10 an hour on average while other manufacturing workers earned $0.25 an hour (location unspecified). In 1903, the average workweek in all manufacturing industries was fifty-seven hours, compared to an average of sixty-two hours in the cotton factories.[52] Moreover, because of the irregularity of employment at the textile factories, a cotton manufacturing operative could expect to work only nine months a year, perhaps a few weeks more if he or she was lucky.[53] The Immigration Commission Report statistically confirms the difficulty of keeping regular employment in the cotton industry. A little less than two thirds (65 percent) of French-Canadian adult male workers (sixteen years of age and over) surveyed in 1908-1909 found employment for twelve months of the year. Compared to male workers of other ethnic/migrant groups, however, French-Canadian men were better able to keep their jobs year-round. About one half of American male workers born in the U.S. to U.S.-born fathers (52 percent) and the Irish (45 percent), and about one third of the Portuguese (33 percent) and the Greek (32 percent) men worked year-round. The figures for female workers were even lower. Among them, French-Canadian women were more regularly employed than any other group, with 57 percent having worked twelve months in a year. The U.S.-born working women of American-born fathers ranked second (56 percent), closely followed by the Irish (54 percent) and the Greek (40 percent). Only one percent of the Portuguese-born women reported having worked twelve months.[54] For women, a combination of household need, workers' skill level, and their seniority in the textile factories likely shaped the tenure of their job year-round.

Wages for textile workers fluctuated frequently. Although available data does not allow one to observe fluctuations in the weekly wages of male textile workers, evidence from the Boott Cotton Mill gives a glimpse of the frequent rises and falls in workers' earnings over a period of less than two decades. In June 1907, for instance, wages earned by those working in the carding sector rose from $11.25 to $11.80 per week for the one fixer, from $10.50 to $11 each for the two grinders, while most of the other eighteen carding workers earned between $5.35 and $6.75 after raises of about $0.25 each. Nine months later, in March 1908, wages fell to levels even lower than before the 1907 increase and remained low until as late as 1910. In neighbouring textile cities, such as Lawrence and Fall River, the average weekly wages of operatives were set no higher in 1911 than they had been in 1893, despite the increase in both productivity levels and the cost of living over the decade.[55]

A series of wage increases began in 1912 that accelerated during the following year. World War I created a demand for increased production and resulted in labour shortages in the textile industry on the American side of the Atlantic. This led to further wage increases in the textile factories. In 1916 and 1917, wages rose twice in the Boott factories each year. After four 10-percent raises in these two years, the wage increases reached their highest levels. The intense competition for labour, steady inflation, and flow of government orders sustained this upswing in earnings until early 1920. Later that year, as the national economy was strained once again, a 23-percent pay reduction was imposed across the board, and this was accompanied by a 25-percent cut in output. The wage cuts continued into the 1920s, with a 20-percent cut being imposed in many Massachusetts factories. By the end of 1924, weekly rates were estimated at $21.63 for spinners, $25.42 for doffers, $22.42-$25.20 for weavers, and $32.81 for loomfixers.[56]

Robert Layer's study of the annual incomes earned by cotton manufacturing operatives in northern New England also provides a similar estimate. According to his study, during the period prior to World War I, the annual earnings of mill workers, making no distinction as to their place of origin, reached their highest level ($397.47 in 1907) before falling into a lengthy period of gradual decrease that lasted until early 1912. Then, later in the same year, earnings took an upward turn. In 1913, just before the war broke out, they reached their highest level($409.26), although according to the real annual earnings index as estimated by Layer, the ratio between average annual earnings and cost of living did not recover the level reached in 1907 (179.2). A worker's real wages remained below that figure throughout the years just prior to World War I.[57]

It must be underlined that these weekly wages were simply an estimate based on average piece-rate earnings, a standard that regulated nearly all measurable jobs in the Lowell textile factories for a long time.[58] The weekly wages and annual incomes calculated above, therefore, do not take into account any unexpected factors such as fines for imperfect products. These penalties were subtracted from the weekly earnings of the workers, uncompensated sick leaves, or the high rates of temporary or seasonal unemployment regularly endured by textile workers.

In 1913, the average annual income of cotton mill workers in Lowell was estimated at $454. In comparison to other Massachusetts cities, this was a fair amount, although well below the average of $625 earned by boot and shoe workers, or the $692 earned by machine shop workers.[59] At about the same time, the Immigration Commission reported an annual average income of $498 for a French-Canadian married man working in the textile industry in Lowell. Again, this average was slightly higher than that of his Irish counterpart, which was estimated at $479 a year.[60]

Looking into the relationship between the income of French-Canadian families and the cost of living lays bare the difficulties in remaining above the poverty line. The average annual earnings of mill workers were far below the estimated minimum cost of living required to sustain a family. For example, economic historian Scott Nearing's national estimation shows that for a couple with three children, an income of between $768 and $1,449 was necessary to maintain a decent standard of living in 1911.[61] In the same year, the U.S. government calculated the minimum cost of living to be between $691 and $732, "depending on the nationality of the families."[62] During the war years, the difference between the minimum cost of living and the average wage had to be made up by work performed by members of the family other than the male household head, or, at times, by the latter taking a second or even third job. When the shortfall could not be filled, families had to live on the verge of poverty.

Even with two or more wage earners, working-class families faced difficulties in making ends meet because of the low wages and the ever-increasing cost of living. Cycles of inflation sharply swelled the prices of commodities and forced working families to stretch their already tight budgets even further. Their grievances gave rise to special legislation introduced by the State of Massachusetts, followed by the creation of a commission on the cost of living. The results of the commission's inquiries, however, only statistically confirmed the harsh reality of working-class life that most already knew all too well. Of all consumer products, the price of food had risen the fastest. By 1908, average food prices had exceeded the 1880-99 levels by 20 percent. Prices of staples such as eggs, bread, and milk increased from 25 to as much as 45 percent during the decade, while meat prices increased more than 90 percent.[63]

In his study, *The Record of a City* (1911), George F. Kenngott examined the family budgets of 287 working-class families in Lowell. Sampled households include a variety of ethnic origins ranging from French-Canadian, Irish, Greek, and Austrian-Polish to American. Their budgets confirmed the financial difficulties experienced by working families who represented, in Kenngott's words, "the respectable, sober, industrious, and thrifty wage earners of Lowell."[64]

One can read on Table 17 a budget of a French-Canadian box maker's family (name unknown). Being the only wage earner in the family, the box maker supported his wife and two small children (aged five months and two years, respectively) with his weekly wage of $7.25. They lived in a large tenement house occupied by families of different migrant groups. The expenditures for provisions, rent, light, and heat amounted to a little less than $6.00 a week, leaving only $1.30 for clothing, medical expenses, or to provide a cushion against sudden and frequent lay-offs. Clearly, this family did not live far from the edge of destitution.[65]

Unlike the box maker's family, when a family had one or more children older than fourteen years who earned wages and contributed to the household, the family was, in general, much better off. This was not the case for a family headed by an unskilled worker, however. A family of one French-Canadian day labourer had a total of eleven people living at home. The husband earned $7.00 a week and his wife stayed home. Of nine children, ranging in age from one-and-half to twenty years old, two worked, earning a total of $11.00 a week. This family lived in an apartment with five rooms including a kitchen. Their expenses for one week in November included $9.73 for food, $1.24 for light and heat, and $2.75 for rent, amounting to $13.72. The family had as little as $0.30 to spend on other expenses.[66]

In another French-Canadian family, the husband was working as a blacksmith's "helper," or assistant, bringing home a weekly wage of $8.00. The

Table 17. Household Budgets of Selected French-Canadian Families in Lowell

	Box maker's family	Labourer's family	Blacksmith's helper's family
Food	$3.34	$9.73	$11.44
Fuel and light	$0.61	$1.24	$1.16
Rent	$2.00	$2.75	$1.25
Total	$5.95	$13.72	$13.85

Sources: Produced by the author. Drawn from the data in George Frederick Kenngott, *The Record of a City: A Social Survey of Lowell* (New York: The Macmillan Company, 1910), 114-19.

wife stayed at home, while of the eleven children aged two to eighteen, four earned wages totaling $29.00. This family of thirteen, living in a four-room apartment (including the kitchen) spent on provisions ($11.44), heat and light ($1.16), and rent ($1.25) a total of $13.85 every week. With $22.15 remaining at the end of the week, this family must have enjoyed comforts that other families could not afford.[67] They had over $15.00 to spend on other expenses such as clothing, furniture, and miscellaneous other needs. Clearly, the most vulnerable sector of the population consisted of families with small children who relied on only one major source of income, while a household with a larger number of workers, be they offspring (many of whom were adult children living with their parents) or spouses, was more secure.[68]

The pre-war difficulties faced by the working-class families Kenngott studied only worsened over the war years and thereafter. In 1918, Lowell saw a brief period of prosperity due to war-related demands that lowered unemployment rates while boosting wages in all industries. In cotton manufacturing, the average hourly wage rose from $0.15 in 1914 to $0.16 in 1916, and, by the beginning of 1918, had jumped to $0.27. These wage hikes were offset by an even higher rise in the cost of living, however. Furthermore, as the stable output of civilian goods and the increase in purchasing power created an inflationary spiral, real wages just barely kept pace with the cost of living.[69]

Layoffs, Turnover, and Labour Inactivism

In addition to the difficulties in making ends meet, Lowell's male and female workers and their families constantly faced job instability and dangerous working conditions. Textile cities were notorious for their high unemployment rates even in good years, and for severe unemployment problems during depressions.[70] In the period from 1900 to 1920, about 20 percent of the workforce was laid off each year.[71] In 1908, when the Lowell factories reduced their production by 20 percent for two months, this entailed a reduction in employment on a similar scale. Once World War I was over, the demand for textile goods dropped substantially. As a result, competition for a smaller share of the market intensified, leading some cotton textile manufacturers to relocate to the South, where the immediate advantages of child labour, long working hours, and geographical proximity to the sources of raw materials and coal could be gained.[72] Other firms simply cut down on the scale of production. In 1920, in the midst of the decline of the Northern industry, the Boott Manufacturing factories ran on a three-day weekly schedule. They closed for an extended period the following year, and in the spring of 1924, "when the business was dull," they only operated one or two days a week. Other factories generally operated at about one half to three quarters of their total capacity.[73] Throughout this post-war recession, business fluctuations made it more economical to reduce or suspend operations. In the interest of economic cuts, workers were simply laid off without any provision for unemployment compensation.

Even without imposed layoffs, a large number of workers left their employment. Historian Laurence Gross observed that with few other means of expressing discontent, quitting became a statement against oppressive working conditions in many factories.[74] The Boott cotton textile factories consistently lost disgruntled workers at a rate exceeding that of other textile factories. An average of 63 percent of workers left the job in 1913-14, despite the recession, and 123 percent—a figure resulting from the fact that the factory had to replace workers in a given position more than once during the period of time in question—walked out the following year when a large labour shortage made other employment alternatives available.[75] In 1916, three quarters of the weavers in the Boott Mill left in six months, and two hundred fifty out of approximately three hundred fifty spinners and spoolers were listed as "fleeing." In addition, one third to one half of the office workers, and forty-one men at the level of second hand or above, quit the Boott Mill between 1914 and 1916.[76] One former female mill worker discussed the facility of leaving one job to find another. She stated: "If you didn't like the job here, you could go next door." "You could come out of one factory and walk into the other one and get hired."[77] Although no comparable account is available among male workers, turnover rates were particularly high among skilled workers, who were predominantly male, and one may thus safely suggest that male workers were generally in a better position to take a stand against exploitation this way.

A more effective way for workers to express their dissatisfaction would have been to strike.[78] But in Lowell, where the organizational power of textile workers remained weak, workers had little bargaining power with which to confront management.[79] In the cotton textile factories, unions existed only among certain skilled workers, such as mule spinners, slashers, weavers, loomfixers, and firemen.[80] Even with these craft unions, Lowell lagged far behind other neighbouring textile centres such as Fall River, New Bedford, and Lawrence in its degree of union organization.[81] Explanations for the limited level of labour activism in Lowell vary, but scholars agree on one point: production of coarse cotton cloth in Lowell required a greater number of easily replaceable semi- and unskilled workers, as opposed to the more specialized products made in neighbouring textile cities. Coupled with a dearth among French-Canadian and

Irish workers of the political radicalism to which Franco-Belgian, Jewish, and Italian workers in the neighbouring cities had been accustomed, the particular composition of Lowell's textile workers created far less fertile ground for their radicalism to take root in that city.[82] One migrant daughter describes her father as too quiet a man to get involved in strikes. She also remembers a strike at the Merrimack, which ended in vain. "We got nowhere," she recounts, "There was no organization. No leadership." And she adds, "Half a loaf is better than none; that was their attitude."[83]

And so, in 1903, when textile workers in Lowell fought for the city's only general strike, the majority of French Canadians did not participate. Instead, many left the city when its factories shut down for an indefinite period, and headed for Canada or elsewhere in search of work. A Lowell newspaper reported that in the first days of April, immediately after the strike hit the city, over two hundred trunks were reportedly checked for operatives returning to Canada on board the two Canadian trains a day. In the first ten days of that month, one thousand two hundred trunks filled the train for departing Canadians; two thirds of these bound for Canada.[84]

It comes as little surprise then, that when asked about how often they participated in union activities, Lowell's many French-Canadian textile mill workers simply stated "never." The contemporary observer George Kenngott endorsed such a state of labour inactivism among French Canadians as he described the city as "remarkably free of labour disputes."[85] True, such a statement overlooked some important strikes such as those occurring in 1900, when weavers in the Bigelow Carpet Company and dyers in the Hamilton Manufacturing Company fought against objectionable foremen as is discussed below, but the management exploited divisions among workers that ran along linguistic and ethnic lines by injecting scab workers specifically hired to replace strikers and thereby undermine the potential gains the workers may have attained in each occasion.

Not infrequently, however, scabs turned into strikers. *L'Étoile de Lowell* reported that in September of 1900, four hundred male print workers at the Merrimack Manufacturing Company refused to work overtime unless they were paid "time and a quarter." The management called Greeks in to replace the strikers. Shortly after, the strike spread to other departments as two hundred employees, mostly women, in the packing department walked out in sympathy for the strikers. The company then asked the mayor to intervene and send the municipal police to escort the Greek workers to and from the mill. The mayor refused. Two days later, two hundred Greeks joined the strikers.[86]

Although workers' radicalism took some prominent form in 1900s and early 1910s Lowell, it failed to bring fruitful results to the city unlike in

Lawrence or other cities. In 1903, the city's textile workers started their first and only general strike, demanding a 10 percent increase in wages. But after nine months of struggle, the strike ended unsuccessfully.[87] The labour activism of Lowell workers pales further when compared to the strong militancy and class-consciousness manifested in the 1912 Bread and Roses Strike in Lawrence. There, men and women demanded "fair days wages," clean water, proper health care, decent housing, schools, and even time "which belonged to us [the workers]."[88] In the aftermath of the 1912 strike, Lowell cotton textile workers fought for three months, which compelled the city's textile corporations to announce a wage hike in order to "equalize Lowell and Lawrence standards." But the result was another disappointment. The management's final offer for a raise was significantly smaller than the 10-percent increase won in Lawrence and elsewhere in New England.[89] Moreover, the 1912 strike in Lowell remained within the cotton textile industry, failing to involve workers outside that industry. A woolen mill worker stated: "I thought they [the cotton mill workers] should get a little more break, you know. They wasn't given them a break."[90] While such words expressed the weaver's sympathy toward the strikers of the cotton mill, they also underline the perceived difference in working conditions between "them" (the cotton workers) and the woolen textile workers, who were more highly skilled than cotton workers in general—a perception that arguably added to the difficulty of building coalitions, rather than facilitating them, among textile workers in Lowell.

Skills, Wages, and the Masculinity of French-Canadian Workers

Although many French-Canadian men and women worked side by side, a distinct logic that dictated the allocation of wages, job opportunities, and the responsibilities of male household heads set the world of male workers apart from the worlds of younger men, boys, and women. Not only did French-Canadian men have a wider variety of occupations available to them than their female counterparts, but they also benefited from greater chances of receiving promotions and pay increases. One female cloth inspector, one of the highest positions women could reach in the textile factories at the time, pointed out that men went into weaving with the idea of getting a job in loom-fixing, slashing, or entering the machine shop. "That [weaving] was their stepping stone to something else. It was almost like a career ladder, up the ladder, you know," she stated. Most female weavers, in contrast, remained weavers because they didn't have "anywhere else to go."[91]

Mary Blewett has observed that the job hierarchy in the textile mill was constructed not only in gender specific manners but that it was also ethnically determined. One could begin working as a bobbin-boy or a filling hand and move up to skilled work such as fixing if one were French Canadian, and even to a position of foreman, if one were Lancashire English or Irish American.[92] Arthur Morrissette was one of many French-Canadian workers who aspired for a position as a loomfixer, a big shot on the factory floor. He began working as a battery boy. After a few months, he went into weaving for another four or five months, and then worked as a changeover man. From this work, he learned how to fix the looms and, eventually, he became a loomfixer. Although his promotion depended on his acquisition of skill, equally if not more, important were his connections and his persistence in striving to achieve the position. Morrissette nagged his overseer constantly each time he saw him. He would say: "When the heck am I going to get on fixing?" or "Hey, I'm due, ain't I?" The boss would respond: "Not yet," or "You've got to learn a little more."[93] Morrissette's personal connection with the boss—the latter was a neighbour and a brother of Morrissette's good friend—likely helped Morrissette speak to the boss with such directness. While Morrissette's straightforwardness was hardly representative, it nevertheless suggests his eagerness to achieve the position of loomfixer as quickly as possible, and in that sense, he was not atypical among contemporary French-Canadian men.

If wages were among the factors that made loom-fixing one of the most desirable jobs for French-Canadian men on the factory floor, that was only part of the attraction. Many aspired to become fixers because it gave them a sense of control over their work and that of others. Referring to his work as a loomfixer, Arthur Morrissette says: "Any machine that runs for twenty-four hours a day is bound to give up. Those pickers sticks [sic], things wear down." Therefore, a fixer checked a machine that a weaver reported as having a problem. As the troubled weaver hailed a fixer, he would go to see the problem immediately. Alternatively, he could also say: "Well, I'm sorry, there's two ahead of you," and make the weaver wait for her or his turn. Moreover, the fixer could decide how much time to spend performing each repair job. He could carefully check the machine that a weaver claimed to have a problem, or he could glance quickly at it and walk away. Because weavers, a large part of whom were female, were paid based on piece work, they would get nervous or distressed if they had to wait for two or three machines that would stop for hours on any given day. They would be losing money. They would call a fixer in desperation, "Come on, come on, it's my turn, it's my turn."[94] The tensions between male fixers and women workers is best captured by one fixer who remembers seeing a weaver crying in anguish because she was kept waiting, her machine kept breaking, and she was not making any money at all for the day.[95]

At times, weavers gave a hard time to fixers they did not like. If a fixer did not find anything wrong with the machine, he would start it back up and leave. That would irritate the weaver because the fixer did not fix the problem. If the machine kept having problems, the weaver would call the fixer repeatedly and keep him going back to the same loom. In order to avoid such situations, one fixer made it a rule to stay on one loom as long as time allowed. He said: "I would stay on that loom for about fifteen or twenty minutes. Look at it run, and if it's all right, I'd go away and do my other jobs, then I'd come back to it. You've got to find it, what causes the problem."[96]

Power and autonomy inherent to the job of loom-fixing, therefore, confirm Blewett's observation that acquiring a skill was synonymous with achieving a respectable manhood.[97] But the reality for French-Canadian male textile workers in early-twentieth-century Lowell was that the fixers remained a privileged few and that the majority worked as semi-skilled or as skilled workers doing jobs other than fixing, such as weaving, spinning, slashing, spooling, warping, or working as change-over men. The question then arises as to what work meant to those French-Canadian male workers whose jobs lacked the advantages, such as the improved wage scale and autonomy, that were enjoyed by fixers.

The evidence that would allow us to draw a conclusive answer to this question is thin. However, it is likely that, partly in an effort to shed off the fear of being defined as a failure, many French-Canadian men would create a logic of their own that allowed them to attain a certain sense of themselves in ways distinct from their elite co-ethnic workers in Lowell and U.S.-born or -raised colleagues elsewhere.[98] On this issue, Alice Kessler-Harris has pointed out a triangle relation of higher skill, wages, and responsibilities that characterized the jobs of male workers at the Hawthorne Works factories in 1920s Chicago. They were attached to what they called "getting ahead," or advancement at work, by which they expected their wages, skill sets, and responsibilities to progress in lock step. Any promotion that failed to assure a wage increase was considered unfair. At the same time, a relatively good wage, if tied to a position that remained stationary, "signaled poor promotion prospects." Put simply, "men associated skill and satisfaction at work with recognition accompanied by higher pay" and a prospect of further advancement. Few women, by contrast, could dream of climbing the ladder of job hierarchy through promotions, the acquisition of new skills, or connections. As a result, they invested little in the job itself as a key to improving their lives—materially and morally—but instead focused exclusively on the advantages of greater income.[99]

Figure 8. Male workers in one of the spinning rooms at the Merrimack Manufacturing. Note the presence of a number of young boys, ca. 1900. (Courtesy of Lowell Historical Society, Lowell Museum Collection.)

French-Canadian male textile workers in early-twentieth-century Lowell bore some similarities to the male workers at the Hawthorne in 1920s Chicago. Like the male workers at the Hawthorne who were attached to the idea of "getting ahead," Arthur Morrissette and many other French-Canadian workers in early-twentieth-century Lowell looked to achieve the position of loomfixer, embodying a triangle of skill, higher wages, and responsibility. Unlike the male workers at the Hawthorne, however, the correlation between skill, income, and status did not present "natural order of things"[100] for the majority of French-Canadian workers. They did not take it for granted that the promotion on the occupational hierarchy was open to everyone. The fact that only a small number could become loomfixers, not to mention the even more prestigious positions of second hands and foremen, meant that the majority who fell below this level of aspiration had to create their own measure of success and satisfaction.

The story of Hubert Lafleur's injured father suggests that one way to do so was to look at one's work through the lens of a male immigrant manual worker, whose worth was arguably equated with his strength to withstand physically taxing working conditions, and to do so even after incurring serious, life-threatening injuries. In other words, mill workers like Lafleur "carried scars as badges of their experience." It is also an example of their strength and resiliency.[101] Another way might be to attach less importance to the triangle of skill, wage, and promotion than to the amount of wages in a way comparable to that employed by female workers—at the Hawthorne or elsewhere—whose occupational prospects were blocked from the beginning. For these female workers, their wages, at least partly, symbolized their worth as responsible daughters or resourceful wives who embodied the working-class immigrant version of womanhood. Similarly, French-Canadian male workers viewed their weekly wages as an indication of their manly strength and thus, as a part of the very foundation of their masculinity and identity.

If wages were central in highlighting French-Canadian male workers' senses of their own masculinity, another set of factors, including everyday family practices and religious rituals, further illuminates men's roles as fathers and husbands. French-Canadian families valued respect and order, as determined by a familial and social hierarchy within which husbands and fathers were placed at the top of the family. Children, on the other hand, were expected to obey and help their parents in every way they could. Arthur Morrissette delivered a hot dinner to his father, a knitter at the Hub Hosiery, when he was ten or eleven years of age. He recalls later his regular errands to the mill during an hour's lunch break from school that amounted to twice or three times a week. As Morrissette put it: "You could not say no to your parents."[102] His words may be imbued with a bit of exaggeration and nostalgia, but regular visits to the mill to perform this and other errands provided him with ample occasions to witness the hard work his father performed, breathe the hot and humid air mixed with floating lint, and smell the sweat and grease in a room filled with ear-piercing noises and vibration. While a glance at these conditions could deter him and many other children from wanting to become mill workers,[103] the same view, perhaps more than any abstract dictate, arguably instilled in the mind of the young boy greater respect for the strength and authority of his father.

In addition to their daily and weekly routines, special holidays such as New Year's Day were an opportunity which served to highlight the parental, and in particular, patriarchal authority in French-Canadian families. On that day, they commonly observed a blessing as one of their valued traditions from Canada. It was an act usually reserved for a priest, but on this special day, the patriarch of the family performed this role. The morning of New Year's Day, the oldest or the first child to get up, depending on the families, would look for the father and ask for his blessing. If children were too small, the mother would ask it for them. The act of blessing thus enacted the family hierarchy, bringing out "a father's role in a positive way," as one migrant daughter stated.[104]

The symbolic importance of blessing notwithstanding, it also revealed the shaky ground on which the authority of a father and husband stood. This was because of the gap between the harsh reality of daily life and the normative ideology of the male breadwinner, which could make the act of blessing a source of embarrassment, rather than a display of the power and authority wielded by the male family head. Irène Desmarais' account illustrates one such instance that conveys the ambiguity her father might have felt. When she was twelve or thirteen, she did something wrong just before or during the holiday and she dreaded asking for a blessing from her father. She was worried that her father might say something. But he never did. Her parents, Desmarais says later, "always felt more embarrassed than we [the children] did, [at] giving the blessing,"[105] adding, "He [her father] did not feel very worthy" partly because of his incapacity to carry out the responsibilities expected of a male breadwinner.

Some children were fortunate enough to experience more amicable relationships with their fathers. Morrissette, for example, remembers the special ways in which his father treated him as the only boy in the family. His father took Morrissette to the cinema every Saturday afternoon. They would stop to buy five and ten cents' worth of candy on their way, then spend ten cents to go to the third balcony, or what they then called "nigger's heaven,"[106] in B.F. Keith's Theatre, and then allow another ten cents for Morrissette's spending money.

Men's and Boys' Leisure Time

French-Canadian boys in early-twentieth-century Lowell did not lack means for amusement. In addition to the movie theatre, a variety of places, such as public parks, dance halls, the YMCA, and even the streets, offered brief moments of diversion which cost little or no money. "Cheap amusement," as Kathy Peiss has skillfully termed it in her analysis, therefore, was not monopolized by young migrant women in turn-of-the-century New York City.[107] Young and older boys as well as adult men of French-Canadian background constructed their own forms of leisure in Lowell.

For young boys, like school-aged Albert Parent, recreational activity was casual, free, and likely interwoven with daily chores. Albert, born and raised in Lowell's Little Canada, delivered a dinner pail to his father, who worked at the Meyers Thread on Pawtucket Street. Albert would pick up discarded bobbins with a little thread still on them in the mill yard and put them in his pocket. Then, he would go to the Aiken Street Park, not far from the Meyers' courtyard, and fly his kite. Albert says, "That (the thread) lasted for a while."[108]

Figure 9. B.F. Keith's Theatre, 1913. (Courtesy of Lowell Historical Society.)

    When they became a little older, sports and dance were added to the roster of leisure activities enjoyed by migrant and American-born sons. As a young boy, Morrissette went skating at Lakeview Park in the winter. Others went to the Lakeview Ballroom on Saturday, a place to meet with friends and girlfriends. The YMCA was another popular place for young men and women to spend their time away from work. Boys' and girls' activities at the "Y", as it was familiarly called, were not the same however. Boys would go there to play sports, such as basketball. Their sisters also did sports such as gymnastics, but the major activity for girls involved taking courses on sewing, cooking, and making fudge in American ways—as part of the Americanization programs advocated with fervour by middle-class, American-born, and, most often, female activists. Progressive reformers promoted such programs in order to save, as they believed, migrant daughters, and often indirectly their foreign-born mothers, from the uncivilized traditions of the migrants' former homes.[109] Migrant daughters, deemed as victims of poverty and ignorance, were thus the specific target of Americanization efforts. But while the objectives of the Americanization program achieved some significant success across the nation, the greater attraction of the YWCA for Lowell's French-Canadian daughters seemed to lie elsewhere. As Blanche Graham and her best friend recounted, what they liked best at the Y was to take a shower, a true luxury that few, if any, working-families could afford, since the norm at their homes was a galvanized bathtub in the kitchen.[110] We do not know whether or not the same comfort was available for the young men and if it was, whether or not they enjoyed that opportunity as much as their sisters did. Given the living conditions of French-Canadian working-class families in Lowell, however, one may safely surmise that a shower, if available, was as important a factor as the pleasure of playing baseball, an activity that inspired Morrissette and his male friends to go to the YMCA more than a few times a week.[111]

The street served as another centre of social life for boys and young men, just as it did for older men and women of all ages among working families. After dinner hours, they would stroll along the street and gatherings on street corners were regular forms of leisure. Boys preferred the streets to proper playgrounds such as the beautiful fields adjacent to St. Louis School, a French-Canadian parish school, and Greenhaldge School. They would play games such as "relative-O" or "tag" on the street even at night. Again, no money was needed to enjoy these activities. As Morrissette says, "It was all clean fun, not a penny used."[112]

Though it was an arena of cheap or free leisure, the street had the potential to become a dangerous place for boys. Occasionally, ethnic fights erupted on the streets. Asked if there were any confrontations with different ethnic groups in the city, Morrissette answered, "Oh, definitely." When he was in fifth, sixth, or seventh grade at St. Louis School, he and his friends would fight with Irish kids in the neighbourhood. "We used to fight among one another with rocks, throwing rocks at one another naturally," says Morrissette. Fights would take the form of territorial disputes between two rival groups of youngsters. Fulton and West was one of the street corners where the Irish kids who lived on one side of the town and the French Canadians who lived on the other scuffled and threw stones at one another. "There used to be a bunch of Irish people up there," recounts Arthur. "This side of the [Saint-Jean-Baptiste] Church were all

French." And he added, "it [the fight] was nothing drastic."[113] More recent arrivals, such as the Portuguese, were also common targets of the French-Canadian boys' antagonism. João da Silva Goes remembers the "bad" part of the town "where the Suffolk Canal was on the other side of Moody Street." There ethnic fights were so common that he was unable to get to the other side without being jumped by French-Canadian boys.[114] A Greek girl also remembers ethnic fights that their boys fought with Irish kids. "You couldn't cross the North Common at that time if you were Greek. The Irish lived from the North Common and up toward Butterfield, and Mt. Vernon. [...] The Greek boys used to go to the YMCA and then they'd come to play in the North Common. There was [sic] always wars. Rock throwing and fighting."[115]

At times, boys formed a coalition among other groups. Greek kids would run after the Irish; the Irish would chase the Greeks. One Greek immigrant son, who came to live in the Acre, an Old Irish neighbourhood, in the 1920s or 1930s, recalls when a group of Irish boys outnumbered his own group of Greek friends. He states, "We [the Greek boys]'d go and join in with the French and fight the Irish," and "if the French weren't handy we'd jump in with the Polish and chase the Irish, and fight them." Such alliances among boys of various backgrounds suggests a partial reflection of power relations in the adult world in the presence of which kids grew up. In Lowell where, in the words of Nicholas Georgoulis, the Irish predominated the city's police force and the city government in early years, "the French and the Greeks got along very well," and so did "the Greeks and Polish [and] all ethnic groups [except for the Irish]." People "banded together for their own protection."[116]

The principle of cheap amusement also dictated the leisure activities of young French-Canadian men. Some discovered a greater range of commercial entertainment, such as pubs, but many gathered at friends' houses for drinking, chatting, and playing cards. Others went to the beach, bowled, or went to dance parties—often all in one weekend.[117] Commercialized forms of entertainment thus made some inroads into the lives of these working young men, but their visits to a pub or a dance hall were more occasional than routine. In addition to the fact that their work stretched from Monday morning to mid-day Saturday, leaving them little time during the week, such forms of diversion cost more than young men could regularly afford. Although one might note a degree of exaggeration, as Morrissette states, "as far as spending money we didn't have any money to spend,"[118] thrift remained the guiding principle for young men.

Adult men did not have large sums of money—or much leisure time—to spend either. But the little extra they had, in addition to a sense of entitlement derived from their weekly hard work and possibly, the need to forget their routine toil and poverty, led them to construct a world of male adulthood distinct from the world enjoyed by the very young. Pubs, and more specifically, alcohol were the major attractions for these men. This is not to deny that French-Canadian husbands and fathers spent part of their time away from work at home with their families. They continued, for instance, the French-Canadian tradition of *veillée*, by which family and friends gathered at someone's home and spent the evening drinking, dancing, singing, and playing music.[119] But men would also go out, if only occasionally, for a drink at a bar. They could afford commercialized forms of diversion more often than younger men, not to mention their spouses, who, like their young children, were socially prevented from entering such spaces. Blanche Graham's father used to frequently have a beer at a local bar. She remembers being sent to fetch him by her mother. Blanche recounts:

> My father had quite a few friends. They'd play cards or go down to Andy Roach's bar room. Have a beer. Many a time I went down there. My mother wanted my father. They had swingin' doors in them days, and you'd open the swingin' doors and holler, "Is my father in there?" They'd say, "Luke, your daughter wants ya."[120]

At times, men's drinking habits could lead to domestic disputes or, worse, violence and abuse in the family. Given the nature of the problems, however, most were reluctant to speak publicly about these issues.[121] Scattered as they are, oral history accounts allow us to glimpse into scenes of discord and tragedy caused by heavy drinking. Blanche Graham endured thirteen years of physical and emotional abuse from her hard-drinking husband because, as she stated, she had nowhere else to go. A Greek immigrant daughter, Mary Rouses Karafelis, remembers her French-Canadian neighbour, a woman in her early twenties, who lived with two children and had a husband who was "a very heavy drinker." He did not drink during the week; he worked. But Saturday and Sunday, he would drink, come home, and beat his wife. One night, at about two o'clock in the morning, someone was banging on the door. Mary says:

> My mother got right out of bed and ran to the door and opened it up. She said, What's the matter? The young [French-Canadian] woman said: "He's trying to kill me!" So she [the mother] took her in, locked the door, and put her to bed. She didn't want to sleep. "Go in the bed; sleep with my daughter; don't worry about him," she says. She got my father, and she said, "If he comes to the door, tell him to go home and take care of the kids and sober up. He's not going to see his wife until tomorrow."[122]

The husband then came looking for his wife. Mary's father, a big, tall man, opened the door, and asked: "What do you want?" The husband said, "I want my wife!" "What for? You hit her; you beat her; no good," said the father, "You're not going to get your wife." The next morning when the young woman got up, Mary's mother did not let her go alone but accompanied her. When she came back, she said: "Everything is fine now. He was sobered up and holding his head when we walked in. He was practically crying." So the mother told him: "You'd better not touch her again, because I'll have the police up here." In those days, "the policeman was your friend," added Mary.[123]

The exact reasons for the husband's heavy drinking habits are not known to us. What is clear is that the neighbour's timely protection saved the young French-Canadian wife from disaster that night. But it is not difficult to imagine more than a few women who suffered similar or even worse fates and who may have had to endure conjugal abuse for a longer period of time.

*****

For French-Canadian men in early-twentieth-century Lowell, to earn wages meant a lifetime of hard work. The notable yet limited improvement in their socioeconomic profiles bore consequences beyond the mere material betterment of their lives and those of their families. Lowell's French-Canadian population was becoming older, more permanent and developed into the largest ethnic group in the city during the first two decades of the twentieth century. This meant that French-Canadian male workers and their families lived transformation and continuity of tradition at work and home in two distinct and yet indelibly connected ways.

For Arthur Morrissette and a small but growing minority who achieved the positions of loomfixer, mechanic or foreman, their work came to signify an increased sense of the autonomy enjoyed by the privileged few. They could go and immediately attend to a weaver who had trouble with his or her machine, or choose to order her or him to wait their turn, and decide how much time to spend on each repair. As skilled mechanics or supervisors, they earned hourly wages, not the piece rate to which most other mill workers were subjected.

For many others who made up the majority of semi- and skilled workers, their jobs did not provide them with the same degree of satisfaction from which loomfixers derived their power and autonomy. But tangible rewards, including being able to earn higher and possibly more stable wages than their predecessors in the late nineteenth century, might have strengthened their sense of power and authority as fathers and husbands. Although money continued to be the central issue for most working families, French-Canadian men's wages also instilled in their minds a greater sense of entitlement to a part of their earnings, which would allow them to enjoy commercialized forms of leisure, such as a drink at a local bar, a practice that few younger men and no women could afford— either financially or socially—with the same regularity.

Either way, the power and prerogative that French-Canadian men derived from their roles as father, husband and male (migrant) worker were not absolute. A sense of ambiguity, like that felt by Irène Desmarais' father, was a reminder that many French-Canadian men in Lowell were unable to conform to the normative ideology by which the family wage was to be earned solely by the father as breadwinner and head of the household.

Figure 10. Despite their recent arrival, some Portuguese workers settled and raised families in Lowell. Here is a family shown enjoying an outing at the beach, ca. 1910. (Courtesy of the University of Massachusetts Lowell.)

CHAPTER FIVE

"You Gotta Keep Going": Paid Work Performed by French-Canadian Women

In the early twentieth century, a large proportion of French-Canadian families in Lowell could not live solely on the wages earned by the male head of the household. A 1909 report of the Immigration Commission shows that the total yearly income of French-Canadian households in Lowell averaged $800, an amount 1.6 times greater than the average annual wage of a single male worker.[1] What other members of the family contributed to the household economy? Whenever possible, wives and children brought home additional wages that eased their families' precarious financial situations. As the amount of family income provided by children declined, the contributions of women became increasingly important.

The Binary Categorization and the Ideology of the Family Wage

Since the 1970s, women's work and family life have constituted important foci for scholarly evaluations of the social impact of industrialization. Until recently, this assessment tended to characterize a woman's relationship to the family in terms of readily definable and oppositional categories that failed to capture the diversity of the roles that women played. Women were viewed as either dependent or independent with regard to their families, either living with the family or "adrift," either supporting others or self-sufficient, and engaging in wage-work either temporarily or permanently. These oppositional categories were derived from the ideology of the family wage—a set of beliefs holding special importance in nineteenth-century social life and remaining influential in the early twentieth century.[2]

Based on such oppositional categories, a large part of academic debate revolved around the significance of women's individual wages, a form of wage-earning that rewarded the labour of an individual, as opposed to that of a family. Edward Shorter set off this debate by arguing that individual wages provided women with new economic independence and encouraged a new type of individualism. Joan Scott and Louise Tilly have taken strong opposition to this view in their study of working women during the period of French and British industrialization. Scott and Tilly argue that women's increased participation in paid employment represented a variant of a traditional family strategy, one aimed primarily at serving purposes related to the family as a collectivity. Young women working outside the home and earning individual wages might have gained some influence over the allocation of family resources,[3] but this did not grant them greater economic independence, nor did it release them from their role of serving the family. Tilly and Scott thus posit that with regard to women's paid work, continuities outweighed discontinuities in the shift from a family economy in the pre-industrial period to a family wage economy in the early industrial period.[4]

The hypothesis advanced by Tilly and Scott has greatly influenced subsequent interpretations of women's wage labour in the United States.[5] Thomas Dublin has explored the experiences of female wage workers from different ethnic/immigrant groups in Lowell's textile industry during the last four decades of the nineteenth century. In *Transforming Women's Work*, Dublin brings to light a series of changes that occurred among the city's female labour force in terms of ethnicity, residence patterns, and family status. In his analysis of these experiences from the lives of an earlier generation of female factory workers—most of whom were young American women recruited from the rural communities surrounding the textile city in the 1830s and 1840s, and more recent arrivals including French-Canadian and Greek factory operatives in 1900—Dublin finds that the latter were significantly more involved in contributing to their families' economic well-being than their "Yankee" predecessors. Dublin's conclusion therefore confirms the hypothesis advanced by Scott and Tilly that the increased participation of women in the paid labour market represented a variant of a traditional family strategy, where the individual served primarily the collective needs of the family.[6]

The importance of his contribution to the history of migrant women notwithstanding, Dublin's inquiry leaves unexamined the variations in economic contribution among women who had the same marital status and ethnicity, but whose household structures and living arrangements differed. This chapter begins its analysis where Dublin left off. To what degree did the roles played by French-Canadian wage-earning women vary? How did the age, marital status, and living arrangements of these workers determine their financial responsibilities? Under what circumstances did a woman's allegiance to her family promote or discourage her participation in wage-earning? And ultimately, what did paid work mean to them? A close focus on the paid work performed by single, married, and widowed women of French-Canadian origin helps one to shed light on the variations that characterized paid work performed by these women and what such divergence meant to them. Contrary to the polarized profiles of women deriving from the family wage ideology, the diversity of French-Canadian women's economic responsibilities forces us to re-examine both the extent and the limitations of the power exerted by the normative ideology of family wage, the life cycle of the family, and culturally rooted values relating to women's paid work outside the home.

The Wage-Earning Women of Lowell

About two fifths of women in early-twentieth-century Lowell worked for wages. Compared to the variety of jobs listed for men, female workers from the five ethnic backgrounds I studied were concentrated in a narrow range of occupations. During the decade between 1910 and 1920, the number of job categories for French-Canadian female workers increased from forty to seventy, and from eighty to one hundred five for Irish female workers, but these numbers represented less than 60 percent of the variety recorded for their male counterparts.[7] The range of French-Canadian men's work was a far cry from ensuring their free choice of employment. However, the number of job titles available for French-Canadian women shows that their choice was even more limited.

Such were the cases with Emma Paquette, Mary-C. Delany, Jessie Hamson, Mary Papas, and Anna Santos—five women of French-Canadian, Irish, American, Greek, and Portuguese origins—who lived in Lowell in 1910.[8] Thirty-year-old Paquette, born in French Canada, was a knitter at a hosiery factory. Delany, an eighteen-year-old daughter of Irish migrants, was a packer at a cartridge factory. Twenty-five-year-old Jessie, born in Massachusetts to parents who had originally lived in Maine, was listed as a bookkeeper at a machine shop. Finally, Papas, forty-five and married, and Santos, thirty-four and also married, both worked as weavers at cotton textile mills.

The rate of gainful employment for women born in French Canada was particularly high. In 1909, the Immigration Commission reported that 42 percent of Lowell women, born in Canada and over the age of fifteen, were working for wages, while the figure was 31 percent for American-born women with American-born fathers, and only 20 percent for Irish-born women. Conversely, an overwhelming majority of Irish-born and American women (80

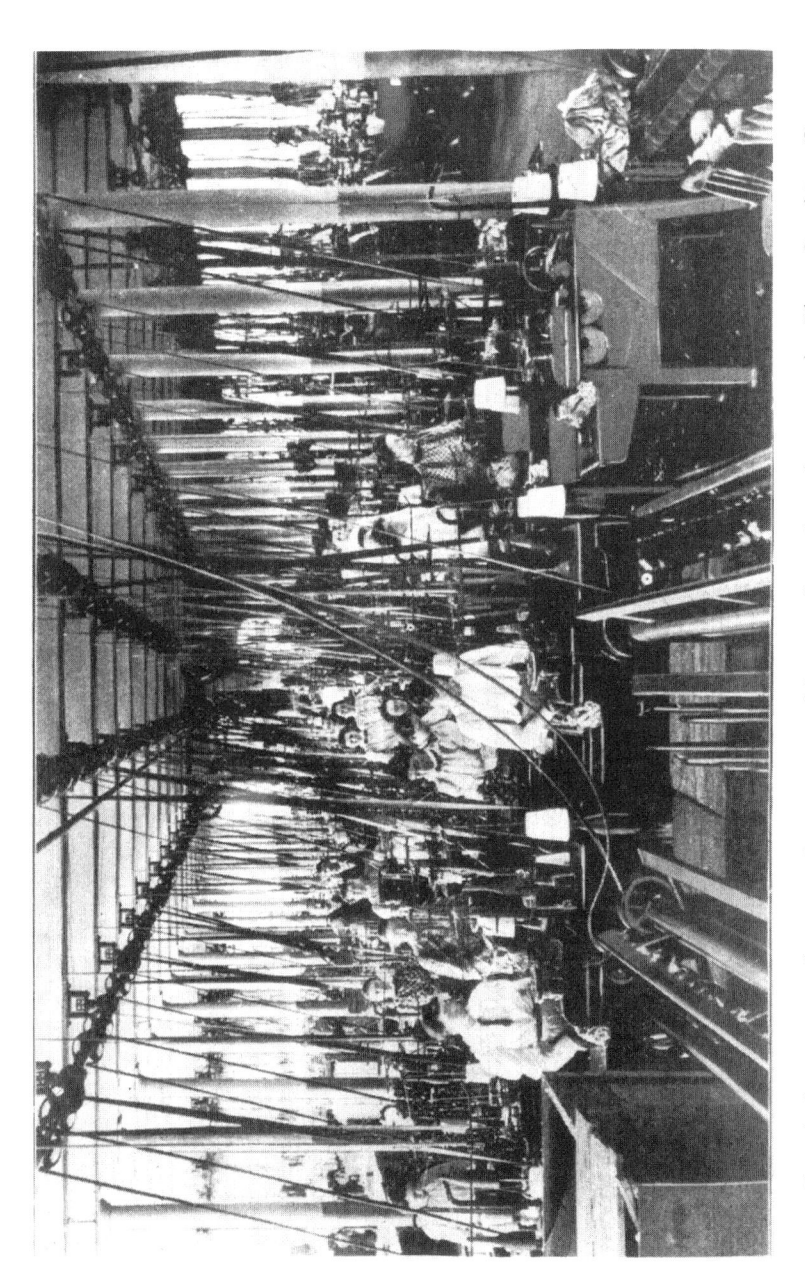

Figure 11. Female knitters working on the automated Jacquard stocking loom in the Shaw Stocking Company, ca. 1915. (Courtesy of the Center for Lowell History, University of Massachusetts Lowell.)

percent and 69 percent, respectively) were listed as staying home, in contrast to only 57 percent for their French-Canadian counterparts.[9] The rates of labour market participation were even higher for Greek and Portuguese women. In 1910, more than five out of every ten Greek women aged sixteen or over in Lowell participated in wage labour, representing the highest rate of female wage-workers among the five migrant/ethnic groups under study. A decade later, the proportion dropped to little more than one in six. Similarly, the proportion of Portuguese women workers decreased from one third to one quarter over the decade (See Tables 18 and 19).

What accounts for the ethnic differences within the participation of women in the labour market? Lowell data suggest that such differences likely reflected a combination of demographic factors, household necessities, and cultural values pertaining to women and their families. Also, my data reveal that in comparison to migrants who had already settled in the city over previous decades (such as Irish and French-Canadian women who were long-time residents), women who

Table 18. Occupational Distribution of Female Workers in Five Ethnic Groups, Lowell, 1910 (Number of Individuals per 100)

	French Canadian	Irish	American	Portuguese	Greek
Manual workers	84.2	72.8	49.3	93.4	92.3
Unskilled	10.1	14.9	9.7	6.7	15.4
Semi- and skilled	74.1	57.9	39.6	86.7	76.9
White collar	6.9	17.1	38.8	-	-
Lower white collar (clerical, etc.)	3.7	7.0	17.2	-	-
Upper white collar	3.2	10.1	21.6	-	-
Professional	2.7	-	0.7	-	-
Independent	8.0	5.5	8.2	6.7	-
Unidentified	2.6	1.5	2.2	-	15.4
Total	100.0	100.0	100.0	100.0	100.0
(N)	(189)	(328)	(134)	(15)	(13)
Labour market participation rate	33.5	38.0	27.1	34.9	43.3
Labour market participation rate of women aged 16 or over	48.6	47.6	36.6	40.0	52.1

Source: Compiled by author from *Thirteenth U.S. Federal Census Schedules*.

Table 19. Occupational Distribution of Female Workers in Five Ethnic Groups, Lowell, 1920 (Number of Individuals per 100)

	French Canadian	Irish	American	Portuguese	Greek
Manual workers	84.0	71.3	45.2	95.0	97.9
Unskilled	10.4	11.8	10.8	20.0	23.4
Semi- and skilled	73.6	59.5	34.4	75.0	74.5
White Collar	15.0	25.3	43.3	-	-
Lower white collar (clerical, etc.)	6.0	13.8	22.3	-	-
Upper white collar	9.0	11.5	21.0	-	2.1
Professional	-	0.3	0.6	-	-
Independent	1.0	2.9	5.1	-	-
Others (Number)	-	-	4.5	5	-
Total	100.0	100.0	100.0	100.0	100.0
(N)	(201)	(348)	(157)	(20)	(47)
Labour market participation rate	33.9	42.2	25.3	24.4	35.6
Labour market participation rate of women aged 16 or over	48.0	48.9	38.3	44.2	60.2

Source: Compiled by author from *Fourteenth U.S. Federal Census Schedules*.

had just moved to Lowell (such as Canadian-born women of recent arrival to the city and Greek and Portuguese women) were more likely to be among those who were able to readily enter the labour market, i.e., those who were young and without children. Moreover, strict enforcement of anti-child labour legislation in New England states made it necessary to explore more fully the wage-earning capacity of married women, both those who had arrived more recently and those who had resided there for a longer period of time, than was the case a half a century earlier. Thus, the wage-earning capacity of adult migrant women—single, married, or widowed—was arguably valued more highly than was the case in the earlier period. At the same time, this put growing pressure on them to work for wages. Pressure may have been felt even more strongly by recent arrivals to the city, since their wages might have paid for the cost of migration itself.

Sharing Unequal Responsibilities: Single French-Canadian Women

The extent to which unmarried women, living either with or without their parents, contributed to a household varied considerably. Among Lowell's French-Canadian women of the same marital status and age group, some supplemented their fathers' earnings; others, living in a single-parent household, assumed the role of principal provider; still others, in a single-parent household, worked together with their siblings or a widowed parent; and another group was self-supporting. The variation within the financial responsibilities assumed by French-Canadian single female workers contests the binary categorization suggested by the family wage ideology, which has placed single wage-earning women in a bracket of supplementary and temporary wage earners.

In Lowell, as in many other textile cities, the majority of female wage earners were never married (Table 20). Two thirds of the French-Canadian labour force were comprised of single women in 1910 and 1920, but they did not constitute a homogeneous group of young daughters. Canadian-born and U.S.-born single female workers diverged in their demographic profiles, skills, and the occupational sectors in which they were engaged. Table 21 shows the

Table 20. Marital Statuses of French-Canadian Female Workers in Lowell, 1910 and 1920 (Number of Individuals per 100)

	French Canadian	Irish	American	Portuguese	Greek
1910					
Single	66.7	76.2	78.4	13.3	69.2
Widowed & divorced	6.9	8.5	6.0	13.3	0
Married	25.4	12.5	14.9	66.7	23.1
Unknown	1.1	2.7	0.7	6.7	7.7
Total	100.0	100.0	100.0	100.0	100.0
(N)	(189)	(328)	(134)	(15)	(13)
1920					
Single	6.2	75.6	68.2	40.0	51.1
Widowed & divorced	9.5	10.1	6.4	0	2.1
Married	23.4	13.5	25.5	60.0	46.8
Unknown	1.0	1.0	0	0	0
Total	100.0	100.0	100.0	100.0	100.0
(N)	(201)	(348)	(157)	(20)	(47)

Sources: Compiled by author from *Thirteenth and Fourteenth U.S. Federal Census Schedules.*

Table 21. Age Distribution of French-Canadian Female Workers in Lowell by Marital Status, 1910 and 1920 (Number of Individuals per 100)

Age group	Single	Married	Widowed
1910			
14 and under	2.3	0	0
15 to 24	68.3	13.2	0
25 to 34	15.9	32.1	16.7
35 to 44	11.1	26.4	25.0
45 and over	13.3	22.6	58.3
Total	100.0	100.0	100.0
(N)	(126)	(53)	(12)
1920			
14 and under	2.3	0	0
15 to 24	60.2	16.0	0
25 to 34	24.8	30.0	26.3
35 to 44	8.3	28.0	26.3
45 and over	12.8	24.0	47.4
Total	100.0	100.0	100.0
(N)	(133)	(50)	(19)

Source: Compiled by author from *Thirteenth U.S. Federal Census Schedules.*

gradual aging of the single French-Canadian female worker, a demographic phenomenon that concerned primarily Canadian-born women, and the relative youthfulness of their American-born counterparts. The average age of the Canadian-born rose from twenty-four in 1910 to thirty years old in 1920, while the average age of the U.S.-born rose only slightly, from twenty to twenty-one.

By 1920, Canadian-born women workers were much more likely than their U.S.-born counterparts to be of age forty-five and over, whereas U.S.-born women were more likely than their Canadian-born colleagues to be under the age of twenty-five. An example of the former is Victoria Bruel, a forty-six-year-old single Canadian-born woman who migrated to the U.S. in 1880. Three decades later, Victoria was working in a hosiery factory as a stitcher.[10] Rose Desjardins illustrates an example of the latter, a U.S.-born female worker of French-Canadian background. The twenty-four-year-old shoe stitcher was born in Massachusetts to French-Canadian parents.[11]

Canadian- and American-born French-Canadian single female workers also differed in their employment patterns. The presence of a few Canadian-born women in skilled jobs in the manufacturing sector indicates the emergence of "elite" workers who had climbed above the lowest rung of the occupational hierarchy where practically the entire French-Canadian female (and male) labour force had clustered earlier. In 1870, these job categories had been inaccessible for 97 percent of French-Canadian female workers regardless of birthplace.[12] In 1910 and 1920, a significant minority of Canadian-born women came to occupy some of the skilled jobs, such as those of finisher or folder, in textile manufacturing. Moreover, a good proportion of Canadian-born women in the early twentieth century were concentrated in skilled and semi-skilled jobs in the textile industry. For example, Ovila and Rosanna Bousquet, sixteen and thirty years old respectively, were both born in Canada and went to the U.S. in 1896, where they worked as weavers in cotton textile mills. A small but growing minority of Canadian-born women worked as inspectors in textile factories, a position that required a high degree of responsibility, skill, and experience. The Federal Census Schedules for 1910 listed a handful of women inspectors at hosiery factories, such as Canadian-born Matilda Depontbriand and Joséphine Matte, another Canadian-born, having migrated to the U.S. in the early 1900s.[13] This was a position that no French-Canadian woman in the late nineteenth century could have achieved.

The socioeconomic profile of American-born women also improved, but with some important differences. Like their Canadian-born colleagues, a significant proportion of American-born workers of French-Canadian descent held skilled and semi-skilled jobs as weavers in woolen mills and as spinners, twisters, and doffers in cotton mills.[14] A small number worked as inspectors in the factories. What distinguished them from the Canadian-born generation was the proportion of American-born women who held white-collar jobs as bookkeepers and salespeople, a category which had been reserved for the Anglo-Celtic population. For example, in 1920, the federal census listed twenty-five-year-old Hélène Grandchamps, born in Massachusetts, working as a saleslady in a department store, and twenty-four-year-old Florence Bissonette and twenty-four-year-old Florette Poirier, both born in Massachusetts, working as bookkeepers in a plumber's office and a hosiery factory, respectively.[15]

One might argue that the emerging presence of single American-born women with French-Canadian backgrounds in white-collar occupations resulted from a considerable increase in the number of jobs available in these occupations. Indeed, the white-collar labour force in Lowell expanded in the early twentieth century, reflecting a broader structural change that had begun earlier in larger northern cities. Evidence from the Federal Census Schedules shows that the proportion of women engaged in jobs in sales, bookkeeping, and inspection increased among long-time residents of the city, in particular among American women (of all marital statuses) and to a lesser extent among their Irish counterparts (see Tables 18 and 19).[16] The expansion of jobs in the white-collar sector, however, did not significantly reduce the ratio of manual-to-white-collar workers, since a large number of single women continued to work in Lowell's textile and shoe factories. Instead, female white-collar workers consisted, in large part, of a separate labour pool from manual labourers.

The emergence of bookkeepers and salespeople among Lowell's American-born daughters of French-Canadian immigrants suggests, therefore, not so much a necessary adjustment on their part to changes in labour market conditions, but rather a larger degree of choice in the jobs available to them. Among the factors that contributed to this broadening of the range of choices were the levels of education and the lengths of residence that came to characterize this demographic. Bookkeeping required basic math and schooling, while shopkeeping required a good command of English, although the latter might not be indispensable for a salesperson in a shop catering to a clientele composed principally of French Canadians. Their acquired skills—basic clerical abilities and English-language capacity—rendered American-born women, rather than Canadian-born women, better suited to such jobs in the white-collar sector. Furthermore, American women's decision was likely influenced by the relative prestige—and not necessarily higher salaries—of white-collar jobs. Also, their values and preferences were increasingly shared with their native-born counterparts of American heritage.[17] Clearly, they were becoming more and more integrated into American society.

Diane Ouellette was one such example. A daughter of French-Canadian immigrants, Diane began working at a textile factory, the U.S. Bunting, at the age of fourteen like many other French-Canadian girls. Unlike many, however, she started working part-time for Bass' Clothing Store on Central Street shortly thereafter, working there on Friday night and Saturday all day for $4.00 each week. "It was good [money she earned at her second job]," she says. While she gave all her pay from the textile mill to her parents, the money she earned at the store was, as she puts it, "my spending money."[18]

It should be underlined, however, that American-born daughters of French-Canadian migrants had no monopoly on white-collar work. A small minority of Canadian-born single women with a good command of English also worked as salespeople. A case in point was Régina Barry. She began working at the textile factory at the age of 14. Soon, though, she left the mill to work in a retail store. She "spoke very good English," as her daughter later recalls,[19] which must have helped her change of occupation. Of additional importance is the fact that Régina had a good connection through her sister Eléanore, a former milliner, who helped Régina find a job in retailing. Régina initially worked at the Gilbrides' store at night after seven to eight hours of work during the day at the mill. Eventually, she became a glove fitter and left the factory. Régina was such a popular fitter that she attracted a following, who then followed her when she left Gilbride's, first for Pelletier Ledoux's, and then for Chalifoux's. It was at the last shop that Régina met her husband.[20]

If facility in the English language was essential for finding a job as a salesgirl, it was also crucial, as some French Canadians came to realize, for work in the textile factories. Diane Ouellette was fluent in both French and English because she was sent to the Immaculate Conception School, an English-speaking school, where she had only a few French-Canadian friends. In addition, school regulations prohibited pupils from speaking French among themselves. The choice of Diane's schooling reflected her mother's belief that Diane would be miserable without English. Her mother wanted her daughter to pick up English. Within a year, Diane learned to speak the language "pretty well." Later, she worked in sections of the textile mill where there were no French speakers, but mostly "all little Irish girls." Thanks to her immersion in the English language, she had few problems at work and learned more English "with a little French accent."[21]

If the English language helped Diane and some other French-Canadian women find, and possibly choose, more attractive jobs, it could also become a source of strain. Blanche Graham spoke very little French until she learned it at a French-Canadian school. This was because of her limited exposure to the French language. As an infant, both her parents, migrants from Québec, worked at the mill full time and Blanche was cared for by an Irish lady, Auntie O'Leary, during the day. At night, she went home with her parents but spent little time with them, since they were in bed by half past seven because of exhaustion from the day-long work at the mill. When she reached school age, she was sent to Immaculate Conception, a decision that decreased the prospect of improving her ability in French. As a result, her command of French was so poor that her sister would have to interpret for her when she spoke with her mother. Blanche recalls: "My mother must have got[ten] sick of that." Finally, Blanche was transferred to St. Joseph's school, a French-Canadian parish school, where she learned to speak French. She said, she could say her "prayers in French," and so, "I was alright."[22]

Diversity in Living Arrangements: Daughters Living at Home?

The household structures and living arrangements of most single French-Canadian female workers conform to templates drawn from the family wage/male breadwinner ideology. The majority were young daughters who lived in households headed by their fathers. But this was not the case for all. Both in

1910 and 1920, the largest proportion of single women (over 70 percent) were daughters living with their parent(s), but the minority was composed of women whose relationship to the head of the household varied considerably (Table 22). Some were sisters, granddaughters or nieces; others were lodgers or boarders, also referred to as "roomers"; and a very small number were, themselves, the heads of their households.

An analysis by birthplace sheds additional light on the diversity in living arrangements made by these single female wage earners. Once again, such diversity runs contrary to the inherent assumption in family wage ideology, which stipulates that all female wage earners were young, single daughters who

Table 22. Distribution of Household Relationships of French-Canadian Wage-Earning Women by Marital Status, Lowell, 1910 and 1920

	Single		Married		Widowed and Divorced	
1910	Percent	(N)	Percent	(N)	Percent	(N)
Household head	2.6	(3)	10.4	(5)	53.8	(7)
Wife	-	-	58.3	(28)	-	-
Daughter	73.0	(92)	16.7	(8)	7.7	(1)
Other family member	9.5	(12)	10.4	(5)	23.1	(3)
Lodger	10.3	(13)	2.1	(1)	7.7	(1)
Servant	4.8	(6)	2.1	(1)	7.7	(1)
Total	100.0	(116)	100.0	(48)	100.0	(13)
1920						
Household head	2.3	(3)	4.3	(2)	57.9	(11)
Wife	-	-	66	(31)	-	-
Daughter	71.4	(95)	10.6	(5)	10.5	(2)
Other family member	12.8	(17)	17	(8)	10.5	(2)
Lodger	13.5	(18)	2.1	(1)	18.8	(3)
Servant	-	-	-	-	5.3	(1)
Total	100	(133)	100	(47)	100	(19)

Source: Compiled by author from *Thirteenth and Fourteenth U.S. Federal Census Schedules.*

worked temporarily in order to supplement the wages earned by their co-resident fathers. Among those born in Canada, the proportion of daughters of all ages who lived with their parents decreased from two thirds in 1910 to just over half in 1920. Conversely, a growing minority, among both the Canadian-born and U.S.-born, came to live with other relatives. Furthermore, the percentage of the Canadian-born who were lodgers or boarders doubled, while the percentage among the American-born remained unchanged. Finally, small numbers of Canadian-born single workers came to head households of their own, while few among U.S.-born women did so (not shown in the tables), All of the women listed as the head of the household were relatively old, falling in the age groups from thirty-five to fifty years old. One of them was Emma Crépeau, forty-four, who migrated to the U.S. in 1889 and was working as a school teacher at a French-Canadian parochial school in Lowell in 1910. Another example was Canadian-born Florida Lapointe, thirty-eight years old, who worked as a stitcher at a hosiery mill in 1910.

Considerable changes in household relations, articulated more pervasively among Canadian-born women, resulted partly from changes in life cycle. As Michael Anderson observed of spinsters in mid-Victorian Britain,[23] many single French-Canadian women in early-twentieth-century Lowell lived in their parental homes. This was especially the case with older single women. Of single French-Canadian female workers who belonged to the age group of thirty-five years and older, as many as 18 percent in 1910 and 47 percent in 1920 resided in their parents' household. For example, Albina Bourgeault, a thirty-six-year-old saleswoman at a grocery store; Eleanor Lelacheur, thirty-seven, a teacher at a public school; and Marie-Anne Baril, thirty-nine years old and a spooler at a cotton textile factory, were all single and resided with their parents.[24] As they became older and their parents died, such arrangements necessarily ended. The pronounced upward shift discussed earlier in the average age of Canadian-born women compared to their U.S.-born counterparts, meant that the event of parental death occurred to a greater proportion of the former than the latter. Accordingly, more single women among the Canadian-born were compelled to find a place outside their parents' residence.

Still, data derived from the U.S. federal census suggest that, in contrast with Anderson's interpretation, for many French-Canadian spinsters, living with parents was less a preference than an obligation, or indeed a constraint, which they accepted more or less willingly. The practice of older single women living with their aged parents reflected a family strategy for assuring the daughters' contribution, both financial and non-financial, to their parents' households. Although daughters, too, benefited from such arrangements in that they could shed the bulk of their living expenses by living with their parents, they had few chances to accept it, largely because of the low wages they earned at the textile mills that prevented them from having any other choice. Unlike the wages of their male siblings, which might have rivaled those of their fathers once the boys reached their late teens, the earning power of female workers in the textile industry remained without significant change over their lifetimes.[25] Canadian-born girls between fourteen and seventeen years of age earned a wage of $6.09 per week, higher than the $5.01 per week received by the Canadian-born boys of the same age group. Canadian-born female cotton workers aged eighteen and older, in contrast, made on average $7.08 (an increase of only 16 percent), considerably surpassed by an average of $9.77 (an increase of 95 percent) for male workers aged eighteen and older.[26]

The differences in wage increases for male and female cotton textile workers resulted largely from differences in job mobility and promotional opportunities within the industry. One of the few ways by which women could get a raise was to leave the factory or the industry altogether. The Great War provided women with such new job opportunities, unprecedented in scale, as the war created acute labour shortages in Lowell's war-related industries, as in other industrial cities. As one female worker who moved to the U.S. Cartridge shop from the textile factory put it: "I made good money there [at the Cartridge shop], I was making up to $6.00 a week." Previously, she earned $5.00 for fifty-seven hours a week at a cotton mill.[27]

Another factor that discouraged single women living alone was the weight of the cultural tradition rooted in both Quebec and the United States which frowned upon such behaviour.[28] This attitude encouraged single wage-earning women to live with their aged parents. Further, comparatively lower wages of female workers also made this practice common among single women. However, there were also exceptions. In Lewiston, Maine, in the 1880s, approximately three quarters of single French-Canadian women lived apart from their families of origin.[29] Cora Pellerin and her siblings remained in Manchester, N.H., when their parents went back to their farm in Canada. The three children, Cora (then thirteen), her older brother (then sixteen), and her older sister (then eighteen), insisted they stay in the United States. After having boarded in a family-style boardinghouse for some time, Cora began living in an apartment all by herself. Acknowledging that, in those days, a woman living alone was rather exceptional, Cora described herself as a "wildcat." Some of her friends' mothers, after learning that Cora was in an apartment alone, did not want their daughters to hang around with her. This was because, as Cora explained, they were afraid that their daughters would "get the idea."[30] In Lowell, too, Emma Crépeau, Florida Lapointe, and a few others lived on their own,[31] but that was hardly the case for the majority of wage-earning single female French Canadians.

Despite the significance of demographic factors such as age, birthplace, and marital status in determining the extent and length of a single woman's paid labour participation, they were textured, and sometimes even cancelled out, by other factors, including the living arrangements and household structures of single female workers, whose function was considered as one of temporarily contributing supplementary income. The extent of financial contributions provided by French-Canadian daughters belonging to the same age group and living in similar households varied considerably. The census manuscripts offer some examples, such as the case of two twenty-four-year-old daughters of household heads, Canadian-born Henrietta Desjardins and American-born Bertha L[a]urier.[32] Henrietta, a stitcher at a shoe factory, and Bertha, a winder[33] at a cotton textile factory, were among a substantial number of single wage-earning women in their twenties who resided with their parent(s).

Henrietta's family consisted of a father, who worked as a stone mason, a mother, who stayed at home, and two younger sisters: Rose, a twenty-year-old stitcher, and Joséphine, a fifteen-year-old who was not listed as working outside the home. The Desjardins family lodged a shoe-cutter, John Desjardins. With the additional income provided by the lodger and the steady work of her father and her younger sister, Henrietta's earnings were not the family's primary source of income. The case of Bertha L[a]urier was quite different. Bertha and her sister, who worked as stitchers, were the principal providers for their family. The two sisters supported their widowed father and a young sister, neither of whom was gainfully employed. Consequently, in comparison with Henrietta, Bertha's economic contribution was far more important to her family.

The case of an older single woman named Angélina Larogne further reveals how the family situation dictated the extent of a single woman's economic responsibility toward her household. Angélina, born in Canada, was thirty-nine years old and working as weaver at a cotton factory. The oldest of six daughters, she lived with her widowed father, who worked as a teamster. Three of her five sisters worked at a cotton factory: nineteen-year-old Louisanna, a stitcher, eighteen-year-old Rose, and fifteen-year-old Liliane, who were both winders. The four daughters supplemented the meagre wages earned by their father, while the second oldest, thirty-one-year-old Georgina, was listed as unemployed. Georgina probably took over the role of her deceased mother, keeping house and caring for her ten-year-old sister.[34] In the household of Émile Gill, a sixty-two-year-old widower, his single sister, Catherine, forty-six years old, likely assumed the responsibilities of domestic tasks, in addition to her work as a rear girl at a cotton textile factory. Financial difficulties were probably not the Gills' principal concern, given the wages brought home by the four adult workers.

Émile worked as a clerk at a hardware store, and his two sons worked as machinists at the Lowell Machine Shop and the Statehouse.[35]

As the pages above have shown, the diversity of financial roles assumed by French-Canadian single women has revealed the limitations of analytical frameworks integral to the family wage ideology. Relying heavily on oppositional categorizations of workers—as either dependent or independent, temporary or permanent [36]—such frameworks explain only partially the significance and complexity of single women's working lives. It would be too simplistic, however, to equate their paid work with a household strategy of working-class families, since to do so risks undermining the liberating effects of wage work. In 1920, Manon, a thirty-five-year-old single wage-earning woman in Lewiston, Maine, embraced her celibacy as an advantage availing her of new options unavailable in Canada. She wrote that she never believed it necessary to marry and that she decided once again to remain single, because "after all," she "much prefer[ed] it that way!"[37] For the majority of French-Canadian single women in Lowell, however, this was hardly the case. As has been discussed above, for the majority, remaining single was not so much a deliberate choice as it was a circumstantial eventuality; participation in wage work was indispensable to the family's survival. True, some left their work at the mill or shop as soon as they got married or gave birth to a child, and they might have considered themselves fortunate to be able to adopt a pattern that suited the male breadwinner family wage ideology as "the best in a very narrow range of unhappy options."[38] But even for those who left the paid labour market at one point, the return to a life of wage-work remained a lifetime possibility. It was because of that type of real possibility, too, that single women's work needs to be understood in relation to, and not in isolation from, married (and, as we will discuss later, widowed) women's work and lives.

"I Had to Keep Going": Intermittent and Continuing Work Patterns of French-Canadian Married Women

A substantial proportion of Lowell's French-Canadian wives and mothers earned wages either continuously or intermittently throughout their lifetimes. While some worked until the birth of their first child and then withdrew from the labour market, a large proportion either continued to work many years more or else re-entered the labour market after childbirth, shuttling between work and home. For the majority of French-Canadian women in early-twentieth-century Lowell, "stay[ing] at jobs throughout their pregnancies" and, for some, "return[ing] to work a few weeks after childbirth" were the norm,

Figure 12. Portuguese female spinners, 1907. (Courtesy of the Center for Lowell History, University of Massachusetts Lowell.)

rather than the exception. These voices confirm in part the observation by Mary Blewett that marriage and motherhood could be a real challenge for female mill workers.[39] At the same time, for Lowell's French-Canadian married women, as the following pages will show, a greater challenge resided less with marriage *per se* than with imperatives to combine their wage work with responsibilities as a wife and mother at home.

Donna Mailloux's grandmother perhaps best illustrates the employment pattern of the largest proportion of Lowell's French-Canadian wives and mothers. Mailloux puts it this way: "She [Grandmother]'d work for a little while, and then she'd, you know, be pregnant again, and she'd stop working. But once the youngest was a few years old, she went back to work full-time again."[40] Once again, such patterns of labour market participation among Lowell's French-Canadian married women diverge sharply from the assumption that wage-earning women were young and single or, if married, working only temporarily until the birth of the first child.

The pattern of intermittent participation by Mailloux and many other French-Canadian wives and mothers in the paid labour market meant that they were on average the oldest in the city's French-Canadian female work force besides widows. While working wives and mothers were found across all age groups, half of them were aged thirty-five years or older, and as much as a quarter were in the upper age category of forty-five years and older. The census manuscripts also show examples of older working wives and mothers who were likely to have worked—some continuously, others intermittently—from the time that they were young women. Since inspectors were likely to have been drawn from experienced workers, Marie Houde, a seventy-year-old inspector in a cotton textile factory, must have worked for many years before assuming this position. Another example is Adeline Goulet, fifty-five years old, who worked as a mender in a hosiery factory, a skilled woman's job that consisted of reconstructing the pattern in defective or damaged woolen or worsted cloth.[41]

The majority of women working in the textile industry were not as fortunate as Houde and Goulet, however. Despite years of work experience, age posed a serious disadvantage to many female workers. Elder women felt bitter about management's preference for younger workers. Speaking to such feelings, a former mender stated: "Most of the older menders resented the younger menders because they could work faster and more productively." Mending required good vision and dexterity, while the mill environment guaranteed poor lighting, which led to "declining eye-sight, and arthritis would take care of the rest." And so, "The young girls were a definite menace," concluded this ex-worker.[42]

Figure 13. A group photograph of mill employees, ca. 1917-1920. This photograph captures the mixed gender of the ranks of floor workers and the homogenously male make-up of the overseers and foremen, who are the ones wearing ties. Note also the small but significant number of young child workers. (Courtesy of the Center for Lowell History, University of Massachusetts Lowell.)

Oral interviews reveal the hardships endured by some of those French-Canadian wives and mothers, who worked over the course of long years of their lives as they tried to make ends meet. For example, Valentine Chartrand, the oldest girl in her family, left school on her fourteenth birthday. She told a nun at her school: "My father needs the extra money, and I have to leave." She worked from that day on—and did so for over fifty years, until she was well past the age of sixty. Even though a doctor once urged her to quit, she recounted: "My husband's pay wasn't that big, so I needed the extra money." "When I was sixty-two," she added:

> I was working part time, and I wasn't well. I had to keep going. Because my husband was sick for four years and a half, in and out of the hospital, and I could see the money going out and getting nothing in. When he died (...), I nearly gave up for two years. I didn't feel like doing nothing, and then I said to myself, 'Well, you can't give up, you gotta keep going.' And I just kept going. I went back to work.[43]

The years between the birth of the first child and the time the child reached working age[44] was the period of greatest need for the household, because it was during this time that the child required food and care, but did not contribute wages. Moreover, mothers who had a child under a year old had a markedly low percentage of employment due to the difficulty of balancing employment with the responsibility of caring for a newborn child.

An examination of French-Canadian married women throughout their family life cycle confirms statistically the difficulty of assuming the twin responsibilities of earning wages and taking care of young children. One can see in Table 23 that in 1910, the rate of married women participating in the labour force is at its highest prior to the birth of the first child (stage I), whereupon it drops to its lowest (stage II), and remains at this level while all the children were under eleven years of age (stage III). A decade later, the labour participation rate of French-Canadian married women was generally higher throughout the entire

Table 23. Paid Labour Participation Rates of French-Canadian Married Women by Life Cycle, 1910 and 1920

Stage	1910 Percent	Working Women	Women in the Category	1920 Percent	Working Women	Women in the Category
I	47.8	(11)	(23)	65.0	(13)	(20)
II	14.3	(1)	(7)	-	-	(7)
III	12.8	(6)	(47)	29.4	(10)	(34)
IV	18.8	(12)	(64)	14.8	(9)	(61)
V	19.5	(8)	(41)	55.0	(11)	(20)
VI	21.4	(6)	(28)	74.0	(20)	(27)
VII	45.5	(5)	(11)	81.3	(13)	(16)

Sources: Compiled by author from *Thirteenth and Fourteenth U.S. Federal Census Schedules*.
Note: 1. Stage I. Wife under forty-five years old, no children
   Stage II. Wife under forty-five years old, one child under one
   Stage III. All children under eleven years old
   Stage IV. Half the children fifteen years old or under
   Stage V. Half the children over fifteen years old
   Stage VI. All children over fifteen years old
   Stage VII. Wife over forty-five years old, no resident children
2. A woman who worked in stage II in 1910 was an autonomous dressmaker working at home.

family life cycle except for when half of the children in a family were aged fifteen or under (stage IV). The general pattern in 1920 was similar to that observed in 1910. A significant proportion worked for wages before the birth of their first children. The rate drops to its lowest point when the family has one infant child, rises considerably once half of the children are over fifteen (stage V), and reaches its highest level during the "empty nest" period (stage VII).

While the overwhelming majority (over three quarters in 1910 and 1920) of French-Canadian married female workers in Lowell earned wages in the textile industry, there was also a substantial minority, about a quarter, who earned their own living elsewhere, or did so in conjunction with their spouses.

Sixty-one-year-old Ida Dextra, who worked as a dressmaker, was one of the latter.[45] A small number ran family-owned businesses such as boardinghouses or variety stores. One might consider running a boardinghouse and working at home to be preferred alternatives for wives and mothers, since working on their own account would allow them a degree of flexibility in organizing their time. However, such work could require of women as many, if not more, hours of work as employment at the mills. We shall discuss this point in greater detail in the following chapter.

As more and more married wives and mothers entered, re-entered or remained in the paid labour market, another change emerged. In contrast to their single colleagues whose relationship to the household varied over the years, the relationship of working French-Canadian wives to their households diverged less and less. In 1910, half of the French-Canadian women in Lowell who were married and employed lived in households headed by their husbands; a decade later, the proportion had grown to two thirds (see Table 24). Conversely, the proportion of married women living with their parent(s) or in-law(s) decreased over the decade; in 1910, one in six French-Canadian wage-earning women lived in the household of their parents or in-laws; ten years later the proportion fell to one in ten. The change in residential pattern—the decrease of multiple households and, conversely, the increase of nuclear households among married French-Canadian female workers—meant that a growing number had to perform domestic work and childcare in addition to their wage work. Few had a female relative around, such as a mother, mother-in-law, aunt, or sister—living with or near the couple—to be called upon to take care of the young children. Dora McGory was one of this growing number of French-Canadian working mothers. This twenty-two-year-old knitter at a hosiery factory was married to a Massachusetts-born Irishman, Frank McGory, twenty-one years old, who worked as a confectioner in an ice cream company. The couple had two infant children. Without any other family members residing in the household, Dora probably had to find someone—

Table 24. Distribution of French-Canadian Married Female Workers According to the Patterns of Wage-Earning in Their Household, Lowell, 1910 and 1920 (Number by Individuals)

Other wage earners in household	Head	Wife	Daughter	Other Family	Lodger	Servant	Total
1910							
Only male household head worked				1			1
Only male household head and spouse worked		23			1	1	26
Only male household head and other family members (spouse excluded) worked		1	6				7
Male household head, spouse, and children worked		4					4
Female household head and other family members worked	4		2				6
Only female household head worked	1						1
Unidentified					3		3
Total (N)	5	28	8	1	5	1	48
Percentage	(10.4)	(50.0)	(16.7)	(2.4)	(10.4)	(2.1)	(100.0)
1920							
Only male household head worked		1				5	6
Only female spouse worked		1					1
Only male household head and spouse worked		17				1	18
Only other family members worked (male household head and spouse excluded)			1				1
Only male household head and other family members worked			3				3
Male household head, spouse, and children worked	1	12			1		14
No one worked (female-headed household)			1			1	1
Only female household head worked						1	1
Female household head and other family members worked			1				1
Only female household head worked (single-woman household)	1						1
Total (N)	2	31	5	-	1	8	47
(Percentage)	(4.3)	(66.0)	(10.6)	-	(17.0)	(2.1)	(100.0)

Source: Compiled by author from *Thirteenth and Fourteenth U.S. Federal Census Schedules*.

a neighbour, friend, distant relative, or a day-care facility—to take care of the two young children while she was at work.[46]

Not surprisingly, more married women tended to work for wages when there was an adult female relative residing in the household, likely reflecting the ease with which they could arrange to share a range of childcare and household responsibilities. In 1910 and 1920, while half of the French-Canadian women living in households with parents or parents-in-law earned wages, less than 20 percent of women residing in households without them did so.[47] These figures statistically confirm the observation by Tamara Hareven that the crucial factor for participation in paid labour for married women was not marriage *per se*, but the living arrangements themselves.[48] Florence Côté and Blanche Rhéaume were among these French-Canadian wage-earning wives who resided with a female member of the family. Florence, a seventeen-year-old stitcher, and her husband Eugène, a twenty-one-year-old machinist, lived with Eugène's parents, Adrien and Émil[i]e Côté. Adrien worked as a labourer and Émil[i]e stayed home, probably in order to take care of domestic work. There were also two of Eugène's sisters and a brother living at home, the women working as a cutter and a turner in a hosiery factory, and the man working as a machinist in a machine shop. Another example is Blanche Rhéaume, a married daughter living in the household of her widowed father, Octavie, a fifty-five-year-old cutter in a hosiery factory. Blanche worked as a stitcher and her twenty-seven-year-old husband was a tanner. Blanche's sister and brother also worked as stitchers. Reine, another sister, stayed at home.[49]

As was the case in the neighbouring mill town of Manchester, New Hampshire,[50] Lowell's French-Canadian wives and mothers had a greater propensity to earn wages than American-born women of American-born parents. Tamara Hareven has suggested that such a difference resulted from an ideological time lag, a lag that reflected that the American middle class ideals relating to the cult of female domesticity and family wage ideology—both of which censured the wage-earning work of married women—had yet to reach the majority of working-class French-Canadian (and other) migrant households.[51] Implicit to Hareven's view is the assumption that the prevalence of traditional values common to rural French-Canadian families in Québec prevented American middle-class values from infiltrating the value systems of working-class French Canadians in the New England textile city. As Bettina Bradbury has argued, however, the American middle-class did not monopolize women's domesticity; on the contrary, religious and political elites in Québec also frowned upon the idea of wives and mothers working outside the home. The significance of such patriarchal ideology was felt among French-Canadian men who held ambivalent feelings toward their wives' participation in paid labour markets.[52] This was the case as late as the 1870s when husbands and fathers had greater difficulty finding work than their wives and children, who could earn wages as unskilled workers in textile factories throughout New England's towns and cities.[53] To what extent the improvement of the male household head's earning power reversed, or maintained, such a process of male marginalization[54] in early-twentieth-century Lowell remains unclear. But we do know that such a process was uneven and far from clear-cut, as was discussed in chapter four. We also know that the memory of these unpleasant, and perhaps dishonourable, arrangements were a part of a not-too-distant past for more than a few among Lowell's French-Canadian men.

Another, more plausible explanation is that the availability of industrial occupations provided part of the structural basis that encouraged, or restricted, the participation of married women in the labour market. Ultimately, these structural factors likely outweighed the cultural factors emphasized by Hareven in her early study.[55] Among the most important factors, perhaps, was the effect of the anti-child labour laws in New England states which compelled a greater proportion of French-Canadian married women to earn wages in comparison to their American counterparts, who likely had fewer difficulties in making ends meet given the higher and possibly more stable wages earned by their spouses. Legal and social sanctions against child labour created another important consequence: a far greater proportion of French-Canadian wives and mothers in Lowell worked for wages compared to women in Québec where such legal restrictions were not enacted until much later in the century. While French-Canadian families in Québec were faced with the same economic needs as their counterparts in Lowell, the absence of child labour laws meant that a woman in Québec had recourse to a more diverse set of options for supplementing her household's income—including having her children earn wages while she engaged in other income-generating or subsistence work, such as cooking, washing, and making clothing for her family, keeping a garden and raising animals, or selling the honey or maple syrup she collected or produced. This created an apparent contradiction: whereas in Québec, French-Canadian women had easier access to family resources such as mothers and female siblings to turn to for assistance in childcare during times of need, far greater numbers of Lowell's French-Canadian married women would have participated in the paid labour market than their counterparts.[56]

A heavy share of work assumed by mothers and wives inevitably led to their overwork. Oral evidence suggests that whereas elsewhere, temporary maternity leaves were at times granted to experienced female workers who had proved themselves to be quick, accurate, and reliable,[57] the textile management in Lowell did not extend special treatment to new mothers. At least in one instance, personal and paternalistic consideration of a supervisor helped an exhausted mother in a Lowell mill who had a large number of children. Her daughter remembered in an interview that the mother never complained or took a leave from work. But when she had to stay up the night before, her exhaustion came to a head. Seeing her tired and worn, her boss would ask her to sit, and sometimes, try to take a nap. He would even have someone watch her machine while she rested. The daughter says: "He felt so bad because she [the mother] had a big family, and, if one was sick, she was up all night. And then work from six to six."[58]

Supervisory consideration as such was hardly representative and its effect remained partial and temporary at best. The rule remained that there was no remunerated leave granted for pregnant women. The absence of such measures posed little concern to the management of the Lowell textile mills because the abundant reserve of labour was continually renewed by the influx of new migrants. In the neighbouring town of Manchester, it was relatively easy for women who had worked in the textile mills to return to work shortly after childbirth, upon the completion of child-rearing, or when changing employers.[59] Oral history accounts of a former Lowell mill worker also suggest a degree of frequency and facility with which the city's textile workers moved from one workplace to another. "You get out of one job and go in for another one," said Martha Doherty.[60] Fragmentary as it is, evidence indicates that although workers' mobility was considerably reduced during times of recession, female workers, including mothers and wives, in Lowell's textile manufacturing sector found it to be less taxing to leave and return to work frequently than it may seem if judged by today's standards. Such mobility among female (and male) workers in the textile factories co-existed with the employment practice of the textile companies which would ordinarily lay off, then re-hire, their workers, including married women, as long as the industry was not too constrained economically. This resulted in the majority of French-Canadian wives and mothers, such as Donna Mailloux's grandmother, going through a life cycle that Louise Tilly has described elsewhere as one in which women "worked for most of their lives, though not necessarily continuously."[61]

Struggling to Make Ends Meet: French-Canadian Widows

Bettina Bradbury has observed that the loss of a male spouse, either by desertion or death, laid bare the fragility of Canadian families in industrializing Montréal. Widows represented but one extreme of an irregular continuum of women who had to manage without a man and his wages, a continuum which included the separated, the deserted, and the non-supported—each different in their legal status but similar in the challenges they faced.[62] Such was also true of French-Canadian women without men in early-twentieth-century Lowell, whose lives revealed the inequality built into local labour markets that invariably offered lower wages to female workers than to their male counterparts.[63] While the majority of these women without spouses did not work, a good proportion did earn wages, and, in order to meet the need to secure sufficient wages, they sent their children into the labour market. When they failed, they sought solutions utilizing the larger circle of extended families, while a handful of them remained self-supporting or the principal wage earners for their families.

Not surprisingly, due to their difficult material conditions, a significant number (40 percent) of French-Canadian widows in early-twentieth-century Lowell worked for wages.[64] Julie Bédard, a fifty-eight-year-old widow, worked as a housekeeper for a private family, and her two sons, Joseph and John, brought home additional income. Thirty-seven-year-old Joseph owned and ran a boardinghouse, and twenty-six-year-old John worked as a printer in a cotton factory. Mary, her eighteen-year-old daughter, did not list any work or indicate attendance at school. She was probably working without wages at her brother Joseph's boardinghouse while taking charge of housekeeping work. The federal census listed two lodgers, who worked as a weaver and a printer at a cotton textile mill.[65]

The majority of widowed female heads of French-Canadian households, however, tried to conform to prevailing social and cultural norms, or family wage ideology, by sending their children to work while staying home themselves. In this way they maintained the employment patterns of the majority of married women who had their spouses. Widow Sarah Bouquet, fifty-eight years old, was recorded as not working for wages, while her son, Louis, aged twenty-four, and three daughters, Rosanne, Emily-A. and Ovilla, thirty, twenty, and sixteen, respectively, worked in cotton textile factories as weavers and winders. The youngest daughter, Georgina, thirteen, was going to school at the time of census-taking in 1910, but likely began working when she reached legal working age the following year.[66]

There may have been another, more pragmatic reason for the majority of French-Canadian widows to stay out of the labour market.[67] Widowed women like Julie Bédard rarely earned enough to compensate for the lost income that their spouses had formerly provided.[68] This was due to the fact that while a man's wage in a textile industry rose considerably when he moved into young adulthood, quickly surpassing his mother's earning capacity, women had few opportunities for promotion and their wage remained one of "perpetual youth."

The average annual earnings of female workers eighteen years of age and older were $283, in comparison to the $463 earned by their male counterparts.[69] Under such a wage structure, according to which a widowed mother earned no more than her young adult daughter and far less than her adult son, it was economically more advantageous for a widowed woman to have her son, rather than herself, work for wages. Thus, in households where there were adult sons, it made sense to send them out to earn wages and for the women to stay home. Similarly, since daughters could expect to earn roughly the same wages as their widowed mothers, the latter might reasonably prefer to stay at home. This led to an organization of the household whereby widowed mothers depended on the wages of their sons and daughters. By sending their adult children to work, therefore, a widowed mother was able to perpetuate the work pattern, one that conformed to the norm of American society and to the practice traditionally performed by women in Québec.

In comparison to their colleagues in two-parent households, more single women and, to a lesser extent, sons in widowed households tended to remain in their parental household for longer periods. Financial constraints were among the factors that compelled them to make such a choice. Among Lowell's single, wage-earning women of French-Canadian background who lived in a household with two parents, only 2 percent in 1910 and 6 percent in 1920 were aged thirty-five and older. In contrast, among single wage-workers who resided in a household headed by a widowed parent, while a majority (84 percent in 1910 and 80 percent in 1920) were under the age of thirty-five, a significant minority (6 percent and 20 percent, respectively) were aged thirty-five or over.[70]

The late departure of women from the parental home frequently coincided with temporarily or permanently postponed marriages, thus ensuring prolonged contribution to the parental household. As the cases of eighteenth-century British and French women and late-nineteenth-century Montréal women have shown, these single daughters diverged from the conventional pattern by working for wages during much of their adult lives.[71]

In Lowell, as observed elsewhere, a working-class household headed by a widowed mother faced different problems than one headed by a widowed father.[72] A widowed French-Canadian mother likely assumed domestic duties while other family members had to find employment adequate for their needs. Bound by the financial constraints, the lives of single, wage-earning daughters were closely tied to the well-being of their widowed mother. Such ties also resulted in the heavier, and often prolonged, commitment of single women to the household of the widowed mother. Underlying such arrangements was the precariousness of the widowed woman's standing in the gendered and ethnically hierarchical orders of local labour markets, as well as the relative power of the family wage ideology.

When French-Canadian daughters were not the sole wage earners in households headed by their widowed mothers, they were much more likely to share this economic responsibility with their siblings than with their widowed mothers.[73] Canadian-born Eugénie Vigneault, twenty-six years old, lived with her widowed mother and supported the household together with her twenty-nine-year-old brother, Alphie. Eugénie worked as an operative at a hosiery factory and Alphie was employed as a box-maker. The Vaillancourts, another widow-headed family, sent three young daughters aged nineteen, seventeen, and thirteen to work as a stitcher, winder, and doffer respectively to support the rest of the family with their earnings. Their forty-two-year-old widowed mother stayed at home to care for their five other siblings, who ranged in age from four to fourteen and did not work.[74]

Another crucial factor underlying widows' limited participation in the wage labour market despite their households' necessities was the advanced age of the women and, concomitantly, their difficulty in keeping pace with the production speed at the textile factories. Widows were the oldest wage earners among Lowell's French-Canadian female workers. The majority were aged forty-five or older (58 percent in 1910 and 50 percent in 1920), and a quarter were between the ages of thirty-five and forty-four (see Table 21). Their relatively advanced age, in addition to the management's preference for young girls who were considered to be quick and accurate, likely rendered it increasingly difficult for widowed workers to assume a sufficient workload in the factories.

It is not surprising, therefore, that a significant proportion of widows sought non-industrial employment, particularly in the service sector. Like single and married French-Canadian (and other) female workers, most widowed French-Canadian women were employed in the textile industry. But their marked presence (as many as one third of widows I studied, in 1910) in boarding and domestic services was by far greater than among single or married women of the same ethnic background (under 4 percent).[75] Selling one's labour power as an experienced housekeeper offered widowed women a practical alternative to industrial employment. And so, Florence Miller, seventy-four; Emma Dubé, thirty-four; Mary Gauthier, fifty-eight; and many other widows like them worked as housekeepers for private families or for boardinghouses.[76] Those with minimal capital but extra space ran their own boardinghouses by converting a part of their home into a rentable space. Cole Octavie, a seventy-two-year-old widow, was listed as a proprietor of a boardinghouse. Her two sons, aged forty-eight and thirty-five, worked as house painters, and her forty-one-year-old daughter, as a spinner.[77] Among widows who did not formally list their homes as boardinghouses, it was common to find one or two lodgers, sometimes referred to as boarders, living with them.

Because the wages earned by women were so low, it was crucial for the families headed by widowed women to secure supplementary sources of income or to reduce the cost of living. Many combined the two strategies. Such was the case with Malvina St. Peter, a spinner in a cotton textile factory. Malvina, in her fifties, lived with her married son, Frank, and his family. He was thirty-three years old, working as a boilerman at a railroad company. His wife, twenty-nine years of age, stayed at home with her two young sons, one several months old, the other six years old.[78]

The need to find alternative housing arrangements was felt even more acutely in the households of widows with children under working age. Emma Guilmet, a thirty-four-year-old widowed spinner at a cotton factory, had a daughter of thirteen and a son of eleven. They lived in the household of Emma's sister, who was married to a labourer and had three children aged ten, nine, and seven. Even with such an arrangement, Emma must have had a hard time keeping her family above the poverty line.[79] A small number of widows were listed as boarders or live-in housekeepers. In such cases, these women were self-supporting or acted as the principal wage earner for the family. Vitaline Bisson, a thirty-three-year-old widow and stitcher at a hosiery factory, boarded with the family of Edward and Victoria Bruel. Edward was a carder at a cotton factory and Victoria occupied the position of stitcher in a hosiery factory.[80]

Women without spouses were clearly the most hard-pressed among French-Canadian female workers in Lowell. Widows were forced by circumstances to be independent of the authority of male family members and this absence also meant a lack of their income which pushed them into the margin of Lowell's economy. Corroborating their financial difficulties was the presence of a considerably higher proportion of French-Canadian widows to their married counterparts. But for the majority of widows of this group, the existing wage hierarchy and the family wage ideology that endorsed it created and at least partially reinforced the patterns of household economy suited to the normative model of non-wage-earning wives and mothers. Consequently, the difficulties of making ends meet bound the lives of widowed women closely to their older, wage-earning, single daughters and sons.

*****

At first glance, French-Canadian mothers, wives, and widows seem to have different interests and responsibilities than the younger, single women who constituted the majority of Lowell's female workers. Yet as this chapter has shown, a minority of older women, either married or single, did not lead lives that can be examined in isolation. Wage-earning women shared the common responsibility of contributing to their household, either as supplementary wage earners, sole providers, or in some other capacity, working continuously or intermittently over their lifetimes. The diversity of wage-earning responsibilities and work patterns along with harsh struggles to meet the daily demands of survival among single, married, and widowed female workers in Lowell's French-Canadian community challenge the binary categorization that characterizes migrant women's relationships to their families. Working French-Canadian women have also pointed to the power and limitations of the ideology of family wage from which such binarisms are derived. Although this normative ideology remained powerful even among households headed by widowed mothers, which were under considerable economic pressure, a woman's age and her marital status were far from the only factors determining the extent of her labour market participation. Women's participation in the paid labour market—both in terms of their rates and patterns of involvement—was a response to a complex set of structural conditions, ranging from industrial demands for cheap and diligent labour power and a series of Progressive laws, to a gendered hierarchical order that endorsed inequalities inherent to the wage structures and promotional opportunities available to working women and men.[81] Their decision to enter or leave the paid labour market and their timing in doing so were also shaped by their families' needs, which were mostly financial, and by the availability of human resources and support, such as access to family and community resources, especially childcare.

A woman's marital status emerged even less as the decisive factor for defining the extent of her responsibility when considering that the two common needs—financial and available sources thereof—bound the lives of a growing number of single daughters (and sons) and their aging, widowed mothers to one another. This was because under the existing wage structure, which seldom allowed women and girls to earn as much as their sons and brothers did, not to mention their husbands or fathers, the absence of a male household head compelled single daughters like Rosanne Bouquet to remain in their widowed mother's household much longer than their peers. Ultimately, for many daughters, delayed departure became synonymous with continued financial contribution to the parental household, which in turn led to the postponement of marriages or lives of spinsterhood.

The emphasis that women placed on the economic needs of their household and the varying levels of their contributions seem to suggest that the financial reality primed over the potentially liberating consequences of the wage-earning practices examined in this chapter. Indeed, few in Lowell praised the opportunities, such as increased autonomy, that individual wages might have brought to them. Without denying that women were committed to their work and took pride in their hard work and endurance, as Valentine Chartrand has demonstrated, one may conclude that many viewed their paid work more as the way things were and that they tended to minimize the value of the long, arduous hours that they toiled in the textile mills, millineries, and offices and the substantial contributions they made to their household budgets.

Despite variations in the responsibility that they assumed in working for wages, Lowell's French-Canadian women all shared a common obligation—that of performing domestic work. Contributing a share of monetary resources to the family budgets was only one aspect of their responsibilities. Their contribution to the family budget was coupled with all the other duties of maintaining the home. In order to understand women's role at work and at home more clearly, the final chapter looks at the importance of their work outside the realm of paid labour.

CHAPTER SIX

More Than a Defence of the Traditional Family: The Unpaid Work of French-Canadian Women

Women and men shared wage work responsibilities in their French-Canadian families in Lowell. However, a vast amount of unpaid work[1] fell onto the shoulders of women. Such tasks were endless, ranging from cooking, washing, cleaning, mending, and managing the household budgets to taking care of children and the elderly. In performing these chores, women helped transform the wages brought into the household into consumable forms. They also helped to stretch and, at times, do without wages. The amount and nature of such work led to a definition of unpaid domestic labour articulated as women's tasks. This further reflected, and at times perpetuated, a gendered hierarchy within the city's French-Canadian families and Lowell's broader economy.

The final chapter of this book explores the significance behind the gendered division of labour and its saliency in French-Canadian families. The following pages draw graciously on the insights advanced by historians and social scientists in women's and gender studies who have explored unequal power relations within migrant and non-migrant (American and Canadian) families on the bases of gender, age, and generation.[2] A few recent studies aside,[3] historians of French-Canadian migration have yet to fully incorporate gendered perspectives into an analysis of this group. To what extent did French-Canadian wives, mothers, and daughters assume unpaid work at home? How did migration help to redefine, or reinforce such division of work at home? What does the share of women's work tell us about the power relationships that regulated the everyday lives of immigrant families? Although available evidence does not allow us to answer all these questions, careful reading of oral histories and other sources[4] discussed in the following pages points to the central and, indeed, indispensable role assumed by French-Canadian women in performing family work, regardless of paid labour status. Based on the evidence drawn from collections of oral histories and other sources, I argue that the sheer amount of unpaid work, coupled with a deep-seated sense of endurance, self-sacrifice and even satisfaction women drew from such responsibilities sustained, rather than levelled, the tenacity of gendered division of work in working-class French-Canadian households.[5] Signs of tension and possibilities for conflict were not absent. Neither did their men and boys remain without offering help with domestic chores, although a share of a man's unpaid work was mostly limited to specific tasks such as cutting wood and carrying coal for long distances.[6] Such tenacity of gendered division of family work, I suggest, stemmed from a mechanism that, for most migrant or American-born wives, mothers and daughters of French-Canadian background in early-twentieth-century Lowell, a family was not so much a site of resistance for greater gender and generational equality; it was above all a site of struggle for everyday survival of the women themselves and family members, a site in which women assumed the central role.

Women's work performed outside the formal economy fell into three main categories: housekeeping, care-giving, and other income-generating practices, which Joan Smith has called subsistence-sector labour.[7] This last category drew much time and energy away from work at home. At times, with the help of children, women sold sandwiches, took in boarders, and when driven by extreme need, scrounged or even stole in order to make a few extra dollars.[8] At other times, they simply did without. However, the very purpose of this type of work—to generate income—differentiated it from other forms of domestic work that did not involve any exchange of money or services. Even when a type of labour, such as the paying of bills, was directly related to the managing of money within the household, women were not financially compensated for it. The difference between income-generating "housework" and other forms of domestic work is even more striking when considered within the context of the early twentieth century, when married women's growing participation in the labour market enabled them to bring home an increasing amount of income on a more regular basis. While the need for other income-generating activities diminished significantly with their participation in the labour market, the number of hours they spent on housekeeping and providing care did not change substantially.[9] In view of these differences, the following discussion focuses on all or part of the three types of unpaid domestic work performed by French-Canadian women: housekeeping (including cleaning, washing, sewing, mending, and cooking), care-giving, and income-generating housework, especially the work involved in running a boardinghouse.

Unpaid Work Performed by French-Canadian Women

In the early twentieth century, dual forces of change—the mass production of food and cloth, and the development of household technology—were spreading rapidly in the United States. As far as working-class households in Lowell were concerned, the so-called time- and labour-saving devices and housekeeping facilities, such as gas stoves, electric lights, running water, and refrigerators, did not have an immediate impact. The majority of French-Canadian families did not have the financial means to take advantage of the new technology available. The domestic space these working families lived in was usually located in the gloomy, crowded cold-water tenements, which often lacked electricity. The tenements were filled with cheap, galvanized objects such as beds, tubs, and lunch pails.[10] A coal stove was essential for heating the apartment, as well as for cooking and heating water for the endless amount of washing. Gas lamps, sometimes even kerosene lamps, lit the kitchen where family members gathered to eat, pass the evening or even take a bath.[11]

In such household settings, the sheer quantity of time and energy required for women's domestic work meant that women had to be healthy, hardy, and strong to carry out physically demanding and time-consuming daily household tasks. Such work made claims on women's time in ways that differed distinctly from those made on men's time. The difference was felt on a daily, weekly, and even lifelong basis. The Lowell factories opened their gates as early as six-thirty in the morning, six days a week. Wives and mothers began their day long before other wage-earning family members in order to ensure that the latter would be awake, fed, and off to work on time. Del Chouinard recalls his mother's tasks in the morning:

> My mother, she'd get up in the morning, and make breakfast for the entire family. My father was a meat-and-potatoes man, three times a day. There was no such thing as just a bowl of corn flakes; that wasn't his bag. He'd need meat and potatoes, three times a day.[12]

Similar accounts were also found among other immigrant working-class families, such as Greeks, Irish, and Swedes, whose mothers "would be up at six o'oclock in the morning trying to wake us [the family] all up," as one son of the Greek immigrants stated. She'd be "[h]ustleing us up, trying to get us fed, and out,"[13] reminiscent of Montréal mothers half a century earlier who also rose long before the sun rose in winter to make sure that the wage earners were awake, fed, and ready to go to work.[14]

While both boys and girls were committed and expected to help with the housework, the kinds of jobs they performed at home differed sharply. Lowell's French-Canadian immigrant girls and boys were exposed from the earliest stages of their lives to the gendered division of work when helping their parents at home. As historian Mary Blewett has noted, boys were responsible for the more physical work outside, whereas girls were expected to do more of the indoor work, even though the latter was equally as time-consuming, and occasionally more physically demanding, than the boys' tasks.[15] An oral interview with an immigrant daughter, Lucie Cordeau suggests that such division of domestic chores along gender lines weighed most heavily on young girls. Because her mother was not well, one of her sisters had to stay with her mother all the time to help her with the housework. Cordeau and her sister had "special household chores" of scrubbing the floors of a large tenement where they lived, while their brothers had to lug the wood and coal and do the chopping. Lucie recalls:

> We had no linoleum, but floors with big wide boards, and every week we had to scrub that floor on our hands and knees. Me and sister. We had [a] toilet in the hallway, and we had to scrub that and scrub the hallway. And the stairways.[16]

In addition, Cordeau and her sister had to do the dishes as well as clean the big, heavy pots and pans. "It was," Madame Cordeau adds, "too much work for us."[17]

Defined within the sphere of women's work, washing embodied the gendered, and increasingly radicalized, division of work perhaps more clearly than any other type of domestic labour.[18] The only exception were a few men, mostly Chinese, who did laundry for fees for "men without women" in many American cities including Lowell.[19] The rising standards of cleanliness affected working families in urban industrial cities as early as the last third of the nineteenth century.[20] With such change in daily practices, washing became one of the central forces in regulating the weekly rhythm of French-Canadian women's lives and those of their families and neighbourhoods. Henry Paradis remembers that for his family, as for his neighbours in Little Canada, Monday was "washday." People in the neighbourhood had clotheslines strung from one building to the other. They would take their washed clothes outside in a basket and hang them on the line. Children would gather under the water dripping from the washed clothes. Paradis recalls: "Every Monday you thought it was raining, it was dripping so much. In the summertime the kids would get underneath there; it looked like a bath."[21]

If washing created memories of playful moments for children, for women it remained, above all, a laborious task. Blanche's mother, like many other French-Canadian women, did the washing for the entire family by hand, using a tub and a washboard, which she shared with her neighbours. "Anybody in the place there [boardinghouse] wanted to wash clothes, could do it [with that board]." Washing involved multiple tasks, some of which necessitated the help of daughters, but rarely that of sons.[22] Irène Desmarais scrubbed clothes by hand using a washboard and two tubs, putting the washed clothes in a ringer and, with the help of Desmarais and her sister, turning the ringer. After putting the clothes in a rinse tub again, she wrung the clothes once more. To wash sheets and pillowcases, Madeline Bergeron's mother filled a big boiler, put it on the stove, and added some potash into the water to bleach them. Finally, for drying, she hung the clothes on the clothesline in the backyard, even in winter. Madeline says: "Two o'clock in the morning, my mother be hanging her clothes out. And had to get to work for six o'clock. Ya, that had it hard."[23]

In an effort to save money, women sewed almost all the clothes for their families. Yvonne Hoar remembers that her mother used to pay a penny for surplus stockings that the bargain basement stores would order in bulk from hosiery factories. She would pick odd stockings, take them home, and then sew them together, trying to match them as best as she could. However, despite her mother's efforts in winter when Hoar wore her long johns with black stockings over them, she'd be bow-legged and lumpy. She recalls: "What a mess! That irritated me more I think in my life than anything. I used to cry every time I put them on in the morning. In fact we all did."[24]

Madeline Bergeron's mother also sewed clothes for her daughters. She made them panties, petticoats and aprons with ruffles to wear over their uniforms. Madeline recounts: "We all got white aprons over the dresses down below the knee. Black stockings, and black high shoes."[25] Her mother even sewed heavy winter clothing for her. If someone gave her an old coat, she would rip it out and make it over for her children. Shoes were among a few items Madeline's family bought from a store. Madeline was proud of her pair of button shoes that her aunt bought for her, since they were different from the more common laced type. Her appreciation was probably enhanced further by the fact that they were one of the rare, if not only, manufactured commodities that came into her possession.

Sewing provided women with an opportunity to extend the geographic boundaries of their activities. In order to shop for bargain fabrics, Madeline's mother went somewhere downtown, or, occasionally, took the trolley as far away as Billerica, a neighbouring town. That trip cost her mother as little as five cents, but it entailed a long ride, including a transfer.[26] Sewing also helped to draw a boundary between the types of social spaces men and women could occupy as they gathered, worked, and socialized. Blanche's mother sewed clothes on her sewing machine in a reception room of the boardinghouse. "She'd work and she'd be sewin', and sewin'. Making shirts for this man or that. [...] Whether it's hers or somebody else's, she sewed. [...] Always fixin' our clothes or doin' somethin' up in the [reception] room," says Blanche. As she

Figure 14. Children standing in front of clothes lines in the Greek tenement district behind the Greek Church, ca. 1910. (Courtesy of the American Textile History Museum, Lowell, Massachusetts.)

worked on her sewing machine, she might have had the opportunity to chat with the people around her, but she rarely did. She was "a quiet woman," busy with her work. Although her reticence may have indeed arisen from her individual nature and her absorption in her needlework, Blanche's account suggests an additional reason: that gendered codes of proper behaviour dictated that her mother refrain from talking too much in that public space. As Blanche put it, "There was mostly men talkin'. And the women were more quiet."[27] The reception room, therefore, can be seen as one part of a gendered ordering of public space in which women worked without talking but where men gathered to socialize.

Given the increased participation in the paid labour market among Lowell's French-Canadian women, like Madeline Bergeron's mother, the tenacity of gendered divisions of labour in cleaning, washing, and sewing discussed above emerged as an apparent contradiction. How can one explain such discrepancy between the increased contribution in wages among French-Canadian women, immigrant or American-born, and their sustained practice that embodies a belief that women's lives would and should continue to evolve around the home? One possible explanation has to do with the very difficulty of upholding the image dictated by the family wage ideology. In their study of working-class Hispanic women and men in Southern California in the late twentieth-century, Patricia Fernandez-Kelly and Anna Garcia have argued that for them "the issue is not so much the presence of the sexual division of labour or the persistence of patriarchal ideologies but the difficulties of upholding both."[28] French-Canadian families in early-twentieth-century Lowell differed in that a growing number of French-Canadian husbands and fathers found jobs that paid higher and more stable wages than three decades earlier when the majority had worked as day labourers or found themselves unemployed or underemployed. Nevertheless, the overwhelming majority of French-Canadian working families continued to live on a very tight, if not precarious, budget. One may argue that in such a household economy, with its internal disparities and asymmetries in power relations, the difficulties of daily survival continued to predominate the daily concerns of most women and men. Pressed by such concerns, or simply by habits of doing such tasks including washing and sewing, working mothers, stay-at-home wives and daughters alike, contributed their time and energy for the well-being of the family, rather than contested to the tenacity of gendered division of labour, in ideology and practice. Doing so, French-Canadian women arguably defended and internalized values and practices relevant to such normative models.

Running a boardinghouse added a set of onerous work to the already busy, well-regimented daily lives of Lowell's French-Canadian women. As a young daughter of French-Canadian parents who were boarding at Polivine Croteau's boardinghouse, Blanche Graham recounts the ways her matron worked. Mrs. Croteau spent a large portion of her time preparing hot, copious, and nutritious meals at the boardinghouse three times a day. In the morning she would cook bacon and eggs and serve toast—French toast or plain—for those who would like it, or oatmeal. For dinner she cooked cornmeal and cabbage. And she cooked a light supper and heated it up as she served it.[29] She would also prepare a hot lunch in a big dinner pail—containing meat, potatoes, vegetables and even a piece of cake for dessert—for boarders working at the mill who did not have the time to leave their workplace at noon. Such work, together with other tasks such as cleaning and washing, meant that her working day stretched to well over twelve hours. As Graham stated, "She was up at four and then to after maybe eight at night, and then went to bed." "That's all there was to it," she further emphasized, "work and eat and sleep. That woman worked hard." Working to provide a range of services, Polivine differed little from boardinghouse keepers of other ethnic groups, such as a Ukrainian boardinghouse keeper in Timmins, a mining town in northern Ontario, the Italian immigrant women in larger towns and cities of the United States, Canada, Belgium, and Australia and even the non-immigrant women in Victorian and Edwardian London and late-nineteenth-century Montréal. All these women took in boarders in order to help sustain the meager wages of their husbands or else struggled to live without them.[30]

The preparation of meals and other tasks necessary to run a boardinghouse regularly left Madame Croteau short-handed. This required Madame Croteau to ask young Graham for help in cleaning and setting the tables in the dining room. At other times, Croteau would say to Blanche Graham: "Would you take this to the Boott [mill] and give it to Mr. so and so? That's his dinner." Graham would reply, "Sure," and would take it over to the mill. Twelve-year-old Alice LaCasse in Manchester, New Hampshire, also helped with a boardinghouse right next door to her family in the mid-1920s. Unlike Graham, who might or might not have received monetary compensation for her work, for LaCasse, working at the boardinghouse was a way to earn a little money in order to help support her family in desperate need. She earned $3.00 a week which she gave to her father. She also received board. "That was a big help," as she recounts, because she had "a big appetite." She adds, "In those days, $3.00 was enormous. Why, at the boardinghouse, they used to serve a meal for thirty-five cents!"[31]

Despite advantages such as occasional free meals set aside, a boardinghouse could be presented as a site of danger and exploitation for the women who worked there. Feminist and gender historians of migration have pointed out that the amount of time and energy demanded of wives, mothers, and daughters who stayed home and who worked for a boardinghouse, and the nature of the work, sacrifice, and even risks—moral and sexual—to those women contrast sharply to earlier depictions of boardinghouses as safe havens from the dehumanizing effects of a larger outside world.[32] Rather, immigrant and non-immigrant boardinghouses alike were double-edged institutions. For labouring men, boardinghouses provided the familiar and familial ambience of a surrogate home, a locus of "fellow feeling," created by gossip and news in an environment where they spoke the same language and shared the same cultural values, as depicted in an influential work by Robert F. Harney. They also served as an important source of income for immigrant families with extra space and women's hands to help run it. But for women like Polivine Croteau who assumed the major, if not sole, share of the work required for running this form of lodging, a boardinghouse can also be seen as a form of exploitation.[33] Commissioned to report on boardinghouses run by Italian immigrants in North America, one middle-class Italian female journalist referred disdainfully to what she saw as "the servitude of the board system,"[34] in which women's labour was exploited and their bodies and souls risked being corrupted, since they had to live in a household with men other than their husbands and sons. The model of the bourgeois family ideal undoubtedly influenced such a view. Nevertheless, the journalist's words capture the close links connecting features of the boardinghouse milieu to that of the paid work, links that suggest that one might redefine boardinghouses as a form of wage-earning, even though contemporaries never did so.[35]

Cooking was yet another way in which Lowell's French-Canadian women stretched and managed their families' limited incomes.[36] Bargain hunting for groceries was part of their daily routine. They baked their own bread and biscuits, made ice cream at home, and prepared lemon drops—little flat cakes spread with bananas and jam, which were covered with another piece of cake and topped with whipped cream—as a Sunday treat. On occasion, they cooked special meals like salmon bread pudding with fried rice. It was a weekly treat for Henry Paradis, for example, that his mother cooked on Friday evening. She would bake bread, hollow out the loaf to make bread pudding and fill the shell "full of salmon." She would then make fried rice and place the dish on the table. "The beautiful bread full of this hot salmon with fried rice," recalls Henry fondly, adding, "Everyone liked it." Paradis and his sisters and brothers were allowed to bring one friend for dinner those nights. They would take turns. And they would ask, "When is it my turn?"[37] Children's voices requesting "my turn" must have brought joy to the mind of the mother, who treated them as best as she could with the little that she had. Standing in sharp contrast to the memories of brief, happy moments around the dinner table like the ones shared by the Paradis family and many of Lowell's other French-Canadians are the lonely dinners experienced by some women in other families, migrant or American.[38]

As Donna Gabaccia has observed in her study of culinary practices among Americans and migrants,[39] French-Canadian mothers and wives played a dual role as they organized their family's dinner table: first, they acted as keepers of culinary conservatism—that is, an inclination toward familiar tastes and dishes—and second, as intrepid explorers of new, that is to say, American, cooking methods. In Lowell, as in Québec, soup was an essential part of the daily meals of French Canadians. It was economical and nutritious, as one French-Canadian immigrant daughter explains, because "in the soup, there's substance." "You had your broth and you had your fat, what you needed." Some families could afford a greater variety of food on their table than just a bowl of soup, as was the case with the Bergerons. They had "bread, meat, potatoes, and vegetables," which, as Madeline Bergeron describes, usually meant "carrots and turnip and cabbage, probably. Not at the same meal. I mean, different times."[40] Even then, the family began the meal with soup.

At times, French-Canadian women varied their dinner table by serving "American" or New England dishes. Bergeron's mother served roasted duck or beef on weekends, recipes she learned from working at a local American restaurant. Her soup ranged from traditional French-Canadian pea soup to chowder. Bergeron says, "If it was vegetable soup [...], [m]y mother used barley to thicken her soups. We had rice soups. And she made a wonderful chowder. And, um, we had pea soup. And of course, we used the soup bone in those days," which they bought for five cents. As Bergeron concludes proudly, her mother "could cook anything," adding "we used very little canned goods."[41]

However typical or atypical the range of Bergeron's mother's cooking was, one thing is clear: her mother's minimal use of mass-produced foods seems to constitute a major commonality between her cooking and that served on most dinner tables around which Lowell's French-Canadian families gathered at that time. Being immigrants and mostly working-class, they had limited budgets for meals. At the turn of the century and early twentieth century, budgetary restraints, coupled with an inclination to eat what was familiar, meant that immigrant families would purchase few processed foods, such as canned goods, which America's food industries increasingly produced, transported, and marketed for the tables of the wealthier, white, native-born Americans.[42] As far as factory-made products were concerned, the cooking habits of Lowell's French-Canadian women confirm the observation that many immigrants' dinner tables were isolated from America's emerging national food market.

Cooking in new and old ways took additional time out of French-Canadian women's already busy schedules. Working mothers needed daughters to pitch in, especially during the week. Madeline and her sister took turns peeling potatoes and putting them on the stove before their mother got home from work. Doing so, they made sure that the potatoes were cooked and that their mother only had to cook the meat.[43] On weekends, women spent an entire day to prepare traditional dishes such as *ragoût*, which involves meatballs cooked with vegetables in a special sauce. Irène Desmarais's mother cooked beans with ham shoulder, another traditional "very good meal," served regularly at French-Canadian homes on Saturday nights. French-Canadian bakeries in Little Canada also cooked beans and ham, but, according to Desmarais, the taste was not quite the same. Referring to her mother's cooked beans, Desmarais says: "Hers were much darker than Rochette's [store-made] beans. I think she added more molasses."[44]

Memories of the dishes mothers prepared etched themselves deeply into the minds of their children. An immigrant daughter told an interviewer how *ragoût* and beans and ham evoked memories of her mother working in the kitchen and the family gathering around the table. French-Canadian *crêpes*, larger and thicker than French ones, were an inexpensive treat, a "standby" of Desmarais's family: "When people were very poor, if you ate them, you weren't hungry till the next meal," Desmarais says. It was also "a very popular thing to have at the fairs." Like many other dishes, the preparation of *crêpes* took time, but "people seem to enjoy them."[45]

For special occasions, such as New Year's Day, French-Canadian women served *tourtière*, a pork-based pie that required a day for preparation. Like other homemade dishes, every family had their own way of making *tourtière*. Desmarais says: "If you can find a pork pie that tastes like your mother's tasted, well you're lucky, because chances are it won't." For Christmas, her mother made stuffed turkey or chicken with pork or beef roast leftovers. Desmarais explains in detail how her mother used different parts from the chicken or turkey. She ground it all together, mashed it with potatoes, adding a little onion and seasoning—such as cinnamon, allspice, and clove—and stuffed the turkey with that mixture, making it "a [whole] meal going into the turkey. (...) And it's a delicacy to this day."[46]

Not only was the preparation for the holiday feast time consuming, it was also particularly trying for the women who prepared it since they had to cook during the period of fasting observed during this occasion. On Christmas, they were not supposed to eat anything until Midnight Mass. "It was really hard for her [mother] to do all the cooking and not, you know, break her fast. 'Til it was, 'til the Mass," Desmarais says. After finishing her preparation of the entire

Christmas dinner, the mother would stay home with the youngest children while the others went to the Mass. The entire family, including the mothers, had to fast all day until the family members who attended the Mass returned for their midnight feast.[47]

If fasting and the preparation of Christmas dinner highlight the difficulty of womanly duty, one of the most arduous tasks at home was the care of the young children. Again, women were almost entirely responsible for this task. As more and more married women with young children were working for wages, spending time and energy of the care of their children posed a serious problem. Fathers would occasionally play with their children or take them out on weekends,[48] but daily care—the changing, bathing, and supervising of the children—was considered "women's work," regardless of how much free time the men in the family had or whether or not the women were also earning wages.[49]

Scholars have pointed out that it was a common practice among working mothers to call upon grandmothers or other female family members outside of their households for help in child-rearing.[50] Numbers of French-Canadian women benefited from such arrangements with female kin, which in turn served to strengthen and extend family networks beyond the confines of the nuclear household in early-twentieth-century Lowell.[51] But exactly how common such practices were for Lowell's French-Canadian women in the first decades of the twentieth century remains unknown. Families who lacked the help of female kin, a group that made up a growing proportion of French Canadians in Lowell, had to seek other solutions. Some sent their young children to the homes of older women—neighbours or friends—who watched over a large number of youngsters for a fee. Another solution was the Lowell Day Nursery, established in 1890,[52] but few appeared to resort to this option, probably because many could not afford to do so.[53]

Other working mothers would put older siblings in charge of the infants.[54] However, when a child was taking care of younger ones, accidents could easily happen, such as dropping a steaming kettle full of boiling water and burning oneself as well as a little sister or brother. Fire could start easily as one could knock over a kerosene lamp, which was commonly used in working-class families in Lowell as late as the 1920s. One night, young Yvonne Hoar looked after her baby sister. She sat her sister on the side of a table where she was doing her homework with a kerosene lamp. The next thing she noticed was that her young sister had both hands on the lamp chimney and burnt all the inside of her hands. The poor baby screamed after she felt the pain and Hoar was petrified; they didn't know any better because they were just kids.[55] Still, other mothers who could not provide necessary care for the very young or sick children, might send them back to Canada. This was the case with Blanche Graham's brother, who stayed in Québec with her grandmother. "He was a strong boy, but I guess he was sickly. So my grandmother took him out there," says Blanche.[56]

Even when they were healthy, some children were sent back to Québec when there was no one to care for them. Diane Ouellette's mother worked as a weaver at the United Bunting Company for over twenty years, starting after her husband's death. At that time, Diane was only two years old and she and her brother were sent to an orphanage in Canada. Shortly after, her brother was brought back to the U.S., while Diane remained in Canada. Her mother worked at the mill and her mother's sister minded him.[57]

Still others who had their children around but preferred not to see them "wandering on the street" took the young ones with them to work and had them sit next to them in the lint-filled spinning rooms or in the deafeningly noisy weaving rooms. When their children were old enough to learn, mothers often taught them some of the techniques of spinning and weaving.[58] Blanche Graham spent her summer vacations helping her mother spin in the textile factory. When she was about eight years old, Blanche delivered dinner to her mother, who worked at the Hamilton Mills, and then she stayed with her mother all afternoon. Occasionally, her mother taught Blanche how to clean the frames and put in the bobbins. But she made a point as she told Blanche: "I don't want you to come work in the mills when you get bigger. I want you to do something else." Yet life did not leave Blanche any other choice but to go and work in the textile factories. At the age of fourteen, she became pregnant. She lost her loving mother and was consequently abandoned by her strict, religious, and unforgiving father. Two years later, she went to work at a hosiery factory, Hub Hosiery, and began a lifelong series of jobs while bearing and raising five children.[59]

Women had to be mindful that family needs took precedence over their own wishes. As a result, aspirations, such as continuing their education beyond the legal schooling age, had to be put aside in order to act as "organizers and perpetuators"[60] of a reciprocal kinship system for their nuclear family and beyond. In Manchester, New Hampshire, for example, Yvonne Dionne remembers skipping school in order to replace her sick aunt, who worked at a textile factory. While Dionne certainly earned daily wages that her aunt could not afford to lose, Dionne probably did not receive any monetary compensation for her work. Rather, her replacement can be understood as an exchange of non-monetary services between her aunt and her own family. In that sense, her work was a type of unpaid work, performed in the guise of paid work, which served to perpetuate a system of reciprocal kinship centring upon female members. In Lowell, evidence of similar accounts is not available. However, given the absence of a corporate or public system of compensation for sickness and injury, one may safely surmise that a similar practice of utilizing the family network, especially that of women, to make up the potential loss of wages was common among French-Canadian working families with comparable financial needs.

In a context slightly different from that of Dionne's, but under similar economic pressure, Valentine Chartrand in Lowell left school on her fourteenth birthday in order to begin working in a textile mill. She, too, earned wages, and the context in which she began her lifelong career in the textile industry had little to do with her own desires. She remembers a painful moment when she and her father had a talk. She recounts:

> He asked me if I would mind quitting school. He was crying, and he needed help, you know. And I was the oldest, the oldest at home then. And he asked me if I wouldn't mind very much if I quit school. And I said, I did like school, and I hated to leave it. I wanted to go to high school. But when he asked me that, I said okay.[61]

Chartrand, then, had to tell one of the nuns at school that she was leaving. Feeling bad about her circumstances, the sister told her that she hated to see Chartrand go because her grades were excellent. Chartrand replied in tears: "Well, my father needs the extra money, and I have to leave." The next day, she went to the employment office at the city hall to find a job. Asked if it was not hard to leave school, she answered, "Yes, it is, but I've got to help my father... I'd take anything."[62] About a week and a half later, she had a job in a woolen manufacturing mill in North Chelmsford, Massachusetts. Tears shed by young Valentine bear little difference from those of immigrant and American women in the late twentieth century, who knew that not only were the wishes of husbands and fathers given priority during a typical family's economic decision-making process, but that they also seem to have dictated the relative weight given to the wishes of other family members.[63]

In addition to performing the labour of keeping the household functioning, French-Canadian women, especially daughters, were expected to take charge of their aging parents and their younger siblings. Two imperatives—securing a minimum household income and having someone take care of domestic tasks—likely determined a daughter's marriage prospects within single parent households, whether or not the lone parent in question was male or female. These households commonly had one or two unmarried daughters (and, to a lesser extent, sons as well) working for wages, taking charge of domestic work, or doing both.[64]

The burden fell most heavily upon the daughters of widow-headed households, who often had to submit to the fate of a temporarily—if not perpetually—postponed marriage. The question of who should care for elderly parents at times became an emotionally charged issue, which created tensions and conflicts, and usually came to a head at the time of a marriage proposal. Oral interviews with Lowell's French-Canadian women do not show the same degree of family tension as that demonstrated by the case of one French-Canadian daughter, Marie-Anne Sénéchal, in Manchester, who postponed her marriage for as long as forty years until she was finally married at age sixty-seven. After five years of marriage, she was widowed. She recalls: "My husband and I waited forty years to get married. Forty years! [...] I could not get married because I had to bring up a family, and he had to take care of his family. I thought I'd never marry. I was sixty-seven years old when I got married."[65] The absence of similar evidence in Lowell notwithstanding, considering French-Canadian women's various domestic tasks and financial contributions, one cannot overstate the pertinence of Louise Tilly and Joan Scott's observation that a daughter's marriage revolved, more often than not, around the question of *when* one should marry, rather than whom.[66]

One might conclude that the tendency among numbers of French-Canadian daughters in single parent households to postpone marriage reinforces the claim made by Tamara Hareven regarding the flexibility of the household unit in determining "family time." The diversity in such timing, described as "flexible" in Hareven's study, was indeed flexible as far as age norms were concerned. Nevertheless, such divergence occurred within a framework that imposed considerable constraints on individual preference, especially that of daughters, subordinating their wishes to the collective goals of the family.[67] What Tamara Hareven has described as the "flexibility" women displayed in the timing of the transitions in their lives thus emerges less as a result of their autonomy than their acceptance of, or compliance with, the pressure to accommodate the needs of their families. After a wife's death, the oldest unmarried daughter was usually expected to take the role of the family's "second mother," managing the household and taking care of younger siblings.

The responsibility of a second mother ranged from making everyday financial decisions to supporting the daily survival of the family members by transforming their wages into sustenance and shelter to providing emotional care within the home. Lucie Cordeau was fourteen when her mother died. Not long after, her older sister also passed away, and Lucie became the only girl left at home. And so, she had to take over the care of her father and three brothers. When she was twenty-nine, her father told her, "Lucie, you better get married. I won't live forever."[68] He never remarried and she married only after her father died. She was then thirty-two, quite late by the norms of the time by which an unmarried woman older than twenty was considered an old maid. Lucie recalled:

> At that time [when the mother died,] the older girl takes over. She's the second mother. She has to supervise. She has to make all the decisions in anything. And if you had a boyfriend, let's say you have to go back home and cook supper for your father or cook meals for your brothers, the boys never stay long. The friendship never lasts. They say, you take your family before me.[69]

Once again, the daughter's marriage was contingent upon the needs of the family. Bound by family responsibilities, single women like Lucie were deeply committed to their families' well-being.

Notwithstanding the precedence of the familial goals over individual interests, the family norm should not make us blind to the liberating consequences of migration that some French-Canadian single women enjoyed in other industrial cities in New England. There are subtle differences and nuances in the circumstances that led to each woman's prolonged celibacy. For example, Manon, a thirty-five-year-old single French-Canadian woman in Lewiston, openly embraced her celibacy. Stating that she felt happy and fulfilled without becoming a wife or mother, she declared: "I have felt so spoiled, and I have been so happy that I've never dreamed it was necessary to marry."[70] Marie Anne Sénéchal in Manchester also confessed that she thought she would "never marry." Like Manon, Marie Anne did not consider herself unhappy, but her postponed marriage in her late sixties changed her earlier view. At the age of seventy-nine, Marie Anne confessed in retrospect: "It was too much of a wait. [...] I would have been happier [..] if I'd got married. But when you don't know, you just stay that way." Cora Pellerin, a weaver in a Manchester mill, did not wait to get married as long as Marie Anne did, but when she did so, she was thirty-one years old. At thirty she called herself "an old maid," but Cora was happy, just like Manon asserted, to be an old maid as she "made a good money, dressed up well, and went dancing." In a word, she "was having a good time." She stated that she had no desire to "switch with her friends who had five or six children and a husband that came in drunk every weekend." Listening closer to her words reveals that Cora's decision not to marry hinged at least as much, if not more, on family circumstances than on her inclination toward wanting personal freedom. Cora was taking care of her aging, sickly mother, who lived with her. She wanted to take care of her and did not feel like getting married as long as her mother was alive. Her fiancé, whom she had known for as long as ten to eleven years, lived with a similar situation: he too was taking care of his mother until she died at the age of eighty-two. Also, he had a sister, who was a spinster, living with him. As Cora puts it, "I didn't want him to break up his house on account of me."[71]

Which woman's assessment of her life as an unmarried woman was the most representative of French-Canadian women in early twentieth century? The question remains open, given the scarcity of available sources. Nevertheless, it is reasonable to assume that while some single women in Lowell might have enjoyed some of the liberating effects stemming from moving to the urban industrial centre, for many others, marriage remained fundamentally a family affair and a pre-determined life course, if not an explicit obligation, given the wage-hierarchy on the job and the gendered division of labour at home, both of which placed female workers at a disadvantage to their male counterparts. Financial considerations—choosing to contribute to one's parental household or to a conjugal household—and family circumstances could therefore easily outweigh possibilities for more personal alternatives.

*****

Examining some of the myriad forms of unpaid work performed by French-Canadian wives, mothers, daughters, and nieces has shown the endless nature of women's tasks and the share of work they performed at home and beyond. Women's roles ranged from acting as caretakers and "second mothers," to being keepers of a familial taste and explorers of new cooking methods, to taking on the responsibilities of organizing and perpetuating kinship networks. The amount and nature of such work have revealed the tenacity of gendered divisions of labour, and the different ways in which such work made demands on the women's and girls' time from the demands made on their male counterparts. Further, they have also pointed to the centrality of female-centered networks of French-Canadian families. The malleability of female-centred networks to support and, indeed strengthen the gendered division of labour has affirmed, rather than contested, the centrality of family in the context of transnational migration.

The tenacity of the gendered division of labour within the French-Canadian working-class household suggest the wide variety of responsibilities that stretched a woman's working day to a double shift at home and a paid work site. But the concept of a double day that many working-class women in the late twentieth and early twenty-first centuries have described as working, as they struggled to support themselves and their families does not fit well with the way that mothers and wives performed money-earning and domestic labour a century before.[72] For instance, in the second half of the nineteenth century in Montréal, only a small number of married women reported employment and the minority that did worked at jobs that "could be fitted in between other domestic tasks" or that "increased such specific domestic tasks" such as washing, sewing, and cooking.[73] A growing number of French-Canadian women in early-twentieth-century Lowell balanced such responsibilities in yet another way that precludes them from being viewed simply as a historical precursor of the double day in our society. The absence of any system of paid leave in the textile factories coupled with the lax enforcement of factory regulations and reform laws in the early twentieth century made it even more difficult for French-Canadian mothers and wives to juggle their responsibilities at work and at home than is the case for many American and immigrant women today. At the same time, these same conditions gave French-Canadian wage-earning mothers a greater margin of autonomy as they helped them to combine their multiple daily responsibilities, exemplified, for instance, by Blanche Graham's mother bringing her daughter to the textile factory and having her sit beside her as she operated the machine. As the twentieth century progressed, an arrangement such as this became impossible as the mill management prohibited small children in the weaving room for fear of a shuttle flying up in the air, which could hit and hurt anyone.[74] Other French-Canadian working wives and mothers charged older children with the care of younger siblings, a risky solution that could easily lead to accidents. Clearly, such flexibility came with a dubious advantage. Nonetheless, it offered a limited range of solutions, which helped wage-earning mothers and wives shift between seemingly separate, impenetrable and hierarchically opposed spheres of paid work and unpaid work over the course of a day, a week, or a lifetime. Therefore, the performance of endless tasks such as cleaning, sewing, washing, cooking, and caring for the young and the elderly did not lead French-Canadian wives and mothers to build a second workday, or "separate sphere," distinct from the world of paid work, even more so than was the case for their American and immigrant working-class sisters a century later. Rather, the sites of paid and unpaid work were tightly linked to one another and even merged to some degree in early-twentieth-century Lowell.

The emphasis on the centrality of the immigrant family, womanly duty, and the apparent complacency among wives, mothers and daughters in accepting their roles should not gloss over increasingly individual characteristics in migration practices. That a small but growing minority came to travel without the company of family and more and more wives and mothers who worked for wages would suggest that the potential for women's independence grew. Yet, evidence discussed in this chapter has revealed that the importance of family for

French-Canadian women with its expanded functionality and, although far less salient, internal tensions and potential conflicts, grew even more remarkably within the framework of transnational migration strategies. More research in new sources and through comparative perspectives will allow one to argue conclusively that the gendered division of labour persisted in French-Canadian families as a reflection and, in turn, a reinforcement of the view held by the majority of the women themselves whereby families were seen to provide the best conceivable way of bringing a better life to themselves, as well as their loved ones. Women's work was more than an act of defending the traditional family structure. Lowell's French-Canadian women were giving new contours and meanings to this repository of traditional values and strengths—the family—in order to respond to the new demands encountered within urban industrial settings.

Epilogue

This book has sought to offer a layered portrait of French-Canadian women and men and their U.S.-born children in Lowell in an attempt to answer the question, "What was the relationship of migration, family, and gender?" The diversity of migration experiences lived by textile workers, shopkeepers, professionals, boardinghouse owners, or stay-at-home housekeepers, who were also husbands, fathers, sons, wives, mothers, and daughters, studied in this book suggests that gender was not the single, nor was it the primary factor, that distinguished the lives of migrant men and women. They all faced social and economic dislocation in Canada; they shared moments of adventure and the risks of travel to Lowell (and their travels back to Canada); and once in Lowell, many found expanding, yet still limited, economic opportunities as wage workers, small business owners, or professionals.

Yet gender mattered in various ways. The skills, experiences, and human networks of the migrant men and women may have led to a new range of possibilities and meanings, but they also closed some doors. Gendered ideologies and practices, such as the family wage ideology and wage hierarchies, further differentiated men's and women's experiences whether *en route* to their destination, earning wages at work, or in familial or social settings, even though they spoke the same language and shared the same religious and familial practices that established the social and cultural boundaries of the French-Canadian immigrant community.

Several important patterns emerged from the process of movement of French-Canadian migration in the twentieth century—patterns that continued and diverged from the pattern of the nineteenth century. As in the earlier time, the overwhelming majority of migrants in the early twentieth century moved as a nuclear family unit. Only a small but growing minority—including both men and a smaller proportion of women, such as the Ducharme sisters—traveled to Lowell without the company of their family members. But to interpret the journeys of the latter as instances of moving alone or outside the family network would be erroneous, since they invariably had a brother, sister (most common among "lone" female migrants), uncle, or aunt awaiting their arrival in Lowell. Even among the minority who carried out "individual" movements independent of a nuclear family unit, migration did not isolate them from their families. For those French Canadians on the move, a family—both as a social unit and as part of an expansive web of networks—continued to serve as the primary motivation and the fundamental means for enabling their spatial movement.

When French Canadians did not move in nuclear family units, it was more likely that a husband, father, or son, rather than a female family member, would begin the chain of migration. Conversely, few French-Canadian women initiated family migration even when they had industrial experience as semi- or unskilled textile workers in Québec. This stands in contrast with the migration of skilled, wage-earning Midland women in Paris, Ontario and female domestics from Sweden, Norway, and Ireland in a number of industrializing cities in North America. Many among the latter migrants were versed in the migration tradition of crossing the Atlantic unaccompanied by a male family member or acting as "pioneers" paving the way for a family's chain migration. Further, evidence discussed in the above pages has shown that having attained paid work experience in Canada made an important difference in migration southward for French-Canadian women of all ages, but it was not a sufficient condition for them to carry out solo migration. What weighed equally, if not more heavily, on the decision of allegedly solitary female migrants such as Béatrice Audet and Anna Aubert was the presence of a female sibling at the destination. Sisters in Lowell, probably more than their male counterparts, were expected to provide a range of support, such as immediate help in finding a job, initial housing, and other practical and emotional means of assistance, for their newly arrived female siblings. The presence of a sister at the destination assured, to some extent, a source of indispensable and reliable support—a source that must have been even more valuable years after the closure of corporate boardinghouses and other amenities for which Lowell's textile companies had once been well known.

More clearly than the process of movement, the process of settlement, or the time after migrants' arrival in Lowell, has shed light on gendered and generational hierarchies that created different expectations and responsibilities for French-Canadian women and men respectively. Child labour laws created one such instance by which the experience and meaning of work diverged sharply for men and women. True, such legislation was far from providing a panacea to what middle-class reformers, Progressives, and political leaders considered as the root of the social vice. True, too, another set of change, ranging from the arrival of "new immigrants," the subsequent halt on transoceanic migration during World War I, and the war-time economic boom created an acute labour need. This temporarily boosted the city's industrial need for child labour. But with the end of World War I, new moral orders of child labour became inevitable and the decline of the textile industry in Lowell as in the rest of New England irreversible. As a result, French-Canadian families were pressed to make up for the loss of the financial contributions formerly brought home by children in their early teens. One can thus understand the growing presence of adult French-Canadian male and female workers in the more skilled positions in Lowell's textile mills as part of micro-level adjustment that French-Canadian men, women, and children made to the city's new political economy. At the same time, the increased presence and the significance of adult workers reflect a larger, i.e., regional or national, transformation that touched the lives of all American and immigrant families, albeit in different ways.

One response to the household needs was an increase in the number of French-Canadian fathers, husbands, and adult sons who worked as skilled loomfixers in the textile factories and as mechanics in non-textile industries. A minority entered white-collar jobs as office clerks, bookkeepers, and salespeople. In contrast, day labourers, who had made up the overwhelming majority of French-Canadian workers a few decades earlier, became a definite minority. But Lowell's ethnically segmented labour markets kept such economic advancement in check. It also had an important effect in shaping these and other French-Canadian male workers' sense of self.

French-Canadian women, especially married women, provided another indispensable source of labour that compensated for the loss of children's financial contributions. Like their male counterparts, more and more female workers moved up into skilled and semi-skilled positions in the textile and cartridge factories. A growing proportion, especially among the U.S-born daughters, came to work as salespeople—a job formerly reserved for Anglo-Celtic workers. Such upward shifts in women's occupational profiles in general and the growth of paid labour market participation among married women in particular, had significance beyond the variety of jobs they held and the levels of income they earned. In the late nineteenth century, the participation of French-Canadian wives and children in the paid labour market resulted from a set of accommodating, rather than competing, demands on their labour: an acute economic need of immigrant households on the one hand, and the advantage these workers presented to the industrial capitalists in need of an inexpensive, easily replaceable, and diligent source of labour, on the other. This symmetry remained basically unchanged throughout the twentieth century. However, the entry of growing numbers of mothers and wives added a new dimension to that familiar order: women's wage-earning was heightened by an edge they held as a legal—as opposed to the now illegal child labour pool—and industrious workforce.

Despite their growing importance as wage earners, French-Canadian women continued to shoulder most, if not all, of the responsibilities of the household work. Regardless of their paid job statuses, wives and mothers commonly got up hours before their husbands and children so that the latter two would be awakened, fed, and arrive on time for work. Wives and daughters cooked, washed, cleaned floors, and mended clothes, frequently before or at the end of hard days of work, or on the weekends. Husbands, fathers, and sons also did certain household chores, such as chopping wood and hauling coal. But they were also likely to spend the greater part of an evening or weekend going out for drinks, chatting with their fellow boarders, or visiting their friends while their mothers, wives, and sisters toiled long hours at home. Frequent pregnancy and little by way of domestic technology made women's work even more difficult. The sheer amount of work and the time it required arguably placed these women in a disadvantaged position within the power relationships at home and in the workplace in early-twentieth-century Lowell. This inequality came to a head when their personal goals and wishes were overridden by those of other family members, such as sons, or the collective needs of the family. Valentine Chartrand, Lucie Cordeau, and many others like them have revealed memories of painful moments when they had to abandon their desire for higher education or when they were obliged to act as the second mother. Looking back, these women also derived a sense of pride and indispensability from the hard work that they performed.

It would be mistaken to conclude, however, that French-Canadian women's struggles to keep their families together were proof of their acquiescence to traditional family practices and patriarchal ideology. As the preceding pages have shown, the need for wages, a myriad of household tasks, and the various obstacles related to familial expectations, compelled French-Canadian women and men to give new contours and meanings to traditional social arrangements—i.e., families. Again, women played a central role in reshaping these repositories of traditional values and strength. At times, female-centred networks extended the narrow confines of a nuclear family as mothers made arrangements with aunts, nieces, and grandmothers for childcare assistance or the replacement of a sick relative at work. Such exchanges of services took place in Lowell, neighbouring localities, and as far away as Canada. At other times, wage-earning mothers regularly shifted across the boundary separating paid and unpaid work. Donna Mailloux's grandmother moved in and out of the paid labour market as she lived through a pattern of pregnancies, births, and the time in-between. This type of intermittent work pattern was familiar to many other

French-Canadian wives and mothers, who had to juggle "double responsibilities" over the course of their lifetimes. Others tried to juggle some of those responsibilities on a daily basis by bringing their children to the mill and having them sit next to an operating machine. Lowell's French-Canadian women thus devised and carried out diverse strategies, certainly not without difficulty. At the same time, in the absence of strict factory regulations which would prohibit working mothers to bring their young children into an operation room, for example, married female wage earners like Blanche Graham's mother seemed to benefit from relatively greater freedom to manage their responsibilities at home and at work than their wage-earning sisters have in the late twentieth and early twenty-first century, when their lives have come under stricter control of state and federal regulations.

Walking in downtown Lowell today, women, men, and children who worked a century ago would find it strange to come across a very different ethnic mixture among the residents of the city. South Asians, mostly from Cambodia, but also from Thailand, Laos, and Vietnam, represent a quarter of the city's population of 106,000 in 2000. Puerto Ricans constitute another significant ethnic/cultural group of the city, who, together with the Spanish-speaking population from other parts of the world, account for a little less than 15,000, or 14 percent of Lowell's population.[1] Many recent migrants arrived in the city during the brief economic upsurge of the 1990s and worked revamping mills for the high-tech electronic industry where French-Canadian and other immigrant workers had spun, woven, fixed machines, and dyed for textile production a century earlier. The huge differences in origin, memories of war and atrocity, transportation, and citizenship status separate the migration experiences of recent migrants from those of earlier groups. And yet, French-Canadian migrants and their sons and daughters who lived and worked in Lowell, not to mention the city's Franco Americans today, would recognize resonances with their lives. These echoes emerge in various sites ranging from ethnically marked labour markets, poverty and unemployment, family and kin networks, and gendered and generational conflicts and cooperation that operate within the family and beyond. All such aspects created and sustained the human complexities called migration. Its asymmetry, intricacy, and inequality that women and men weaved together and continue to do so today make up a fundamental part of North American history on both sides of the border and across the oceans.

Appendix A

Longitudinal Data and the Nominal Record-Linkage Method

In chapter three, I presented evidence drawn from nominative linkages of data derived from three sources, the U.S. federal manuscript schedules, the *Soundex Index to Canadian Border Entries through the St. Albans, Vermont, District, 1895-1924* (*Border Entry*), and the *Case History Records for the Overseers of the Poor*. Nominative linkages enable historians to systematically follow the lives of immigrants at municipal levels over a period of time in a way that few other sources have previously allowed. Certain key moments of the immigrant itineraries can be reconstructed from the birthplace of the recorded individuals and from their children's birthplace through to the time just before their departure (i.e., place of last permanent residence), up to the moment they entered the United States to head for their destination, in the case of this present study, Lowell. This may have created some ambiguity when immigrants changed their destination after they crossed the border. Yet, given that most French-Canadian immigrants listed a person to be met upon their arrival at the U.S. destination, one can speculate that few changed their destination after filling out the border entry form. As for the mobility of Lowell-bound immigrants after their entry into the United States, *Case Histories* provides detailed information at the level of municipality on a selected population.

The analyses in chapters three, four and five are based on three sets of samples created from the three nominal sources. The first set of data, which I compiled from the U.S. Federal Census Schedules (1910 and 1920), Middlesex County, City of Lowell, represents a sample of 5 percent, or 11,901 individuals (5,120 in 1910; 5,781 in 1920). In this sample, French Canadians account for 2,258 (1,103 in 1910; 1,153 in 1920) individuals.

The second sample consists of two data sets compiled from the *Border Entry*, U.S. Immigration and Naturalization Service, Record Group 85, Washington D.C.[1] The first set includes 150 French Canadians whose last name began with the letter A, who resided in Canada just before their emigration during the period from 1900 to 1920, and who listed Lowell, Massachusetts, as their destination. The second set is composed of individuals who appeared both in

Border Entry and in the census manuscript schedules of 1910 or 1920. I selected all those who immigrated to Lowell between 1900 and 1920 from the census manuscripts and, with the help of the Soundex coding system, traced these individuals and families to the *Border Entry* files. A total of eighty-nine individuals and twenty-nine families were successfully identified.

Finally, I created the third sample from the *Case History* files. This data bank includes 178 French Canadians whose records were completed from the year 1900 onward. *Case Histories* lists each individual's name, birthplace, age, marital status, birth date or year of arrival in Lowell, the names and addresses of parents or children, and most importantly, individual residential itineraries prior to arriving in Lowell.

Appendix B

The Classification of Work

Gérard Bouchard and his research group, the IREP (*Institut interuniversitaire de recherches sur les populations*), have developed a scale for classifying different occupations present in the Saguenay region of Québec from 1842 to 1971.[1] First, occupations are divided into two major categories—manual labour and non-manual labour. These categories are then grouped into nine sub-categories based on the technical difficulty and the level of responsibility that each job involves. The sub-categories include: (a) semi- and unskilled manual workers, (b) skilled manual workers, (c) craftsmen, (d) farmers, (e) semi- and unskilled white-collar workers, (f) administrators and skilled white-collar workers, (g) those who work in the liberal professions, (h) industrialists and small shopkeepers, and (i) undetermined.

The logic of the above classification notwithstanding, one must be aware of the arbitrariness of terms such as skilled and unskilled. One such example of arbitrariness was pointed out by David Montgomery, who alerts us to the extent of the judgement and experience required by many types of operative work, despite its repetitive nature. The case of an experienced power-loom weaver, Cora Pellerin, an immigrant daughter of French-Canadian immigrants in Manchester, New Hampshire, illustrates this point. Pellerin's work as a power-loom weaver, classified as "semi-skilled," nevertheless required comprehensive knowledge of power-loom functions, and swift judgment to be able to respond promptly to any kind of unforeseen abnormality. Pellerin once said about her work: "You have to have it in you to be a good weaver. You either fit in or you don't." Pellerin's interview further reveals how her work would proceed. It consisted primarily of watching for breaks in the yarn that would spoil the machine's output. When the loom would get out of order, a bobbin would drop and sprout a whole new warp. The warp would have to be cut out and the weaver would have to start the entire process all over again. In order to manage such a situation quickly, the weaver had to learn the patterns with five or six colours "not just in your hands" but "in your head too."[2] This brief account suggests therefore that the terms "skilled" and "unskilled" constituted only one way of classifying the levels of knowledge, judgment, and supervision required for various kinds of work.

In addition, the boundaries between skills often shifted, in response to cultural changes or workplace struggles. Gender is one of such dimensions of the skills. As Christina Burr has highlighted, bearing little relationship to the level of training or ability required to perform them, "skill" classifications define men's work as skilled and women's work as unskilled or semi-skilled. Further, the nature of work and the attendant skills were also constantly changing.[3] The machinist in the pre-Civil War period was described by pioneer trade unionist Jonathan Fincher as "a cross between a millwright and a whitesmith, a fitter, finisher, locksmith, etc." Within half a century, "machinists" saw their job description evolve from builders of machinery to those who cut and shaped metal parts on machine tools.[4] A question rises then about how to classify the "machinist," "mechanic," and "engineer" in the first two decades of the twentieth century.

Heeding to these and other ambiguities inherent in terms such as "skilled," "semi-skilled," and "unskilled," I have used a modified scale of Bouchard's classification in chapters four and five of this book. All operatives such as weavers, spinners, and carders, craft workers, and the more skilled workers are thus grouped into one category. Under that category, however, I have created sub-categories which will enable us to distinguish trades according to the degree of difficulty of the work they require. The first sub-category includes the semi-skilled and skilled, ranging from operatives to machinists, mechanics, engineers, carpenters, other craft workers, and loomfixers. The second includes other less qualified workers, such as bobbin boys, sweepers, and labourers, who are treated as unskilled workers.

Notes

Note on Language and Terminology

1 Charles-Édouard Boivin, de Fall River, "La presse française des États-Unis," *La revue canadienne* 47, 1904 : 146. Cited in Yves Roby, *Les Franco-Américains de la Nouvelle-Angleterre, 1776-1930* (Sillery, Québec: Septentrion, 1990), 232.

Introduction

1 Historians, geographers and demographers have produced a number of studies on French Canadians in New England and Mid-West localities. Early works on the subject include Marcus Lee Hansen, *The Mingling of the Canadian and American Peoples*. Completed and prepared by John B. Brebner (New Haven: Yale University Press, 1940); Ralph Dominic Vicero, "Immigration of French Canadians to New England, 1840-1900: Geographical Analysis" (Ph.D. diss, University of Wisconsin, 1968); Albert Faucher, "L'émigration des Canadiens français au XIXe siècle: position du problème et perspectives," *Recherches sociographiques* 5, no. 3 (septembre-décembre, 1964): 217-317; Yolande Lavoie, "Les mouvements migratoires des Canadiens entre leur pays et les *États-Unis au XIXe et au XXe siècle: études quantitatives*," in *La population du Québec: études rétrospectives* (Montréal: Éditions Fides, 1973); Yolande Lavoie, *L'émigration des Canadiens aux États-Unis avant 1930: mesures du phénomène* (Montréal: Les Presses de l'Université de Montréal, 1972); Yolande Lavoie, *L'emigration des Québécois aux États-Unis de 1840 à 1930* (Québec: Gouvernement du Québec, Conseil de la langue française, Direction des Études et recherches, 1979; rev. ed., 1981); James P. Allen, "Migration Fields of French Canadian Immigrants to Southern Maine," *Geographical Review* 62, no. 1 (1974): 32-66. Among more recent work, see Roby, *Les Franco-Américains de la Nouvelle-Angleterre*; Bruno Ramirez, *On the Move: French-Canadian and Italian Migrants in the North Atlantic Economy, 1860-1914* (Toronto: McClelland & Stewart, 1991); Ramirez with Otis, *Crossing the 49th Parallel: Migration from Canada to the United States, 1900-1930* (Ithaca: Cornell University Press, 2001); Yves Frenette, "La genèse d'une communauté canadienne française en Nouvelle-Angleterre, Lewiston, Maine, 1800-1880," (Ph.D. thesis, Université Laval, 1988); Sylvie Beaudreau and Yves Frenette, "Les stratégies familiales des francophones de la Nouvelle-Angleterre. Perspective diachronique," *Sociologie et société* 26, 1 (printemps 1994): 167-78; Yves Frenette, "Macroscopie et microscopie d'un mouvement migratoire: les Canadiens français à Lewiston au XXe siècle," in *Les chemins de la migration en Belgique et au Québec: XVIIe–XXe siècles*, ed. Yves Landry, John A. Dickinson, Suzy Pasleau and Claude Desma (Louvain-la-Neuve: Éditions Academia, 1995), 221-31; Yves

Frenette, *Les Francophones de la Nouvelle-Angleterre, 1524-2000* (Sainte-Foy, Québec: INRS-Culture et société, 2000); Jean Lamarre, *Les Canadiens français du Michigan: Leur contribution dans le développement de la vallée de la Saginaw et de la péninsule de Keweenaw 1840-1914* (Sillery, Québec: Les editions du Septentrion, 2000); David R. Smith, "Borders that Divide and Connect: Capital and Labour Movements in the Great Lakes Region," *Canadian Review of American Studies* 25, no. 2 (1995): 1-25.

2   Lavoie, *L'émigration des Canadiens aux États-Unis avant 1930* (Montréal: Les Presses de l'Université de Montréal, 1972), 45, Tableau 7. See also Gilles Paquet "L'émigration des Canadiens français vers la Nouvelle-Angleterre, 1870-1910, prises de vue quantitatives," *Recherches historiographiques* 5 (1964): 319-70; Albert Faucher, "L'émigration des Canadiens français."

3   The burgeoning field of borderland studies is producing a growing amount of work in this direction on both Canadians and non-Canadians. On the Canadian-U.S. border, see Randy William Widdis, *With Scarcely a Ripple: Anglo-Canadian Migration into the United States and Western Canada, 1880-1920* (Montreal: McGill-Queen's University Press, 1998); Ramirez, *On the Move*; Ramirez with Otis, *Crossing the 49th Parallel*; Ramirez, "Canada in the United States: Perspectives on Migration and Continental History" *Journal of American Ethnic History* (Spring 2001): 50-70; Stephen J. Hornby, Victor A. Konrad, and James J. Herlan, eds., *The Northeastern Borderlands: Four Centuries of Interaction* (Orono, ME: Canadian American Center, University of Maine; Fredericton, N.B.: Acadiensis Press, 1989); Robert Lecker, ed., *Borderlands: Essays in Canadian-American Relations* (Toronto, 1991); John J. Bukowczyk, Nora Faires, David R. Smith and Randy William Widdis, *Permeable Border: The Great Lakes Basin as Transnational Region, 1650-1990* (Pittsburgh: University of Pittsburgh Press; Calgary, AL: University of Calgary Press, 2005). Far more voluminous work has been written about the Mexican-U.S. border. Among these titles, see for example Lawrence Cardoso, *Mexican Emigration to the United States, 1891-1932* (Tucson: University of Arizona Press, 1980); George J. Sánchez, *Becoming Mexican American: Ethnicity, Culture, and Identity in Chicano Los Angeles, 1900-1945* (New York: Oxford University Press, 1993); Miguel Tinker Salas, *In the Shadow of the Eagles: Sonora and the Transformation of the Border during the Porfiriato* (Berkeley: University of California Press, 1997); Mae Ngai, *Impossible Subjects: Illegal Aliens and the Making of Modern America* (Princeton: Princeton University Press, 2004), chap. 4.

4   A dozen of the most important industrial centres in New England and the American Mid-West have monographs which depict the arrival of French-Canadian immigrants and the establishment of their community. For a comprehensive review of the scholarship produced before the 1990s see Yves Roby, "Quebec in the United States: A Historiographical Survey," *Maine Historical Society Quarterly* 26, no. 3 (Winter 1987): 126-59.

5   In line with this argument, I have chosen to use the terms "migrants" and "migration," in place of "immigration" and "emigration," unless they became repetitious. This is because I consider that, as Donna Gabaccia has stated, these terms better describe the reality of multidirectional and multiple movements of migration within and across the border. Donna R. Gabaccia, *Italy's Many Diasporas* (Seattle: University of Washington Press, 2000).

6   Oscar Handlin, *The Uprooted: The Epic Study of the Great Migrations That Made the American People* (Boston: Little Brown, 1951); John Bodnar, *The Transplanted: A History of Immigrants in Urban America* (Bloomington: University of Indiana Press, 1985). See also Rudolph J. Vecoli, "*Contadini* in Chicago: a Critique of the Uprooted," *Journal of American History* 51, no. 3 (1964): 404-17; Rudolph Vecoli, "From the Uprooted to the Transplanted: The Writing of

American Immigration History, 1951-1989," in *From Melting Pot to Multiculturalism: The Evolution of Ethnic Relations in the United States and Canada*, ed. Valeria Gennaro Lerda (Roma: Bulzoni, 1990), 25-53.

7   Donna Gabaccia, "Immigrant Women: Nowhere at Home?" *Journal of American Ethnic History* 10 (Summer 1991): 62-87.

8   Franca Iacovetta, *Such Hardworking People: Italian Immigrants in Postwar Toronto* (Montreal: McGill-Queen's University Press, 1993), xxvi. See also, "Introduction" in *Sisters or Strangers? Immigrant, Ethnic, and Racialized Women in Canadian History*, ed. Marlene Epp, Franca Iacovetta and Frances Swyripa (Toronto: University of Toronto Press, 2004), 11-13; Franca Iacovetta with Paula Draper and Robert Bentresca, ed., *A Nation of Immigrants: Women, Workers, and Communities in Canadian History, 1840s-1960s* (Toronto: University of Toronto Press, 1998); Donna R. Gabaccia and Franca Iacovetta, "Preface" in *Women, Gender, and Transnational Lives: Italian Workers of the World*, ed. Donna R. Gabaccia and Franca Iacovetta (Toronto: University of Toronto Press, 2002), ix; Donna Gabaccia, *Seeking Common Ground: Multidisciplinary Studies of Immigrant Women in the United States* (Westport, CT: Praeger, 1992).

9   Thomas Dublin, *Transforming Women's Work: New England Lives in the Industrial Revolution* (Ithaca and London: Cornell University Press, 1994).

10 Dublin, *Transforming Women's Work*, 11-12; Tamara K. Hareven, *Family Time and Industrial Time: The Relationship between the Family and Work in a New England Industrial Community* (Cambridge: Cambridge University Press, 1982).

11 Exception to this tendency is work by FlorenceMae Waldron, "The Battle over Female (In)Dependence: Women in New England Quebecois Migrant Communities, 1870-1930," *Frontiers: A Journal of Women Studies* 26, no. 2 (2005): 158-205.

12 Hareven, *Family Time and Industrial Time*; Frances Early, "French-Canadian Beginnings in an American Community: Lowell, Massachusetts, 1868-1886" (Ph.D. thesis, Concordia University, 1979).

13 For American studies including the literature on women workers and radicals, see Alice Kessler-Harris, *Out to Work: a History of Wage-Earning Women in the United States* (Oxford: Oxford University Press, 1982); Leslie Tentler, *Wage-Earning Women: Industrial Work and Family Life in the United States, 1900-1930* (Oxford: Oxford University Press, 1979); Mari Jo Buhle, *Women and American Socialism, 1870-1920* (Urbana: University of Illinois Press, 1991); Sarah Eisenstein, *Give Us Bread but Give Us Roses: Working Women's Consciousness in the United States, 1890 to the First World War* (London: Routledge & Kegan Paul, 1983); Dana Frank, "Housewives, Socialists and the Politics of Food: The 1917 Cost of Living Protests," *Feminist Studies* 11, no. 2 (Summer 1985): 254-85; Ruth Milkman, ed., *Women, Work and Protest: A Century of US Women's Labor History* (Boston: Routledge & Kegan Paul, 1985); Linda Gordon, *Heroes of Their Own Lives: The Politics and History of Family Violence* (New York: Viking, 1988); Lynn Y. Weiner, *From Working Girl to Working Mother: The Female Labor Force in the United States, 1820-1980* (Chapel Hill: University of North Carolina, 1985). On Canada, see Bettina Bradbury, *Working Families: Age, Gender, and Daily Survival in Industrializing Montreal* (Toronto: Oxford University Press, 1993); Joan Sangster, *Dreams of Equality: Women on the Canadian Left, 1920-1950* (Toronto: McClelland & Stewart, 1989); Alison Prentice et al., eds., *Canadian Women: A History* (Toronto: Harcourt Brace Jovanovich, 1988); Joy Parr, *The Gender of Breadwinners: Women, Men, and Change in Two Industrial Towns, 1880-1950* (Toronto: University of Toronto Press, 1990).

14 For a similar observation concerning migrant families of different ethnic and cultural backgrounds, see Donna R. Gabaccia, *From Sicily to Elizabeth Street: Housing and Social Change among Italian Immigrants, 1880-1930* (Albany: State University of New York Press, 1984); Gabaccia, *From the Other Side: Women, Gender, and Immigrant Life in the U.S., 1820-1990* (Bloomington: University of Indiana Press, 1994); Miriam Cohen, *Workshop to Office: The Generations of Italian Women in New York City, 1900-1950* (Ithaca: Cornell University Press, 1991); Ardis Cameron, *Radicals of the Worst Sort: Laboring Women in Lawrence, Massachusetts, 1860-1912* (Urbana: University of Illinois Press, 1993); Carole Turbin, *Working Women of Collar City: Gender, Class, and Community in Troy, New York, 1864-86* (Urbana: University of Illinois Press, 1992); Michael Di Leonardo, *The Varieties of Ethnic Experience: Kinship, Class, and Gender among California Italian-Americans* (Ithaca: Cornell University Press, 1984); and Louise Lamphere, *From Working Daughters to Working Mothers: Immigrant Women in a New England Industrial Community* (Ithaca: Cornell University Press, 1987); Iacovetta, *Such Hardworking People*.

15 Also, feminist anthropologists have closely examined the subject. As early as the 1970s, Jane Collier looked at the family not as a unified entity, but as a political arena. Michelle Zimbalist Rosaldo, "Women, Culture, and Society: A Theoretical Overview," in *Women, Culture, and Society*, ed. Michelle Zimbalist Rosaldo and Louise Lamphere (Stanford: Stanford University Press, 1974).

16 U.S. Bureau of the Census, *Thirteenth Census of the United States: 1910*, vol. 2, *Population* (n.p., 1914), 868; U.S. Bureau of the Census, *Fourteenth U.S. Federal Census: 1920*, vol. 1, *Population* (Washington, D.C.: GPO, 1923), 229, vol. 2, 854-55; George F. Kenngott, *The Record of a City: A Social Survey of Lowell, Massachusetts* (New York: Macmillan, 1912), chaps. 1 and 2; Dublin, *Transforming Women's Work*, 77, 230; Thomas Dublin, *Women at Work: The Transformation of Work and Community in Lowell, Massachusetts, 1826-1860* (New York: Columbia University Press, 1979), especially chaps. 2 and 9.

17 Kenngott, *The Record of a City*, 147-55.

18 David J. Goldberg, *A Tale of Three Cities: Labor, Organization and Protest in Paterson, Passaic, and Lawrence, 1916-1921* (New Brunswick, New Jersey: Rutgers University Press, 1989); Gary Gerstle, *Working-Class Americanism: The Politics of Labor in a Textile City, 1914-1960* (Cambridge: Cambridge University Press, 1989), chap. 2; Laurence F. Gross, *The Course of Industrial Decline: The Boott Cotton Mills of Lowell, Massachusetts, 1835-1955* (Baltimore: Johns Hopkins University Press, 1993), 18-22, 152.

19 Calculation based on the data provided by Gross, *The Course of Industrial Decline*, 144-49.

20 Lavoie, "Les mouvements migratoires des Canadiens," 45, Tableau 7.

21 U.S. Bureau of the Census, *Fourteenth Census of the United States. Population: 1920*, 745, 929.

22 Calculated by the author based on the data derived from a 5-percent sample of the manuscript schedules of the *Thirteenth and Fourteenth Federal Censuses*, City of Lowell, Middlesex County, Massachusetts.

23 Marian L. Smith, "By Way of Canada: U.S. Records of Immigration across the U.S.-Canadian Border, 1895-1954," *Prologue* 32, 3 (Fall 2000), 192-99; Yukari Takai, "The Family Networks and Geographic Mobility of French-Canadian Immigrants in Early-Twentieth-Century Lowell, Massachusetts," *Journal of Family History* 26, no. 3 (July 2001), 373-94. See also Ramirez with Otis, *Crossing the 49th Parallel*, Appendix, 189-92; Yukari Takai, "Transnational Movements of Japanese and French Canadian Migrants: A Discussion of

Concepts, Methodology and Sources," *Journal of Aïchi Kenritsu Daigaku* 35 (March 2003), 71-93.

24 For further discussion on sources and methodology, see Appendix A of this book.

25 Early, "French-Canadian Beginnings"; Frances Early, "Mobility Potential and the Quality of Life in Working-Class Lowell, Massachusetts: The French Canadians ca. 1870," *Labour/Le Travailleur* 2 (1977): 214-28; Early, "The French-Canadian Family Economy and Standard-of-Living in Lowell, Massachusetts, 1870," *Journal of Family History* 7, no. 2 (1982): 180-99; Early, "The Settling-In Process: The Beginnings of the Little Canada in Lowell, Massachusetts, in the Late Nineteenth Century," in *Steeples and Smokestacks: A Collection of Essays on the Franco-American Experience in New England*, edited by Claire Quintal (Worcester, Massachusetts: French Institute, Assumption College, 1996), 89-108.

Chapter One

1 An article from an unnamed Lowell newspaper, published February 19, 1909, and reproduced by U.S. Congress, Senate, 61st Congress, 2d Session, in Document No. 633, Reports of the Immigration Commission, *Immigrants in Industries*, part 3-4, vol. 10, *Cotton Goods Manufacturing in the North Atlantic States. Woolen and Worsted Goods Manufacturing* (Washington, D.C.: U.S. GPO, 1911; reprint, New York: Arno & The New York Times, 1970), 228. Hereafter referred to as *Immigrants in Industries*.

2 Virginia Yans-McLaughlin, "Introduction," in *Immigration Reconsidered: History, Sociology, and Politics*, ed. Virginia Yans-McLaughlin (New York: Oxford University Press, 1990). See also Bodnar, *The Transplanted*; Vecoli, "Contadini in Chicago"; Ewa Morawska, "The Sociology and Historiography of Immigration," in *Immigration Reconsidered*, ed. Yans-McLaughlin, 187-238, especially 189; Gabaccia, *From Italy to Elisabeth Street*.

3 Studies that explore the continuity and complexity of trans-Atlantic migrants include Dirk Hoerder, *People on the Move: Migration, Acculturation, and Ethnic Interaction in Europe and North America*, German Historical Institute Washington D.C. Annual Lecture 1993, 6 (Oxford: Berg Publishers, 1993); Dirk Hoerder, "International Labor Markets and Community Building by Migrant Workers in the Atlantic Economies," in *A Century of European Migrations*, ed. Rudolph J. Vecoli and Suzanne M. Sinke (Urbana : University of Illinois Press, 1991), 78-107; Ewa Morawska, *For Bread with Butter: Life-Worlds of East Central Europeans in Johnstown, Pennsylvania, 1890-1940* (Cambridge: Cambridge University Press, 1985); Ewa Morawska, "Return Migrations: Theoretical and Research Agenda," in *A Century of European Migrations*, ed. Vecoli and Sinke, 277-92, especially 277-78; June Granatir Alexander, "Moving into and out of Pittsburgh: Ongoing Chain Migration," in *A Century of European Migrations*, ed. Vecoli and Sinke, 200-20.

4 Notable exceptions are Frenette, "La genèse d'une communauté," and Ramirez, *On the Move*.

5 Ramirez, *On the Move*; Frenette, "Macroscopie et microscopie."

6 Paul-André Linteau, René Durocher and Jean-Clayde Robert, *Histoire du Québec contemporain*, vol. 1 (Montréal: Boréal, 1989, new ed.), 469-70.

7 Ibid., 170, 474-75

8 Ibid., 474-75.

9   La Commission de toponymie, Noms et lieux du Québec: dictionnaire illustré, (Sainte-Foy, Québec : Publications du Québec, 1994); Gouvernement du Québec, http://www.toponymie.gouv.qc.ca/.

10 Linteau et al., Histoire du Québec contemporain, vol. 1, 170, 474-75.

11 Ibid.

12 John McCallum, Unequal Beginnings: Agriculture and Economic Development in Quebec and Ontario until 1870 (Toronto: University of Toronto Press, 1980), 49-50.

13 Ibid.

14 Normand Perron, "Genèse des activités laitières 1850-1960," in Agriculture et colonisation au Québec: aspects historiques, ed., Normand Séguin (Montréal: Boréal Expresse, 1980), 113-40, especially 121, Tableau 4.

15 The number of butter and cheese manufactories increased rapidly: it more than doubled, going from 728 in 1891 to 1,867 in 1919. The total value of manufactured products also increased: during the same period it went from $2,919 000 to $15,305,488 for cheese, and from $268,000 to $1,369,384 for butter. See Marjorie Cohen, Women's Work, Markets, and Economic Development in Nineteenth-Century Ontario (Toronto: University of Toronto Press, 1988), 109. Chapter 5 of this study focuses on Québec's agriculture.

16 Ibid., 109.

17 Linteau et al., Histoire du Québec contemporain, vol. 1: 129-35.

18 Ibid., 132-33; Cohen, Women's Work, 109; Marjorie Cohen, "The Decline of Women in Canadian Dairying," Histoire Sociale/Social History 17, no. 34 (1984): 307-34.

19 Serge Courville and Normand Séguin, Le monde rural québécois au XIXe siècle (Ottawa: La Société historique du Canada, 1989), 19; Linteau et al., Histoire du Québec contemporain, vol. 1, 492-93.

20 Ibid., 170.

21 Roby, Les Franco-Américains de la Nouvelle-Angleterre, 341, nt. 17.

22 Jean Hamelin and Yves Roby, Histoire économique du Québec, 1851-1896 (Montréal: Fides, 1971), 88-98; McCallum, Unequal Beginnings, 5.

23 Ramirez with Otis, Crossing the 49th Parallel, 15.

24 Small holdings of up to fifty acres comprised about one third of the Berthier County's acreage, and the relatively low income of their owners may be inferred by the fact that one out of three worked as journaliers to supplement their earnings. Ramirez, On the Move, 25.

25 Linteau et al., Histoire du Québec contemporain 1: 498-99.

26 Ibid.

27 Cohen, Women's Work, 104-10.

28 Edward Wiest, The Butter Industry in the United States: An Economic Study of Butter and Oleomargarine (New York: Columbia University Press, 1916), 40; Cohen, Women's Work, 104-10.

29 Martine Tremblay, "La division sexuelle du travail et la modernization de l'agriculture à travers la presse agricole, 1840-1900," Revue d'histoire de l'Amérique française 47, no. 2 (automne 1993): 226-29.

30 Journal d'agriculture et transaction de la Société d'agriculture du Bas-Canada 6, no. 2 (February 1853); Gazette des campagnes, 7 (20 April 1893), 54. See also Tremblay, "La division sexuelle du travail": 227-29.

31 *Gazette des campagnes* 12 (21 March 1878); 33 (4 June 1886). See also Tremblay, "La division sexuelle du travail": 229.

32 Micheline Dumont-Johnson et al., *L'histoire des femmes au Québec depuis quatre siècles* (Montréal: Le Jour, 1992), 200. See also Sophie-Laurence Lamontagne, *La production textile domestique au Québec, 1827-1941: une approche quantitative et régionale* (Ottawa: Museé national des sciences et de la technologie, 1997), chap. 2.

33 Denise Lemieux and Lucie Mercier, *Les femmes au tournant du siècle 1880-1940: âge de la vie, maternité et quotidien* (Québec: Institut québécois de recherche sur la culture, 1989), 90.

34 Agusutine M. Linteau, *Douce mémoire*, (Charlesbourg: manuscript in possession of the author, 1983), 61, reprinted in *Les femmes au tournant du siècle*, ed. Lemieux and Mercier, 90. Translation by Yukari Takai. Hereafter, translation of French texts has been provided by Yukari Takai unless otherwise specified.

35 Ibid.

36 Linteau et al., *Histoire du Québec contemporain*, vol. 1, 137-45. See also Vicero, "Immigration of French Canadians," 50-59. The proponents of colonization envisaged the establishment of French Canadians in other regions as well, such as the Canadian Prairies. However, the Laurentian hinterlands remained the primary focus of concrete colonization schemes.

37 Ramirez, *On the Move*, 84.

38 Ibid.

39 Linteau et al., *Histoire du Québec contemporain*, vol. 1, 137-45.

40 Télesphore Saint-Pierre, *Les Canadiens des États-Unis: ce qu'on perd à émigrer* (Montréal: printed by la Compagnie d'imprimerie "La Gazette", 1893).

41 Ibid.

42 *L'Étoile du Nord*, September 8, 1904.

43 Linteau et al., Histoire *du Québec contemporain*, vol. 1, 137-45.

44 Christian Pouyez, Yolande Lavoie with collaboration of Gérard Bouchard, *Les Saguenayens: introduction à l'histoire des populations du Saguenay XIXe et XXe siècles* (Sillery, Québec: Les Presses de l'Université du Québec, 1983), 236, tableau 6.2.

45 In 1900, the Canadian-born population alone (and excluding the American-born descendants of Canadian background) numbered 14,674 in Lowell and 20,172 in Fall River. By 1910, French Canadians (including both Canadian-born and U.S.-born) in Lowell numbered 23,208; in Fall River, 32,033. Figures for the French Canadian population (either Canadian-born or U.S.-born) in 1900 are not available. U.S. Bureau of the Census, *Thirteenth Census of the United States: 1910, Population* (Washington, D.C.: GPO, 1913), 868. See also Bruno Ramirez, "Crossroad Province: Quebec's Place in International Migrations: 1870-1915," in *A Century of European Migration, 1830-1930*, ed. Vecoli and Sinke, 243-60, especially 247.

46 Canada, *Census of 1901*, I, 4-5; Linteau et al., *Histoire du Québec contemporain*, vol. 1, 41 and 17o.

47 Jean-Charles Fortin and Antonio Lechasseur, *Histoire du Bas-Saint-Laurent* (Québec: Institut québécois de recherche sur la culture, 1993), 203, Table 5.5.

48 Frenette, "Microscopie et macroscopie," 221-23.

49 Société de colonisation de Montréal, *Rapport spécial du Secrétaire* (mars 1908). The report of this colonization society shows the number of repatriates as follows: 1898, 68 "Canadiens

des États-Unis"; 1899, 31; 1900, 92; 1901, 102; 1903, 119; 1904, 228; 1905, 295; 1906, 310; 1907, 330.

50   Canada, *Sessional Papers*, 1896, no. 29, 10; Canada, *Report of the Department of Interior*, 1895, 54-56. See also Robert G. LeBlanc, "Colonisation et rapatriement au Lac-Saint-Jean, 1895-1905," *Revue d'histoire de l'Amérique française* 38, no. 3 (hiver 1985): 379-408, especially 392.

51   LeBlanc, *ibid.*, esp. 392; Pierre Anctil, "La Franco-Américainie ou le Québec d'en bas," *Cahier de Géographie du Québec* 58 (1979): 39-52; Dear R. Louder and Eric Waddell, eds., *Du continent perdu à l'archipel retrouvé: le Québec et l'Amérique française* (Québec: Les Presses de l'Université Laval, 1983); Dear R. Louder and Eric Waddell, eds., *French America: Mobility, Identity, and Minority Experience Across the Continent*, tranlated by Franklin Philip (Baton Rouge: Louisiana University Press, 1993).

52   Ramirez, *On the Move*, 80-81; Frenette, "Macroscopie et microscopie," 223; René Hardy and Normand Séguin, *Forêt et société en Mauricie. La formation de la région de Trois-Rivières 1830-1930* (Montréal: Boréal; Ottawa: Musée national de l'Homme, Musées nationaux du Canada, 1984), 150-51.

53   Fortin and Lechasseur, *Histoire du Bas-Saint-Laurent*, 297-302.

54   John Willis, "Urbanization, Colonization and Underdevelopment in the Bas-Saint-Laurent: Fraserville and the Témiscouata in the Late Nineteenth Century," *Cahier de géographique du Québec* 27, nos. 73-74 (1984): 125-61.

55   Between 1880 and 1890, 6,782 people left Rimouski out of a population of 18,809. See Fortin and Lechasseur, *Histoire du Bas-Saint-Laurent*, 203.

56   Ramirez, *On the Move*, chap. 5, especially 118-25.

57   Yves Bourdon and Jean Lamarre, *Histoire du Québec. Une société nord-américaine* (Laval, Québec: Beauchemin, 1998), 124-25.

58   Roby, "Quebec in the United States," 126-259, Ramirez, *On the Move*, chap. 5; Ramirez with Otis, *Crossing the 49th Parallel*, 17-20, 72-75.

59   Jean-Baptiste Proulx, *Les pionniers du lac Nominingue ou les avantages de la colonisation. Drame en trois actes*, (Montréal: Beauchemin & Valois, 1883), 5; Jean-Baptiste Proulx, *Voyage au lac Long, dans le canton de Preston*, (Saint-Jérôme, Québec: s.n. 1882), reproduced in *Mélanges littéraires* (Montréal: Beauchemin & Valois, 1884), 34. See also Gabriel Dussault, *Le Curé Labelle: Messianisme, utopie et colonisation au Québec 1850-1900* (Montréal: Hurtubise HMH, 1983), nts. 56-60.

60   Linteau et al., *Histoire du Québec contemporain*, vol. 1, 501-05.

61   Ramirez, *On the Move*, 84-85.

62   Unless otherwise stated, data used in this section are derived from *Soundex Index to Canadian Border Entries through the Saint Albans, Vermont, District*, the U.S. Immigration and Naturalization Services, Record Group 85, National Archives, Washington D.C. Microfilmed copies are housed at the Bibliothèque municipale de Montréal. For discussion of the *Border Entry*, see Appendix B of this book. See also Appendix in Ramirez with Otis, *Crossing the 49th Parallel*.

63   Linteau, *Histoire du Québec contemporain*, vol. 1, 475. La Commission de toponymie, *Noms et lieux du Québec*.

64   Raoul Blanchard, *Le Centre du Canada Français* (Montréal: Beauchemin, 1947), 65-119. See also Ramirez, *On the Move*, 24.

65 See Yves Frenette for a similar account with migrants to Lewiston, Maine, whose origin included urban centres such as Montréal and Québec. Frenette, "Macroscopie et microscopie": 225-26.
66 *Border Entry*, reel no. 5.
67 *Ibid.*
68 *Ibid*, reel no. 16.
69 Linteau et al., *Histoire du Québec contemporain*, vol. 1, 177, 475.
70 For details of the life and work of forestry workers, see Hardy and Séguin, *Forêt et société en Mauricie*, 126-34, 156, 203-10.
71 Gérard Bouchard, "Co-intégration et reproduction de la société rurale. Pour un modèle saguenayen de la marginalité," *Recherches sociographiques* 29, nos. 2-3 (1988): 283-305; Bouchard and Lise Bergeron, "Aux origines d'une population régionale: mythes et réalités démographiques et sociales," *Revue d'histoire d'Amérique française* 42, no. 3 (hiver 1989): 389-409.
72 Hardy and Séguin, *Forêt et société*, 203-210. Léon Gérin, *L'habitant de Saint-Justin: contribution à la géographie sociale du Canada* (Ottawa: J. Hope et Fils; Toronto: Copp-Clark; London, U.K.: Bernard Quaritch, 1898).
73 *Le Nouvelliste*, 28 septembre 1933. See also Hardy and Séguin in *Forêt et société*, 130. The outbreak of the Great Depression continued this downward spiral of wages so that by 1931, the father of a family would likely earn as little as $26 a month.
74 Hardy and Séguin, *Forêt et société*, 126-34.
75 The population of the latter rose from just below 10 000 in 1901 to 13 691 in 1911 to 22 267 in 1921. Linteau et al., *Histoire du Québec contemporain*, vol. 1, 177, 475.
76 *Ibid.*, 412.
77 *L'Étoile du Nord*, 2 June, 1904.
78 *Border Entry*, reel no. 4.
79 Ramirez with Otis, *Crossing the 49th Parallel*, 17.

Chapter Two

1 The number of French Canadians who left for the United States declined from 150,000 in 1880-90 to just 80,000 in 1910-20. See Yolande Lavoie, *L'émigration des Québécois*, 45, Tableau 7.
2 U.S. Department of Commerce, Bureau of the Census, *Thirteenth Census of the United States Taken in the Year 1910*, 1, 229; 2, 854-55; U.S. Congress, Senate, *Immigrants in Industries* 10: 227-28, 232.
3 Early, "French Canadian Beginnings," 35.
4 Thomas Dublin, *Women at Work: The Transformation of Work and Community in Lowell, Massachusetts, 1826-1860* (New York: Columbia University Press, 1993, 2nd ed.), 17-22; Thomas Dublin and Paul Marion, *Lowell: The Story of an Industrial City: A Guide to Lowell National Historical Park and Lowell Heritage State Park, Lowell, Massachusetts* (Washington, D.C.: U.S. Dept. of the Interior, 1992), 30.

5   Dublin and Marion, Ibid., 30.
6   Nathan Appleton, *Introduction of the Power Loom and Origin of Lowell* (Lowell: Printed by B.H. Penhallow, 1858), 13; Dublin, *Women at Work*, 19; H.C. Meserve, *Lowell, an Industrial Dream Come True* (Boston: The National Association of Cotton Manufacturers, 1923), 46-47.
7   Among other firms that rapidly came into being were Hamilton (1826), Appleton (1828), Lowell (1829), Middlesex (1831), Suffolk and Tremont (1832), Lawrence (1833), Boott (1836), and Massachusetts (1832).
8   Dublin and Marion, *Lowell*, 39; Dublin, *Women at Work*, 20.
9   Gross, *The Course of Industrial Decline*, 18-22; Dublin, *Women at Work*, chap. 2.
10 Ibid., 18-20.
11 Dublin, *Women at Work*, 21; Dublin and Marion, *Lowell*, 39; Frances W. Gregory, *Nathan Appleton, Merchant and Entrepreneur, 1779-1861* (Charlottesville: University Press of Virginia, 1975), 196; Gross, *The Course of Industrial Decline*, 18-20.
12 Turbin, *Working Women of Collar City*, 21-24.
13 Charles Dickens, *American Notes for General Circulation* (New York: Harper & Brothers, 1842). See also the U.S. Senate, *Immigrants in Industries* 10: 280-81. For other comments by foreign visitors to Lowell, see Michel Chevalier, *Society, Manners, and Politics in the United States* (New York, A. M. Kelley, 1966), reprint of the ed. published in 1839, which was translated from the 3d Paris ed. 142; Early, "French-Canadian Beginnings," 36-38, 40; Dublin, *Women at Work*, 77-78; Dublin and Marion, *Lowell*, 52.
14 Dublin, *Women at Work*, 86-107.
15 Ibid., chap. 3; Meserve, *Lowell*, 39. The influx of a large number of young rural women into Lowell also reflected the presence of "idle" females due to rapid changes sweeping across southern New England. As cheap factory-made cloth became available to New England farmers, farm women were no longer burdened with spinning and weaving duties at home, but were driven by the need for cash to buy machine-made fabrics instead. Some young rural women found a solution to this problem by working in textile centres such as Lowell.
16 Dublin, *Women at Work*, note 4, 271; 109-10. See also "Early, French-Canadian Beginnings," 41-44; Frances E. Piva, "An Idyl Confronted: The New England Mill Girls and the Lowell Female Labor Reform Association" (M.A. thesis, Sir George Williams University, 1973), 31-32, 68.
17 Dublin, *Women at Work*, chap. 8, especially 138.
18 Ibid., 138-48.
19 Massachusetts Bureau of Statistics of Labor, *Census of the Commonwealth of Massachusetts, 1875* (Boston: Wright & Potter Printing, 1876-1877), I, 743.
20 Dublin and Marion, *Lowell*, 67.
21 Immigration Commission, *Immigrants in Industries* 10 : 232.
22 Lavoie, "Les mouvements migratoires," 78.
23 Lowell was not the only industrial centre in the region that saw a sudden increase in the French Canadian population during the last three decades of the nineteenth century. In Holyoke, Massachusetts, for example, the French Canadian population totaled over 10,000 in 1895. See Peter Haebler, "Habitants in Holyoke: The Development of the French-Canadian Community in a Massachusetts City, 1865-1910" (Ph.D. thesis, University of New Hampshire, 1976), 337, appendix B. Similarly, the bulk of French Canadians

• NOTES •

emigrated—the peak taking place between 1870 and 1890—to Fall River, Woonsocket, and Lawrence, as well as to other textile centres. See Yolande Lavoie, "Les mouvements migratoires," 78.

24 I calculated these figures myself from the data drawn from U.S. Department of Commerce, U.S. Bureau of the Census, *Thirteenth Census of the United States, 1910. Population* (Washington, D.C.: GPO, 1912-13), 228, 716.

25 *Ibid.*, 868.

26 Immigration Commission, *Immigrants in Industries* 10: 232-33

27 U.S. Department of Commerce, U.S. Bureau of the Census, *Thirteenth Census of the United States, 1910. Manufacturers* (Washington, D.C.: GPO, 1913), vol. 9, 160-164, 527, 540; Mary H. Blewett, *The Last Generation: Work and Life in the Textile Mills of Lowell, Massachusetts, 1910-1960* (Amherst: University of Massachusetts Press, 1990), 5-8.

28 U.S. Bureau of the Census, *Thirteenth Census of the United States, 1910. Manufacturers*, 527; U.S. Department of Commerce, U.S. Bureau of the Census, *Fourteenth Census of the United States, 1920. Occupations* (Washington, D.C.: GPO, 1922), 172-73; Dublin and Marion, *Lowell*, 81.

29 Gross, *The Course of Industrial Decline*, 166.

30 Dublin and Marion, *Lowell*, 65.

31 In his study of French Canadians in Holyoke, Peter Haebler brings to our attention an important point: those who left the city during the Depression years were mostly single, while immigrants who were part of a family tended to stay in the city. Peter Haebler, "Habitants in Holyoke: The Development of the French-Canadian Community in a Massachusetts City, 1865-1910" (Ph.D. thesis, University of New Hampshire, 1976), 182-83.

32 Levine et al., *Who Built America?* II, 264-76.

33 *Ibid.*, 276.

34 Walter F. Willcox and Imre Ferenczi, ed., *International Migrations* (New York: The National Bureau of Economic Research, 1929), vol. 1, Statistics, table 3, pp. 391-93. See also, Ramirez with Otis, *Crossing the 49th Parallel*, 49-51.

35 Gross, *The Course of Industrial Decline*, 144-49.

36 Charles T. Main, "Report" (1926, private collections), 1-5. See also Gross, *The Course of Industrial Decline*, 165-66.

37 Immigration Commission, *Immigrants in Industries* 10: 236.

38 *Ibid.*, 228.

39 U.S. Congress, Senate, *Report on the Conditions of Women and Children Wage-Earners in the United States* (Washington, D.C.: GPO, 1910), 28.

40 Ramirez, *On the Move*, 126-28.

41 *U.S. Bureau of the Census, Fourteenth Census of the United States, 1920*, 592, Table 6.

42 I calculated the Lowell figures myself from the sample created from U.S. Department of Commerce, Bureau of the Census, *Thirteenth Census of the United States Taken in the Year of 1910* and *Fourteenth Census of the United States Taken in the Year of 1920. Federal Census Schedules. City of Lowell (Middlesex County, Massachusetts)*. Hereafter, these two sources will be referred to as *Thirteenth Federal Population Census Schedules, 1910* and *Fourteenth Federal Population Census Schedules, 1920*. For Massachusetts figures, see U.S. Department of Commerce, U.S. Bureau of the Census, *Thirteenth Census of the United States: Population*, 346.

· GENDERED PASSAGES ·

In 1880, more than eight out of ten French Canadian children aged eleven to fifteen in Rhode Island were working, while only 8.5 percent attended school. See Ramirez, *On the Move*, 120.

43   Jacques Rouillard, *Les travailleurs du cotton au Québec: 1900-1915* (Montréal: Les Presses de l'Universié du Québec, 1974), 54-55, especially Tableau XII.

44   My calculation is derived from the census sample.

45   Beaudreau and Frenette, "Les stratégies familiales des francophones," 171-73.

46   Kessler-Harris, *Out to Work*, especially chap. 7.

47   Owen R. Lovejoy, "Child Labor Laws in Massachusetts," in *The New Encyclopedia of Social Reform*, ed. William Dwight Porter Bliss (New York: Funk & Wagnall Co., 1908), 170-81.

48   *Ibid.*

49   Kenngott, *The Record of a City*, 138-47.

50   Gloria Vollmers, "Industrial Home Work of the Dennison Manufacturing Company of Framingham, Massachusetts, 1912-1935," *Business History Review* 71, no. 3 (Autumn 1997): 444-70; Lovejoy, "Child Labor Laws," 170-81. See also David Montgomery, *The Fall of the House of Labor: The Workplace, the State, and American Labor Activism, 1865-1925* (New York: Cambridge University Press, 1987), 132; Ramirez, *On the Move*, 127. For discussion of the city's enforcement to eliminate children from the textile mills in Lawrence, Massachusetts, see Cameron, *Radicals of the Worst Sort*, 104-06.

51   Viviana A. Rotman Zelizer, *Pricing the Priceless Child: The Changing Social Value of Children* (New York: Basic Books, 1985) chap. 2, especially 57; Cameron, *Radicals of the Worst Sort*, 104-06.

52   Florence Kelly, *Some Ethical Gains through Legislation* (New York: Macmillan, 1905; reprint, New York: Arno Press, 1969), 132-33.

53   David Montgomery, *The Fall of the House of Labor*, 132, 167; Robert H. Wiebe, *The Search for Order: 1877-1920* (New York: Hill and Wang, 1967), 168-69.

54   Zelizer, *Pricing the Priceless Child*, 57-59.

55   *Ibid.*

56   Editorial, *New York Times*, 17 December 1902, 8. Cited in Zelizer, *Pricing the Priceless Child*, 59. Progressive reform working toward curbing the number of children in work places also resulted in legislation regulating the children's attendance at school. See Forest Chester Ensign, *Compulsory School Attendance and Child Labor. A Study of the Historical Development of Regulations Compelling Attendance and Limiting the Labor of Children in a Selected Group of States* ([New York?] 1921; Reprint, New York: Arno Press, 1969), chap. 4.

57   Zelizer, *Pricing the Priceless Child*, 59. See also Cameron, *Radicals of the Worst Sort*, 104-7.

58   Montgomery, *Fall of House of Labor*, 132. See also Virginia Yans-McLaughlin, *Family and Community: Italian Immigrants in Buffalo, 1880-1930* (Urbana: University of Illinois Press, 1982, c1977); Florence Kelly, *Some Ethnical Gains through Legislation* (New York: Macmillan, 1905), 132-33.

59   Tamara K. Hareven and Randolph Langenbach, *Amoskeag: Life and Work in an American Factory City* (New York: Pantheon Books, 1978), 202. See also Roby, *Franco-Américains*, 70-71.

60   *Fourteenth U.S. Federal Census*, 15-192-2-3. 665-52-338.

61   *Ibid.*, 210-7-572, 2-39-147.

62   Hareven, *Family Time and Industrial Time*, 126-29.

63 For more discussion on this issue, see chap. 6 of this book.
64 Viviana Zelizer reminds us that the precise nature of the relationship between changes in the economic roles of women and that of children remains unclear. Zelizer, *Pricing the Priceless Child*, Introduction, especially 9-11. Winifred D. Wandersee, for instance, suggests that between 1920 and 1940 the decline in child labour pushed mothers into the labour force. Married women's work, therefore, represented a substitution of secondary wage-earnings. Christopher Lasch presents a very different interpretation of changes in family and child life. According to Lasch, the elimination of children from the workplace was part of a general effort by Progressive reformers to remove children from family influence, especially in the case of immigrant families. He contends that public policy contributed "not to the sentimentalization of domestic ties, but to their deterioration, specifically through the appropriation of parental function by new agencies of socialized reproduction such as educators, psychiatrists, social workers, penologists." Demographic historians' theories, on the other hand, claim that the newly emerging emotional value of children is best explained by declining birth and mortality rates in the twentieth century. See Winifred D. Wandersee, *Women's Work and Family Values, 1920-1940* (Cambridge, MA: Harvard University Press, 1981), 66; Christopher Lasch, *Haven in a Heartless World: The Family Besieged* (New York: Basic Books, 1979), 13; Lawrence Stone, *The Family, Sex, and Marriage in England, 1500-1800* (London: Weidenfeld & Nicolson, 1977), 105; Philippe Ariès, *L'enfant et la vie familiale sous l'Ancien Régime* (Paris: Plon, 1960).
65 Ramirez, *On the Move*, 120-24. Changes in the migrating population will be further discussed in chap. 4.
66 See chap. 5 of this book for further discussion on this issue.
67 Montgomery, *The Fall of the House of Labor*, 123-24; Ramirez, *On the Move*, 127-28.
68 Ibid.
69 City of Lowell, *Annual Report of the Board of Health of the City of Lowell* (Lowell: C.I. Hood, 1881), 126-27; Margaret Terrell Parker, *Lowell: a Study of Industrial Development* (New York: Macmillan, 1940): 86-88; Peter F. Blewett, "The New People," in *Cotton Was King: A History of Lowell, Massachusetts*, ed. Arthur Jr. Eno (Somersworth, N.H.: New Hampshire Pub. Co., 1976), 209; Early "French-Canadian Beginnings," 170.
70 City of Lowell, *Annual Report*, 126-27. See also Pierre Anctil, "Chinese of the Eastern States, 1881," *Recherches sociographiques* XXII, 1 (1981): 125-31.
71 Ibid.
72 Frederick W. Coburn, *History of Lowell and Its People* (New York: Lewis Historical Pub. Co., 1920), vol. 1, 343-44.
73 George Frederick Kenngott, *The Record of a City: A Social Survey of Lowell* (New York: Macmillan, 1910), 59.
74 Martin Thétrault, "La santé publique dans une ville manufacturière de la Nouvelle-Angleterre: Lowell, Massachusetts, 1965-1900" (Ph.D. thesis, Université de Montréal, 1985), 218.
75 *Lowell Daily Citizen*, 2 September 1882.
76 Kenngott, *The Record of a City*, 59.
77 Ibid.
78 Early, "French-Canadian Beginnings," 161. A study by Martin Thétrault shows that in 1880, the French-Canadian population in Little Canada was comprised of 1,464 dwellings and

3,477 individuals, divided into 538 families. See Thétrault, "La santé publique," 215. See also Thétrault, "De la difficulté de naître et de survivre dans une ville industrielle de la Nouvelle-Angleterre au XIX siècle: mortalité infantile, infanticide et avortement à Lowell, Massachusetts, 1870-1900," *Revue d'histoire de l'Amérique française* 47, no. 1 (été 1983): 53-82.

79 Kenngott, *The Record of a City*, 101; Blewett, "The New People," 209.

80 Kenngott, *The Record of a City*, 52-54.

81 Ibid.

82 Immigration Commission, *Immigrants in Industries* 10: 295, 297.

83 There were several churches in the city; each immigrant group built their own church or shared the building with another group and often held services in their own language. For the French Canadians in Lowell, their l'Église Saint-Jean-Baptist, nicknamed by Jack Kérouac as "the Chartres of Little Canada," undoubtedly constituted one of the most important institutions in their lives. See Blewett, "The New People," 190-217; Lane, *Franco-American Folk Traditions*, 331.

84 Yvonne Lagassé, interview by Lane in Lane, *French Canadian Folk Traditions*, 331.

85 Dirk Hoerder, "International Labor Markets and Community Building by Migrant Workers in the Atlantic Economies," in *A Century of European Migrations, 1830-1930*, ed. Vecoli and Sinke, 78-107, especially 96-97.

86 Father Morrissette, *Journal de Lowell* (août 1977), 4. In Lane, *Franco-American Folk Traditions and Popular Culture in a Former Milltown: Aspects of Ethnic Urban Folklore and the Dynamics of Folklore Change in Lowell, Massachusetts* (New York: Garland Publishing, 1990), 332.

87 Lane, *ibid*.

88 Father Morrissette, "Faits et gestes," *Journal de Lowell* (October 1977), 4, in Lane, *Franco-American Folk Traditions*, 332-33. Photographs taken between 1905 and 1919 in the Lowell Historical Society's collection provide some visual evidence of the economic expansion and social consolidation that occurred in Lowell during this period. See Lewis T. Karabatsos and Robert W. McLeod, Jr., eds., *Fixed in Time: Photographs of Lowell, Massachusetts, 1860-1940* (Lowell: Lowell Historical Society, 1983), Photographs 57, 61 and 87. See also interview transcripts with Yvonne Lagassé in Lane, *Franco-American Folk Traditions*, Appendix J, I "Les rues et les magasins," 514-25.

89 Father Morrissette, Lane, *ibid.*, 332-33.

90 Another French-Canadian resident of the city, Roger Lacette, mentioned that there were 24 *buvettes* (cafés) on the Moody and the Merrimack combined (date unspecified). See Lane, *Franco-American Folk Traditions*, 371, nt. 31.

91 Early, "French-Canadian Beginnings," 159. In the 1870 census sample there were only traders, one dry goods dealer, one huckster shop owner, one saloon keeper, and three physicians among French Canadians in Lowell.

92 Lane, "Histoire orale des Franco-Américains de Lowell, Massachusetts: mémoire, histoire et identité(s)," *Francophonie d'Amérique* 5 (1995): 155-72, especially 162-64.

93 Yvonne Lagassé, interview transcripts in Lane, *Franco-American Folk Traditions*, Appendix J. III "The Peddlers," 528-32, especially, 525.

94 Ibid.

95 Ibid.

96 Ibid.

97 Ibid.
98 Ibid.
99 Cornelius Chiclis, Oral History Project, Mogan Center, Lowell (hereafter referred to as OHPMC).
100 Denyse Baillargeon discusses the issue of infant morality, breast-feeding, and the quality of milk. Denyse Baillargeon, *Ménagères au temps de la crise* (Montréal: Éditions du Remue-ménage, 1991), 94-97.
101 Kenngott, *The Record of a City*, 83-86. Kenngott points out that since it was impossible to determine the number of infants in each immigrant group examined, the figures in his study show the percentage of infant deaths in one immigrant group compared to the total population of that group. It should be also emphasized that under similar conditions, an ethnic group in which mothers breast-fed their babies for a longer period of time exhibited lower rates of infant mortality in comparison to a group that practiced earlier weaning. Denyse Baillargeon has shown that in 1910 Montréal, the rate of infant mortality among French-Canadian mothers was considerably higher than among mothers in other cultural groups. Whereas among Anglo-Protestant families, the infant mortality rate was 163 per 1,000, among French-Canadian families this proportion reached 224 per 1,000, in comparison to 207 per 1,000 for Catholics of other origins and 94 per 1,000 for Jewish families. French-Canadian mothers weaned their babies at an earlier stage compared to these other mothers. Baillargeon explains that early weaning probably led to a greater number of pregnancies among French-Canadian women, which in turn resulted in the exhaustion of mothers and increased risks for the lives of newborns. See Denyse Baillargeon, "Fréquenter les Gouttes de lait. L'expérience des mères montréalaises, 1910-1965," *Revue d'histoire de l'Amérique française* 50, no. 1 (été 1996): 29-68, esp. 29-31. See also Martin Tétreault, "L'état de santé des Montréalais, de 1880 à 1914" (M.A. thesis, Université de Montréal, 1979); Patricia Thornton, Sherry Olson and Quon Thuy Thach, "Dimensions sociales de la mortalité infantile à Montréal au milieu du XIXe siècle." *Annales de démographie historique* (1988): 299-325.
102 According to George Kenngott, from 1880 to 1909, while the mortality rates for the Irish, the English, and the native-born Americans fell significantly (2.0, 1.5, and 3.9, respectively), the rates for the French Canadians, after a period of steady decline, rose again between 1905 and 1909. In the latter year, the French-Canadian group recorded the highest rate (2.3) among the four studied here. Kenngott, *The Record of a City*, 83.
103 Ibid., 57.
104 Blewett, *The Last Generation*, 32.
105 Mabel Delehanty Managan, OHPMC.
106 Madeline Bergeron, OHPMC.
107 Gross, *The Course of Industrial Decline*, 64.
108 Cornelia Chicklis, OHPMC.
109 Ibid.
110 Mangan, OHPMC.
111 Kenngott, *The Record of a City*, 96-97.
112 Blewett, *The Last Generation*, 151.
113 Gross, *The Course of Industrial Decline*, 64.

114 Ibid.

115 Valentine, Tead and Gregg, Industrial Counselors, "The Industrial Audit of the Boott Mills, Lowell, Massachusetts," (1916), box 45, The Flather Collection, Lowell Museum, 33-38, 40-41, 43-44, 46-52; L.A. Hackett, "Report on the Boott Mills," 1/9/1911, p. 12, box 45, FC; "Textile Development Corporation Report," (1928), box 45, FC (n.p.), 134-35. Cited in Gross, *The Course of Industrial Decline*, 133-38.

116 Blanche Graham, OHPMC.

117 Ibid.

118 Sydney Muskovitz, OHPMC.

119 Blanche Graham, OHPMC.

120 Muskovitz, OHPMC. Oral history accounts reveal many other cases of work injuries common to workers in textile mills elsewhere. See, for instance, Hareven and Langenbach, *Amoskeag*, 190-91. For records of earlier accidents in Lowell, see Gross, *The Course of Industrial Decline*, 68-74.

Chapter Three

1   Leon E. Truesdell, *The Canadian Born in the United States 1850 to 1930* (New Haven: Yale University Press, 1943), 10; Ramirez with Otis, *Crossing the 49th Parallel*, 35.

2   Department of Commerce and Labor, Bureau of Naturalization, *Annual Report of the Commissioner-General of Immigration to the Secretary of Commerce and Labor: For the Fiscal Year Ended June 30, 1900* (Washington, D.C.: U.S. Dept. of Labor, 1900), 4.

3   Donna R. Gabaccia, "Is Everywhere Nowhere? Nomads, Nations, and the Immigrant Paradigm of United States History," *Journal of American History* 86, 3 (1999), 1115-34.

4   Hareven, *Family Time and Industrial Time*, chaps. 5 and 6.

5   Ralph D. Vicero, "Immigration of French Canadians to New England, 1840-1900: A Geographical Analysis" (Ph.D. thesis, Universtiy of Wisconsin, 1968); James P. Allen, "Migration Fields of French Canadian Immigrants to Southern Maine," *Geographical Review* 62, no. 3 (1972): 366-83; Frenette, "Macroscopie et microscopie," 221-33; Bruno Ramirez, "L'émigration canadienne vers les États-Unis, perspective continentale et comparative," in *Amérique sans frontière: Les États-Unis dans l'espace nord-américain*, ed. Catherine Collomp and Mario Menéndez (Vincennes: Les Presses Universitaires de Vincennes, 1995), 91-113; Ramirez with Otis, *Crossing the 49th Parallel*, chaps. 3, 4, and 5.

6   Frank Thistlethwaite, "Migration from Europe Overseas in the Nineteenth and Twentieth Centuries," paper originally presented at the Eleventh International Congress of Historical Sciences, Stockholm, 1960; reprint in *A Century of European Migrations, 1830-1930*, ed. Rudolph J. Vecoli and Suzanne M. Sinke (Urbana: University of Illinois Press, 1991), 17-57. For work in the burgeoning field of borderland studies, see John J. Bukowczyk, "Introduction," *Mid-America* 80, no 3 (Fall 1998): 160-70; David R. Smith, "Borders That Divide and Connect: Capital and Labor Movements in the Great Lakes Region," *Canadian Review of American Studies* 25, no. 2 (1995): 1-25; Widdis, *With Scarcely a Ripple*; Ramirez with Otis, *Crossing the 49th Parallel*; Lee, *At America's Gates*; Nora Faires, "Poor Women, Proximate Border: Migrants from Ontario to Detroit in the Late Nineteenth Century," *Journal of American Ethnic History* (2001); Roger Gibbins, "The Meaning and Significance of the

American-Canadian Border," in *Borders and Border Regions in Europe and North America* ed. Paul Ganster et al. (San Diego, California: San Diego State University Press and Institute for Regional Studies of the Californias, 1997), 315-32; Bukowczyk et al., *Permeable Border: The Great Lakes Basin as Transnational Region*. These and other scholars in borderland studies have sophisticated insights which contest the "immigration paradigm."

7   My analysis in chapter 3 is based on longitudinal data derived from three kinds of nominative sources: the U.S. Federal Census Manuscript Schedules, the *Soundex Index to the Canadian Border Entry* and the *Case History Records for the Overseers of the Poor*. Bruno Ramirez and his research group have undertaken the task of creating part of the data set out of microfilmed collections of *Border Entry*, covering the period from 1891 to 1952. I gratefully acknowledge the access to this sample accorded to me by this research group. I have compiled records for the rest, as well as additional information for the first data set collected by Ramirez' research group. Most important were names of the sample individuals for the purpose of record linkage with data drawn from the census schedules. For discussion of longitudinal data and nominal-linkage method used for my analysis, see Appendix A.

8   Karen Fog Olwig, "New York as a Locality in a Global Family Network" in *Islands in the City: West Indian Migration to New York*, ed. Nancy Foner (Berkeley: University of California Press, 2001), 142-60, especially 143-45. For further discussion critical to the immigration paradigm and the incorporation paradigm, see Constance R. Sutton and Elsa M. Chancey ed., *Caribbean Life in New York City* (New York: Center for Migration Studies, 1987); Mary C. Waters, "Ethnic and Racial Identities of Second-Generation Black Immigrants in New York City, *International Migration Review* 28 (1994): 795-820.

9   Marian L. Smith, "INS at the U.S.-Canadian Border, 1893-1993: An Overview of Issues and Topics," paper presented at the meeting of the Organization of American Historians, Toronto, 23, April 1999; Ramirez with Otis, *Crossing the 49th Parallel*, 42-43: Lee, *At America's Gates*, 176-78.

10 Ramirez with Otis, *Crossing the 49th Parallel*, 46.

11 Ibid.

12 For Asian immigrants inspected by U.S. immigration officials at Angel Island, the detention lasted on average for two weeks. Europeans arriving at Ellis Island were processed in a matter of hours. Lee, *At America's Gates*, chap. 3, especially 82.

13 Ramirez with Otis, *Crossing the 49th Parallel*, chap. 2.

14 Committee on Immigration, *RICI*, LXXVIII.

15 Pierre Anctil, "Chinese of the Eastern States, 1881," 125-31. Massachusetts Department of Labor and Industry, *Twelfth Annual Report of the Bureau of Statistics of Labor* (Boston: Wright & Potter Printing Co., 1881), 469-70. See also Yves Roby, *Les Franco-Américains*, 185-88; Ramirez, *On the Move*, 111-13.

16 Ramirez with Otis, *Crossing the 49th Parallel*, 53.

17 Catherine Collomp, "Immigrants, Labor Markets, and the State, A Comparative Approach: France and the United States, 1880-1930," *Journal of American History* 86, no. 1 (1999): 41-66, especially 60; Ramirez with Otis, *Crossing the 49th Parallel*, 52-53.

18 Everette C. Hughes, *French Canada in Transition* (Chicago: The University of Illinois Press, 1963, c1943).

19 Early, "Mobility Potential," 217; Early, "The French-Canadian Family Economy," 181-82. Early, "The Settling-In Process," 90.

20 Ramirez, *On the Move*, 28-29.

21 Hareven, *Family Time and Industrial Time*, 123.

22 The criteria for distinguishing a city (with a population over 6,000) from a town (with a population over 3,000), or a village (with a population of 3,000 or less) are taken from those applied by Linteau et al. in *Histoire du Québec*, vol. 1, 472-73. Colonization regions are not easy to determine because their frontiers moved constantly. Considering that by the early twentieth century most of the province's colonization frontiers were no longer designated as *régions de colonisation* but had become agricultural regions with an increasingly settled population, one might safely speculate that only a small proportion of the reported rural origins had been from the colonization region.

23 Madame Ouellette, interview with Brigitte Lane, February 16, 1983, reproduced in Lane, *Franco-American Folk Traditions*, 316.

24 Four individuals are recorded as having been born in Lowell (3) and Manchester (1) and having lived in Canada before crossing the border southward to Lowell. One individual listed Lowell as his last permanent place of residence. He was probably visiting Québec and then filled out the *Border Entry* card on his way back to Lowell.

25 The birthplace of one individual (name unknown) is not indicated. Rudolph Allard was listed as having been born in Lowell, moved to Canada, and gone back to Lowell.

26 *Border Entry*, reel number 49; *Fourteenth U.S. Federal Population Census Schedules, 1920*, 570-38-85.

27 Ibid., 117-18.

28 Immigration Commission, *Immigrants in Industries* 10: 243-44.

29 *Border Entry* and the *Thirteenth U.S. Federal Census, 1910*.

30 Ramirez, *On the Move*, chap. 1. Labourers, farmers, and farm labourers continued to form leading occupational categories among French-Canadian men migrating out of Québec and the Maritimes to the United States in the first three decades of the twentieth century. In contrast, the proportion of male migrants with factory-related work experience was limited in the overall migration of French Canadians to the United States. Bruno Ramirez and Yves Otis claim that this was a predictable result, given the strong labour demand for semi- and unskilled workers in the large urban and industrial centres such as Montréal. These workers filled the growing industrial workforce in Canada and, subsequently, had little need to migrate elsewhere including the United States. Ramirez with Otis, *Crossing the 49th Parallel*, 88-89.

31 Ramirez, *On the Move*, 117.

32 A second hand was a person in charge of production who ranked between foremen and operatives in a textile factory. A second hand was invariably male and acted as an intermediary between overseers and operative workers. Hareven, *Family Time and Industrial Time*, 261.

33 The Immigration Commission provided a similar figure for the pre-migration occupational background of French-Canadian women in the New England cotton industry. Immigration Commission, *Immigrants in Industries* 10: 363-64. See also Ramirez with Otis, *Crossing the 49th Parallel*, 85-87.

34 Jean-Charles Fortin and Antonio Lechasseur, *Histoire du Bas-Saint-Laurent*, 203.

35 Rouillard, *Les travailleurs du coton au Québec*.

36 Ramirez, *On the Move*, 117-18.
37 *Ibid.*, 125.
38 According to data derived from the sampled French-Canadian migrants listed on the U.S. Federal Census Schedules, among the male wage workers, the percentage of the unskilled decreased from 24 percent in 1910 to 17 percent in 1920. Conversely, the percentage of the semi-skilled and skilled rose from 53 percent to 63 percent. Among the female wage workers, the percentage of the semi-skilled and skilled remained higher than that for men over the decade (74 percent in 1910 and 1920), while the percentage of the unskilled was 10 percent in 1910 and in 1920. The occupational classification used here is based on the occupational scale developed by Gérard Bouchard. Gérard Bouchard, *Tous les métiers du monde: le traitement des données professionnelles en histoire sociale* (Québec: Les Presses de l'Université Laval, 1996).
39 Immigration Commission, *Immigrants in Industries* 10: 268, 270.
40 Early, "The French-Canadian Beginning": 186; Immigration Commission, *Immigrants in Industries* 10: 271.
41 *Border Entry*, reel number 50; *Fourteenth Federal Population Census Schedules, 1920*, 205-3-217-187-12-54.
42 *Border Entry*, reel number 76; *Thirteenth Federal Population Census Schedules, 1910*, 940-2-14-33.
43 Narcissa Fantini Nodges, OHPMC. Reports by the Industrial Commission state that by the dawn of the twentieth century, the improvement of textile machinery contributed to de-skilling formerly skilled labour. Although the report does not specify how much time was needed to learn to weave, it does point to the shortened time period needed to operate certain machines. For instance, only a week or two was needed to learn to operate the ring-spinning machine, which replaced mule-spinners and three or four weeks were needed to run four looms and thus earn some money doing so. U.S. Industrial Commission, *Reports of the Industrial Commission on Immigration, Including Testimony, with Review and Digest, and Special Reports. And on Education, Including Testimony, with Review and Digest* vol. XV (Washington, G.O.P., 1901), xxxvi, xxxvii. See also Hareven, *Family Time and Industrial Time*; Parr, *The Gender of Breadwinners*.
44 Joy Parr, "The Skilled Emigrant and Her Kin: Gender, Culture, and Labour Recruitment." *Canadian Historical Review* 68, no. 4 (1987): 528-51.
45 *Thirteenth Federal Population Census Schedules*, 1910, 860-6-1-90-327.
46 Louise A. Tilly and Joan W. Scott. *Women, Work, and Family.* (New York: Routledge, 1978, reprinted in 1989), 109.
47 Dublin, *Transforming Women's Work*, 232.
48 This interpretation is influenced by the argument made by Donna Gabaccia in "Women of Mass Migrations," especially pp. 96-99.
49 Parr, *The Gender of Breadwinners*, 26.
50 Cameron, *Radicals of the Worst Sort*, 79.
51 *Border Entry*, reel number 147; *Fourteenth Federal Population Census Schedules, 1920*, 218-3-13-33.
52 Yvonne Lagassé, interview transcript, in Lane, *Franco-American Folk Traditions*, 318-21.
53 *Ibid.*
54 *Ibid.*
55 *Ibid.*
56 *Ibid.*

57 Roger Brunelle, interview transcript, in Lane, *Franco-American Traditions*, 325-26.
58 Cynthia R. Comacchio, "Beneath the 'Sentimental Veil': Families and Family History in Canada." *Labour/Le Travail* 33 (Spring 1994): 279-302, especially 287-88; Phillis Moen and Elaine Wethington, "The Concept of Family Adaptive Strategies," *Annual Review of Sociology* 18 (1992): 233-51, especially 237.
59 *Border Entry*, reel number 76; *Thirteenth Federal Census Schedules, 1910*, 861-6-1, 39-203-497. Birthplaces are important indicators for reconstructing the geographic itineraries of immigrants. It should be noted, however, that when there was no record of birth for a period of time (usually, from five to six years) with the result that historians do not have proof that immigrants moved, this does not exclude the possibility that there might have been displacements. Such ambiguities notwithstanding, this study reproduced, by way of illustration, some of the itineraries from the reconstruction of the birthplace data. For the use of birthplace records for the reconstruction of migratory itineraries, see Bruno Ramirez and Yves Otis, "French-Canadian Emigration to the USA in the 1920s: A Research Report" (Montréal: Université de Montréal, 1992), 19-20; Jean Lamarre, "Modèles migratoires et intégration socio-économiques des Canadiens français de la vallée de la Saginaw, Michigan, 1840-1900," *Labour/Le Travail* 41 (Spring 1998): 9-33.
60 Yves Frenette, "La genèse d'une communauté canadienne-française en Nouvelle-Angleterre : Lewiston, Maine, 1800-1880" (Ph.D. thesis, Université Laval, 1988), 170-71 and Frenette, "Macroscopie et microscopie," 221-33; Ramirez, *On the Move*, 78-84.
61 Immigrants' letters are also an important source for revealing the extent of information networks among family and friends. See, for instance, Father Casgrain's "Lettres américaines," *L'opinion publique* (Montréal, 30 mars 1882), a description of an emigrant who visited home, reproduced in part by Yves Roby in *Franco-Américains*, 50-51.
62 Unfortunately, the data derived from the *Border Entry* do not allow a researcher to distinguish the gender of cousins listed as contact persons.
63 Ramirez and Otis, "French Canadian Emigration," 10-11.
64 Bruno Ramirez, "French Canadian Immigrants in the New England Cotton Industry: A Socioeconomic Profile," *Labour/Le Travail* 11 (Spring 1983): 125-42.
65 "Cultural distance" and "mental map" are other expressions that Dirk Hoerder uses in reference to this concept. Bruno Ramirez, "Migration and Regional Labour Markets," in *Class, Community and the Labour Movement: Wales and Canada, 1850-1930* (LLFUR/CCLH, 1989), 119-33; Hoerder, *Cultures in Contact*, 14. See also, Jean Lamarre, *Les Canadiens français du Michigan*, chap. 1.
66 Dirk Hoerder, "Segmented Macrosystems and Networking Individuals: The Balancing Functions of Migration Processes," in *Migration, Migration History, History*, ed. Jan Lucassen and Leo Lucassen (Bern: Peter Lang, 1999), 73-84.
67 Yves Roby, *Les Franco-Américains de la Nouvelle-Angleterre*, 14.

Chapter Four

1 Industrial Commission, *Report of the Industrial Commission on Immigration*, LXXVIII, 39.
2 Ramirez with Otis, *Crossing the 49th Parallel*, 52-53.

3 Anctil, "Chinese of the Eastern States, 1881," 125-31. Massachusetts Bureau of Statistics of Labor, *Twelfth Annual Report* (Boston), 469-70.

4 See for instance, Stephan Thernstrom, *The Other Bostonians: Poverty and Progress in the American Metropolis, 1880-1970* (Cambridge, MA: Harvard University Press, 1973); Thernstrom, *Poverty and Progress, Social Mobility in a Nineteenth Century City* (Cambridge, MA: Harvard University Press, 1964); Iacovetta, *Such Hardworking People*, chap. 3; Lilian Petroff, *Sojourner and Settler: The Macedonian Community in Toronto 1940* (Toronto: Toronto University Press, 1994); Carmela Patrias, *Patriots and Proletarians: Politicizing Hungarian Immigrants in Interwar Canada* (Montreal and Kingston: McGill-Queen's University Press, 1994).

5 Recent advance of scholarly interest in formation and expression of masculinities at home, work, school, and on the street has reversed earlier observations that labour historians showed little interest in the relations between men and their families. See for instance *International Labor and Working-Class History* 69 (Spring 2006) on working-class subjectivities and sexualities; Robert W. Connell, *Masculinities* (Berkeley: University of California Press, 1995); John Tosh, "What Should Historians Do with Masculinity? Reflections on Nineteenth-Century Britain," *History Workshop* 38 (Fall 1994), 179-202. In the Canadian context, Franca Iacovetta has pointed out that important corrections begun in the 1990s including work by Mark Steven Rosenfeld, "'It Was a Hard Life': Class and Gender in the Work and Family Rhythms of a Railway Town, 1920-1950," *Historical Papers/Communications historiques*, (Canadian Historical Association/Société historique du Canada, 1988), 237-79; Mark Steven Rosenfeld, "'She Was a Hard Life': Work, Family, Community, Politics, and Ideology in the Railway Ward of a Central Ontario Town, 1900-1960" (Ph.D. thesis, University of Toronto, 1990); Joy Parr, *The Gender of Breadwinners*; Iacovetta, *Such Hardworking People*; and more recently, a groundbreaking contribution by Craig Heron, "Boys Will Be Boys: Working-Class Masculinities in the Age of Mass Production," *International Labor and Working-Class History* 69 (Spring 2006), 6-34. Literature on the family wage has shed light on a number of issues relating to gender, breadwinning, class-consciousness, and the persistence of patriarchal family structures. Martha May, "The Historical Problems of the Family Wage: The Ford Motor Company and the Five Dollar Days," *Feminist Studies* 8 (Summer 1982): 399-424; Lawrence Glickman, *A Living Wage: American Workers and the Making of Consumer Society* (Ithaca: Cornell University Press, 1997); Alice Kessler-Harris, *In Pursuit of Equity: Women, Men, and the Quest for Economic Citizenship in Twentieth-Century America* (New York: Oxford University Press, 2001).

6 Extensive scholarship on whiteness expanded since the 1990s. Noel Ignatiev, *How the Irish Became White* (New York: Routledge, 1995); George Lipsitz, *The Possessive Investment in Whiteness: How White People Profit from Identity Politics* (Philadelphia: Temple University Press, 1998; rev. ed., 2006); David R. Roediger, *The Wages of Whiteness: Race and the Making of the American Working Class* (London and New York: Verso, 1991, revised edition, 1999); Matthew Frye Jacobson, *Whiteness of a Different Color: European Immigrants and the Alchemy of Race* (Cambridge, MA: Harvard University Press, 1998). Among the sharp criticisms of whiteness studies, see an essay by Eric Arnesen with responses by six historians, also mostly critical, entitled "Scholarly Controversy: Whiteness and the Historians' Imagination," *International Labor and Working-Class History* 60 (Fall 2001): 1-92; Andrew Hartman, "The Rise and Fall of Whiteness Studies," *Race & Class* 46, no.2 (2004): 22-38.

7 FlorenceMae Waldron is one of the first to explore ways in which French-Canadian men's and women's perceptions of gender identities shaped their process of becoming Americans or remaining Canadians. I offer in this chapter another take on the issue with regard to

working-class French-Canadian men. Waldron, "The Gendered Worlds of New England's Quebecois Migrants, 1870-1930," paper presented at the Conference: Histoire, Genre et Migration, Paris, March 2005.

8   Lawrence Glickman makes an important distinction in the use of the terms "family wage" and "living wage." Labour unions in the nineteenth and early twentieth centuries used "living wage," a more gender-neutral term, whereas the middle-class reformers in the Progressive-era first employed "family wage," a term later adopted by historians in the 1970s and 1980s to refer to the "living wage." Glickman, *A Living Wage*.

9   See especially Linda Gordon, "Black and White Visions of Welfare: Women's Welfare Activism, 1890-1945," in ed., Vicki L Ruiz and Ellen Carol DuBois, *Unequal Sisters: A Multicultural Reader in U.S. Women's History* (New York: Routledge, 2000, 3rd ed.), 214-41, esp. 228-31.

10 Cameron, *Radicals of the Worst Sort*, 40.

11 *Ibid.*, 42. For similar situations in other textile cities in New England, see *Le Travailleur*, 6 February 1880. See also Ramirez, *On the Move*, 119.

12 Early, "French-Canadian Beginnings," 110, 112; Ramirez, *On the Move*, 118-19.

13 Early, "French-Canadian Beginnings," 186; Massachusetts Bureau of Statistics of Labor, *Sixth Annual Report*, 1875, 203, 235-36, 275-76, 307, 311-14, 337. The Immigration Commission, *Immigrants in Industries* 10: 271. The Immigration Commission data do not specify the age of the children but include all those who appear as sons or daughters of the household head on the Commission's inquiry.

14 Figures calculated by Yukari Takai from the data drawn from the *Thirteenth and Fourteenth U.S. Federal Census Schedules, 1910, 1920*. The issue of women's paid labour participation shall be discussed in greater details in chap. 5.

15 Unless otherwise specified, statistical data presented in the following discussion are calculated by the author based on a 5-percent sample of the manuscript schedules of the *Thirteenth and Fourteenth Federal Censuses, 1910, 1920*, City of Lowell, Middlesex County, Massachusetts.

16 Border Entry 394-25-20, 50-42-8, and unidentified number.

17 Charter 494, Acts of 1898, *the Statues of the Commonwealth of Massachusetts*. The legislation underwent several modifications since 1840. Kenngott, *The Record of a City*, 138-47.

18 David Montgomery, *The Fall of House of Labor*, 123-24, 131.

19 *L'Etoile de Lowell*, December 30, 1905.

20 *Ibid.*, October 28, 1905.

21 See chap. 2 of this book. See also Tamara K. Hareven and Randolph Langenbach, *Amoskeag: Life and Work in an American Factory City* (New York: Pantheon Books, 1978), 202. See also Roby, *Franco-Américains*, 70-71; Cameron, *Radicals of the Worst Sort*, 70-72.

22 For discussion on the classification of work, see Appendix A in this study.

23 In the following analysis, I have used a modified version of an occupational classificatory scheme developed by Gérard Bouchard and his research group, the IREP (Institut Interuniversitaire de Recherches sur les Populations). In an effort to take into account some of the ambiguities inherent in terms such as "skilled," "semi-skilled," and "unskilled," all operatives such as weavers, spinners, and carders, and craft workers such as machinists, mechanics, and engineers are grouped into one category. Bouchard, *Tous les métiers du monde*, 67, 78, see Appendix B in this book for greater discussion on the issue.

24 Early, "French-Canadian Beginnings," 110, 112. The marked presence of day labourers among French-Canadian male workers was, by no means, a unique phenomenon in Lowell. During the last three decades of the nineteenth century, French-Canadian men worked in a dozen New England textile communities concentrated overwhelmingly in unskilled occupations. In Fall River, Massachusetts, for example, the 1869 city directory shows that about half of the French-Canadian heads of family were working as day labourers, whereas no more than one out of four was employed in textile manufacturing. At about the same time in Holyoke, more than one quarter of French-Canadian adult men worked as day labourers, forming the largest occupational group. Textile mill employment made up the second largest occupational group after that of day labourers, with 18 percent of the working population employed in the cotton textile industry and 4 percent in the woolen textile industry. Following closely in third place were construction and building-related workers. In Lewiston, Maine, as many as 41 percent of French-Canadian family heads were listed as day labourers. Philip T. Silva, Jr., "The Spindle City: Labor, Politics, and Religion in Fall River, Massachusetts, 1870-1905" (Ph.D. thesis, Fordham University, 1973), 345-46; Haebler, "Habitants in Holyoke," 66-68.

25 *Fourteenth U.S. Federal Census Schedules, 1920*, 185-2-41-86.

26 Ibid., 576-10-28-65.

27 Ibid., 195-2-28-34.

28 Hareven, *Family Time and Industrial Time*, chap. 5. See also Blewett, *The Last Generation*, 147.

29 *Fourteenth U.S. Federal Census Schedules, 1920*, 179-3-5-52. Given Alfred Parent's indication of workplace (house) and occupation (carpenter), he might well be classified as a self-employed or a small entrepreneur. Yet the census schedule also reported that Alfred was an employee and not an independent business owner (or someone working on his own account). Accordingly, I have classified Alfred in the category of skilled workers and not among the small business owners.

30 Immigration Commission, *Immigrants in Industries* 10: 253.

31 Calculation by the author based on the data drawn from the *Thirteenth and Fourteenth Federal Census Schedules*.

32 Roediger, *The Wages of Whiteness*, especially chap. 7.

33 James R. Barrett and David R. Roediger, "Inbetween Peoples: Race, Nationality, and the 'New Immigrant' Working Class," *Journal of Ethnic History* 16 (Spring 1997), reprinted in David R. Roediger, *Colored White: Transcending the Racial Past* (Berkeley: University of California Press, 2002), 138-68.

34 Timothy J. Meagher, *Inventing Irish America: Generation, Class, and Ethnic Identity in a New England City, 1800-1923* (Notre Dame, Indiana: University of Notre Dame, 2001), 15-16.

35 Henry Paradis, OHPMC.

36 Hubert LaFleur, OHPMC.

37 Ibid.

38 Ibid.

39 *Fourteenth U.S. Federal Population Census Schedules, 1920*, 570-38-85.

40 The classification of police officers here may raise some eyebrows. This categorization adheres to criteria developed by Gérard Bouchard, including the nature of effort (manual or

non-manual), level of responsibility, and level of technical difficulty. Bouchard, *Tous les métiers du monde*, chap. 4, especially 89.

41 *Fourteenth U.S. Federal Population Census Schedules, 1920*, 177-1-10-10.

42 *Fourteenth U.S. Federal Census Schedules, 1920*, 183-4-17-60; 199-4-57-96.

43 In 1910, sixteen French-Canadian men in my sample were listed in this category of independent shopkeepers and professionals as either employer or self-employed: proprietors of wood yards (2), one candy store owner, one boardinghouse owner, one caretaker; variety store dealer and wood dealer (1 each); barbers (3); contractors in a butcher shop and in an unspecified sector (1 each); a grocer and a storekeeper (1 each); a clothier and a fruit peddler (1 each). Ten years later, there were eleven people of my sample in this category: proprietors of wood yards (2); a restaurant owner and a meat market owner (1 each); contractors (2), a roofer and a carpenter (1 each); and a barber, baker, and jeweller (1 each).

44 Yvonne Lagassé in Lane, *Franco-American Folk Traditions*, Appendix J, I. Les rues et les magasins: 514-25, especially 515-16.

45 Franca Iacovetta discusses the significance of becoming a shop owner in the case of Italian immigrants in post-World War II Toronto. Iacovetta, *Such Hardworking People*, 64.

46 Lagassé in Lane, *Franco-American Folk Traditions*, Appendix J, I. Les rues et les magasins: 514-25, especially 514-15.

47 *Ibid.*, 520-21.

48 *Ibid.*, 518-19.

49 Nicholas Georgoulis, OHPMC.

50 For a discussion of French-Canadian shop owners and professionals in the neighbouring city of Fall River, see Brigitte Violette, "Formation et développement d'une petite-bourgeoisie Franco-Américaine de la Nouvelle-Angleterre (Fall River, 1870-1920)" (Ph.D. thesis, Université de Montréal, 2000).

51 See Virginia Yans-McLaughlin, "Metaphors of Self in History: Subjectivity, Oral Narrative, and Immigration Studies," in *Immigration Reconsidered*, ed. Virginia Yans-McLaughlin, 254-90, especially 267.

52 Shirley Zebroski does not specify the geographic extent of "all manufacturing industries," but the context of her writing suggests this refers to the manufacturing in New England. See Shirley Zebroski, "The 1903 Strike in the Lowell Cotton Mills," in *Surviving Hard Times: The Working People of Lowell*, ed. Mary H. Blewett, (Lowell, MA: Lowell Museum, 1982), 45-62.

53 *Ibid.*

54 Immigration Commission, *Immigrants in Industries* 10: 274.

55 Gross, *The Course of Industrial Decline*, 144-49; Silvia, "Spindle City," 696-705; Jean-Claude Simon, "Textile Workers, Trade Unions, and Politics: Comparative Case Studies, France and the United States, 1885-1914" (Ph.D. thesis, Tufts University, 1980), 306-08. See also, Montgomery, *Fall of the House of Labor*, 169-79.

56 Gross, *Course of Industrial Decline*, 144-49.

57 Robert George Layer, *Earnings of Cotton Mill Operatives, 1826-1914* (Cambridge, MA: Committee on Research in Economic History, 1995), 48. Layer's real annual earnings index represents the rate of relative annual earnings per full-time worker divided by the cost of living index estimated by Alvin Hansen. Layer, *Earning of Cotton Mill Operatives*, 15. Layer

calculated the relative annual earnings per worker based on the relative increase in annual earnings in relation to the 1844-46 level taken as 100.
58 Gross, *Course of Industrial Decline*, 144-49.
59 Ibid.
60 Immigration Commission, *Immigration in Industries*, vol. 10, 261.
61 R. C. Chapin, *The Standard of Living in New York City* (New York: Charities Publication Committee, 1909), 259. Cited by Scott Nearing in *Financing the Wage-Earner's Family: A Survey of the Facts Bearing on Income and Expenditures in the Families of American Wage-Earners* (New York: Huebsch, 1914), 45.
62 Valentine, Tead, and Gregg, Industrial Counselors, "The Industrial Audit of the Boott Mills, Lowell, Massachusetts" (1916), box 45, Flather Collection, Lowell Museum at the University of Massachusetts Lowell, 170-74. Cited in Gross, *The Course of Industrial Decline*, 149.
63 Massachusetts, Commission on the Cost of Living, *Report on the Cost of Living* (Boston: Wright & Potter Printing Co., 1910), 21. See also Cameron, *Radicals of the Worst Sort*, chap. 3, especially 98. For comparison with other cities, see also Kessler-Harris, *Out to Work*, 121; Margaret Frances Byington, *Homestead: The Household of a Mill Town* (1910; reprint, Pittsburgh: University Center for International Studies, 1974), chap. 10 and especially 152; Donald B. Cole, *Immigrant City: Lawrence, Massachusetts, 1845-1921* (Chapel Hill: University of North Carolina Press, 1963), 118.
64 Kenngott, *The Record of a City*, chap. 5, especially page 110.
65 Ibid., 121. Budget number 55.
66 Ibid., 114-15. Budget number 86.
67 Ibid., 115-19. Budget number 17.
68 Hareven made a similar observation. Hareven, *Family Time and Industrial Time*, 207-08.
69 Edward Scollan, "World War I and the 1918 Cotton Textile Strikes," in *Surviving Hard Times*, ed. Blewett, 105-14.
70 Gross, *The Course of Industrial Decline*, 148.
71 Alexander Keyssar, *Out to Work: The First Century of Unemployment in Massachusetts* (Cambridge: Cambridge University Press, 1986), 58, 118.
72 Kenngott, *The Record of a City*, 169.
73 Gross, *The Course of Industrial Decline*, 148-49.
74 Ibid., 151-55. See also Shirley Zebroski, "The 1903 Strike in the Lowell Cotton Mills," in *Surviving Hard Times*, ed. Blewett, 44-62; Mary T. Mulligan, "Epilogue to Lawrence: The 1912 Strike in Lowell, Massachusetts," *Surviving Hard Times*, ed. Blewett, 82-83; Edward J. Scollan, "World War I," in *Surviving Hard Times*, ed. Blewett, 105-14.
75 Gross, *The Course of Industrial Decline*, 151. The author would like to thank Laurence Gross for extended accounts on this point.
76 Irving Bernstein, *The Lean Years: A History of the American Worker, 1920-1933* (Boston: Houghton Mifflin Company, 1960), 7; James R. Green, *World of the Worker: Labor in Twentieth-Century America* (New York: Hill and Wang, 1980; reprint, Urbana: University of Illinois Press, 1998), 109; Caroline Ware, *The Early New England Cotton Manufacture: A Study in Industrial Beginnings* (Boston and New York: Houghton Mifflin Company, 1931; reprint, New York: Russel and Russel, 1966), 244. See also Gross, *The Course of Industrial Decline*, 151-52.

77 Blanche Graham and Martha Doherty, OHPMC.
78 Yves Roby acknowledges heightened labour activism among French-Canadian workers in New England textile factories in the first decades of the twentieth century. And yet, numbers of them crossed the picket line at the time of strikes. Roby, *Franco-Américains de la Nouvelle-Angleterre*, 236.
79 Kenngott, *The Record of a City*, 147-55.
80 Blewett, *The Last Generation*, 6.
81 Lawrence, Massachusetts, though only twelve kilometres away and equally dominated by the textile industry, experienced labour strikes which occurred far more frequently. Divided ownership of several major textile corporations, unlike Lowell's united ownership, made it easier for Lawrence workers to form a united front against the management. Also, the greater number of highly skilled jobs in woolen and worsted mills in that city attracted more experienced immigrant workers. Many of these skilled workers brought with them experience in labour organization at the turn of the century. The Franco-Belgians and Italians, in particular, came with a highly developed, politically radical belief-system as well. The difference in production lines was another factor. In Lowell, production of coarse cottons was encouraged. Mass production of the latter required hiring of mostly unskilled and/or uneducated workers, who had been relatively unfamiliar with labour organization. In addition, the growing presence of migrant workers of more recent arrival and their diverse languages likely reduced further the workers' prospects for organization. A combination of these factors enabled the manufacturing owners to maintain Lowell's longstanding managerial system, composed of joint ownership and joint action and their strong anti-craft union attitudes. David J. Goldberg, *A Tale of Three Cities: Labor, Organization and Protest in Paterson, Passaic, and Lawrence, 1916-1921* (New Brunswick, New Jersey: Rutgers University Press, 1989); Gary Gerstle, *Working-Class Americanism: The Politics of Labor in a Textile City, 1914-1960* (Cambridge: Cambridge University Press, 1989), chap. 2; Gross, *The Course of Industrial Decline*, 152.
82 Gross, *ibid.*, 152; Gary Gerstle, *Working-Class Americanism*, chaps. 4 and 6.
83 Mangan, OHPMC.
84 Immigration Commission, *Immigrants in the Industries*, vol. 10, 292.
85 Kenngott, *The Record of a City*, 151-54.
86 *L'Étoile de Lowell*, September 19, 20, 21, 24, 25, 27, October 2 and 6, 1900.
87 Immigration Commission, *Immigrants in Industries* 10: 291-93; Kenngott, *The Record of a City*, 152-53.
88 Cameron, *Radicals of the Worst Sort*, 3.
89 Gross, *The Course of Industrial Decline*, 153.
90 Diane Ouellette, OHPMC.
91 Narcissa Fantini Hodges, OHPMC.
92 Blewett, *The Last Generation*, 151-52.
93 Arthur Morrissette, OHPMC.
94 *Ibid.*
95 Blewett, *The Last Generation*, 152.
96 Albert Côté, OHPMC.
97 Blewett, *The Last Generation*, 151.

98 On the manhood of skilled textile workers in a neighbouring city of Fall River and New England in the second half of the nineteenth century, see Mary H. Blewett, "Manhood and the Market: The Politics of Gender and Class among the Textile Workers of Fall River, Massachusetts, 1870-1880," in *Work Engendered: Toward a New History of American Labor*, ed. Ava Baron (Ithaca: Cornell University Press, 1991), 92-113; Blewett, *Constant Turmoil: The Politics of Industrial Life in Nineteenth-Century New England* (Amherst: University of Massachusetts Press. 2000).

99 Kessler-Harris, *In Pursuit of Equity*, 54-55.

100 Ibid, 51-56.

101 Blewett, *The Last Generation*, 151.

102 Arthur Morrissette, OHPMC.

103 Blewettt, *The Last Generation*, 295.

104 Desmarais, OHPMC.

105 *Ibid.*

106 Morrissette, OHPMC. The expression "nigger's heaven," or "nigger heaven," to be more precise, was a commonly used phrase. The title of a 1926 novel, referring to the cheap balcony seats reserved for African Americans exemplifies this. The usage of this term in Lowell is curious, however, given only a small number of African Americans in Lowell at the time. Carl Van Vechten, *Nigger Heaven* (New York: Grosset & Dunlap, 1926.

107 Kathey Peiss, *Cheap Amusements: Working Women and Leisure in Turn-of-the-Century New York* (Philadelphia: Temple University Press, 1986), especially 45-55, chaps. 4-6.

108 Albert Parent, OHPMC.

109 Cameron, *Radicals of the Worst Sort*, 178-79.

110 Blewett, *The Last Generation*, 31.

111 Morrissette, Martha Doherty, and Graham, OHPMC.

112 Morrissette, OHPMC.

113 *Ibid.*

114 João da Silva Goes, OHPMC.

115 Conelia Chiklis, OHPMC.

116 Georgoulis, OHPMC.

117 Blewett, *The Last Generation*, 149-50.

118 Morrissette, OHPMC.

119 Lane, *Franco-American Folk Traditions*, chaps. 2 and 3.

120 Graham, OHPMC.

121 Migration historians have been reluctant to discuss domestic violence until recently. This issue will be discussed in greater details in chapter 6. Franca Iacovetta, "Introduction" in Epp, Iacovetta and Swyripa eds., *Sisters or Strangers*, 11-13. Among emerging studies on the subject, see Angelo Principe, "Glimpses of Lives in Canada's Shadow: Insiders, Outsiders, and Female Activism in the Fascist Era," in *Women, Gender, and Transnational Lives*, ed. Gabaccia and Iacovetta, 349-85; Lisa R. Mar, "The Table of Lin Tee: Madness, Family Violence, and Lindsay's Anti-Chinese Riot of 1919," in *Sisters or Strangers?* ed. Epp, Iacovetta and Swyripa, 108-29.

122 Mary Rouses Karafelis, OHPMC.

123 *Ibid.*

Chapter Five

1. Immigration Commission, *Immigrants in Industries* 10: 264.
2. See Introduction of chap. 4.
3. Scott and Tilly, *Women, Work, and Family*, 116.
4. *Ibid.*, 104, 134-36. See also Dublin, *Transforming Women's Work*, 10-12.
5. Carole Groneman, "She Works as a Child; She Pays as a Man: Women Workers in a Mid-Nineteenth Century New York City Community," in *Class, Sex, and the Women Workers*, ed. Milton Cantor and Bruce Laurie (Westport, CT: Greenwood Press, 1977), 83-100, especially 90; Yans-McLaughlin, *Family and Community*, 170, 187, 200-02; Hareven, *Family Time and Industrial Time*, especially 75. See also, Dublin, *Transforming Women's Work*.
6. Dublin, *Transforming Women's Work*, 8-14, 232-33.
7. These figures are drawn from a random sample of the *Thirteenth and Fourteenth U.S. Census Schedules, 1910, 1920* and calculated by the author. Figures used in the following pages are also derived from the same sources unless otherwise stated. According to this Lowell data, during the same period the number of job titles held by French-Canadian male workers increased from 107 to 127; that of Irish males declined from 185 to 172.
8. *Thirteenth U.S. Census Schedules, 1910*, 865-6-3-7-24; 857-5-2-59-124; 841-2-2-18-18; 852-4-2-46-80.
9. My own calculation, based on the data provided by the Immigration Commission, *Immigrants in Industries* 10: 246.
10. *Thirteenth U.S. Census Schedules, 1910*, 861-6-1-81-259.
11. *Thirteenth U.S. Census Schedules, 1910*, 839-2-1-1-1.
12. Early, "French-Canadian Beginnings," 110, 112, Tables 9, 10.
13. *Thirteenth U.S. Census Schedules, 1910*, 861-6-324-899-958; 860-6-1-29-149-354.
14. Bergeron and Valentine Chartrand, OHPMC.
15. *Fourteenth U.S. Census Schedules, 1920*, 237-3-44-60, 231-3-193-234 and 557-3-2-96.
16. From 1910 to 1920, the percentage of American-born women of American parentage rose from 39 percent to 43 percent and that of women of Irish background (both those born in the U.S. and in Ireland) from 17 percent to 25 percent. Author's calculation based on the data drawn from *Thirteenth and Fourteenth U.S. Census Schedules, 1910, 1920*.
17. This interpretation is influenced by the one advanced by Carole Turbin. Turbin, *Working Women of Collar City*, 52-60.
18. Ouellette, OHPMC.
19. Desmarais, OHPMC.
20. *Ibid.*
21. Ouellette, OHPMC.
22. Graham, OHPMC.
23. Michael Anderson, "The Social Position of Spinsters in Mid-Victorian Britain," *Journal of Family History* 9 (Winter 1984): 377-93, especially 388.

24 *Thirteenth U.S. Census Schedules, 1910,* 861-6-1-16-60; *Fourteenth U.S. Census Schedules, 1920,* 237-3-2-24-34; 218-158-482.
25 Immigration Commission, *Immigrants in Industries* 10: 260, 263.
26 Ibid., 251-54.
27 Bergeron, OHPMC.
28 Tamara Hareven and Louise Tilly, "Solitary Women and Family Mediation in American and French Textile Cities," *Annales de démographie historique* (1981), 253-71.
29 FlorenceMae Waldron, "'I've Never Dreamed It Was Necessary to Marry!' Women and Work in New England French Canadian Communities, 1870-1930," *Journal of American Ethnic History* 24, no. 2 (Winter 2005): 34-64, especially 55-56.
30 See an interview with Cora Pellerin, Hareven and Langenbach, *Amoskeag*, 201-11; Waldron, "'I've Never Dreamed It Was Necessary'": 55-56.
31 *Thirteenth Federal Census Schedules, 1910,* 861-6-1-205-649, 861-6-1-81-267.
32 *Thirteenth U.S. Census Schedules, 1910,* 839-2-1-1, 861-6-81-225.
33 A winder attends to the mechanical transfer of yarn from one size or form of package to another, such as from bobbins to cones to tubes. Blewett, *The Last Generations,* 323.
34 *Fourteenth U.S. Census Schedules, 1920,* 180-6-25-148. The family name was illegible from the microfilmed copy.
35 *Thirteenth Federal Census Schedules, 1910,* 842-2-3-199.
36 Turbin, *Working Women of Collar City,* 74.
37 Waldron, "'I've Never Dreamed It Was Necessary'": 55.
38 Barbara Taylor, *Eve and the New Jerusalem: Socialism in the Nineteenth Century* (Cambridge, MA: Harvard University Press, 1993), 112. See also Blewett, *The Last Generation,* 41.
39 Blewett, *The Last Generation,* 41.
40 Donna Mailleux, OHPMC.
41 *Fourteenth U.S. Federal Census Schedules, 1920,* 133-6-193-80; *Thirteenth U.S. Federal Census Schedules, 1910,* 860-6-1-683.
42 Evelyn Winters, OHPMC.
43 Valentine Chartrand, OHPMC. In the neighbouring city of Manchester, New Hampshire, women followed similar intermittent patterns of employment, working three to four months a year when their husbands were out of work or "entre les accouchements," as Evelyn Desruisseaux recalls. Even pregnant women, anticipating large expenses for their newborn babies, went back to "donner un coup" at the textile factories. Others worked three or four months so that they could save just enough to buy a piece of furniture for the bedroom or replace a pot in the kitchen. Elmire Boucher and Evelyn Desruisseaux, interviews by Rouillard, *Ah! Les États!,* 87-100; 101-12, especially 93 and 109.
44 The State of Massachusetts prohibited the employment of children under fourteen years of age in any factory, workshop, or mercantile establishment starting in 1898. A number of bills and laws followed this change, specifying in detail the working hours and age limits of children and women workers. In 1903, it was resolved that the age limit for work in the mill should be raised from fourteen to sixteen but this resolution did not receive final approval. For the textile workers, the age limit for these two groups of workers remained at fourteen for the period under study here. See chapters 2 and 4 of this book for further discussion.

45 *Thirteenth U.S. Federal Census Schedules, 1910,* 861-6-184-597, 860-6-683; *Fourteenth Census Schedules, 1920,* 185-2-22-36.
46 *Fourteenth U.S. Federal Census Schedules, 1920,* 218-23-158-484.
47 *Thirteenth U.S. Federal Census Schedules, 1910,* 861-6-102-356, 861-6-81-256.
48 Hareven, *Family Time and Industrial Time,* 198-99.
49 *Thirteenth U.S. Federal Census Schedules, 1910,* 861-6-102-356; 861-6-81-256.
50 Hareven, *Family Time and Industrial Time.* Bettina Bradbury has pointed to low rates of involvement among French-Canadian wives in different towns with similar socioeconomic structures. Bradbury, *Working Families,* 172. See also Early, "The French-Canadian Economy," 183; McGaw, "A Good Place to Work," 240.
51 Hareven, *Family Time and Industrial Time.* In another study, Tamara Hareven claims, however, that economic rather than cultural factors were more influential in raising employment rates of married women. "Women's Work," 209. See also Bradbury, *Working Families,* 172.
52 Bradbury, *ibid.*
53 Ramirez, *On the Move,* 118-19.
54 *Ibid.*
55 Bradbury, *Working Families,* 172.
56 My calculation is based on data drawn from *Thirteenth and Fourteenth U.S. Federal Census Schedules.* Studies of other New England textile centres reveal the increased presence of married women in the labour market. In Rhode Island, for example, only 3 percent of married French-Canadian women brought wages home in 1880. Twenty years later, their proportion rose to 15 percent. A New England-wide survey undertaken by the Immigration Commission also confirms this tendency. In the cotton textiles, the industry that continued to draw the largest number of French Canadians in 1908, more than one third of French-Canadian female wageworkers were married women. Moreover, while the ages of these married women spanned between twenty to forty-four years old, a large proportion was found to belong to the category of thirty to forty-four years old. See Immigration Commission, *Immigrants in Industries* 10: 396-99. See also Ramirez, *On the Move,* 131-33; Cuthbert Brandt, "Weaving It Together," *Labour/Le Travail* 7 (Spring 1981): 113-25.
57 In Paris, Ontario, for instance, hosiery factories accorded temporary leaves of absence for childbirth to their experienced female workers. Such allowances encouraged many wives to return to the factories after giving birth. Parr, *The Gender of Breadwinners,* 80-81. To my knowledge, there is no evidence of such a practice in the Lowell textile industry during this period.
58 Chiklis, OHPMC.
59 Hareven, *Family Time and Industrial Time,* chap. 9, especially 243-58.
60 Martha Doherty, OHPMC.
61 Scott Tilly, "Paths of Proletarianization: Organization of Production, Sexual Division of Labor and Women's Collective Action," *Signs* 7 (1978): 400-17, especially 415.
62 Bradbury, *Working Families,* 183.
63 Immigration Commission, *Immigrants in Industries* 10: 251-54.
64 A similar pattern for the participation of widowed women in the labour force has been found in Tullylish, Ireland. Marilyn Cohen, "Survival Strategies," 307-08.

65 *Thirteenth U.S. Federal Census Schedules, 1910*, 846-3-213-391.

66 Ibid., 504-6-48-48.

67 According to my calculation, based on the Federal Census data, among widow-headed households, when adult sons or daughters were working for wages, widows themselves tended to stay home. In 1910, of eighteen households where male and female children were earning wages, seven widows also worked whereas eleven stayed out of the labour market. In 1920, the figures are eighteen, six, and twelve, respectively.

68 For the labour market participation and the organization households headed by widows, see Bradbury, *Working Families*, chap. 6; Suzanna Morton, *Ideal Surroundings: Domestic Life in Working-Class Suburbs in the 1920s* (Toronto: University of Toronto Press, 1995), chap. 5.

69 Immigration Commission, *Immigrants in Industries* 10: 260, 263.

70 Calculated by the author from *Thirteenth and Fourteenth Federal Census* data.

71 Bradbury, *Working Families*, 205, Olwen Hufton, "Women without Men: Widows and Spinsters in Britain and France in the Eighteenth Century," *Journal of Family History* 9 (Winter 1984): 355-75; Cohen, "Survival Strategies," 308. See also, Cohen, "Survival Strategies," 303-18; Houghton, "Women without Men": 362.

72 Bradbury, *Working Families*, chap. 6; esp. 196-97. See also Turbin, *Working Women of Collar City*, 85-91; Cohen, "Survival Strategies," 303-18, especially 308; Tamara Hareven, "Family and Work Patterns of Immigrant Laborers in a Planned Industrial Town, 1900-1930," in *Immigrants in Industrial America, 1850-1920*, ed. Richard L. Ehrlich, published for the Elentherian Mills-Hagley Foundation and the Balch Institute (Charlottesville: University Press of Virginia, 1977), 47-66, especially 62.

73 Cohen, "Survival Strategies," 307; Hufton, "Women without Men," 362; Turbin, *Working Women of Collar City*, 87.

74 *Fourteenth U.S. Census Schedules, 1920*, 537-16-79-257, 570-4-221-84.

75 My calculation is based on the data drawn from the *Thirteenth and Fourteenth U.S. Census Schedules, 1910, 1920*.

76 *Thirteenth U.S. Federal Census Schedules, 1910*, 877-8-3-239-293; 860-6-1-70-257; *Fourteenth U.S. Federal Census Schedules, 1920*, 554-3-2-205-238.

77 *Fourteenth U.S. Federal Census Schedules, 1920*, 186-2-10-39.

78 Ibid., 576-102-179.

79 Ibid., 1920, 219-6-20-33.

80 *Thirteenth U.S. Federal Census Schedules, 1910*, 861-6-81-259.

81 Immigration Commission, *Immigrants in Industries* 10: 251-54.

Chapter Six

1 Eileen Boris, "The Home as a Workplace: Deconstructing Dichotomies," *International Review of Social History* 39 (1994): 415-28; Dorothy Sue Cobble, *Dishing It Out: Waitresses and Their Unions in the Twentieth Century* (Urbana: University of Illinois Press, 1991); Deborah Gray White, *Ar'n't I A Woman? Female Slaves in the Plantation South* (New York: Norton, 1985; rev. ed., New York: W.W. Norton, 1999); Jacqueline Jones, *The Dispossessed: America's Underclasses from the Civil War to the Present* (New York: Basic Books, 1992). For discussion on the relationship between women's paid and unpaid work, see Jeanne Boydston, *Home and Work: Housework, Wages, and the Ideology of the Early Republic* (New York: Oxford University

Press, 1990); Susan Strasser, *Never Done: A History of American Housework* (New York: Pantheon Books, 1982; 1st Owl Books ed., New York: Henry Holt, 2000); Ruth Schwartz Cowan, *More Work for Mother: The Ironies of Household Technology from the Open Hearth to the Microwave* (New York: Basic Books, 1983); Meg Luxton, *More Than a Labour of Love: Three Generations of Women's Work in the Home* (Toronto: Women's Press, 1980); Meg Luxton and June Corman, *Getting By in Hard Times: Gendered Labour at Home and on the Job* (Toronto: University of Toronto Press, 2001); Anne Forrest, "The Industrial Relations Significance of Unpaid Work," *Labour/Le Travail* 42 (Fall 1998): 199-225.

2 A new look at migrant family, either as a bastion of resistance or a locus of negotiations, has generated a body of recent work critical of earlier depictions of migrant families—both in its capacity to offer, exchange and exploit the paid and unpaid work of their members—as invariably providing, using the phrase of Elaine Bauer and Paul Thompson, the "structural context within which an individual decides to migrate." Pierrette Hondagneu-Sotelo, ed., *Gender and U.S. Immigration: Contemporary Trends* (Berkeley and Los Angeles: University of California Press, 2003); Patricia Pessar, "Engendering Migration Studies: The Case of New Immigrants in the United States," *American Behavioral Scientist* 42 (1999): 577-600; Sheba Mariam George, *When Women Come First: Gender and Class in Transnational Migration* (Berkeley: University of California Press, 2005), especially 25-30; Elaine Bauer and Paul Thompson, "'She's Always the Person with a Very Global Vision': The Gender Dynamics of Migration, Narrative Interpretation and the Case of Jamaican Transnational Families," *Gender & History* vol. 16, no. 2 (August 2004), 334-75.

3 Frances Early has revealed the gendered context of Franco-American culture by which the primacy of economic and cultural *survivance* helped to sustain the limited upward mobility among women and men of this group in the 1870s and 1880s. Early, "The Settling-In Process," 89-108. See also Yukari Takai, "Shared Earnings, Unequal Responsibilities: Single French-Canadian Wage-Earning Women in Lowell, Massachusetts, 1900-1920," *Labour/Le Travail* 47 (Spring 2001), 115-32; Takai, "The Family Networks and Geographic Mobility of French Canadian Immigrants in Early-Twentieth-Century Lowell, Massachusetts," *Journal of Family History* (July 2001) 373-94, especially 383; FlorenceMae Waldron, "'I've Never Dreamed It Was Necessary to Marry!'" Women and Work in New England French Canadian Communities, 1870-1930," *Journal of American Ethnic History* 24, 2 (Winter 2005), 34-64.

4 In the following discussion, I have drawn on a collection of oral histories with Lowell's French-Canadian former mill workers and their children conducted between 1979-81 and 1984-86. These and other interviews with mill workers and their families were directed by Mary H. Blewett, Martha Mayo and Judith K. Dunning. Transcripts from these projects are housed at the Center for Lowell History, University of Massachusetts in Lowell. Selected interviews from these projects are edited and published in Blewett, *The Last Generation*.

5 I acknowledge the anonymous reviewer for pointing out this interpretation.

6 Hareven, *Family Time and Industrial Time*, 206.

7 Joan Smith, "Non-Wage Labor and Subsistence," in *Households and the World Economy*, ed. Joan Smith, Immanuel Wallerstein, and Evers Hans-Dieter (Beverly Hills: Sage Publications, 1984), 64-89, especially 70. Michaela Di Leonardo posits the existence of another category of women's work, "kinship work," by which Italian women in San Francisco brought extended families together for holiday celebrations and took charge of ritual observances like birthdays, decided upon visits, wrote cards, and exchanged presents. Michaela Di Leonardo, "The

Female World of Cards and Holidays: Women, Families, and the Work of Kinship," *Signs* 12 (Spring 1987): 440-53; Di Leonardo, *The Varieties of Ethnic Experience: Kinship, Class, and Gender among California Italian-Americans* (Ithaca, New York: Cornell University Press, 1984).

8   Bradbury, *Working Families*, 168-69; Christine Stansell, "Women, Children and the Uses of the Streets: Class and Gender Conflict in New York City, 1850-1860," *Feminist Studies* 8, no. 2 (Summer 1982), 309-335, especially 316.

9   Joan Smith, "Non-wage Labor and Subsistence," 64-89, especially 70. Nicholas Georgoulis, son of Greek immigrants, recounts the experience of stealing coal and coke by the railroad tracks in twentieth-century Lowell, Massachusetts. Georgoulis, OHPMC

10 Blewett, *The Last Generation*, 31.

11 Paradis, Chiklis, Georgoulis, OHPMC.

12 Del Chouinard, OHPMC.

13 Georgoulis, OHPMC.

14 Bradbury, *Working Families*, 160.

15 Blewett, *The Last Generation*, 32-34, 144-45. This gendered division of labour between boys and girls was not unique to Lowell in the early twentieth century. In industrializing Montréal, daughters "served an apprenticeship in the reproduction of labour power," helping their mothers in taking care of babies, cleaning, mending, sewing, cooking and shopping. In mid-twentieth century Vancouver, gendered division of work among English-speaking children likely played a considerable role in forming their gendered identities. Bradbury, *Working Families*, 143; Neil Sutherland, "'We Always Had Things to Do': The Paid and Unpaid Work of Anglophone Children between the 1920s and the 1960s," *Labour/Le Travail* 25 (1990): 105-41.

16 Lucie Cordeau, OHPMC.

17 *Ibid.*

18 Nancy M. Forestell, "Bachelors, Boarding-Houses, and Blind Pigs: Gender Construction in a Multi-Ethnic Mining Camp, 1909-1920," in *A Nation of Immigrants*, eds. Franca Iacovetta, Paula Draper and Robert Ventresca. (Toronto: University of Toronto Press, 1998): 251-90, especially 263.

19 Men without wives, daughters or boardinghouse keepers, who could wash clothes for them, sent their shirts and underwear to commercial laundries run by "Chinamen," who would "pick it up every week." See Joan S. Wang, "Race, Gender, and Laundry Work: The Roles of Chinese Laundrymen and American Women in the United States, 1850-1950," *Journal of American Ethnic History* (Fall 2004) 24, no. 1: 58-99. Such practices among "men without women" enacted a form of commercialization of labour-intensive domestic tasks, practices commonly carried out by Chinese male migrants who owned and ran laundry businesses, made up an indispensable part of the urban landscape in Lowell, New York, Boston and many other American cities. Similarly, in a remote frontier settlement such as Timmins with a highly multiethnic and predominantly male population, men who lived in "bachelor families" without women to perform domestic tasks sent out many of the functions of "normal" nuclear families—composed of men, women and children—to local businesses owned by Chinese male migrants. By relegating these tasks to women and men of colour, who "substituted for American women" and who chose this trade as a form of accommodation in the United States among the few economic niches open to them, Lowell's French-Canadian (and other immigrant) men arguably protected their sense of

masculinity. See Sucheng Chan, "Chinese American Experiences in a New England Mill City: Lowell, Massachusetts, 1876-1967," in *Remapping Asian American History*, ed. Sucheng Chan (Lanham, MD: Rowman & Littlefield Publishers, 2003), 3-29. For further discussion on Chinese laundrymen and the impact of race and gender see Renqui Yu, *To Save China, To Save Ourselves: The Chinese Hand Laundry Alliance of New York* (Philadelphia: Temple University Press, 1992); Rose Hum Lee, *The Growth and Decline of Chinese Communities in Rocky Mountain Region* (New York: Arno Press, 1978); Betty Lee Sung, *The Story of the Chinese in America: Their Struggle for Survival, Acceptance, and Full Participation in American Life* (New York, 1967); Forestell, "Bachelors, Boarding-Houses, and Blind Pigs," 263.

20   Arwen Mohun, *Steam Laundries: Gender, Technology, and Work in the United States and Great Britain, 1880-1940* (Baltimore: The Johns Hopkins University Press, 1999), 15-16.

21   Paradis, OHPMC. An interview by Evelyn Desruisseaux in Manchester, New Hampshire, also reveals an orderly day-to-day schedule of household tasks. Her interview illustrates the fact that domestic chores assigned to men and women moulded their social time differently. Evelyn Desruisseaux, interview by Rouillard, reproduced in Rouillard, *Ah! Les États!*, 101-11, especially 106.

22   There were also exceptions such as the case of Nicholas Georgoulis, who helped his mother with washing. He recalls in an interview that he used to stay home from school when his mother was not feeling too well. Once he was in the backyard doing the scrubbing on a board, the truant-officer came along to check on him, thinking perhaps that he was playing hookey. When the officer found out that young Nicholas was washing, he just laughed and took off. Georgoulis, OHPMC.

23   Madeline Bergeron, OHPMC.

24   Yvonne Hoar, OHPMC.

25   Bergeron, OHPMC.

26   *Ibid.*

27   Graham, OHPMC.

28   Fernandez-Kelly and Garcia, "Power Surrendered," 148.

29   *Ibid.*

30   Forestell, "Bachelors, Boarding-Houses, and Blind Pigs," especially 259-63; Caroline Waldron Merithew, "Anarchist Motherhood: Toward the Making of a Revolutionary Proletariat in Illinois Coal Towns," in *Women, Gender, and Transnational Lives*, ed. Gabaccia and Iacovetta, 217-46; Anne Morelli, "Nestore's Wife? Work, Family, and Militancy in Belgium," in *ibid.*, 327-46; Angelo Principe, "Glimpses of Lives in Canada's Shadow," in *ibid.*, 350-85; Roselyn Pesman, "Italian Women and Work in Post-Second World War Australia: Representation and Experience," in *ibid.*, 386-409; Bradbury, *Working Families*, chap. 5; Ellen Ross, *Love and Toil: Motherhood in Outcast London, 1870-1918* (New York: Oxford University Press, 1993).

31   Alice LaCase, in Hareven and Langenbach, Amoskeag, 254-73, especially 264.

32   Gabaccia and Iacovetta, *Women, Gender, and Transnational Lives*, 8-9, 359-60; Robert Harney, "Men without Women," in *The Italian Immigrant Woman in North America*, ed. Betty Boyd Caroli, Robert F. Harney, and Lydio F. Tomasi (Toronto: Multicultural History Society of Ontario, 1978), 79-102.

33   Principe, "Glimpses of Lives in Canada's Shadow," 359-60.

34 Amy A. Bernardy, "Relazione sulle condizioni delle donne e dei fanciulli italiani negli Stati del Centro e dell'Ovest della Confederazione del Nord-America," in *Bollettino dell'Emigrazione* (1911), 78. Cited by Principe, "Glimpses of Lives in Canada's Shadow," 359-60.

35 This interpretation has been raised by the anonymous reviewer.

36 The emerging literature on ethnically-marked cultural practices surrounding food emphasizes the value of these practices—including preparation, display, and most importantly, sharing—as expressions par excellence of familial unity and collective identity. One cannot question the importance of daily routines, rituals and memories revolving around the eating habits of migrants in promoting and sustaining the process of their Americanization and ethnicization. However, as historian Simone Cinotto has skillfully revealed in his study of Italians in East Harlem during the early twentieth century, the ethnic consensual approach, which underlines the role of food as a means for building ethnic identity, says little about the multiple roles women played and the power relations at work within immigrant families or about the inner contentions, especially among immigrant parents and U.S.-born and raised daughters and sons, over the value of ethnic food practices and rituals performed within the ethnic group in question. Marlene Epp, for her part, has offered an evocative study of the intimate and complex relationships between food, gender, and ethnicity in her analysis of Mennonite women in the first half of the twentieth century. Mennonite women took very seriously their responsibility to ensure the physical well-being of their families and protect them against the emotional costs of hunger. They blamed themselves for hungry families even when it was beyond their control. They also acted as "primary conveyors of ethnic cultural traditions" in the context of refugee sojourning, where one shifted quickly from famine to feast and in which long-held food identities are challenged and modified. See Simone Cinotto, "Leonard Covello, the Covello Papers, and the History of Eating Habits among Italian Immigrants in New York," *Journal of American History* 91, no. 2 (September 2004), 497-521; Marlene Epp, "The Semiotics of Zwieback: Feast and Famine in the Narratives of Mennonite Refugee Women," in *Sisters or Strangers?* ed. Epp, Iacovetta and Swyripa, 314-40.

There is little historical literature on culinary practices among French-Canadian immigrants upon which to build an analysis of the subject. In light of such limitations, collections of transcripts drawn from interviews with French Canadians and their children made available by ethnographers and historians of the working class become all the more valuable for the purposes of this study. Fragmentary as they are, they shed light on the significance of eating habits—including the preparation, serving, and consumption of meals—and the multiple roles women played and the meanings they drew from preparing daily and special meals for their families.

37 Paradis, Irène Demarais, OHPMC.

38 For example, Korean military brides who arrived in the United States half a century later cooked American food on demand for their families as part of their obligation as wives and mothers. At the same time, they ate *kimchi* or other Korean foods that reminded them of home, alone or only in the company of other Korean women, or went without and craved it. Ji-Yeon Yuh, *Beyond the Shadow of Camptown: Korean Military Brides in America* (New York and London: New York University Press, 2002), chap. 4.

39 Gabaccia, *We Are What We Eat*, chap. 2.

40 Bergeron, OHPMC.

41 Desmarais, OHPMC.
42 Gabaccia, *We Are What We Eat*, 55-61.
43 Bergeron, OHPMC.
44 Desmarais, OHPMC.
45 *Ibid.*
46 *Ibid.*
47 *Ibid.*
48 Arthur Morrissette, OHPMC. See chap. 4 of this book.
49 Alice LaCasse, one of the daughters of a French-Canadian couple that had emigrated from St. Clothilde, Québec, to Manchester, New Hampshire, recalls her father's negative reaction to her mother's decision to work outside the home. Her mother's part-time work at one of the Amoskeag factories meant that her father had to look after children. For him, child-minding was "women's work; his work was outside." The LaCasse Family, interview by Hareven and Langenbach, reprinted in Hareven and Langenbach, *Amoskeag*, 254-73, especially 255.
50 Parr, *The Gender of Breadwinners*, 92-93.; Blewett, *The Last Generation*, 41. In the neighbouring city of Manchester, New Hampshire, a French-Canadian immigrant daughter, Yvonne Dionne, recollects having been sent to replace her sick aunt at work. See Yvonne Dionne, interview by Hareven and Langenbach, reproduced in Hareven and Langenbach, *Amoskeag*, 196-200. Joy Parr describes an interesting practice whereby women—an aunt and a niece, or two sisters—sharing a household divided their responsibilities between income-earning and taking charge of domestic chores.
51 Yvonne Hoar, who went back to work during the Depression years, considered herself "lucky" for having a family member nearby to take care of her young son the first years following his birth. She arranged for her mother-in-law to care for her three-year-old son while she and her husband worked for wages. Yvonne's husband would take the baby to his mother's, and she would go to work. Then at night, on her way home from work, she went to pick up the baby from her mother-in-law.
52 Blewett, *The Last Generation*, 41.
53 Later on, Yvonne Hoar and her husband were among the few who took their boy to the nursery, rather than to his grandmother's house, as he started to "get rambunctious." "Grammy was having a hard time chasing after him," explained Yvonne, and the nursery was "a nice place with a yard with swings and teeters and everything." In addition, the nursery fed him during the day. Yvonne gave the boy breakfast and the nursery provided a light lunch in the morning, dinner at noon, and another light lunch in the afternoon. Yvonne Hoar, OHPMC.
54 See, for instance, Marie Anne Sénéchal, interview by Hareven and Langenbach, reproduced in Hareven and Langenbach, *Amoskeag*, 197-200.
55 Yvonne Hoar, OHPMC.
56 Graham, OHPMC.
57 Ouellette, OHPMC.
58 Blewett, *The Last Generation*, 70-72, 301-94.
59 Graham, OHPMC.
60 Tilly and Scott, *Women, Work and Family*, 144. See also Di Leonardo, *The Varieties of Ethnic Experience*, chap. 6.

61 Chartrand, OHPMC.

62 *Ibid.* A similar example can be found in the oral history account of Yvonne Dionne. Her case illustrates the unequal and asymmetrical nature of the family's organization of work. Yvonne Dionne, interview by Hareven and Langenbach, reproduced in Hareven and Langenbach, *Amoskeag*, 197-200.

63 Scott Tilly, "Beyond Family Strategies, What?" *Historical Methodology* 20, no. 3 (1987): 123-25; Nancy Folbre, "Family Strategy, Feminist Strategy," *ibid.*: 115-18; Chiara Saraceno, "The Concept of the Family Strategy and Its Application to the Family Work Complex: Some Theoretical and Methodological Problems," *Marriage and Family Review* 14, no. 1-2 (1989): 1-18; Moen and Wethington, "The Concept of Family Adaptive Strategies," 239.

64 A comparative study of several New England textile communities conducted by the United States Bureau of Labor in 1910 reported that while sons contributed 83 percent of their income to their parents' households, daughters delivered 95 percent of their pay to their families' budgets. Clearly, the daughters' commitments to their families' incomes were more critical than the sons'. U.S. Department of Labor, *The Share of Wage-Earning Women in Family Support*, Women's Bureau Bulletin, no. 30 (Washington, D.C.: GPO, 1923): 137-40; Hareven, "Family and Work Patterns," 47-66, especially 62.

65 Marie-Anne Sénéchal, interview with Hareven and Langenbach, reproduced in Hareven and Langenbach, *Amoskeag*, 197-200.

66 Tilly and Scott, *Women, Work, and Family*, 192.

67 Hareven, *Family Time and Industrial Time*, 187-88.

68 Cordeau, OHPMC.

69 *Ibid.*

70 Waldron, "'I've Never Dreamed It Was Necessary'": 55-56

71 Cora Pellerin, interview with Hareven and Langenbach, reproduced in Hareven and Langenbach, *Amoskeag*, 201-11.

72 Bradbury, *Working Families*, 154-55. See also Linda K. Kerber, "Separate Spheres, Female Worlds, Woman's Place: The Rhetoric of Women's History," *Journal of American History* 75 (June 1988): 9-39.

73 *Ibid.*

74 Narcissa Hodges, OHPMC.

Epilogue

1 U.S. Census Bureau, http://www.census.gov/.

Appendix A

1 For discussion on the *Border Entry*, see also Marian L. Smith, "By Way of Canada," 192-99; Takai, "The Family Networks and Geographic Mobility" 373-94; Appendix by Randy William Widdis in Bukowczyk et al., *Permeable Border: The Great Lakes Basin as Transnational*

Region, 1650-1990, 183-85; Appendix in Ramirez with Otis, *Crossing the 49th Parallel*; Takai, "Transnational Movements of Japanese and French Canadian Migrants."

Appendix B

1   Bouchard, *Tous les métiers du monde*, especially 67, 68, Annex.
2   Hareven, *Family Time and Industrial Time*, 79-82. See also Montgomery, *The Fall of the House of Labor*, 116.
3   Christina Burr, "Defending 'the Art of Preservative': Class and Gender Relations in the Printing Trades Unions, 1850-1914," *Labour/Le Travail 31* (Spring 1993): 47-73.
4   Jonathan C. Fincher, "Early History of Our Organization," *Machinists and Blacksmiths International Journal* (February 1872): 520. Cited in Montgomery, *Fall of the House of Labor*, 181-82.

Selected Bibliography

Primary Sources

Manuscript Collections

Bibliothèque Municipale de Montréal, Salle Gagnon.
> U.S. Immigration and Naturalization Service. Record Group 85. *Soundex Index to Canadian Border Entries through the St. Albans, Vermont, District.* Microfilm.

Boston Public Library, Massachusetts
> Richard Santerre Collection

City of Lowell
> *Case History Records for the Overseers of the Poor*

Université de Montéal, Bibliothèque de Lettres et Sciences Sociales
> U.S. Department of Commerce. Bureau of the Census. *Thirteenth Census of the United States, 1910.* Federal Census Schedules. City of Lowell. Middlesex County, Massachusetts. Microfilm.
>
> U.S. Department of Commerce. Bureau of the Census. *Fourteenth Census of the United States, 1920.* Federal Census Schedules. City of Lowell. Middlesex County, Massachusetts. Microfilm.

University of Massachusetts, Lowell, Center for Lowell Hisory
> Lowell Oral History Collections
>
> Flather Collection

Government Documents

Canada. Census Office. Statistics Canada. *Fourth Census of Canada, 1901.* Bulletin. I. Ottawa: Census Office/Bureau du recensement, 1901-1903.

Canada. Parliament. *Sessional Papers,* 1896.

Canada. *Report of the Department of Interior,* 1895.

City of Lowell. *Annual Report of the Board of Health of the City of Lowell.* Lowell: C. I. Hood, 1881.

Massachusetts. Bureau of Statistics of Labor. Census of the Commonwealth of Massachusetts: 1875. Boston: Wright & Potter Print. Co., 1876-1877.

Massachusetts. Bureau of Statistics of Labor. *Annual Report of the Bureau of Statistics of Labor.*

Boston: Wright & Potter Printing Co., 1872-1906.

Massachusetts. Commission on the Cost of Living. *Report of the Commission on the Cost of Living*. Boston: Wright & Potter Printing Co., State Printers, 1910.

U.S. Congress. Joint Select Committee on Immigration and Naturalization. *Report of the Select Committee on Immigration and Naturalization, and Testimony Taken by the Committee on Immigration of the Senate and the Select Committee on Immigration and Naturalization of the House of Representatives under Concurrent Resolution of March 12, 1890.* 51st Congress, 2d sess. Washington, D.C.: Government Printing Office, 1890-1891.

U.S. Congress. Senate. *Report on the Conditions of Women and Children Wage-Earners in the United States*. Washington, D.C.: Government Printing Office, 1910.

U.S. Department of Commerce and Labor. Bureau of Naturalization. *Annual Report of the Commissioner-General of Immigration to the Secretary of Commerce and Labor: For the Fiscal Year Ended June 30, 1900*. Washington, D.C.: Government Printing Office, 1900.

——. *Annual Report of the Commissioner-General of Immigration to the Secretary of Commerce and Labor: For the Fiscal Year ended June 30, 1903*. Washington, D.C: Government Printing Office, 1903.

U.S. Department of Commerce. U.S. Bureau of the Census. *Thirteenth Census of the United States, 1910*. Washington, D.C.: Government Printing Office, 1912-1914.

——. *Fourteenth Census of the United States, 1920*. Washington, D.C.: Government Printing Office, 1921-25.

U.S. Department of Labor. *The Share of Wage-Earning Women in Family Support*. Women's Bureau Bulletin. No. 30. Washington, D.C.: Government Printing Office, 1923.

——. *Lost Time and Labor Turnover in Cotton Mills: A Study of Cause and Extent*. Women's Bureau Bulletin. No. 52. Washington, D.C.: Government Printing Office, 1926.

U.S. Immigration Commission. *Immigrants in Industries (In Twenty-Five Parts)*. Part 3-4, vol. 10, Cotton Goods Manufacturing in the North Atlantic States. Woolen and Worsted Goods Manufacturing. 61st Cong., 2d sess. Senate Doc. 633. Washington, D.C.: Government Printing Office, 1911.

——. *Reports of the Industrial Commission on Immigration, Including Testimony, with Review and Digest, and Special Reports on Education, Including Testimony, with Review and Digest*. Washington, D.C.: Government Printing Office, 1901.

Periodicals

Courrier-Citizen. Lowell, Massachusetts. 1906-1910.
Gazette des campagnes: journal du cultivateur et du colon. Kamouraska, Québec. 1878-1893.
L'Action française. Montréal : Ligue des droits du français, 1918.
Le Devoir. 1912-1918.
L'Etoile de Lowell. Lowell, Massachusetts, 1900-1910.
L'Étoile du Nord. Joliette, Québec. Various years.
Lowell Daily Citizen. Lowell, Massachusetts. Various years.
Le Nouvelliste. Trois-Rivières, Québec. 1933.

Institutional Records

Congrès de Colonisation. *Le Problème de la colonisation au Canada français. Rapport officiel du Congrès de Colonisation tenu par l'A.C.J.C. à Chicoutimi, du 29 juin au 2 juillet 1919.* Montréal : Bureau de L'A.A.C.J.C., 1920.

Dissertations and Theses

Dauphinais, Paul Raymond. "Structure and Strategy: French Canadians in Central New England, 1850-1900." Ph.D. thesis. University of Maine, 1991.

Early, Frances H. "French-Canadian Beginnings in an American Community: Lowell, Massachusetts, 1868-1886." Ph.D. thesis, Concordia University, 1979.

Frenette, Yves. "La genèse d'une communauté canadienne française en Nouvelle-Angleterre, Lewiston, Maine, 1800-1880." Ph.D. diss., Université Laval, 1988.

Haebler, Peter. "Habitants in Holyoke: The Development of the French-Canadian Community in a Massachusetts City, 1865-1910." Ph.D. thesis, University of New Hampshire, 1976.

Piva, Frances E. "An Idyl Confronted: The New England Mill Girls and the Lowell Female Labor Reform Association." M.A. thesis, Sir George Williams University, 1973.

Tétreault, Martin. "L'état de santé des Montréalais, de 1880 à 1914." M.A. thesis, Université de Montréal, 1979.

———. "La santé publique dans une ville manufacturière de la Nouvelle-Angleterre: Lowell, Massachusetts, 1965-1900." Ph.D. thesis, Université de Montréal, 1985.

Vicero, Ralph Dominic. "Immigration of French Canadians to New England, 1840-1900: Geographical Analysis." Ph.D. diss, University of Wisconsin, 1968.

Violette, Brigitte. "Formation et développement d'une petite-bourgeoisie Franco-Américaine de la Nouvelle-Angleterre (Fall River, 1870-1920)." Ph.D. thesis, Université de Montréal, 2000.

Articles, Books, Reports, Brochures, and Miscellaneous Items

Albert, Félix. *Histoire d'un enfant pauvre.* [*Immigrant Oddysey : A French-Canadian Habitant in New England.*] Bilingual edition. Introduction by Frances H. Early. Translation by Arthur L. Éno, Jr. Orono, ME: University of Maine, c1991.

Alexander, June Granatir. "Moving into and out of Pittsburgh: Ongoing Chain Migration." In *A Century of European Migrations.* Edited by Rudolf J. Vecoli and Suzanne M. Sinke, 200-20. Cambridge: Cambridge University Press, 1985.

Allen, James P. "Migration Fields of French Canadian Immigrants to Southern Maine," *Geographical Review* 62, no.1 (1974): 366-83.

Anctil, Pierre. "La Franco-Américainie ou le Québec d'en bas." *Cahier de Géographie du Québec* 58 (1979): 39-52.

———. "Chinese of the Eastern States, 1881." *Recherches sociographiques* 22, no. 1 (1981): 125-31.

Anderson, Michael. "The Social Position of Spinsters in Mid-Victorian Britain." *Journal of Family*

History 9 (Winter 1984): 377-93.

Appleton, Nathan. *Introduction of the Power Loom and Origin of Lowell.* Lowell: Printed by B.H. Penhallow, 1858.

Ariès, Philippe. *L'enfant et la vie familiale sous l'Ancien Régime.* Paris: Plon, 1960.

Arnesen, Eric. "Scholarly Controversy: Whiteness and the Historians' Imagination." *International Labor and Working-Class History* 60 (Fall 2001): 1-92.

Baillargeon, Denyse. *Ménagères au temps de la crise.* Montréal: Éditions du Remue-ménage, 1991.

Barrett, James R., and David R. Roediger, "Inbetween Peoples: Race, Nationality, and the 'New Immigrant' Working Class." *Journal of Ethnic History* 16 (Spring 1997). Reprinted in Roediger, *Colored White: Transcending the Racial Past,* 138-68. Berkeley: University of California Press, 2002.

Bauer, Elaine, and Paul Thompson. "'She's Always the Person with a Very Global Vision': The Gender Dynamics of Migration, Narrative Interpretation and the Case of Jamaican Transnational Families." *Gender & History* 16, no. 2 (August 2004): 334-75.

Beaudreau, Sylvie, and Yves Frenette. "Les stratégies familiales des francophones de la Nouvelle-Angleterre. Perspective diachronique." *Sociologie et société* 26, no. 1 (printemps 1994): 167-78.

Bernstein, Irving. *The Lean Years: A History of the American Worker, 1920-1933.* Boston: Houghton Mifflin Company, 1960.

Blanchard, Raoul. *Le Centre du Canada Français.* Montréal: Beauchemin, 1947.

Blewett, Mary H. *Men, Women, and Work: Class, Gender, and Protest in the New England Shoe Industry, 1780-1910.* Urbana: University of Illinois Press, 1988.

——. *The Last Generation: Work and Life in the Textile Mills of Lowell, Massachusetts, 1910-1960.* Amherst: University of Massachusetts Press, 1990.

Blewett, Peter F. "The New People." In *Cotton Was King: A History of Lowell, Massachusetts.* Edited by Arthur Jr. Eno, 191-93. Somersworth, N.H.: New Hampshire Pub. Co., 1976.

Bodnar, John. *The Transplanted: A History of Immigrants in Urban America.* Bloomington: University of Indiana Press, 1985.

Boris, Eileen. "The Home as a Workplace: Deconstructing Dichotomies," *International Review of Social History* 39 (1994): 415-28.

Bott, Elizabeth. *Family and Social Network: Roles, Norms, and External Relationships in Ordinary Urban Families.* London: Tavistock Publications, 1957.

Bouchard, Gérard. "Co-intégration et reproduction de la société rurale. Pour un modèle saguenayen de la marginalité." *Recherches sociographique* 29, no. 2-3 (1988): 283-305.

——. *Tous les métiers du monde: le traitement des données professionnelles en histoire sociale.* Saint-Nicolas, Québec: Les Presses de l'Université Laval, 1996.

Bouchard, Gérard, and Lise Bergeron. "Aux origines d'une population régionale: mythes et réalités démographiques et sociales." *Revue d'histoire d'Amérique française* 42, no. 3 (hiver 1989): 389-409.

Bourdon, Yves, and Jean Lamarre. *Histoire du Québec. Une société nord-américaine.* Laval, Québec: Beauchemin, 1998.

Boydston, Jeanne. *Home and Work: Housework, Wages, and the Ideology of the Early Republic.* New York: Oxford University Press, 1990.

Bradbury, Bettina. *Working Families: Age, Gender, and Daily Survival in Industrializing Montreal.*

Toronto: Oxford University Press, 1993.

Brandt, Cuthbert. "Weaving It Together." *Labour/Le Travail* 7 (Spring 1981): 113-25.

Bukowczyk, John J., Nora Faires, David R. Smith, and Randy William Widdis. *Permeable Border: The Great Lakes Basin as Transnational Region, 1650-1990*. Pittsburgh: University of Pittsburgh Press; Calgary, Alberta: University of Calgary Press, 2005.

Byington, Margaret Frances. *Homestead: The Household of a Mill Town*. New York, Charities Publication Committee, 1910. Reprint, Pittsburgh: University Center for International Studies, 1974.

Buhle, Mari Jo. *Women and American Socialism, 1870-1920*. Urbana: University of Illinois Press, 1981.

Burr, Christina. "Defending 'the Art of Preservative': Class and Gender Relations in the Printing Trades Unions, 1850-1914." *Labour/Le Travail* 31 (Spring 1993): 47-73.

Cameron, Ardis. *Radicals of the Worst Sort: Laboring Women in Lawrence, Massachusetts, 1860-1912*. Urbana: University of Illinois Press, 1993.

Cardoso, Lawrence A. *Mexican Emigration to the United States, 1891-1932*, Tucson: University of Arizona Press, 1980.

Chan, Sucheng. "Chinese American Experiences in a New England Mill City: Lowell, Massachusetts, 1876-1967." In *Remapping Asian American History*. Edited by Sucheng Chan, 3-29. Lanham, MD: Rowman & Littlefield Publishers, 2003.

Chang, Grace. "Undocumented Latinas: The New 'Employable Mothers.'" In *Mothering: Ideology, Experience, and Agency*. Edited by Evelyn Nakano-Glenn, Grace Chang, and Linda Rennie Forcey, 259-85. New York: Routledge, 1994.

Cinotto, Simone. "Leonard Covello, the Covello Papers, and the History of Eating Habits among Italian Immigrants in New York." *Journal of American History* 91, no. 2 (September 2004): 497-521.

Cobble, Dorothy Sue. *Dishing It Out: Waitresses and Their Unions in the Twentieth Century*. Urbana: University of Illinois Press, 1991.

Coburn, Frederick W. *History of Lowell and Its People*. Vol. 1. New York: Lewis Historical Pub. Co., 1920.

Cohen, Marjorie. "The Decline of Women in Canadian Dairying." *Histoire Sociale/Social History* 17 no. 34 (1984): 307-334.

———. *Women's Work, Markets, and Economic Development in Nineteenth-Century Ontario*. Toronto: University of Toronto Press, 1988.

Cohen, Miriam. *Workshop to Office: The Generations of Italian Women in New York City, 1900-1950*. Ithaca: Cornell University Press, 1991.

Cole, Donald B. *Immigrant City: Lawrence, Massachusetts, 1845-1921*. Chapel Hill: University of North Carolina Press, 1963.

Coleman, James S. "Social Capital in the Creation of Human Capital." *American Journal of Sociology* 94 (1988): 95-120.

Collomp, Catherine. "Immigrants, Labor Markets, and The State, A Comparative Approach: France and the United States, 1880-1930." *Journal of American History* 86, no. 1 (1999): 41-66.

Comacchio, Cynthia R. "Beneath the 'Sentimental Veil': Families and Family History in Canada." *Labour/Le Travail* 33 (Spring 1994): 279-302.

Courville, Serge, and Normand Séguin, *Le monde rural québécois au XIXe siècle*. Ottawa: La Société historique du Canada, 1989.

Cowan, Ruth Schwartz. *More Work for Mother: The Ironies of Household Technology from the Open Hearth to the Microwave.* New York: Basic Books, 1983.

Cunningham, Hillary. "Transnational Politics at the Edges of Sovereignty: Social Movements, Crossings and the State at the U.S.-Mexican Border." *Global Networks* 1, no.4 (October 2001): 369-87.

Dickens, Charles. *American Notes for General Circulation.* New York: Harper & Brothers, 1842.

Di Leonardo, Micaela. *The Varieties of Ethnic Experience: Kinship, Class, and Gender among California Italian-Americans.* Ithaca: Cornell University Press, 1984.

———. "The Female World of Cards and Holidays: Women, Families, and the Work of Kinship." *Signs: Journal of Women in Culture and Society* 12 (Spring 1987): 440-53.

Diner, Hasia R. *Hungering for America: Italian, Irish, and Jewish Foodways in the Age of Migration.* Cambridge, MA: Harvard University Press, 2001.

Donato, Katharine M., Donna Gabaccia, Jennifer Holdway, Martin Manalansan IV, and Patricia R. Pessar. "A Glass Half Full? Gender in Migration Studies." *International Migration Review* 40, no. 1 (Spring 2006): 3-26.

Dublin, Thomas, and Paul Marion. *Lowell: The Story of an Industrial City: A Guide to Lowell National Historial Park and Lowell Heritage State Park, Lowell, Massachusetts.* Washington, D.C.: U.S. Department of the Interior, 1992.

Dublin, Thomas. *Women at Work: The Transformation of Work and Community in Lowell, Massachusetts, 1826-1860.* 2nd ed. New York: Columbia University Press, 1993.

———. *Transforming Women's Work: New England Lives in the Industrial Revolution.* Ithaca and London: Cornell University Press, 1994.

Dumont-Johnson, Micheline et al. *L'histoire des femmes au Québec depuis quatre siècles.* Montréal: Le Jour, 1992.

Dussault, Gabriel. *Le Curé Labelle: Messianisme, utopie et colonisation au Québec 1850-1900.* Montréal: Hurtubise HMH, 1983.

Early, Frances H. "Mobility Potential and the Quality of Life in Working-Class Lowell, Massachusetts: The French Canadians ca. 1870." *Labour/Le Travailleur* 2 (1977): 214-28.

———. "The French-Canadian Family Economy and Standard-of-Living in Lowell, Massachusetts, 1870." *Journal of Family History* 7, no. 2 (1982): 180-99.

———. "The Settling-In Process: The Beginnings of the Little Canada in Lowell, Massachusetts, in the Late Nineteenth Century." In *Steeples and Smokestacks: A Collection of Essays on the Franco-American Experience in New England.* Edited by Claire Quintal, 89-108. Worcester, Massachusetts: French Institute, Assumption College, 1996.

Eisenstein, Sarah. *Give Us Bread but Give Us Roses: Working Women's Consciousness in the United States, 1890 to the First World War.* London: Routledge and Kegan Paul, 1983.

Ensign, Forest Chester. *Compulsory School Attendance and Child Labor. A Study of the Historical Development of Regulations Compelling Attendance and Limiting the Labor of Children in a Selected Group of States.* Iowa City, IA.: The Athens Press, 1921. Reprint, New York: Arno Press, 1969.

Epp, Marlene. "The Semiotics of Zwieback: Feast and Famine in the Narratives of Mennonite Refugee Women." In *Sisters or Strangers? Immigrant, Ethnic, and Racialized Women in Canadian History.* Edited by Marlene Epp, Franca Iacovetta, and Frances Swyripa, 314-40. Toronto:

University of Toronto Press, 2004.

Epp, Marlene, Franca Iacovetta, and Frances Swyripa. *Sisters or Strangers? Immigrant, Ethnic, and Racialized Women in Canadian History.* Toronto: University of Toronto Press, 2004.

Faucher, Albert. "L'émigration des Canadiens français au XIXe siècle: position du problème et perspectives." *Recherches sociographiques* 5, no. 3 (septembre-décembre, 1964): 217-317.

Fernandez-Kelly, Patricia, and Anna Garcia. "Power Surrendered, Power Restored: The Politics of Home and Work among Hispanic Women in Southern California and Southern Florida." In *Women, Politics, and Change.* Edited by Louise A. Tilly and Patricia Guerin, 130-49. New York: Russell Sage Foundation, 1990.

Folbre, Nancy. "Family Strategy, Feminist Strategy." *Historical Methodology* 20, no. 3 (1987): 115-18.

Forestell, Nancy M. "Bachelors, Boarding-Houses, and Blind Pigs: Gender Construction in a Multi-Ethnic Mining Camp, 1909-1920." In *A Nation of Immigrants.* Edited by Franca Iacovetta, Paula Draper, and Robert Ventresca, 251-90. Toronto: University of Toronto Press, 1998.

Forrest, Anne. "The Industrial Relations Significance of Unpaid Work." *Labour/Le Travail* 42 (Fall 1998): 199-225.

Fortin, Jean-Charles, and Antonio Lechasseur, *Histoire du Bas-Saint-Laurent.* Québec: Institut québécois de recherche sur la culture, 1993.

Frank, Dana. "Housewives, Socialists and the Politics of Food: The 1917 Cost of Living Protests." *Feminist Studies* 11, no. 2 (Summer 1985): 254-85.

Frenette, Yves. "Macroscopie et microscopie d'un mouvement migratoire: les Canadiens français à Lewiston au XXe siècle." In *Les chemins de la migration en Belgique et au Québec: XVIIe–XXe siècles.* Edited by Yves Landry, John A. Dickinson, Suzy Pasleau, and Claude Desma, 221-31. Louvain-la-Neuve: Éditions Academia, 1995.

———. *Les Francophones de la Nouvelle-Angleterre, 1524-2000.* Sainte-Foy, Québec: INRS-Culture et société, 2000.

Gabaccia, Donna R. *From Sicily to Elizabeth Street: Housing and Social Change among Italian Immigrants, 1880-1930.* Albany: State University of New York Press, 1984.

———. "Immigrant Women: Nowhere at Home?" *Journal of American Ethnic History* 10 (Summer 1991): 62-87.

———. *Seeking Common Ground: Multidisciplinary Studies of Immigrant Women in the United States.* Westport, CT: Praeger, 1992.

———. *From the Other Side: Women, Gender, and Immigrant Life in the U.S., 1820-1990.* Bloomington: University of Indiana Press, 1994.

———. *We Are What We Eat: Ethnic Food and the Making of Americans.* Cambridge, MA: Harvard University Press, 1998.

———. "Is Everywhere Nowhere? Nomads, Nations, and the Immigrant Paradigm of United States History." *Journal of American History* 86, no. 3 (December 1999): 1115-34.

———. *Italy's Many Diasporas.* Seattle: University of Washington Press, 2000.

Gabaccia, Donna R., and Fraser Ottanelli, eds. *Italian Workers of the World: Labor Migration and the Formation of Multiethnic States.* Urbana-Champaign, Illinois: University of Illinois Press, 2001.

Gamboa, Erasmo. *Mexican Labor and World War II: Braceros in the Pacific Northwest, 1942-1947.*

Austin, Texas: University of Texas Press, 1990.

Gérin, Léon. *L'habitant de Saint-Justin : contribution à la géographie sociale du Canada.* Ottawa: J. Hope et Fils; Toronto: Copp-Clark; London, U.K.: Bernard Quaritch, 1898.

Gerstle, Gary. *Working-Class Americanism: The Politics of Labor in a Textile City, 1914-1960.* Cambridge: Cambridge University Press, 1989.

Gibbins, Roger. "The Meaning and Significance of the American-Canadian Border." In *Borders and Border Regions in Europe and North America.* Edited by Paul Ganster, Alan Sweedler, James Scott and Wolf Dieter-Eberwein, 315-32. San Diego: San Diego State University Press and Institute for Regional Studies of the Californias, 1997.

Glickman, Lawrence. *A Living Wage: American Workers and the Making of Consumer Society.* Ithaca: Cornell University Press, 1997.

Goldberg, David J. *A Tale of Three Cities: Labor, Organization and Protest in Paterson, Passaic, and Lawrence, 1916-1921.* New Brunswick, New Jersey: Rutgers University Press, 1989.

Green, James R. *World of the Worker: Labor in Twentieth-Century America.* New York: Hill and Wang, 1980. Reprint, Urbana: University of Illinois Press, 1998.

Gregory, Frances W. *Nathan Appleton, Merchant and Entrepreneur, 1779-1861.* Charlottesville: University Press of Virginia, 1975.

Gross, Laurence F. *The Course of Industrial Decline: The Boott Cotton Mills of Lowell, Massachusetts, 1835-1955.* Baltimore: Johns Hopkins University Press, 1993.

Gordon, Linda. *Heroes of Their Own Lives: The Politics and History of Family Violence.* New York: Viking, 1988.

Glenn, Evelyn Nakano. "Split Household, Small Producer and Wage Earner: An Analysis of Chinese-American Family Strategies." *Journal of Marriage and Family* 45 (1983): 35-46.

Gordon, Linda. "Black and White Visions of Welfare: Women's Welfare Activism, 1890-1945." In *Unequal Sisters: A Multicultural Reader in U.S. Women's History.* Edited by Vicki L. Ruiz and Ellen Carol DuBois, 214-41. New York: Routledge, 1990. 3rd ed., 2000.

Gotanda, Neil. "Race, Citizenship, and the Search for Political Community among 'We the People': A Review Essay on Citizenship without Consent." *Oregon Law Review* 76 (1997): 233-58.

Groneman, Carole. "She Works as a Child; She Pays as a Man: Women Workers in a Mid-Nineteenth Century New York City Community." In *Class, Sex, and the Women Workers.* Edited by Milton Cantor and Bruce Laurie, 83-100. Westport, CT: Greenwood Press, 1977.

Hamelin, Jean, and Yves Roby, *Histoire économique du Québec, 1851-1896.* Montréal: Fides, 1971.

Handlin, Oscar. *The Uprooted: The Epic Study of the Great Migrations That Made the American People.* Boston: Little Brown, 1951.

Hansen, Marcus Lee. *The Mingling of the Canadian and American Peoples.* Completed and Prepared by John B. Brebner. New Haven: Yale University Press, 1940.

Hardy, René, and Normand Séguin. *Forêt et société en Mauricie. La formation de la région de Trois-Rivières 1830-1930.* Montréal: Boréal; Ottawa: Musée national de l'Homme, Musées nationaux du Canada, 1984.

Hareven, Tamara, K. "Family and Work Patterns of Immigrant Laborers in a Planned Industrial Town, 1900-1930." In *Immigrants in Industrial America, 1850-1920.* Edited by Richard L. Ehrlich, 47-66. Published for the Elentherian Mills-Hagley Foundation and the Balch Institute. Charlottesville: University Press of Virginia, 1977.

———. *Family Time and Industrial Time: The Relationship between the Family and Work in a New England Industrial Community*. Cambridge: Cambridge University Press, 1982.

Hareven, Tamara K., and Randolph Langenbach. *Amoskeag: Life and Work in an American Factory City*. New York: Pantheon Books, 1978.

Hareven, Tamara K., and Louise Tilly. "Solitary Women and Family Mediation in American and French Textile Cities." *Annales de démographie historique* (1981): 253-71.

Harney, Robert. "Men without Women: Italian Immigrants in Canada." In *The Italian Immigrant Woman in North America: Proceedings of the Tenth Annual Conference of the American Italian Historical Association Held in Toronto, Ontario (Canada) October 28 and 29, 1977 in Conjunction with the Canadian Italian Historical Association*. Edited by Betty Boyd Caroli, Robert F. Harney, and Lydio F. Tomasi, 79-102. Toronto: Multicultural History Society of Ontario, 1977.

Hartman, Andrew. "The Rise and Fall of Whiteness Studies." *Race & Class* 46, no.2 (2004): 22-38.

Hartmann, Heidi. "The Family as the Locus of Gender, Class, and Political Struggle: The Example of Housework." *Signs: Journal of Women in Culture and Society* 6, no. 3 (1981): 366-94.

———. "Change in Women's Economic and Family Roles in Post-World War II United States." In *Women, Households, and the Economy*. Edited by Lourdes Beneria and Catherine Stimpson, 33-64. New Brunswick, New Jersey: Rutgers University Press, 1987.

Heron, Craig. "Boys Will Be Boys: Working-Class Masculinities in the Age of Mass Production." *International Labor and Working-Class History* 69 (Spring 2006): 6-34

Hoerder, Dirk. "International Labor Markets and Community Building by Migrant Workers in the Atlantic Economies." In *A Century of European Migrations*. Edited by Rudolf J. Vecoli and Suzanne M. Sinke, 78-107. Urbana: University of Illinois Press, 1991.

———. *People on the Move: Migration, Acculturation, and Ethnic Interaction in Europe and North America*, German Historical Institute Washington D.C. Annual Lecture 6. Oxford: Berg Publishers, 1993.

———. "Segmented Macrosystems and Networking Individuals: The Balancing Functions of Migration Processes." In *Migration, Migration History, History*. Edited by Jan Lucassen and Leo Lucassen, 73-84. Bern: Peter Lang, 1999.

———. *Cultures in Contact: World Migrations in the Second Millennium*. Durham, N.C.: Duke University Press, 2002.

Hondagneu-Sotelo, Pierrette, ed. *Gender and U.S. Immigration: Contemporary Trends*. Berkeley and Los Angeles: University of California Press, 2003.

Hondagneu-Sotelo, Pierrette, and Ernestine Avila. "'I'm Here, but I'm There': The Meaning of Latina Transnational Motherhood." *Gender and Society* 11, no. 5 (October 1997): 548-71.

Hornby, Stephen J., Victor A. Konrad, and James J. Herlan, eds. *The Northeastern Borderlands: Four Centuries of Interaction*. Orono, ME: Canadian American Center, University of Maine; Fredericton, N.B.: Acadiensis Press, 1989.

Hufton, Olwen. "Women without Men: Widows and Spinsters in Britain and France in the Eighteenth Century." *Journal of Family History* 9 (Winter 1984): 355-75.

Hughes, Everette Cherrington. *French Canada in Transition*. Chicago: University of Illinois Press, 1963, c1943.

Iacovetta, Franca. *Such Hardworking People: Italian Immigrants in Postwar Toronto*. Montreal: McGill-Queen's University Press, 1993.

Iacovetta, Franca with Paula Draper, and Robert Bentresca, eds. *A Nation of Immigrants: Women,*

Workers, and Communities in Canadian History, 1840s-1960s. Toronto: University of Toronto Press, 1998.

Ignatiev, Noel. How the Irish Became White. New York: Routledge, 1995.

Jacobson, Matthew Frye. Whiteness of a Different Color: European Immigrants and the Alchemy of Race. Harvard University Press: Cambridge, MA, 1998.

Jones, Jacqueline. The Dispossessed: America's Underclasses from the Civil War to the Present. New York: Basic Books, 1992.

Karabatos, Lewis, and Robert McLeod Jr., eds. Fixed in Time: Photographs of Lowell, Massachusetts, 1860-1940. Lowell, MA: Lowell Historical Society, 1983.

Kenngott, George Frederick. The Record of a City: A Social Survey of Lowell. New York: The Macmillan Company, 1910.

Kessler-Harris, Alice. Out to Work: A History of Wage-Earning Women in the United States. Oxford: Oxford University Press, 1982.

———. In Pursuit of Equity: Women, Men, and the Quest for Economic Citizenship in Twentieth-Century America. New York: Oxford University Press, 2001.

Kessler-Harris, Alice, and Karen Brodkin Sacks. "The Demise of Domesticity in America." In Women, Households, and the Economy. Edited by Lourdes Benería and Catherine Stimpson, 65-84. New Brunswick, New Jersey: Rutgers University Press, 1987.

Kerber, Linda K. "Separate Spheres, Female Worlds, Woman's Place: The Rhetoric of Women's History." Journal of American History 75 (June 1988): 9-39.

Keyssar, Alexander. Out to Work: The First Century of Unemployment in Massachusetts. Cambridge: Cambridge University Press, 1986.

Lamphere, Louise. From Working Daughters to Working Mothers: Immigrant Women in a New England Industrial Community. Ithaca: Cornell University Press, 1987.

Lamarre, Jean. "Modèles migratoires et intégration socio-économiques des Canadiens français de la vallée de la Saginaw, Michigan, 1840-1900." Labour/Le Travail 41 (Spring 1998): 9-33.

———. Les Canadiens français du Michigan: Leur contribution dans le développement de la vallée de la Saginaw et de la péninsule de Keweenaw 1840-1914. Sillery, Québec: Éditions du Septentrion, 2000.

Lamontagne, Sophie-Laurence. La production textile domestique au Québec, 1827-1941: une approche quantitative et régionale. Ottawa: Museé national des sciences et de la technologie, 1997.

Lane, Brigitte. Franco-American Folk Traditions and Popular Culture in a Former Milltown: Aspects of Ethnic Urban Folklore and the Dynamics of Folklore Change in Lowell, Massachusetts. New York: Garland Publishing, 1990.

———. "Histoire orale des Franco-Américains de Lowell, Massachusetts: mémoire, histoire et identité(s)." Francophonie d'Amérique 5 (1995): 155-72.

Lasch, Christopher. Haven in a Heartless World: The Family Besieged. New York: Basic Books, 1979.

Lavoie, Yolande. L'émigration des Québécois aux États-Unis de 1840 à 1930. Rev. ed. Québec: Gouvernement du Québec, Conseil de la langue française, Direction des Études et recherches, 1981.

———. L'émigration des Canadiens aux États-Unis avant 1930: mesures du phénomène. Montréal: Les Presses de l'Université de Montréal, 1972.

Layer, Robert George. Earnings of Cotton Mill Operatives, 1826-1914. Cambridge: Committee on Research in Economic History, 1955.

LeBlanc, Robert G. "Colonisation et rapatriement au Lac-Saint-Jean, 1895-1905." *Revue d'histoire de l'Amérique française* 38, no. 3 (hiver 1985): 379-408.

Lecker, Robert ed., *Borderlands: Essays in Canadian-American Relations*. Toronto: ECW Press, 1991.

Lee, Erika. "Enforcing the Borders: Chinese Exclusion along the U.S. Borders with Canada and Mexico, 1882-1924." *Journal of American History* 89, no. 1 (June 2002): 54-86.

———. *At America's Gates: Chinese Immigration During the Exclusion Era, 1882-1943*. Chapel Hill: University of North Carolina Press, 2003.

Lee, Rose Hum. *The Growth and Decline of Chinese Communities in Rocky Mountain Region*. New York: Arno Press, 1978.

Lemieux, Denise, and Lucie Mercier, *Les femmes au tournant du siècle 1880-1940: âge de la vie, maternité et quotidien*. Québec: Institut québécois de recherche sur la culture, 1989.

Levitt, Peggy, and Rafael de la Dehesa. "Transnational Migration and the Redefinition of the State: Variations and Explanations." *Ethnic and Racial Studies* 26, no. 4 (July 2003): 587-611.

Linteau, Paul-André, René Durocher, and Jean-Clayde Robert. *Histoire du Québec contemporain*. Vol. 1. New ed. Montréal: Boréal, 1989.

Lipsitz, George. *The Possessive Investment in Whiteness: How White People Profit from Identity Politics*. Philadelphia: Temple University Press, 1998.

Lovejoy, Owen R. "Child Labor Laws." In *The New Encyclopedia of Social Reform*. Edited by William Dwight Porter Bliss, 170-81. New York: Funk Wagnall Co., 1908.

Louder, Dear R., and Eric Waddell eds. *Du continent perdu à l'archipele retrouvé: le Québec et l'Amérique française*. Québec: Les Presses de l'Université Laval, 1983.

Lucassen, Jan, and Leo Lucasen, eds. *Migration, Migration History, History. Old Paradigms and New Perspectives*. Bern: Peter Lang AG, 1999.

Luxton, Meg. *More Than a Labour of Love: Three Generations of Women's Work in the Home*. Toronto: Women's Press, 1980.

———. "Two Hands for the Clock: Changing Patterns in the Gendered Division of Labour in the Home." In *Through the Kitchen Window: The Politics of Home and Family*. Edited by Luxton, Harriet Rosenberg, and Sedef Arat-Koc, 39-55. Toronto: Garamond Press, 1986; 2nd ed., 1990.

Luxton, Meg, and June Corman. *Getting By in Hard Times: Gendered Labour at Home and on the Job*. Toronto: University of Toronto Press, 2001.

Mar, Lisa R. "The Table of Lin Tee: Madness, Family Violence, and Lindsay's Anti-Chinese Riot of 1919." In *Sisters or Strangers? Immigrant, Ethnic, and Racialized Women in Canadian History*. Edited by Marlene Epp, Franca Iacovetta, and Frances Swyripa, 108-29. Toronto: University of Toronto Press, 2004.

May, Martha. "The Historical Problems of the Family Wage: The Ford Motor Company and the Five Dollar Days." *Feminist Studies* 8 (Summer 1982): 399-424.

McCallum, John. *Unequal Beginnings: Agriculture and Economic Development in Quebec and Ontario Until 1870*. Toronto: University of Toronto Press, 1980.

Meagher, Timothy J. *Inventing Irish America: Generation, Class, and Ethnic Identity in a New England City, 1800-1923*. Notre Dame, Indiana: University of Notre Dame, 2001.

Merithew, Caroline Waldron. "Anarchist Motherhood: Toward the Making of a Revolutionary Proletariat in Illinois Coal Towns." In *Women, Gender, and Transnational Lives*. Edited by Donna R. Gabaccia and Franca Iacovetta, 217-46. Toronto and Buffalo: University of

Toronto Press, 2002.

Meserve, H. C. *Lowell: An Industrial Dream Come True.* Boston: The National Association of Cotton Manufacturers, 1923.

Milkman, Ruth, ed. *Women, Work and Protest: A Century of US Women's Labor History.* Boston: Routledge & Kegan Paul, 1985.

Modell, John. "Patterns of Consumption, Acculturation, and Family Income Strategies in Late Nineteenth-Century America." In *Family and Population in Princeton in Nineteenth-Century America.* Edited by Tamara K. Hareven and Maria A. Vinovskis, 206-40. Princeton: Princeton University Press, 1978.

Moen, Phillis, and Elaine Wethington. "The Concept of Family Adaptive Strategies." *Annual Review of Sociology* 18 (1992): 233-51.

Mohun, Arwen. *Steam Laundries: Gender, Technology, and Work in the United States and Great Britain, 1880-1940.* Baltimore: The Johns Hopkins University Press, 1999.

Montgomery, David. *The Fall of the House of Labor: The Workplace, the State, and American Labor Activism, 1865-1925.* New York: Cambridge University Press, 1987.

Morawska, Ewa. *For Bread with Butter: Life-Worlds of East Central Europeans in Johnstown, Pennsylvania, 1890-1940.* Cambridge: Cambridge University Press, 1985.

———. "Return Migrations: Theoretical and Research Agenda." In *A Century of European Migrations.* Edited by Rudolf J. Vecoli and Suzanne M. Sinke, 277-92. Cambridge: Cambridge University Press, 1985.

———. "The Sociology and Historiography of Immigration." In *Immigration Reconsidered: History, Sociology, and Politics.* Edited by Virginia Yans-McLaughlin, 187-238. New York: Oxford University Press, 1990.

Morelli, Anne. "Nestore's Wife? Work, Family, and Militancy in Belgium," In *Women, Gender, and Transnational Lives.* Edited by Donna R. Gabaccia and Franca Iacovetta, 327-46. Toronto and Buffalo: University of Toronto Press, 2002.

Morton, Suzanna. *Ideal Surroundings: Domestic Life in Working-Class Suburbs in the 1920s.* Toronto: University of Toronto Press, 1995.

Mulligan, Mary T. "Epilogue to Lawrence: The 1912 Strike in Lowell, Massachusetts." In *Surviving Hard Times: The Working People of Lowell.* Edited by Mary H. Blewett, 82-83. Lowell, MA: Lowell Museum, 1982.

Nearing, Scott. *Financing the Wage-Earner's Family: A Survey of the Facts Bearing on Income and Expenditures in the Families of American Wage-Earners.* New York: Huebsch, 1914.

Ngai, Mae. *Impossible Subjects: Illegal Aliens and the Making of Modern America.* Princeton: Princeton University Press, 2004.

Noiriel, Gérard. *La tyrannie du national: Le droit d'asile en Europe, 1793-1993.* Paris: Calmann-Lévy, 1991.

Nugent, Walter T. K. *Crossings: The Great Transatlantic Migrations, 1870-1914.* Bloomington: Indiana University Press, 1992.

Olwig, Karen Fog. "New York as a Locality in a Global Family Network." In *Islands in the City: West Indian Migration to New York.* Edited by Nancy Foner, 142-60. Berkeley: University of California Press, 2001.

Paquet, Gilles. "L'émigration des Canadiens français vers la Nouvelle-Angleterre, 1870-1910, prises de vue quantitatives." *Recherches historiographiques* 5 (1964): 319-70.

Parker, Margaret Terrell. *Lowell: A Study of Industrial Development*. New York: The Macmillan Company, 1940.

Parr, Joy. "The Skilled Emigrant and Her Kin: Gender, Culture, and Labour Recruitment." *Canadian Historical Review* 68, no. 4 (1987): 528-51.

———. *The Gender of Breadwinners: Women, Men, and Change in Two Industrial Towns, 1880-1950*. Toronto: University of Toronto Press, 1990.

Patrias, Carmela. *Patriots and Proletarians: Politicizing Hungarian Immigrants in Interwar Canada*. Montreal and Kingston: McGill-Queen's University Press, 1994.

Peiss, Kathey. *Cheap Amusements: Working Women and Leisure in Turn-of-the-Century New York*. Philadelphia: Temple University Press, 1986.

Perron, Normand. "Genèse des activités laitières 1850-1960." In *Agriculture et colonisation au Québec: aspects historiques*. Edited by Normand Séguin, 113-40. Montréal: Boréal Expresse, 1980.

Pesman, Roselyn. "Italian Women and Work in Post-Second World War Australia: Representation and Experience." In *Women, Gender, and Transnational Lives*. Edited by Donna R. Gabaccia and Franca Iacovetta, 386-409. Toronto and Buffalo: University of Toronto Press, 2002.

Pessar, Patricia R. "Engendering Migration Studies: The Case of New Immigrants in the United States." *American Behavioral Scientist* 42 (1999): 577-600. Reprinted in *Gender and U.S. Immigration: Contemporary Trends*. Edited by Pierrette Hondagneu-Sotelo, 20-42. Berkeley: University of California Press, 2003.

Petroff, Lilian. *Sojourner and Settler: The Macedonian Community in Toronto to 1940*. Toronto: Toronto University Press, 1994.

Pouyez, Christian, Yolande Lavoie, with collaboration of Gérard Bouchard. *Les Saguenayens: introduction à l'histoire des populations du Saguenay XIXe et XXe siècles*. Sillery, Québec: Les Presses de l'Université du Québec, 1983.

Prentice, Alison et al., eds. *Canadian Women: A History*. Toronto: Harcourt Brace Jovanovich, 1988.

Principe, Angelo. "Glimpses of Lives in Canada's Shadow: Insiders, Outsiders, and Female Activism in the Fascist Era." In *Women, Gender, and Transnational Lives*. Edited by Donna R. Gabaccia and Franca Iacovetta, 350-85. Toronto and Buffalo: University of Toronto Press, 2002.

Proulx, Jean-Baptiste. *Les pionniers du lac Nominingue ou les avantages de la colonisation. Drame en trois Actes*. Montréal: Beauchemin & Valois, 1883.

———. *Voyage au lac Long, dans le canton de Preston*. Saint-Jérôme, Québec: s.n. 1882. Reproduced in *Mélanges littéraires*. Montréal: Beauchemin & Valois, 1884.

Ramirez, Bruno. *On the Move: French-Canadian and Italian Migrants in the North Atlantic Economy, 1860-1914*. Toronto: McClelland & Stewart, 1991.

———. "Crossroad Province: Quebec's Place in International Migrations: 1870-1915." In *A Century of European Migration, 1830-1930*. Edited by Rudolf J. Vecoli and Suzanne M. Sinke, 243-60. Urbana: University of Illinois Press, 1991.

Ramirez, Bruno, and Yves Otis. *French-Canadian Emigration to the USA in the 1920s: A Research Report*. Montréal: Université de Montréal, 1992.

Ramirez, Bruno, with the assistance of Yves Otis. *Crossing the 49th Parallel: Migration from Canada to the United States, 1900-1930*. Ithaca: Cornell University Press, 2001.

Roby, Yves. "Quebec in the United States: A Historiographical Survey." *Maine Historical Society Quarterly* 26, no. 3 (Winter 1987): 126-59.

———. *Les Franco-Américains de la Nouvelle-Angleterre, 1776-1930*. Sillery, Québec: Septentrion, 1990.

Rodriguez, Marc Simon. "A Movement Made of 'Young Mexican Americans Seeking Change': Critical Citizenship, Migration, and the Chicano Movement in Texas and Wisconsin, 1960-1975." *Western Historical Quarterly* 34, no. 3 (Autumn 2003): 275-99.

Rodriguez, Marc Simon, ed. *Repositioning North American Migration History: New Directions in Modern Continental Migration, Citizenship, and Community.* Rochester, New York: University of Rochester Press, 2004.

Roediger, David R. *The Wages of Whiteness: Race and the Making of the American Working Class.* London and New York: Verso, 1991. Rev. ed., 1999.

Rosaldo, Michelle Zimbalist. "Women, Culture, and Society: A Theoretical Overview." In *Women, Culture, and Society.* Edited by Michelle Zimbalist Rosaldo and Louise Lamphere, 263-80. Stanford: Stanford University Press, 1974.

Rosenfeld, Mark. "'It Was a Hard Life': Class and Gender in the Work and Family Rhythms of a Railway Town, 1920-1950." In *Historical Papers/Communications historiques*, 237-79. Ottawa: Canadian Historical Association/Société historique due Canada, 1988.

Rouillard, Jacques. *Les travailleurs du cotton au Québec: 1900-1915.* Montréal: Les Presses de l'Université du Québec, 1974.

Sangster, Joan. *Dreams of Equality: Women on the Canadian Left, 1920-1950.* Toronto: McClelland & Stewart, 1989.

Sánchez, George J. *Becoming Mexican American: Ethnicity, Culture, and Identity in Chicano Los Angeles, 1900-1945.* New York: Oxford University Press, 1993.

Saraceno, Chiara. "The Concept of the Family Strategy and Its Application to the Family Work Complex: Some Theoretical and Methodological Problems." *Marriage and Family Review* 14, no. 1-2 (1989): 1-18.

Scollan, Edward. "World War I and the 1918 Cotton Textile Strikes." In *Surviving Hard Times : The Working People of Lowell.* Edited by Mary H. Blewett, 105-14. Lowell, MA: Lowell Museum, 1982.

Sinke, Suzanne M. "Gender and Migration: Historical Perspectives." *International Migration Review* 40, no. 1 (Spring 2006): 82-103.

Smith, David R. "Borders that Divide and Connect: Capital and Labour Movements in the Great Lakes Region." *Canadian Review of American Studies* 25, no. 2 (1995): 1-25.

Smith, Joan. "Non-Wage Labor and Subsistence." In *Households and the World Economy.* Edited by Joan Smith, Immanuel Wallerstein, and Evers Hans-Dieter, 64-89. Beverly Hills: Sage Publications, 1984.

Smith, Marian L. "By Way of Canada: U.S. Records of Immigration Across the U.S.-Canadian Border, 1895-1954." *Prologue* 32, 3 (Fall 2000) : 192-99.

———. "The Immigration and Naturalization Service (INS) at the U.S.-Canadian Border, 1893-1993: An Overview of Issues and Topics," *Michigan Historican Review* 26, no. 2 (2000): 127-47.

Stansell, Christine. "Women, Children and the Uses of the Streets: Class and Gender Conflict in New York City, 1850-1860," *Feminist Studies* 8, no. 2 (Summer 1982): 309-35.

Stone, Lawrence. *The Family, Sex, and Marriage in England, 1500-1800.* London: Weidenfeld &

Nicolson, 1977.

Strasser, Susan. *Never Done: A History of American Housework*. New York: Pantheon Books, 1982. New York : Pantheon Books, 1982; New York: Henry Holt, 2000.

Sung, Betty Lee. *Mountain of Gold: The Story of the Chinese in America: Their Struggle for Survival, Acceptance, and Full Participation in American Life*. New York: The Macmillan Company, 1967.

Sutherland, Neil. "'We Always Had Things to Do': The Paid and Unpaid Work of Anglophone Children between the 1920s and the 1960s." *Labour/Le Travail* 25 (1990): 105-41.

Takai, Yukari. "Transnational Movements of Japanese and French Canadian Migrants: A Discussion of Concepts, Methodology and Sources." *Journal of Aïchi Kenritsu Daigaku* 35 (March 2003): 71-93.

———. "The Family Networks and Geographic Mobility of French Canadian Immigrants in Early-Twentieth-Century Lowell, Massachusetts." *Journal of Family History* 26, no.3 (July 2001): 373-94.

———. "Shared Earnings, Unequal Responsibilities: Single French-Canadian Wage-Earning Women in Lowell, Massachusetts, 1900-1920." *Labour/Le Travail* 47 (spring 2001): 115-32.

———. "Sexe et expérience de travail comme critères migratoires: le cas des immigrantes canadiennes-françaises à Lowell, Massachusetts au début du vingtième siècle." *Francophonies d'Amérique* 11 (2001) : 183-93.

Taylor, Barbara. *Eve and the New Jerusalem: Socialism in the Nineteenth Century*. Cambridge, MA: Harvard University Press, 1993.

Télesphore, Saint-Pierre. *Les Canadiens des États-Unis: ce qu'on perd à émigrer*. Montréal: la Compagnie d'imprimerie "La Gazette," 1893.

Tentler, Leslie. *Wage-Earning Women: Industrial Work and Family Life in the United States, 1900-1930*. Oxford: Oxford University Press, 1979.

Thernstrom, Stephan. *Poverty and Progress, Social Mobility in a Nineteenth Century City*. Cambridge, MA: Harvard University Press, 1964.

———. *The Other Bostonians: Poverty and Progress in the American Metropolis, 1880-1970*. Cambridge, MA: Harvard University Press, 1973.

Thétrault, Martin. "De la difficulté de naître et de survivre dans une ville industrielle de la Nouvelle-Angleterre au XIX siècle: mortalité infantile, infanticide et avortement à Lowell, Massachusetts, 1870-1900." *Revue d'histoire de l'Amérique française* 47, no. 1 (été 1983): 53-82.

Thistlethwaite, Frank. "Migration from Europe Overseas in the Nineteenth and Twentieth Centuries." Paper originally presented at the Eleventh International Congress of Historical Sciences, Stockholm, 1960. Reprint in *A Century of European Migrations, 1830-1930*. Edited by Rudolph J. Vecoli and Suzanne M. Sinke, 17-57. Urbana: University of Illinois Press, 1991.

Thornton, Patricia, Sherry Olson, and Quon Thuy Thach. "Dimensions sociales de la mortalité infantile à Montréal au milieu du XIXe siècle." *Annales de démographie historique* (1988): 299-325.

Tichnor, Daniel J. *Dividing Lines: The Politics of Immigration Control in America*. Princeton: Princeton University Press, 2002.

Tilly, Scott A. "Paths of Proletarianization: Organization of Production, Sexual Division of Labor and Women's Collective Action." *Signs: Journal of Women in Culture and Society* 7 (1978): 400-17.

———. "Beyond Family Strategies, What?" *Historical Methodology* 20, no. 3 (1987): 123-25.

Tilly, Louise A., and Joan W. Scott. *Women, Work, and Family*. New York: Routledge, 1978. Reprinted in 1989.

Tinker Salas, Miguel. *In the Shadow of the Eagles: Sonora and the Transformation of the Border during the Porfiriato*. Berkeley: University of California Press, 1997.

Tremblay, Martine. "La division sexuelle du travail et la modernization de l'agriculture à travers la presse agricole, 1840-1900." *Revue d'histoire de l'Amérique française* 47, no. 2 (automne 1993): 226-29.

Trotter, Joe William. "The Great Migration, African Americans, and Immigrants in the Industrial City." In *Not Just Black and White: Historical and Contemporary Perspectives on Immigration, Race, Ethnicity in the United States*. Edited by Nancy Foner and George M. Fredrickson, 82-99. New York: Russell Sage Foundation, 2004.

Turbin, Carole. *Working Women of Collar City: Gender, Class, and Community in Troy, New York, 1864-86*. Urbana: University of Illinois Press, 1992.

Valdés, Dennis Nodin. *Al Norte: Agricultural Workers in the Great Lakes Region, 1917-1970*. Austin, Texas: University of Texas Press, 1991.

———. *Barrios Nortenos: St. Paul and Midwestern Mexican Communities in the Twentieth Century*. Austin, Texas: University of Texas Press, 2000.

Vargas, Zaragosa. *Proletarians of the North: A History of Mexican Industrial Workers in Detroit and the Midwest, 1917-1933*. Berkeley, California: University of California Press, 1993.

Vecoli, Rudolph J. "*Contadini* in Chicago: a Critique of the Uprooted." *Journal of American History* 51, no. 3 (1964): 404-17.

——— "From the Uprooted to the Transplanted: The Writing of American Immigration History, 1951-1989." In *From Melting Pot to Multiculturalism: The Evolution of Ethnic Relations in the United States and Canada*. Edited by Valeria Gennaro Lerda, 25-53. Roma: Bulzoni, 1990.

Vollmers, Gloria. "Industrial Home Work of the Dennison Manufacturing Company of Framingham, Massachusetts, 1912-1935." *Business History Review* 71, no. 3 (Autumn 1997): 444-70.

Waldron, FlorenceMae. "'I've Never Dreamed It Was Necessary to Marry!' Women and Work in New England French Canadian Communities, 1870-1930." *Journal of American Ethnic History* 24, no. 2 (Winter 2005): 34-64.

———. "The Battle over Female (In)Dependence: Women in New England Quebecois Migrant Communities, 1870-1930," *Frontiers: A Journal of Women Studies* 26, no. 2 (2005): 158-205.

Wandersee, Winifred D. *Women's Work and Family Values, 1920-1940*. Cambridge, MA: Harvard University Press, 1981.

Ware, Caroline. *The Early New England Cotton Manufacture: A Study in Industrial Beginnings*. Boston and New York: Houghton Mifflin Company, 1931. Reprint, New York: Russel and Russel, 1966.

Wang, Joan S. "Race, Gender, and Laundry Work: The Roles of Chinese Laundrymen and American Women in the United States, 1850-1950." *Journal of American Ethnic History* (Fall 2004) 24, no. 1: 58-99.

Weil, François. *Les Franco-Américains. 1860-1980*. Tours: Belin, 1989.

Weiner, Lynn Y. *From Working Girl to Working Mother: The Female Labor Force in the United States, 1820-1980*. Chapel Hill: University of North Carolina, 1985.

White, Deborah Gray. *Ar'n't I a Woman? Female Slaves in the Plantation South.* New York: Norton, 1985. Rev. ed., New York: W. W. Norton, 1999.

White, Richard. "Is There a North American History?" *Revue française d'études américaines* 79 (1999): 8-28.

Widdis, Randy William. *With Scarcely a Ripple: Anglo-Canadian Migration into the United States and Western Canada, 1880-1920.* Montreal: McGill-Queen's University Press, 1998.

Wiest, Edward. *The Butter Industry in the United States: An Economic Study of Butter and Oleomargarine.* New York: Columbia University Press, 1916.

Willcox, Walter F., and Imre Ferenczi, eds. *International Migrations.* Vol. 1. New York: The National Bureau of Economic Research, 1929-31.

Willis, John. "Urbanization, Colonization and Underdevelopment in the Bas-Saint-Laurent: Fraserville and the Témiscouata in the Late Nineteenth Century." *Cahier de géographique du Québec* 27, nos. 73-74 (1984): 125-61.

Yans-McLaughlin, Virginia. *Family and Community: Italian Immigrants in Buffalo, 1880-1930.* Urbana: University of Illinois Press, 1982, c1977.

Yans-McLaughlin, Virginia, ed. *Immigration Reconsidered: History, Sociology, and Politics.* New York: Oxford University Press, 1990.

Yu, Renqiu. *To Save China, To Save Ourselves: The Chinese Hand Laundry Alliance of New York.* Philadelphia, Temple University Press, 1992.

Yuh, Ji-Yeon. *Beyond the Shadow of Camptown: Korean Military Brides in America.* New York and London: New York University Press, 2002.

Zebroski, Shirley. "The 1903 Strike in the Lowell Cotton Mills." In *Surviving Hard Times: The Working People of Lowell.* Edited by Mary H. Blewett, 44-62. Lowell, MA: Lowell Museum, 1982.

Zelizer, Viviana A. Rotman. *Pricing the Priceless Child: The Changing Social Value of Children.* New York Basic Books, 1985; Princeton, N.J.: Princeton University Press, 1994.

Index

Note: page numbers in *italics* indicate a table or illustration.

Adam, Herménégilde and Leah, 26
Adam, Alexandria, Alphonsa, Hermine, and Philomena, 26
Adélard, Victor, 99
agriculture, 25, 194n.15; commercialization, 11, 13,14, 16, 18, 31; dairy production 13-14, 194n.15; indebtedness and emigration of Québec farmers, 71; specialization, 13, 18; transformation of in Québec and Ontario, 10, 13-15, 19; transition from subsistence farming to commercial farming, 75
alcohol, 27, 125-127, 176, 183
Allen, James P., 189n.1
American Federation of Labour (AFL), 65, 87
Americans, 89, 112, 170; born of American-born parents, 46, 87, 110, 123, 124; demography of, 92-94, *136*, 142, 144, 161, 162, 203n.102, 216n.16;
Amoskeag Manufacturing Company, 3, 29, 48, 66, 100, 152, 173, 176, 200, 204, 210, 217, 223, 224n.49, 225
Appleton Manufacturing Company, 198n.8.
Appleton, Nathan, 33
Archambault, Céline, 26
Asians, 2, 62, 65, 79, 205n.12. *See also* South Asians
Aubert, Anna, 84, 181
Audet, Béatrice, 84, 86, 181
Auger, Isidore, 30
Ayotte, Edmont, 68

Baril, Marie-Anne, 142
Barrett, James, 102
Barry, Régina and Eléanore, 139-140

Bas-Saint-Laurent, *xix*, 20, 22-23
Bauer, Elaine, 220n.2
Beaudry, Gaspard, 77-78
Beauregard, Irène, 68, 103
Beauregard, Maria, 68
Bédard, Julie and Joseph, 155
Bergeron, Madeline, 165, 167, 170
Bergeron, Samuel, 67
Bigelow Carpet Company, 116
Bissonette, Florence, 138
Blewett, Mary H., 57, 118, 119, 147, 164
boardinghouses, 8, 33-34, 36, 84, 104, 143, 150, 155, 157-158, 169, 181, 212 n.43, 221n. 19; and women's work, 150, 157-158, 162, 164-165, 167-169
Boisvert, Joseph, 71
bookkeepers, 132, 138-139, 182
Boott, Kirk, 33
Boott Manufacturing Company, 5, 33, 44, 58, 110-111, 114-115, 168, 198n.7.
Border, porous nature of the Canada-U.S., 1-2, 62, 85. *See also* migration across the Canada-U.S. border
Border Entry
See Soundex Index to Canadian Border Entries through the St. Albans, Vermont, District
Boston Associates, 33-34
Bouchard, Gérard, 27, 187-188, 207n.38, 211n.23, 212n.40
Boudreau, Laura, 71
Bouquet, Sarah, Louis, Roseanne, Emily-A., Ovilla, 155, 159
Bradbury, Bettina, 152, 154, **218n.50**
Breton, Raymond, 24
Brière, Annie, 1, 74, 85; Brières, Arthur,

Béatrice, Delphis, Joseph, William, 1, 80-81
Brisson, T.A., 22. *See also* Société Général de la Colonisation
Bruel, Edward and Victoria, 137, 158
Brunelle, Roger, 78, 79
Bureau of Immigration, U.S., 64, 87

Cadorette, James, 67, 91
Cameron, Ardis, 76, 89
Canada-U.S. border, 2, 66, 68, 72-74, 76, 79, 81, 85, 185, 206n.24; enforcement of, 62, 64, 65, 66. *See also* migration across the Canada-U.S. border
carder, 71, 98, 158, 188, 210n.23
care, of ageing parents and younger siblings, 19, 150, 159, 161, 172, 175-178, 221n.15; and single French Canadian women, 18-19, 150, 153, 157, 162, 177; of young children, 19, 140, 149-150, 152, 172-173, 183-184, 221n.15, 224n.51
Catarette, Yvonne, James, Miralda, 49
change of family strategy, 49, 57
Chartrand, Valentine, 148, 160, 174, 183, 217n.43
Chinese, 50, 51, 55, 102, 105, 164, 221-222n.19
"Chinese of the East [Coast]", 51, 65, 87. *See also* French Canadians
child labour, 5, 37, 39, 45, 46, 48, 49, 50, 72, 73, 91, 94, 95, 96, 102, 114, 130, 148, 155, 164, 173, 199n.42; anti-child labour legislation, 24, 45, 46, 47, 48, 50, 58, 61, 64, 72, 76, 89, 95, 135, 153, 181, 182, 183, 200n.56, 218n.44; decrease of, 46, 47, 49-50, 72, 76, 89, 91, 95, 96, 130, 153, 181, 182, 200n.56, 201n.64; discourse of French-Canadian elite, 95-96. *See also* change in family strategy; French-Canadian female workers and child labour law
Chouinard, Del, 163
Chouinard, Marie, Mary, George, 75, 91
Cinotto, Simone, 223n.36
Cinqmars, Phillip, 104
circular migration, 2
Clément, Alfred, 104
Clermont, Mary Louise, Annie, Remeus, 1, 73
Clermont, Maxime, 91
Coburn, Frederick W., 51
Collomp, Catherine, 65
colonization, 10-11, 19, 20-24, 27, 30; régions de la colonisation, 21-23, 25, 31, 81, 195n.36, 195n.45, 206n.22; Société Générale de la Colonisation, 22, 195n.49. *See also* Société Général de la Colonisation
Comacchio, Cynthia, 79
contact person, 82-83, 84-85, 208n.62
Cordeau, Lucie, 164, 175, 183
corporate paternalism, of textile mills, 32, 34, 36, 61
cost of living, 111-112, 113-114, 158, 213n.57
Côté, Emma, 74; Florence and Eugène, 71, 152; Adrien and Émilie, 152
Crépeau, Emma, 142, 143
Croteau, Polivine, 168-169

Depontbriand, Matilda, 138
Desjardins, Henrietta, 144
Desjardins, Joséphine and John, 144
Desjardins, Rose, 137, 144
Desmarais, Irène, 122, 128, 165, 171
De[s]marais, Michel and Angélina, 98
Dextra, Ida, 150
Dickens, Charles, 36
Doherty, Martha, 154
domestic violence, 126-127, 215n.121
double day, 177-178
Dubé, Emma, 157
Dublin, Thomas, 3, 36, 75, 131

Early, Frances, 55, 66, 220n.3
Église Saint-Jean-Baptiste, 39, 124, 202n.83
engineers, 96, 98, 100, 127, 182
Epp, Marlene, 223n.36
European migrants, 2, 5, 23, 32, 39, 43, 45, 46, 50, 66, 72, 79, 101, 102, 205n.12; at the Canada-U.S. border, 62, 65, 79

Fall River, Massachusetts, *xviii*, 21, 24, 41, 42, 80, 109, 111, 115, 195n.45, 198-199n.23, 211n.24, 212n.50, 215n.98
family, and kin networks, 1, 2, 8, 62, 84; budgets, 4, 28, 112, 113, 158, 160, 161, 167, 170, 225n.64; economic needs, 8,

24, 27, 28, 89, 104, 130, 153, 182; of immigrants, 3, 4, 81, 130, 220n.2; labour system, 82-85, 100; reunification and separation, 8, 27, 77-79, 81, 84, 85, 86. *See also* reciprocal kinship; networks, women-centred,
family life cycle, 132, *149*, 150; and colonization settlers, 19
family strategy, change in, 75, 79, 130, 131, 142, 145, 225n.63. *See also* anti-child labour legislation; child labour
family units, of French-Canadian migrants, 1, 4, 37, 74, 81, 180, 181
family wage, ideology, 2, 76, 88-89, 128, 130-132, 136, 140-141, 145, 152, 155, 157-159, 167, 180, 209n.5, 210n.8. *See also* living wage
Fernandez-Kelly, Patricia, 167
food, 5, 18, 42, 56, 57, 112, *113*, 149, 163, 170; and immigrant women's roles, 223n.36, 224n.38; and Korean women, 224n.38; and women in French Canadian families, 169-172, 177
foreman, 49, 104, 118, 127
Franco Americans. *See* French Canadians
French Canadians, ageing of, 49, 94, 127; arrival in Lowell, 1, 181, 190n.4, 198n.23; in Lowell, 1, 2, 6, 8, 31, 32, 34, 37, 39, 42, 45, 51, 52, 55, 61, 62, 65, 91, 92, 93, 94, *95*, 114, 127, 184; born in the U.S., 1, 8, 39, 62, 138; *Canadiens*, 1, 37; demography of, 91-92, 93-95, 189n.1, 197n.1, 202n.91, 203n.101, 203n.102, 208n.59; folk society, 66; *habitants*, 66; household relationship of, 18, 75, 88, 91, *94*, 121, 141, *151*, 152, 164, 167, 223n.36, 224n.49; and increase of, 1, 37, 39, 42, 82, 195n.45, 198n.23; marital status of, 65, 75, 84, 86, *136-137*, *141*, 159, 218n.50, 218n.56; parish school, 24, 124, 140, 199n.42; upward mobility of, 71, 88, 89, 96, 98, 99, 100, 101, 102, 120, 127, 182, 220n.3. *See also* "Chinese of the East [Coast]"; of French Canadians; living conditions; occupations; textile industry
French-Canadian female workers, and birthplace, 66, 67, 75, 208n.59; and child labour law, 47, 49, 58, 61, 64, 73, 130, 135, 153, 181-182, 183, 184, 201n.64; industrial occupations, 131, 132, *133-134*, 153, 159, 173, 181, 184, 218n.56; and life cycle, 145-147, *149*, 150, 154, 218n.57, 224n.51; and living arrangements, 94, 144, *151*, 152; married and age, *136*, 147, 159, 218n.56; and postponed marriage, 65, 156, 159, 175, 176, 177; *See also* child labour; widowed household; single women
Frenette, Émil and Napoléon, 72
Frenette, Emma, Hermine, Napoléon, Émile, Albertine, and Ovila, 74
Frenette, Yves, 11, 46, 81, 197n.65

Gabaccia, Donna, R. 3, 63, 170, 190n.5
Garcia, Anna, 167
Gauthier, Mary, 157
Gill, Émile and Catherine, 144-145
Gill, Louis, 67-68
Gompers, Samuel, 65-66, 87
Goulet, Adeline, 147
Graham, Blanche, 60, 124, 126, 140, 168, 173, 178, 184
gender, and division of labour, 2, 17, 172; of French-Canadian households in Canada, 17, 18, 19, 30; and housework for children, 121, 162, 163, 164, 221n.15; in Lowell, 89, 161, 162, 163, 164, 165, 166, 167, 177, 179, 183, 221n.15, 224n.49; and sewing, 123, 162, 165, 167, 178; and transnational migration, 71, 72; unpaid work performed by French-Canadian women, 2, 9, 16-19, 28, 31, 57, 75, 89, 110, 130, 134, 149, 152, 161-163, 173, 177, 178, 183; and washing, 153, 160, 162-164, 167, 168, 178. *See also* single women
geographical proximity, 2, 114. *See also* railroad
Greeks, 44, 52, 57, 59, 101, 106, 110, 116, 125, 132, 134, 221n.9; coffeehouses, 57, 106; demography of, 39, 52, 92, 93, 94, 136; household relationship of, 93, 94, 112-113, 126, 163
Gross, Laurence, 115, 127, 213n.75
Guilmet, Emma, 158

Hamilton Manufacturing Company, 103, 116, 173, 198n.7
Hareven, Tamara K., 3, 49, 63, 152, 153, 175, 213n.68, 218n.51
Hoar, Yvonne, 165, 172, 224n.51, 224n.53
Hoerder, Dirk, 53, 85, 193n.3, 208n.65
Houde, Marie, 147
housekeepers, 155, 157, 158, 180
household, budgets of French-Canadian, 4, 18, 28, 89, 112, 113, 114, 130, 161, 167, 182, 225n.64; composition of French-Canadian migrant, 7, 9, 18, 52, 73, 75, 88, 91, 94, 121, 141, 142, 150, 151, 152, 164, 167, 223n.36, 224n.49, 224n.50; headed by skilled worker, 94, 104, 113, 114; headed by unskilled worker, 94, 113, 114, 224n.50

Iacovetta, Franca, 3, 209n.5, 212n.45, 215n.121
Immigration Act of 1891, 64
Immigration Commission Report, 52, 68, 110, 112, 130, 206n.33, 210n.13, 218n.56
Immigrants in Industries, 44, 68, 71, 193n.1, 210n.13, 216n.9, 218n.56
injury, of labourers, 50, 57, 60, 102, 103, 120, 174, 204n.120
Irish, 33, 37, 39, 44, 52, 55, 58, 92-94, 97, 99-102, 105, 106, 110, 112, 15, 118, 124, 125, 132, 134, 135, 136, 138, 140, 150, 163; demography of, 33, 37, 39, 44, 45, 52, 55, 58, 92, 93, 94, 97, 99, 100, 102, 105, 106, 110, 112, 115, 118, 124, 125, 132, 134, 136, 138, 140, 150, 163; household relationship of, 55, 93, 94

Jackson, Patrick Tracy, 33
Joliette, xix, 12, 14, 21, 22, 25, 26, 29, 68, 69, 70
journaliers, 8, 15, 16, 71, 75, 194n.24

Katranes, Michael, 106
Kenngott, George F., 51, 52, 112, 113-114, 116, 203n.101, 203n.102; *The Record of a City*, 112, 113
Kessler-Harris, Alice, 119
kinship, reciprocal, 173. *See also* family, and kin networks; networks, women-centred

Labelle, François-Xavier-Antoine, 20
labour process, intensifying, 8, 32, 46, 50, 95
labour turnover, and irregular employment, 16, 95, 110, 112, 114, 115, 131, 147, 154, 178, 184
labourer, 10, 24, 31, 33, 49, 67, 71-75, 78, 91, 98, 99, 105, 113, 139, 152, 158, 188; day, 8, 16, 29, 66, 71, 96, 98, 100, 104, 113, 139, 167, 182, 211n.24; farm, 15, 16, 17, 71, 72, 206n.30. *See also* French Canadians; *journaliers*
LaCasse, Alice, 168, 224n.49
LaFleur, Hubert, 102, 103, 120
Lagassé, Yvonne, 53, 55, 56, 77-79, 85, 104, 105
Lalonde, Pierre and Amanda, 98
Lanaudière, xix , 2, 12, 21, 22, 25-27, 30, 77
Lane, Brigitte, 55
Langlois, 105
Lapointe, Florida, 142, 143
Larogne, Angélina, Louisianna, Rose, and Liliane, 144
Layer, Robert, 111, 212n.57
Lechasseur, Antonio, 23
Leclair, William, Louis, Mélanie, Yvonne, Théodore, Janette, and Issne, 49
leisure, 55, 122-125, 127; and drinking, 125, 127; and ethnic fights, 124, 125; of French Canadian boys, 122-125, 127; of French Canadian girls, 124
Linteau, Augustine, 19
Linteau, Paul-André, 21, 206n.22
Little Canada, 50-52, 53- 56, 104-106, 122, 164, 171, 201n.78, 202n.83; *peddleurs* in, 55; *Petit Canada*, 33, 39, 52, 53, 55, 78; streets in, 33, 50-52, 57, 58, 122; street vendors in, 53, 56
living conditions, 50-53, 55, 57-59, 112-113, 124, 163; blocks, 33, 51, 53, 55, 57
living wage, 87-89, 210n.8
longitudinal analysis, 6-8, 63, 185, 205n.7
loomfixers, 59, 71, 98, 111, 115, 118, 120, 127, 182, 188
Lowell, Francis Cabot, 33
lumber camp, 27-29; as a rite of passage, 29. *See also* manhood
lumber industry, of Québec, 27; agro-forestry, 23, 28

· INDEX ·

Mailloux, Donna, 147, 154, 183
Manchester, New Hampshire, *xviii*, 3, 29, 48, 63, 66, 69, 80, 100, 143, 152, 154, 168, 173, 175, 176, 187, 206n.24, 217n.43, 222n.21, 224n.49, 224n.50
Mandeville, Arthur, 72
manhood, 27, 88-91, 119, 215n.98; masculinity, skill and wages of French-Canadian
male workers, 88, 101, 117, 119, 121; and whiteness of French-Canadian male workers, 101, 102. *See also* lumber camp as a rite of passage; skill; textile industry, and wage increase; wage
Massachusetts Bureau of Statistics of Labor, 87, 89
Massachusetts Manufacturing Company, 59, 111
Matte, Joséphine, 138
Mauricie, *xix*, 12, 20, 21, 25, 27-30, 67, 81
McGory, Dora and Frank, 150
Meagher, Timothy J., 102
Mercier, Honoré, 20
Mercier, Lucie, 19
Merrimack Manufacturing Company, 33, 34, 58, 116, 120
Merrimack Street, *xx*, 54, 58, 202n.90. *See also* Little Canada
migration, 1-11, 20, 22-24, 26, 29, 31, 32, 43, 46, 62-64, 66, 71-77, 79, 81, 82, 84-86, 88, 96, 135, 161, 168, 176-179, 181, 184; across the Canadian-U.S. border, 1, 2, 5, 6, 10, 11, 24, 26, 31, 32, 46, 62-64, 66, 71-74, 76, 77, 79, 81, 82, 84, 86, 96, 176; of African Americans, 2, 44; of Anglo Canadians, 2; of Asians, 65; of Europeans, 42, 43, 62, 65, 102; field, 1, 66; of French Canadians, 2, 4, 6-8, 11, 20, 31, 32, 46, 71, 73-77, 79, 81, 82, 84-86, 88, 96, 135, 161, 168, 176, 177; of Mexicans, 2, 62; process of, 2, 8, 63, 64, 66, 86; unit of migration, 76. *See also* geographical proximity; border; Settlement, process of
Miller, Florence, 157
mobility, transnational, 2, 62, 85
Montréal, *xviii*, *xix*, 11, 12, 68; as a birthplace, 68; as a place of sojourning, 68

Morrissette, Arthur, 118, 120-125, 127
Morrissette, Father, 55

Nearing, Scott, 112
networks, women-centred, 172, 174, 177, 183, 184. *See also* family, and kin networks; kinship reciprocal
newspaper, 6, 10, 21, 29, 39, 45, 57, 95, 101, 116, 193n.1; *l'Étoile de Lowell*, 95, 116; *l'Étoile du Nord*, 21; *Daily Citizen*, 51

occupations, of Americans, 87, 97, 101-102, 106, 110, 131-132, *134-135*, *137-138*, 152; crafts workers, 71, 76, 100, 101; of French Canadians, before migration, 49, 66-67, 153, 206n.30, 206n.33, 207n.38; after migration, 44, 71, 72, 76, 96, 97, 98, 99, 100, 110, 117, 157, 206n.30, 211n.24, 212n.43, 216n.7, 218n.56; of Greeks, 52, 97, 101, 106, 110, 131, *134*, *135*; of Irish, 37, 44, 45, 96, 97, 99, 100, 101, 105, 106, 110, 112, 115, 118, 132, *134*, *135*, 163; of Portuguese, 59, 97, 101, 106, *107*, 132, *134*, *135*; manual workers, 59-60, 71, 73, 76, 96, 97, 98, 110, 117-119, 120, *134*. *See also* upward mobility of French Canadians

Octavie, Cole, 157
Octavie, 152 (father of Blanche Rhéaume)
Olwig, Karen Fog, 64
Otis, Yves, 82, 206n.30
Ouellette family, 67, 105
Ouellette, Diane, 139, 140, 173

Paradis, Henry, 102, 164, 169, 170
Parent, Albert, 122
Parent, Alfred, 100, 211n.29
Parr, Joy, 74, 224n.50
peddleurs, 55. *See also* Little Canada, street vendors in
Pellerin, Cora, 48, 143, 176, 187
Poirier, Florette, 138
Poirier, Joseph, 104
Poles, 39, 52, 59, 65, 112, 125
Portuguese, 39, 44, 52, 59, 92, 93, *94*, 97, 101, 106, *107*, 110, 125, 132, *134*, *135*, 136, 146; demography of, 39, 44, 52, 92, 93,

101, 106, 110, 125, 134, *135*, 136; household relationship of, 52, 92-94. See also occupations, of Portuguese
Powderly, Terrence Vincent, 65
Progressivism, 5, 46, 48, 50, 62, 64, 89, 124, 159, 181, 200n.56, 201n.64, 210n.8

Québec, 11, 19, 20, 21, 23, 24, 37, 66, 143; agriculture, transformation of, 13, 14, 16, 23, 72, 75, 194n.15; industrialization, 7, 11, 16, 18, 25, 31, 67, 74; and urbanization of, 7, 11, 12, 25, 31, 67. See also lumber industry
Québec City, *xviii, xix*, 11, 12, 14, 25, 29

race, 20, 64, 89, 102; and citizenship of cross-border migrants, 64; lack of racial reference to French-Canadian male workers, 89, 102
railroad, 2, 16, 21, 23, 24, 29, 41, 78, 158, 221n.9; expansion of, 23, 29, 41. See also geographic proximity
Ramirez, Bruno, 11, 15, 20, 24, 30, 71, 72, 81, 82, 205n.7, 206n.30
recruiting agents, 82, 83
repatriation, 10, 19-22, 30
Rhéaume, Blanche, 152, 164, 165
Roby, Yves, 14, 15, 85, 214n.78
Roediger, David, 102. See also whiteness

Saint-Pierre, T., 20
salespersons, 138, 139, 180, 182
Scott, Joan, 75, 131, 175
Second hand, 71, 103, 104, 115, 120, 206n.32
semi-skilled and unskilled, ambiguous distinction among skilled, semi-skilled, and unskilled, 187-188, 210n.23; semi-skilled, 71, 73, 96, 97, 98, 99, 100, 103, 115, 119, 127, *134*, *135*, 138, 181, 182, 187-188, 206n.30, 207n.38; unskilled, 5, 36, 37, 71, 73, 97, 98, 99, 101, 113, 115, *134*, *135*, 153, 181, 187-188, 206n.30. See also manhood; skill and wage
Sénéchal, Marie-Anne, 175
settlement, process of, 62, 63, 75, 181. See also migration
shop owners, independent, among Americans, 104-106, 134; among French Canadians, 104-105, 106, 109, 134, 202n. 91, 212n.43 212n.50; among Greeks, 106, 134; among Irish, 104-106, 134, among Italians, 202n.45; among Portuguese, 106, 134
Single women: age, birth place, and occupations of French-Canadian workers, 5-7, 34, 36, 37, 74, 75, 131, 132, 134-139, 141-145, 155-158; American-born, *136*-138; Canadian-born, 84, *136*-137, 138, 140-*141*, 142, 143, 145, 175, 176; and living arrangements, 94, 136, 140-*141*, 142-143, 144, 145; remaining in parental household, 19, 136, 140-142, 143-145, 175-176, 225n.64; skill, 5, 8, 17, 26, 30, 36, 37, 50, 71-75, 84, 88, 96, 97, 98, *99*, 199, 193, 194, 110, 115, 117-121, 127, *134*, 136-139, 180-182, 187, 188; French Canadians in skilled work, 8, 17, 26, 30, 72-75, 84, 88, 97, 98, 99, 100, 103, 104, 113, 115, 118-121, 127, *134*, *135*, 136, 137-139, 147, 181, 182, 207n.38; lack of industrial, 30; mechanics, 108. See also engineers; loomfixers; manhood; semi-skilled and unskilled; textile industry, and wage increase; wage
Soundex Index to Canadian Border Entries through the St. Albans, Vermont, District, 6, 7, 72, 74, 82, 85, 185, 186, 196n.62, 205n.7, 206n.24, 208n.62
South Asians, 184. See also Asians
speed-up, 36
St. Peter, Malvina, 158
stretch-out, 36
Stump, Herman, 62, 87

textile industry, 5, 8, 26, 32, 37, 41, 44-46, 65, 71, 73, 76, 100, 111, 112, 117, 131, 138, 143, 147, 150, 155, 157, 174, 182, 211n.24, 214n.81; age, 8, 32, 37, 41, 45, 76, 143, 182; ethnicity, 37, 44, 45, 71, 73, 76, 100, 112, 131, 138, 143, 150, 155, 157, 182; gendered job hierarchy in textile factories, 71, 88, 101, 117-119, 120, 132, 138, 147; gender and marital status of workers in Lowell's, 41, 45, 65, 71, 73, 76, 100, 111, 112, 117, 131, 138, 143, 147, 150, 155, 157, 174, 182, 218n.57; in Lowell, 5, 32, 36, 41, 76, 112, 117, 131, 150, 182; recomposition of the workforce in Lowell, 32, 36, 37, 45, 182, 211n.24; regional competition, 8, 32, 34, 41, 50, 52, 61, 72, 76, 111; and wage increase, 2, 4, 5, 36, 44, 109-111, 119, 143, 155; working conditions in Lowell's textile industry, 36, 58, 60, 110, 114, 115, 117, 121. See also French Canadians; Hareven, Tamara K.; injury; manhood; skill; wage; work, paid of French-Canadian women

Thistlethwaite, Frank, 63

Thompson, Paul, 230n.2

Tilly, Louise, 75, 131, 154, 175

Trois-Rivières, *xix*, 12, 22, 27, 29, 67, 68, 69, 70

Turks, 39, 52

Turner, Frederick Jackson, 20; Frontier Thesis in reverse, 20

Vaillancourt family, 157

velvet finisher, 77

Vigneault, Alphie, Eugénie, 157

wage, 15, 16, 18, 19, 24, 25, 27, 28, 34, 46, 49, 52, 65, 72-75, 79, 87-89, 91, 93, 96, 110-114, 125, 130-132, 135, *141*-145, 149, 150, 152, 156, 158-160, 161, 167, 168, 172-175, 178, 180, 183, 197n.73, 219n.67; wage and skill, 8, 87-89, 100-102, 104, 117-121, 127, 153; *See also* manhood; skill; textile industry, and wage increase

Waldron, Florencemae, 191n.11, 210n.7

weaver, 26, 48, 59, 71, 73, 74, 81, 98, 104, 111, 115-119, 127, 132, 138, 144, 155, 173, 176, 187, 188, 210n.23

whiteness, 88, 101, 102, 209n.6. *See also* David Roediger

Widows, and household, 156, 219n.67; French-Canadian, 156; and living arrangements, 140-141, 155, 156, 175

work, paid of French-Canadian women, 17-19, 39, 58, 71-73, 76, 91, 116-118, 134-141, 143-145, 147, 149, 150, 152-160, 182, of married French-Canadian women, growing participation, 18, 45, 49, 72, 73, 76, 91, 102, 130-132, 134-136, *137*, 138, 139, *141*, 145, 147, 149, 150, 152-154, 201n.64, 218n.56, 224n.49; of men, 39, 56, 61, 72, 76, 87-89, 91-93, 95-107, 109, 110, 115, 117, 120, 127, 132, 161, 164, 181; unpaid, in Ontario, 168, 181; in Québec. *See* gender and division of labour; care; reciprocal kinship; textile industry

workers, white collar, 97, 103, 104, 109, *134*, *135*, 138, 139, 182, 187, 212n.43

Wright, Carroll Davidson, 87

Yankee girls, 34, 36, 37, 75, 131

Yans-McLaughlin, Virginia, 109

Zebroski, Shirley, 110, 212n.52